THE POLITICAL ECONOMY OF
CONTEMPORARY AFRICA

VOLUME I

SAGE SERIES ON AFRICAN MODERNIZATION AND DEVELOPMENT

The Political Economy of
CONTEMPORARY
AFRICA

PETER C.W. GUTKIND
and
IMMANUEL WALLERSTEIN
Editors

 SAGE Publications   Beverly Hills / London

For information address:

SAGE Publications, Inc.
275 South Beverly Drive
Beverly Hills, California 90212

SAGE Publications Ltd
28 Banner Street
London EC1Y 8QE

Printed in the United States of America

International Standard Book Number 0-8039-0506-8 (cloth)
International Standard Book Number 0-8039-0592-0 (paper)
Library of Congress Catalog Card No. 75-33470

FOURTH PRINTING

CONTENTS

INTRODUCTION

PETER C.W. GUTKIND
McGill University

IMMANUEL WALLERSTEIN
State University of New York, Binghamton

This book is concerned with what Barrington Moore has called "the chains of historical causation." Lionel Cliffe in his essay "Rural Political Economy of Africa" has expressed this orientation from a similar perspective when he writes, "The full task of a political economy of Africa must . . . start with an analysis of the precapitalist modes" of production.

The contemporary economy and polity of Africa, while its antecedents are indigenous, must be analyzed in the context of the specifics of an evolving world system of economic and political relations starting in the sixteenth century, leading at first to the gradual involvement of Africa with worldwide exchange relations and later, by the middle of the nineteenth century, into more direct incorporation and finally, by the early twentieth century, to the subordination of the continent to the economic and political needs and objectives of the major Western powers.

This "chain of historical causation" is best studied, in our view, by means of the model of "political economy." This approach, Chris Allen writes, "is still a relatively recent, minority trend, and since it must draw on the large body of work that is derived from other approaches, it seems more fruitful at present to define it in deliberately broad terms." More specifically, the notion of political economy, Steve Langdon (1974:123) has suggested, emphasizes "the intermeshing of so-called 'political,' 'economic' and social factors of change in one ongoing historical process. The dynamics of such change emerge from the

EDITORS' NOTE: This volume has been assisted financially by a grant from McGill University, Faculty of Graduate Studies and Research. The editors and contributors hereby express their appreciation of this assistance. The views expressed in this volume are those of the authors alone.

continuing interplay of economic forces and related social classes; and those dynamics are reflected and furthered through institutional innovation and change." However, the authors of this volume are also likely to share the following view expressed by Lukacs (1971:8) when he wrote, "Only in [a] context which sees the isolated facts of social life as aspects of the historical process and integrates them in a totality, can knowledge of the facts hope to become knowledge of reality." (See also Onitiri, 1973; Baran, 1970.)

Essentially, all the authors, directly or otherwise, ask the same question: What are the reasons for the poverty and the "underdevelopment" of the continent? The question is approached historically, for it is the past, rather than some evolutionary dynamics, which has shaped the present, and it is past events and "experience" which so many contemporary analysts have elected to ignore. It is the "decline of the historical perspective," Barrington Moore (1958:136-137) writes, "and the use of a formalist deductive tradition in search of laws [which] has been accompanied by an increasing static bias in much contemporary social science." At the same time he warns us that "The search for categories that apply without reference to time or place easily introduces a static bias unless we are extremely careful to notice the historical limits of our generalizations. . . . The investigator discovers, or thinks he has discovered, a relationship that actually holds for a limited period of history, and extends it unjustifiably into the future."

All the authors of this volume see historical analysis, and in particular the multidisciplinary approach, as a way of explaining realities—the realities of the introduction and spread of colonialism and capitalism or, more precisely, colonial capitalism, all the major and complex processes as revealed in the specific political, economic, and social matrix of colonial and postcolonial Africa. Our contributors are not Marxist in the same manner in which some French colleagues have declared themselves. Yet our contributors have certainly made extensive use of the various modifications of this influential approach which is now being given more serious attention than perhaps at any time during this century. We assume that all the authors may share the fruitfulness of this approach while they are also likely to subscribe to the caution expressed by the editors of the *Review of African Political Economy* ("Editorial," 1975:2):

All too often, Marxist analyses, in attempting to correct . . . [various bourgeois] tendencies, mechanically transposed to African societies schema of the class relations characteristic of Western capitalism, and its development from European feudalism. These Marxists tended to proceed by assertion, from some inexorable historical precedent, rather than through the analysis of African societies and their relations to the rest of the world. Marxist analysis cannot proceed from textbook definitions of classes removed from their history and their society. It is not a matter of a theory or a model claiming universal validity. Marxist analysis requires examination and analysis of the material conditions which determine the possibilities for and obstacles to revolutionary action by the exploited classes. It demands a political analysis, in terms of class struggle, of the steps necessary to fashion the conditions under which a class, in alliance with other classes, can transform its own situation and end its exploitation. It is not a matter of disputing, say, the relative revolutionary capacity of workers against peasants in the abstract, but of examining the relations of workers and peasants to their exploiters and to one another, in order to identify the conditions under which the struggles of the exploited classes may converge in opposition to the entire system of exploitation.

At the same time Harvey, in his recent book *Social Justice and the City* (1973:126-127), pointedly makes this suggestion directed at skeptic and antagonist alike.

> The Marxist theory was [and is] clearly dangerous in that it appeared to provide the key to understanding capitalist production from the position of those *not* in control of the means of production. Consequently, the categories, concepts, relationships and methods which had the potential to form a new paradigm were an enormous threat to the power structure of the capitalist world.

It is the hope of the editors that caution has been combined with commitment; that the "message" contained in this volume states clearly that the incorporation of Africa into, and its subsequent subjugation to, the world capitalist system led to the destruction of varied and culturally rich polities and social structures and to the installation of new productive activities based on the needs of the capitalist system, but that all this was achieved by means of conquest, oppression, and exploitation.

Thus Bernard Magubane in his essay points his finger directly at the roots of Africa's poverty. He insists that "the political economy in Africa can only be understood in terms of the relation of various African countries to the international power structure and the social classes this power structure reproduced within the dominated formations," while Philip Ehrensaft suggests that "Underdevelopment is not a condition of being several centuries behind the kinds of transformations experienced in the capitalist center, but a condition of satellitization forced upon the periphery since 1500."

It may be argued that the weakness of these arguments stems from a Eurocentric perspective, however strongly denied but nevertheless subtly expressed, which casts the countries of Africa (as well as Latin America and much of Asia) in a common mold, a largely passive recipient of historical forces unleashed in Europe (and later in North America) to which no response was possible. This, of course, is neither historically correct nor the orientation of any of the authors. Each African country responded differently according to the degree of incorporation and subjugation experienced—that is, according to their historical background and experiences (slavery, forced labor, administrative fiat, destruction of basic institutions), their ecology and resources, and their trade and exchange relationships during precolonial, colonial, and neocolonial times. Alpers in his recently published *Ivory and Slaves in East Central Africa* (1975:267) comments on this perspective as follows:

> Interpretations which look to the structure of African societies for the roots of underdevelopment err in confusing a lack of economic development for the dynamic of underdevelopment. Those who seek these roots in colonialism err in assuming that trade between Europe and Africa, not to mention that between India and Africa, was equally beneficial to all parties. The evidence presented here suggests, quite to the

contrary, that the historical roots of underdevelopment in East Central Africa must be sought in the system of international trade which was established by Arabs by the thirteenth century, seized and extended by the Portuguese in the sixteenth and seventeenth centuries, and finally by a complex admixture of Indian, Arab and Western capitalism.

Thus, rather than search for inflexible categories (to heed Moore's warning) and common responses, the authors treat specific countries and regions within countries or concentrate on particular problems to build up a mosaic of African experiences and reactions. Thus rather than either a Eurocentric or Afrocentric perspective, the various contributors have concentrated on what they perceive to be "objective" conditions as revealed in the "chains of historical causation." Marxist and non-Marxist alike will surely share the conclusion reached by Marx that much of Asia, Africa, and Latin America were "swept by universal commerce into the universal competitive struggle" (Marx and Engels, 1963:58).

The "traditional" social, economic, political, and cultural structures of African societies, in their vast variety, form the background of most presentations in this volume. It is important to recognize that none of the authors treats these structures as static and immutable; change has taken place particularly in the exchange relations between groups and in political relations, i.e., the contraction or expansion of influences beyond the area occupied by any particular ethnic group. This dynamic and often very fluid situation and the initiatives taken by Africans are clearly demonstrated by Madame Coquery-Vidrovitch. Therefore, it is accepted as basic that every society has its transformational sources, that is, its own internal contradictions generated from the forces of production, the ownership of property, and the use of surplus and, possibly, from class antagonism (in all but the smallest scale societies). However, this does not imply the inevitability of a linear development but rather that few societies are wholly homogeneous and totally resistant to external influences. Marxist analysis does not, therefore, coerce observed changes into a "stages" theory of social and economic evolution. Rather, emphasis is given to how indigenous structures articulate with external influences. In the context of our essays, this means the ways in which the African continent has been involved commercially with Europe, the Islamic world, and India and, eventually, in the seventeenth and eighteenth centuries, with a worldwide system of mercantile capitalism. These consequences Alpers (1975:165) summarizes as follows:

> The dangers of attempting to achieve economic development [of the indigenous African economies] as opposed to mere economic growth by linking a significant sector of one's economy to capitalist economies, and of surrendering basic decision-making power over the developmental path to be followed by one's society exist whatever the nationality of the dominating capitalist power.

Thus it is not a matter of "integration" with these powerful external intrusions, but rather of hegemony over, and fluctuating fortunes for, non-European countries. The indigenous structures came to serve new ends as African societies were drawn into new commercial and political relationships which during the nineteenth and twentieth centuries were controlled by an imperialist outpouring of Western European competition for raw material resources, trade, and markets and for outlets for mercantile and, later, industrial capital (Kay, 1975). Indigenous economic structures largely lost their functions, legitimacy, and autonomy as they were incorporated into the colonial capitalist state with its primary objective of extraction of resources both physical and human. Subsistence economies were transformed into peasant or wage-labor structures. Africa's rural economy was transformed into a vast reservoir of labor to be shunted about according to the fortunes of the capitalist economies; and, as a result, there was set in motion the processes of proletarianization dependency, and internal center-periphery relations, i.e., the dominance of towns over the rural areas, one region over another, or one (African) country over another. (See O'Brien, 1975; Galting, 1972; Gonzalez, 1974; Gonzalez-Casanova, 1969.)

All the authors in this volume stress that there was an asymmetrical and unequal economic relationship between Africa and the industrially highly developed world and that the "change process on the periphery of the world capitalist system is not an endogenous path through stages, but a process subject to powerful exogenous factors" (Langdon, 1974:124). These structural inequalities have generated internal class divisions, often intensifying older forms of stratification and various subimperialisms (as in parts of West Africa), with the result that local elites, whose economic and political power stems from their incorporation into the colonial capitalist state (the "insiders"), control any possible transformation of the rural economy which must be made to serve the extractive export sector of the economy. Thus the progressive evolution of a class system and its rapid crystallization, as revealed in enormous income differentials and massive unemployment (Kay, 1975), are all an indication of the (negative) interaction between internal and external developments in the peripheral colonial and neocolonial economies. A vital aspect of this interaction is the alliances and strategies between various groups internally and the linkages of such groups to the external (metropolis) forces. To put it briefly, it is the function of local power groups to assist the metropolis in the export of surplus created by local labor power. Therein lie the fundamental roots of the "contradictions" extant in the various African countries. Frank (1971:23) sums this up as follows: "for the generation of structural underdevelopment, more important still than the drain of economic surplus . . . is the impregnation of the satellite's domestic economy with the same capitalistic structure and its fundamental contradictions." Although Frank has been criticized for the "economistic" character of his model and the absence of the specifics of economic and class formations, this aspect of his model can be readily applied to the African continent as a whole, although regional differences may call for various modifications.

The exact nature of the "contradictions" and their evolution and systemic operation in precolonial African societies still require much detailed research. However, those contradictions revealed in present-day Africa have their origin in the incorporation of the continent into international trade and the operations of an updated form of merchant capital. Kay makes this clear in two important passages which are worth quoting in full (1975:125, 124):

> The collapse of primary commodity prices during the depression of the 1930's brought all the pressures bearing on merchant capital to a head. The savagely reduced prices it was forced to pay producers in a desperate attempt to protect its profits carried the crisis [from the developed] into the underdeveloped world, which responded with nationalist opposition to the whole political and economic order established in the nineteenth century.

Hence merchant capital, caught in a serious crisis which threatened its very existence, began to operate alongside investment-industrial capital.

> As [the] profits dwindled merchant capital began to lose the last remnant of independence and was forced to act simply as the agent of industrial capital. To survive as capital it was forced out of trade directly into the sphere of production; that is, it was forced to act as productive capital openly. At the same time productive capital which had previously restricted its activities to the developed world, finding its role of profit from the underdeveloped countries ceasing to grow if not actually decline, was obliged to intervene directly. The result was a new phase in the history of underdevelopment: the inception of a capitalist mode of production proper in the underdeveloped world. But capital could not wipe out its own history and begin [in the 1930s] as though nothing had happened previously; it was forced to operate in the conditions of underdevelopment which it had itself created: conditions that were quite different from those that prevailed in the developed countries in the eighteenth and nineteenth centuries.

Underdevelopment, then, is the product of the operations and contradictions *within* the capitalist system (a once fashionable assertion now being fleshed out by careful analytical research), and it is just as clearly revealed in the relations between England and Scotland, as between Great Britain and Nigeria, in terms of the modes of expropriation of surplus value and the structure of its appropriation. It is, therefore, not a matter (alone) of the rich world versus the poor world. (See Hechter, 1975; Brown, 1975.)

During the colonial era development took place only in those sectors producing for export, in the import trade, and in the structures and services required to collect raw materials and distribute imports; and much of this took place in Britain between 1790 and 1945. Thus it eventually has become evident that the continued expansion of the so-called "modern sector," to the detriment of the needs of the vast majority of Africans, has led them to escape from rural poverty only to join the ranks of the unemployed in the towns and cities. Today these export-import oriented enclaves and the totally asymmetrical urbanization, "overurbanization" and parasitism of the primate city force "the subordination of the peasant communities to a trade, always induced from outside, and the subsequent deterioration of the rural sector to the benefit of the commercial and industrial capitalist sector" (Meillassoux, 1971:85). Capitalism, Meillassoux notes (1971:76), acts in two ways.

> On [the] one hand it elicits a sector of production built up in its own image through the presence of capital and its corollaries—private control of the means of production and wage earning. On the other hand it feeds off the pre-capitalist sectors through the

mechanism of primitive accumulation—with the contradictory results of both perpetuating and destroying them at the same time. The introduction of capitalism had the dual effect of maintaining a dependent African commercial sector and of competing eventually with traditional trade.

Such a model does not, however, indicate support for Boeke's dualism theory, which describes two sectors static in nature and isolated from each other and governed by separate institutions (Singer, 1970). Rather, the dualism that did emerge from the middle of the nineteenth century reveals the dialectical relationship of the two sectors. The growth of the "modern" imperialist-oriented export-import sector required the destruction of the more traditional economies. This more current assessment of the roots of poverty of the African nations (as well as those of Latin America and parts of Asia) contrasts strongly with the view expressed by Lewis in 1961 (pp. 274, 411-412), who suggested that

> at low levels of economic activity, production for the foreign market is usually the turning point which sets a country on the road to economic growth. . . . Foreigners bring new skills, new tastes, capital and expanding markets. They may also bring exploitation, but if in one's zeal to prevent exploitation one keeps them out altogether, the country is deprived equally of their stimulus.

This conceptualization opened the door to the multinational corporations. Africans would respond like rational (American?) economic men! All that was required was to develop further the task which the colonial power had started but not quite completed: to bring into being a powerful domestic capitalist class "linked to and dependent on the very institutions which must be changed fundamentally" (Seidman, n.d.). State capitalism will not restructure the cannibalized African economies—even if this model parades under the name of socialism.

It is the emergence of a distinctive bourgeoisie in virtually every African nation which reveals as clearly as the statistics do when, how, and why Africa was incorporated into the world capitalist system. Today, the African bourgeoisie, much in evidence, is part of and the inheritors of what Magubane has called the "colonial capitalist mode of production" (CCMP), an amalgam of previous modes of production with a modern capitalist variant. The "greatest impact of the CCMP" writes Magubane, "was on the level of the working class which produced the super profits in the plantations and mines." While in classic capitalist societies the proletariat broke away completely from the subsistence economy, in Africa—because of the extractive nature of colonial capitalism—"the integration of African peasants into the world capitalist system was marginal. It led to impoverishment without [as yet] complete proletarianization." Yet today this class structure of neocolonial Africa is far from simple. (See Arrighi and Saul, 1968; Cohen, 1972; Kitching, 1972.) Explicit class divisions among the elites, the bourgeoisie, the proletariat, and the peasantry have yet to reveal themselves, and when they do they might well take different forms from that we may daringly predict. At the same time the present political and economic power holders derive their elevated position from the forces of imperialism which both reared them and currently still protect them.

Immanuel Wallerstein, the first contributor, introduces us to the idea of the world-system and Africa's place in and relationship to this system, "whose fundamental dynamic largely controlled the actors located in both sectors of one united arena" (see also Wallerstein, 1973, 1974). He sets out to "draw an interpretive sketch of the historical outlines of the political economy of contemporary Africa, . . . an outline of the various stages (and modes) of its involvement in this capitalist world-economy." He draws a fundamental distinction between the early luxury trade between distinct "external arenas" and the later core-periphery trade in primary products (essentials), with the result that eventually the external arenas merge into a single (world) system.

The first incorporation, 1750-1900, transformed relations from relative autonomy to peripheralization and the expansion of the geographical boundaries of the capitalist world economy. As peripheralization proceeded, a newly created bourgeoisie "might come to utilize the local state structures to erect mercantilist barriers. Ideally what the core countries wanted was a direct channel to primary producers, an unencumbered economic alliance," which then allowed any consequences of reduced demand to be shifted directly to the producer rather than the owners of enterprise.

The second phase of incorporation, 1900-1975, the period which eventually revealed the extent and implications of peripheralization, rested heavily on the extraction of raw materials and on the exploitation of the low-cost labor available. This phase, Wallerstein suggests, was brought to an end by the contradictions which revealed themselves in the world capitalist system—and Africa's role within it.

The third phase, the present, is one which presents Africa with a major challenge: dependent development or revolutionary transformation? (Wallerstein, 1975). Wallerstein suggests that an attempt will be made to increase effective demand in the Third World by expanding the forces of production, resulting in a new hierarchy within the world system. This might strengthen the power of semiperipheral areas but also result in the further decline of truly peripheral areas—hence, possibly, massive unemployment.

Philip Ehrensaft, the second contributor, concentrates on the semiperipheral areas. He suggests that

> Underdevelopment is not a condition of being several centuries behind the kinds of transformations experienced in the capitalist center but a condition of satellitization forced upon the periphery since 1500 by this very center. Integration of a peripheral power structure, which benefits from satellitization, with corporate capital from the center results in structures which permit, at most, a limited degree of industrialization through import-substitution. Fundamental economic transformation is thus precluded within a peripheral capitalist mode of production. The choice for the masses, again, is stagnation or socialist revolution.

Specifically, Ehrensaft is putting forward a more refined model of (a) the dynamics of peripheralization and (b) satellitization. His purpose is to examine the role of a given peripheral territory from the moment of its initial integration into world capitalism. Peripheral societies, he suggests, are not necessarily those transitional toward capitalism "but rather constitute a particular and distinctive form of modern capitalism which developed pari passu and in direct relation to the world economy. It is thus incorrect to speak of 'modernizing' the periphery. Latin America, Asia, and Africa have been modernized for some centuries now, but in ways that render them distinctive from and dependent upon the center."

His central interest is to ask "whether there is at least a possibility that some peripheral societies might advance beyond stagnation within a capitalist mode of production." He suggests that "some of the larger and more strategic units of the periphery" might succeed in achieving "polarized accumulation" rather than a mere "semi-industrial capitalism." Hence the "theory of dependence should be reformulated to account for this possibility." A primary product exporter does not lead necessarily to the "development of underdevelopment," because polarized accumulation is *one possible* path through which *some* semi-industrial capitalist economies *might* move beyond semi-industrialism [i.e., stagnation] while remaining within the capitalist orbit." The critical issue is whether the semi-industrial capitalist societies are of the "classic" or "dominion" type. Ehrensaft concludes that certain stronger peripheral states will be able to drive increasingly hard bargains vis-à-vis the multinationals.

In her essay, Catherine Coquery-Vidrovitch returns to the topic of the African mode of production, contrasting it with the (controversial) Asian mode of production, a variant which Jean Suret-Canale attempted to locate in pre-colonial Africa. (See Coquery-Vidrovitch, 1969; Krader, 1975; Suret-Canale, 1964.) In 1969 she had expressed her skepticism on the ground that this attempt had eliminated the dynamic element in African history—namely, the foreign contacts, such as long distance trade, which she sees as the major feature of the African mode of production. The evolution of economic, political, and social structures in Africa, she suggests, was the consequence of a dualistic organization based on subsistence agriculture and long-distance trade. "The real process of African history," she writes, "was that of the collision of two heterogeneous modes of production, capitalist and 'African,' and the overthrow of one by the other."

In contrast to the Asian mode of production, the privileged minority groups in power, exploited less their "own subjects than the neighboring tribes." Hence, no "African regime, no matter how despotic, felt the need to eliminate communal village structures within its borders." While the Asian mode of production exercised direct control, the African mode did so more indirectly; the former employed extensive internal exploitation, and the latter sought gain primarily by means of external relations; the former exercised control over land and the latter over long-distance trade; and the former was based on an autocratic state system while in Africa authority often rested within the community and its local economy. Thus the dialectical interplay in African history is between heterogeneous socioeconomic levels within the same unit—i.e., communal clan structures, territorial entities, subsistence activities, and long-distance trade. Agricultural surplus was rarely available; where it did exist it was in nonagricultural goods (salt in West Africa and ivory in East Africa). Thus, Coquery-Vidrovitch puts forward the view that the "mode of circulation" was probably as important as "mode of production." The issue was not so much how to transport the goods, but to "procure" them—in a sense, to "produce" them.

The African mode of production is "based upon the combination of a patriarchal agrarian economy . . . and the exclusive ascendancy of one group over long-distance trade. The form of power at any given moment depended upon the nature of this group." Political and economic power of the bureaucracy and the ethnic group declined if control over long-distance trade was lost or the exchange of goods went into recession. Yet the African mode of production is not dependent on the exploitation by a despot of a peasant class. Two systems, supportive of each other yet largely independent, the village and state, facilitated the African mode of production. Eventually African societies moved away from this particular mode of production into the worldwide capitalist orbit, moving from the exploitation of (foreign) neighbors to the exploitation of individuals within their own communities. African societies, in this process, were "adulterated" in that "capitalist relationships of production are [now] closely linked to the more archaic forms of relationship, to the greater profit of the privileged." The days were now past when an African bureaucracy interfered only indirectly with the local community and respected the structures of rural life. Once again the "chains of historical causation" are demonstrated with the impact of foreign intrusion—i.e., the expansion of Islam, the slave trade, early merchant activities, the introduction of cash-cropping in the nineteenth century, and eventually the arrival of industrial capital, all of which destroyed the African mode of production, although its precise empirical roots, if roots there are, call for further research.

Lionel Cliffe in his "Rural Political Economy of Africa" asks a number of questions. What are the causes of agrarian underdevelopment? Why has Africa become a major food importer? Why has African agriculture not developed along capitalist lines? Why do precapitalist modes of production persist? Cliffe raises the seminal issues whether or not merchant and commercial capital can transform precapitalist modes (Kay, 1975) and, like Marx, observes that this depends "on the character of the old mode of production" and not alone on the impact of commerce.

Essentially Cliffe argues that Africa was subjected to politically enforced incorporation without economic transformation.

> The continued existence in rural Africa of precapitalist elements in the social formation is at once the measure of the continent's underdevelopment and also its cause and continually reproduced result. . . . The transformations that have occurred have stalled, essentially because the wider international system has wanted the societies to be a source of primitive accumulation, not of expanded reproduction. African rural societies have thus been structured so as to provide the required commodities—peasant products and labor power—below the price of their reproduction through the market. . . . The artificial preservation of precapitalist modes is a crucial counterrevolutionary measure as well as one which allows primitive accumulation.

What then will transform the rural political economy of Africa? Cliffe points in the following direction.

[If] the forces of international capital acting in a variety of ways on rural Africa are not in the end capable of fully transforming Africa's forces or relations of production . . . one must logically go on to ask the question . . . can rural social forces be their own instrument for change? . . . Identification of the forces of change can only come from a class analysis of particular social formations, which would reveal region by region those strata whose interests are likely to steer them into support of (or opposition to) a particular alternative to the existing political economy.

The role of peasants and their transformation into urban workers is taken up in the next two papers, by Gavin Williams and Robin Cohen respectively. "Modernization and development," Williams observes, "have been achieved only on the backs and over the dead bodies of peasants or by the liquidation of peasants as a class," because colonialism has incorporated the African producer into the capitalist world market, with only minimal advantage to a few, and has subjected the majority to the authority and control of the colonial state. Development has failed because it has been brought from the outside by the state and its "experts." Despite failures, Nigeria, for example, encourages capitalist and state-farming enterprises with the result that "Conflict within rural communities is the result of peasant hostility to the local allies of an oppressive government." Governments have failed in their relations with peasants because the political economy of rural Africa cannot be treated "independently of its relation to commodity exchange"; the peasant farm is more than an enterprise, it is the only source of livelihood. A major failure is that "Commodity production by family farms is [wrongly] interpreted as one of the ways in which capitalist production assimilates precapitalist modes of production to itself." But a mere recognition by governments of inequalities is not sufficient evidence for the fundamentally capitalist tendencies of the development of the peasant economy. The real issue is that "Class relations, not inequality as such, define production as capitalist."

It is assumed that peasants can produce goods and services at lower prices than capitalists can, *because they are peasants* and because of the innovative ways in which they have, allegedly, incorporated changes into the peasant economy. But this innovation has not increased their wealth or power under capitalist or socialist African governments. Peasants "have sought to defend their gains [however modest] within the frontiers of peasant society, but have not [been able in most cases] to seize state power and thus control the instrument of their own exploitation," simply because they lack the resources to do so. Hence they tend to "remain committed to the institutions which are the means of their exploitation and oppression." The way out of this dilemma is that "the development of peasant production is a condition for the development of industrial production."

Robin Cohen warns us of the dangers of placing "concepts in an historical deep freeze, embalmed around a particular historical conjuncture, conditioned by an image of an ideal or pure form of the social object. A purist position can take no account of a changing context within which a previous identification of a social category finds new expression." Cohen is concerned with labels, peasants, cultivators and workers, and process and, as far as the last is concerned, begs us to "comprehend the processual character involved in all social change." He protests that the charge of ethnocentrism, often directed against Marxists, "can in fact more accurately be leveled against those who wish to isolate European or North American experiences from the mainstream of common social processes."

He is concerned with a number of processes—such as peasantization ("the widening and depersonalization of market relations consequent on the introduction of a pervasive cash economy and a colonial state"), proletarianization (consequent on the spread of capitalism and the colonial state), the market economy, and wage labor. Africa's involvement in both the market economy and wage labor started, in his view, "the chain of proletarianization," the creation of an often landless group unable to meet cash demands either to pay taxes or to purchase basic necessities. He thus points to the central contradiction of the colonial economy, which tried to maintain a delicate balance between supplying agricultural products (for export and market garden needs) and supplying labor wherever needed and which, above all, tried to prevent the rural economy from becoming too viable. The chains of proletarianization, and the consciousness associated with it, move more or less in "harness with changing economic realities."

In the next essay, Bernard Magubane sees these changing economic realities in the unfolding of the class structure in Africa. He asks: "By means of what concept or what set of concepts is it possible to think of the determination of a subordinate structure by a dominant structure?" He puts forward the concept of the "colonial capitalist mode of production" (CCMP) as "useful in the analysis of particular, concrete, historical realities of incorpoation [and] the articulation and combination of various modes of production that are subsumed by capitalism under the special conditions of colonialism." The "class situation" arises as follows:

> Insofar as the capitalist mode of production dominates the precapitalist modes and subjects their manpower to its need and the logic of its own mode of functioning, i.e., integrates them more or less in the mechanism of its own reproduction, then we have a class situation.

Magubane is explicit. "The bourgeois sociologists," he writes, "have trivialized class as simply one aspect of a graded system of social stratification" while in classical sociology it was understood that "class relationships could not be studied apart from the study of political economy." A class analysis, as Dos Santos insisted (1970:181), exposes the "relations or modes of relations conditioning the possibilities of interaction among men, given a determinate mode of production." The classes that emerged in Africa, after the continent's incorporation into the world capitalist system, says Magubane, "were not reflective of an autonomous economy, but were auxiliary to the world class structure." Hence an understanding of Africa's class structure "must begin with an inquiry into the degree of exploitation of African resources and labor, and must proceed to follow the surplus to its destination outside Africa—into the bank accounts of the world capitalist class."

This world capitalist class refused to allow Africa to become capitalist—or indeed even to develop a wholly capitalist milieu. Here Magubane quotes Ernest Mandel (1972:96), who characterized this condition neatly.

> Capitalism, and especially imperialism, combined development and underdevelopment, the rapid growth of some nations with the retarded growth of others, not by making all produce under the same capitalist conditions of production, but precisely by maintaining varying degrees of pre-capitalist or semi-capitalist relations of production in most colonial and semi-colonial countries.

Although the African societies were kept in this condition, they were subjected to "violent penetration and rupture . . . and the subjugation of their economic life to the profit impulse of the Western bourgeoisie [which] constitute[s] the fundamental reality of modern Africa."

The satellite predicament of the African nations "sets limits to the evolution of social classes," for it is this condition which "ensures that no independent bourgeoisie emerges and that the working class will remain as segments within the peasant subsistence economies." In current radical writing on Africa, this is controversial enough, since Fanonists, old-style Marxists, and, now, Maoists will differ in their interpretations. Magubane himself notes that the term "wage worker" in Africa embraces a large group of various semiproletarian elements. Thus, clearly, the filtering out of various strata is still taking place.

Independence "aggravated rather than resolved the class contradictions because some inheritors of the colonial estate further entrenched the full range of colonial privileges." This privileged class is now firmly established in the cities of Africa, which have become the "focus of the accumulated contradictions of colonial capitalism and its class conflict." A weak middle class is unable to resolve its predicament because it cannot act autonomously so long as its position is underwritten by foreign monopolies. Hence it turns to populism and African socialism and may support military takeovers.

The theme is continued in the next paper by Claude Ake, who turns our attention from structures to ideologies, although their interdependence is obvious. This is made clear when he writes that "ideologies are not autonomous but derivative," because the "colonial relation demands, indeed imposes, a particular political system and particular ideologies congruent with its objective character." Class interests had to be defended, with the appropriate ideologies, and popular sovereignty or substantive democracy could not be allowed without undermining colonial capitalist production. Ideologies were and are rigid: "The political stance and the political style of both the colonizers and the nationalist leaders were rigidly defined by the colonial situation."

Enemies fought one another with the same weapons or, as Ake puts it, "one exclusive claim to power against another." But the position changed once the colonizers departed and the conflict between the new rulers and the masses appeared. The ideology of the former explicitly guided their policies.

> They decided to maintain the exploitative relations and a stratification system that they dominated. They decided to firmly discourage demands for redistribution of wealth and for mass participation.

Clearly, the stakes were and are enormous. Who should control the power and the structure of the state, its law and order machinery, and, above all, how might the state be used to guide the economy both internally and externally? To safeguard the privileges of the elite, they proclaimed, as did their Western counterparts, the "end of ideology"; the ideology of fascism replaced the ideology of liberty; conformism and order were "necessary for maximum effectiveness in dealing with the problems of development"; the insistence on "unity" turned out to be "blatantly self-serving." Ake, harshly, sums up the significant features of the postindependence ideology of the leaders: it is the ideology always "associated with the establishment and consolidation of the dictatorship of the bourgeoisie."

But despite, or because of this, two revolutionary pressures remain: poverty and "the consciousness of the burden of poverty and the injustices of economic inequality." The needed transformation can be summed up as the need to develop the forces of production instead of the extraction of surplus by coercion. So far this has not taken place in Africa. Instead, the ideology of the bourgeoisie—what Ake has called "defensive radicalism"—is a sham which, ideologically, presents itself in many disguises but whose real intent is to buy time for the bourgeoisie while its long range (positive) effect is to develop the consciousness of the masses and reveal the contradictions within the structures of the contemporary political economy of Africa. Defensive radicalism creates exploitation which cannot be satisfied in the context of the existing order.

P-Kiven Tunteng, in the following essay, turns to a new theme which remains largely unexplored in African studies: subimperialism within the African continent. He challenges the idea that the "retreat of the colonial powers" has meant "that imperialism remains only as an aberrant exception in a few areas of the continent."

He thus suggests that it is not sufficient to limit the analysis of imperialism to actions by foreign powers. His concentration is really on neocolonialism (rather than economic and political relations between various African powers) and on the various agreements and linkages which remain between Francophone West Africa and France. Most of these arrangements, which indicate how "the chain of historical causation" is brought into the present, are unstable and pragmatic arrangements which allow the continued exploitation of France's old imperial domains. The thrust behind various agreements, while predominantly economic, also reveal an aspect of imperialism in which France excelled, namely cultural dominance. Nothing must be allowed to disturb the "pattern of tranquility, the illusion of harmonious change" in Franco-African relations. The French government has taken upon itself to oversee and determine the road of economic and political development of France's once extensive African empire. "The various accords signed by France and its African colonies on the eve of their independence," Tunteng suggests, "provided the juridical framework for [a] patron-client relationship." In the process, France carefully manipulates the relations between the main contenders (Senegal, the Ivory Coast, and the Congo) for subimperial influence in West Africa and tilts the wealthier states against the poorer and the poorer against the others. French loyalties and assistance shift according to French economic and political objectives. "The 'real' imperialists," Tunteng notes, "just as the 'real' bourgeoisie, are resident abroad, while their agents advance their predetermined objectives within the region."

Tunteng points to the inherent difficulties in the promotion of African unification while West Africa is the scene of an intense struggle for leadership between Senegal, the Ivory Coast, and Nigeria. Within Francophone West Africa this struggle has been won, for the moment, by President Houphouët-Boigny, while within the Anglophone region Nigeria is the undisputed dominant influence. All the major West African powers vie for hegemonic influence over their neighbors—aspirations and actions unlikely to affect the economic conditions of the masses of Africans. Tunteng concludes:

> Indeed, throughout Africa, the majority has been subjected to economic injustices from their black rulers just as they did from the colonial regimes. This situation has been concealed by the illusion of the alleged communal African spirit which makes for a preference to share with one's brethren. . . . That the elites can remain indifferent to such awesome inequality . . . indicates that, barring revolutionary upheavals, the prospects of change are indeed limited.

Research into hegemonic relations within the African continent, particularly the fate of small ethnic minorities, has so far received relatively little attention from the perspective of the structure of inequality.

Clearly, the most hegemonic imperialism is identified with Southern Africa and in particular with South Africa. No treatment of the contemporary political economy of Africa would be complete without some concentration on that region of the continent. Ben Turok and Kees Maxey in their essay make this position clear from the start:

> The subcontinent will remain in a condition of continuous conflict until all the white regimes and especially that of South Africa have fallen. And that particular task remains especially difficult since its ruling class regards itself as indigenous, having no metropole to retreat to, and since imperialist interests still regard this class as the bastion of Western economic, political, and military interests in the region as a whole.

The authors, like others writing on the same theme, are torn between optimism that change will follow in the wake of new pressures to relax the hegemony of white domination (the collapse of Portuguese colonialism has inspired a part of this optimism) and the pessimism they reveal when they note that the South African system has congealed into one of the most undemocratic, unequal, and authoritarian in the world, with white political power being used to enforce and entrench white privilege in every sphere.

Various liberation movements threaten the white laagers of southern Africa. But more threatening yet would be the consequences of dismantling the migrant labor system or the land-apportionment and group-areas regulations or to underwrite economically the Bantustans in such a way that labor would no longer need to seek employment elsewhere. The industrialization of South Africa was "contingent on the maintenance of a cheap migrant labor system. The greater the intensity of exploitation of black workers, the faster the economy could grow, and the greater the surplus to syphon off for white appropriation." For the time being, no changes will take place to alter the structure of inequality while the Western powers do whatever they consider necessary to protect their investments and their sources of basic raw materials and maintain South Africa as a link in the chain of defense.

The South African economy depends heavily on migrant labor, and despite the brutal control exercised over the movements of Africans, the influx into urban areas continues. It is probably the urbanization of South Africa, the most extensive in Africa, and the secularization of the African population, which is generating the kind of pressures which are now revealing themselves in strikes, new wage agreements, and an intensifying demand for such other political rights as the right to form and join trade unions that are not government inspired and controlled. (See Institute for Industrial Education, 1974; Dekker et al., 1974.) Turok and Maxey observe that it is such pressures, and the changing geopolitical map of southern Africa, that matter, and it is their "effects on the root structures that will determine whether history has really moved." Whether these pressures are the result of geopolitical change or spring from the "increasing contradictions in the system of apartheid" is uncertain. What is certain, however, is that white domination and exploitation are not eternal.

In the next paper, Tamas Szentes turns our attention to the critical issue of investment in African economic development. He appraises various strategies and their operationalization. Investment is needed but of what kind? Szentes turns to what he calls a contradiction. "Why" is it, he asks, that,

> in general, the more intensive the penetration of foreign capital has been, the higher the level of commodity production, accumulation, GNP per capita, etc. has become on the one hand, and the more marked the disastrous socioeconomic consequences have been on the other.

Whether these consequences are the result of foreign investment or result from the broader complex of transformation is a matter to be debated. Thus it might be suggested that rather than capital investment being the guilty party, the broader spectrum of capitalism caused the havoc that we now see before us. Szentes seems to share this view, for he writes:

> Social transformation following the rise of capitalist relations in the enclave sectors not only was more painful as a result of having been governed by foreign interests but

also resulted in a misbirth: the old did not completely disappear, and the new was built not on the ruins but among the remnants of the old. . . . Thus modern relations become associated with traditional conditions [because in peripheral countries] the steps of real development were taken in forms, under conditions, and with consequences that have erected new obstacles to further development.

This is a theme which runs through virtually all the papers; the old had to be sacrificed, to be left in a liminal state, uncertain between two worlds, but made to serve the needs of capitalist exploitation.

Szentes suggests that the old international division of labor, between industrial and primary producers, is changing to one between

centers of scientific and technological progress and the periphery of all those countries relying on the regular imports of the technical achievements and scientific results of the former. Although it may add new features to the economy of developing countries by a certain type and level of industrialization, it may result in an even wider gap between center and periphery than the present one.

In the light of this, investment patterns have changed over the years and now point clearly in the direction of capital-intensive activities. Apart from the inevitable increase in unemployment, and its likely political consequences, Szentes suggests other disadvantages to the economy.

Since the imported capital-intensive techniques with their relatively high technical level . . . mean the exclusion of local labor from the training process or at least the restriction of this training process to a narrow worker elite, the old mechanisms which ensure the predominance of those sectors and techniques that produce hardly any linkage effects are, strangely enough, left unchanged in the rest of the economy.

The importation of ready-made technology increases the dependency of all the African nations, and, in the urge to modernize, "there is hardly any room for technological experimentations, innovations, and research."

Almost every development plan in Africa now calls for considerable investment in the rural economy, although the classic pattern of an economy based on "extractive imperialism" will continue to be the main source of national revenue, to be used in an effort to transform this important sector. However, a close study of many of these development plans reveals that the political and economic elite (almost totally urban-based) continue to look upon the rural areas as a source of cash crops for export and as a market garden economy to supply the needs of the cities. A symbiotic relationship between rural and urban areas threatens the hegemony of the cities over the rural areas.

A small number of African scholars in particular have suggested complete disengagement from various capitalist metropoles. Szentes considers such a policy neither realistic nor the exclusive alternative "in view of [present] structural relations" and that it is likely to be harmful to Africa to "underestimate the growing dimensions of production, science, and technology and the concentration of their centers in the advanced sectors of capitalist world economy." This is a conclusion with very far-reaching implications and surely raises the issue of "dependence in an interdependent world."

In the end, Szentes comes down on the side of loan capital rather than direct foreign investment capital; but this is only a partial solution, because without a "structural transformation" of the rural economy the prospect of decreasing dependency is small.

Chris Allen brings the book to a close with a bibliographical essay pointing out the best of the critical literature on the political economy of contemporary Africa. Those acquainted with his "Radical Africana," which now appears regularly in *The Review of African Political Economy* (RAPE), will know how exceedingly useful his work has been to a large number of scholars. His essay is a major teaching aid. However, Allen does not merely annotate; his essay sets out the outlines of a model of political economy, namely, a concern with a temporal dimension—the ways in which change may occur and be induced, the ways in which phenomena are reproduced or reproduce themselves, the possible economic basis of ostensibly noneconomic phenomena, and the sensitivity to other disciplines. Theoretically, he suggests that we view colonial economic policy as a consequence of the continued use of primitive accumulation and the uneven transformation of precapitalist economic and social structures.

A common theme among all the contributors is that the capitalist mode of production requires the extraction of surplus from labor to be retained by the capitalist-owner-investor. In Africa, as in other "underdeveloped" nations, the early stages of capitalist formation are violent and socially more destructive than, perhaps, at a later stage when the capitalist mode and capitalists are more established and secure in their ability to control. Until such a time, an extractive economy geared to exports and fueled by cheap labor is the basic mode of primitive accumulation in a colonial context (Levin, 1960). By definition, this produces both dependence and dominance, the destruction of political autonomy, the evisceration of the rural economy (depriving it of investments and savings), and the subordination of the nation to the imperial design. But dominance and dependence affect the various groups in the economy and polity differentially. Non-African settlers lord it over the indigenous population while they themselves remain under the dominance of the metropole; and, of course, the indigenous population is divided, roughly, between elites and masses. Each category relates both specifically and generally to the processes of capital accumulation and the authority of the colonial state.

Again, every contributor to this volume has something to say about underdevelopment, a condition resulting from externally imposed capitalist economic development strategies which seek to freeze, as it were, traditional forms of production and technology. Underdevelopment, therefore, is manifest during a period of change over which an indigenous people have virtually no control because their economic and political institutions are subordinated to the objectives of colonial and imperial power. The people were largely powerless to alter their situation in the face of "legal" and military repression, the expropriation of land, racial segregation, forced (and "recruited") labor, various forms of taxation (Van Zwanenberg, 1975), and, above all, a low-wage economy, which has made saving impossible and held the population in economic bondage.

This wage economy, and the migratory system which provided the labor, gave rise to proletarianization, the appearance of a disposed or landless class—a grouping dependent on the "sale" of its labor and resulting from the new relations of capitalist modes of production. Primitive accumulation requires an assured yet flexible supply of labor that is easily obtainable from the rural areas yet is not allowed to stabilize, not in any numbers at least, in the urban areas (Hooker, 1969). Yet shortages have persisted even during periods of modestly rising wages. Wage levels have determined labor supply, although rural to urban migration has steadily increased since 1920, generally independent of economic conditions. Not only were low wages essential for primitive accumulation (and for more highly developed capitalist systems too), but the imperial powers insisted that the rural sector provide the African with economic support and that labor be given wages tied to subsistence economies rather than to market conditions. In short, the colonial state in Africa administered the economy for the prosperity of a distant metropole and for the prosperity of a few local notables, all the while that poverty and stagnation increased. Apart from the consequences enumerated already, the result was (and is) an internal polarization—consisting of an elite, a bourgeoisie, professionals, traders, artisans, laborers, and the poor.

The dialectics of the political economy of Africa are now as much influenced by this polarization as by neocolonial hegemony. Each group stands in a particular relationship to the particular brand of metropolitan capitalism which is explicated in a complex class structure that varies from country to country. In the majority of African countries the present political leaders, and their "expert" advisors, have failed to resist the entry of the multinational corporations, the latest addition to the growing complexity of political and economic structures. Indeed, many leaders have encouraged their entry, which leads to the further consolidation of the power of local elites and an enlargement of their opportunity to expropriate their share of the surplus. Steve Langdon, writing about Kenya (1974:145), portrays this situation quite explicitly.

> The result has been remarkably favourable for the dominant African political-bureaucratic bourgeoisie in the political economy—and also significantly beneficial for those petty bourgeois and wage-earning elements, particularly in Nairobi and Central Province, with sources of access to the system; it is the interests of these "inside" classes that defend and perpetuate the structure of [this particular] political economy.

Yet no single wing of the bourgeoisie can command enough power to prevent it from being ousted by another wing. The corporate power of the bourgeoisie has firm control over the formal (nonagricultural) sector of the economy, leaving the informal sector to the impoverished African masses (ILO, 1972). The "insiders" have access to the state, while the "outsiders" must depend on brokers and patron-client networks. "State capitalism" has accentuated inequalities ever more strongly as revealed by conspicuous consumption by the administrative elite living off wealth often unethically obtained. The full productive capacity of African economies is inhibited deliberately by the few who stand to gain from the present stagnation. Perhaps more serious still are the consequences of ethnic and regional tensions which have their roots in the internal center-periphery imbalances, a condition which has so far received far too little analytical attention.

Let us then briefly summarize this Introduction. The approach taken in this volume might be seen as an alternative to the enormous influence which has flowed from the imperial historians and their Eurocentric perspective. Likewise, the essays are a challenge to anthropologists, economists, sociologists, and some contemporary historians. At present, the political scientists seem to be in search for a new direction. In all too many studies the underlying forces were never made explicit, largely because the concentration was on microunits. Analytical models were used which reflected a narrow ethnocentrism and often were totally removed from reality. Such has been the case in the field of labor history, which Van Onselen has recently critically reviewed (1975; see also MacRae, 1974). Van Onselen's conclusion sets out his criticism and also serves as a warning (p. 246):

> An evolutionary perspective, the notion of "race" to the exclusion of class, the concept of the *laissez faire* economy, and the idea of the backward "tribesman" are all singularly inappropriate tools for the study of industry in a colonial political economy. Until such time as the historiography and sociology reflect a greater understanding of the process of proletarianization, class formation and class conflict, the literature will remain one of the most unprofitable sources for the student of African labour history.

Likewise, the economists have failed to expose the underlying processes of the labor supply and wage policy, the operations of the imperial markets, the ways in which the world capitalist economy impinges on different sectors of the colonial economy, or the character of peripheralization and internal colonialism, even though economic historians have recently turned with determination to these topics. In short, the economists, like some historians, have been staunchly ahistorical, because they have considered the laws of capitalism to be eternal. But now we are beginning to look at the significance of merchant capital and its operation and at the distinctions between circulation and production (industrial capital), between appropriation of surplus product and expropriation of surplus value, and between different controls over the means of production (Kay, 1975).

However, a diachronic approach is not enough. It is the model that matters. The basic sources, yet largely untapped and often hard to find, are certain to be rich, and the analysis and interpretation are likely to be controversial. That Africa is "underdeveloped" is common knowledge, a cruel fact perhaps better understood by Africans than by those who make their living by studying this condition, but why this is so is the subject of this book. The authors have pointed to many cold empirical conditions which must be taken into account —including the import-export economy that results in a dependence on world commodity markets; the underdevelopment of the rural economy at the expense of the development of a bourgeoisie; the consequences of an extractive agri-culture; cash-cropping; peasantization and proletarianization; oligopolistic control of trade; and the arrival of multinationals. To understand these complex processes, which deserve concentrated study in the years ahead, the authors have "resurrected" the concept and the methods of political economy. (See Coleman, 1967; Chattopadhyay, 1974.) They have done so not merely because they consider themselves progressive, or radical, but also because this interdisciplinary model solicits our understanding of realities. As Chattopadhyay points out, Marx failed to define his use of this long-established concept (though he used it repeatedly), but Engles did. Political economy, he wrote, studies "laws governing the production and exchange of the material means of subsistence." It is both as simple and as complex as that.

Why is Africa (or for that matter Latin America and much of Asia) so poor? At the risk of soliciting criticism for using intellectual shorthand, the answer is very brief: we have made it poor. But to bring us up to date, we cannot objectively leave it at that. We shall therefore conclude with a passage from Steve Langdon's article about Kenya (1974:146). His analysis and summary have applicability to almost every African nation, be it ex-British, ex-French, ex-Belgian, or ex-Portuguese.

> What, then, has happened in Kenya? During the colonial period a metropolis-satellite relationship with British capitalism shaped the political economy. As the new African nationalist elite emerged, the benefits open to it from maintaining that exchange structure encouraged a neo-colonial option—which has changed Kenya's metropolis-satellite relationship only relatively marginally. By remaining in a position of dependence on world capitalism, the political-bureaucratic bourgeoisie has been able to exercise lucrative dominance in Kenya—accumulating wealth to solidify its own class-power and providing economic opportunities to placate its petty bourgeois clients, through control and manipulation of the metropolis-periphery exchange structure. This system of state-centered, metropolis-oriented exchange has polarized the African community inside Kenya. As a result, staggering inequalities have emerged. And broadly-based growth, benefitting all Kenyans, has been inhibited. In short, the underdevelopment of Kenya has been perpetuated and deepened.

This present condition turns our minds once again to Barrington Moore (1966:523), for in many respects he put forward a view likely to be shared by most of our contributors.

> In any society the dominant groups are the ones with the most to hide about the way society works. Very often, therefore, truthful analyses are bound to have a critical ring, to seem like postures rather than objective statements. . . . For all students of human society sympathy with the victims of historical process and skepticism about the victors' claims provide essential safeguards against being taken in by the dominant mythology. A scholar who tries to be objective needs these feelings as part of his working equipment.

This book is an attempt to continue the effort, alongside our colleagues everywhere, to "set the record straight." The "chains of historical causation" are being linked together. The end result is to achieve freedom and liberty for all Africans, the oppressed, the poor, the exploited everywhere.

REFERENCES

ALPERS, E. (1975). Ivory and slaves in East Central Africa: Changing patterns of international trade to the later nineteenth century. London: Heinemann.

ARRIGHI, G., and SAUL, J.S. (1968). "Socialism and economic development in tropical Africa." Journal of Modern African Studies, 6(2):141-169.

BARAN, P.A. (1970). "On the political economy of backwardness." Pp. 285-301 in R.I. Rhodes (ed.), Imperialism and underdevelopment: A reader. New York: Monthly Review Press.

BROWN, G. (ed., 1975). The Red Paper on Scotland. Edinburgh: Edinburgh University Student Publication Board.

CHATTOPADHYAY, P. (1974). "Political economy: What's in a name." Monthly Review, (April):23-33.

COHEN, R. (1972). "Class in Africa: Analytical problems and perspectives." Pp. 231-255 in R. Miliband and J. Saville (eds.), The Socialist Register, 1972. London: Merlin.

COLEMAN, J.S. (1967). "The resurrection of political economy." Mawazo, 1(1):31-40.

COQUERY-VIDROVITCH, C. (1969). "Recherches sur un mode de production africain." La Pensée, (no. 44):61-78.

DEKKER, L.D., HEMSON, D., KANE-BERMAN, J.S., LEVER, J., and SCHLEMMER, L. (1974). "Case studies in African labour action in South and Southwest Africa." African Review, 4(2):205-236.

DOS SANTOS, T. (1970). "The concept of social classes." Science and Society, (summer): 166-193.

"Editorial" (1975). Review of African Political Economy, (no. 3):2.

FRANK, A.G. (1971). Capitalism and underdevelopment in Latin America. Harmondsworth, Eng.: Penguin.

GALTUNG, J. (1972). "A structural theory of imperialism." African Review, 1(4):93-138.

GONZALEZ, G.G. (1974). "A critique of the internal colonialism model." Latin American Perspectives, 1(1):154-161.

GONZALEZ-CASANOVA, P. (1969). "Internal colonialism and national development." Pp. 118-139 in I. Horowitz, L. Josue de Castro, and J. Gerassi (eds.), Latin American radicalism. New York: Vintage.

HARVEY, D. (1973). Social justice and the city. Baltimore: Johns Hopkins University Press.

HECHTER, M. (1975). Internal colonialism. Berkeley: University of California Press.

HOOKER, J.R. (1969). "Shortages among the surplus: European views of African unemployment in British central Africa between the wars." Canadian Journal of African Studies, 3(2):421-429.

Institute for Industrial Education (1974). The Durban Strike, 1973. Durban-Johannesburg: Author (in association with Raven Press).

International Labor Office (1972). Employment, incomes and equality for increasing productive employment in Kenya. Geneva: Author.

KAY, G. (1975). Development and underdevelopment: A Marxist analysis. London: Macmillan.

KITCHING, G. (1972). "The concept of class and the study of Africa." African Review, 2(3):327-350.

KRADER, L. (1975). The Asiatic mode of production. Assen: Van Gorcum.

LANGDON, S. (1974). "The political economy of dependence: Note toward analysis of multinational corporations in Kenya." Journal of Eastern African Research and Development, 4(2).

LEVIN, J.V. (1960). The export economies: The pattern of development in historical perspective. Cambridge, Mass.: Harvard University Press.

LEWIS, W.A. (1961). The theory of economic growth. London: Allen and Unwin.

LUKACS, G. (1971). History and class consciousness. London: Merlin.

MacRAE, P. (1974). "Race and class in southern Africa." African Review, 4(2):237-257.

MANDEL, E. (1972). "The driving force of imperialism in our era." In Spheres of influence in the age of imperialism. Nottingham: Spokesman Books.

MARX, K., and ENGELS, F. (1963). The German ideology. New York: International Publishers.

MEILLASSOUX, C. (ed., 1971). The development of indigenous trade and markets in West Africa. London: Oxford University Press.

MOORE, B. (1958). "Strategy in social science." In Political power and social theory: Six studies. Cambridge, Mass.: Harvard University Press.

——— (1966). Social origins of dictatorship and democracy: Lord and peasant in the making of the modern world. Boston: Beacon Press.

NEALE, W.C. (1962). Economic change in rural India: Land tenure and reform in Uttar Pradesh, 1800-1955. New Haven, Conn.: Yale Unversity Press.

O'BRIEN, P.J. (1975). "A critique of Latin American theories of dependency." Pp. 7-27 in I. Oxall, T. Barnett, and D. Booth (eds.), Beyond the sociology of development: Economy and society in Latin America and Africa. London: Routledge and Kegan Paul.

ONITIRI, H.M.A. (1973). "The international aspects of economic independence." In D.P. Ghai (ed.), Economic independence in Africa. Nairobi: East African Literature Bureau.

SAUL, J.S. (1969). "Africa." In G. Ionescu and E. Gellner (eds.), Populism: Its meanings and national characteristics. London: Weidenfeld and Nicolson.

SEIDMAN, A. (n.d.). "Changing theories of political economy in Africa. Unpublished manuscript.

SINGER, H.W. (1970). "Dualism revisited: A new approach to the problems of a dual society in developing countries." Journal of Development Studies, 7(1):60-75.

SURET-CANALE, J. (1964). "Les sociétés traditionnelles en Afrique noire et le concept du mode de production asiatique." La Pensée, (no. 117):19-42.

VAN ONSELEN, C. (1975). "Black workers in central African industry: A critical essay on historiography and sociology of Rhodesia." Journal of Southern African Studies, 1(2):228-246.

VAN ZWANENBERG, R.M.A. (1975). Colonialism capitalism and labour in Kenya, 1919-1939. Nairobi: East African Literature Bureau.

WALLERSTEIN, I. (1973). "Africa in the capitalist world." Issue, 3(3):1-11.

——— (1974). The modern world system: Capitalist agriculture and the origins of the European world-economy in the sixteenth century. New York: Academic Press.

——— (1975). "Alternative development strategies." Paper read at the symposium on "Development Strategies in the Third World," Institute for International Studies and Department of Government and International Studies, University of Notre Dame, April 11-12.

1

THE THREE STAGES OF AFRICAN INVOLVEMENT
IN THE WORLD-ECONOMY

IMMANUEL WALLERSTEIN

State University of New York, Binghamton

The historiography of modern Africa has been a battleground of so-called Eurocentric versus so-called Afrocentric interpretations, and we have passed from early crude versions of each to a state of sophisticated and subtle arguments about analytical primacy. This intellectual battle of course reflects a wider social battle. But in the end both versions seem to me to be wrong. At a certain point in time, both Europe and Africa (or at least large zones of each) came to be incorporated into a single social system, a capitalist world-economy, whose fundamental dynamic largely controlled the actors located in both sectors of one united arena. It is in the reciprocal linkages of the various regions of the capitalist world-economy that we find the underlying determinants of social actions at a more local level.

It will be said that this ignores the relative autonomy of the acting groups. It does indeed in the sense that all systemic analysis denies the real autonomy of parts of a whole. It is not that there are no particularities of each acting group. Quite the contrary. It is that the alternatives available for each unit are constrained by the framework of the whole, even while each actor opting for a given alternative in fact alters the framework of the whole.

An analysis then must start from how the whole operates, and of course one must determine what is the whole in a given instance. Only then may we be able to draw an interpretative sketch of the historical outlines of the political economy of contemporary Africa, which is in my view an outline of the various stages (and modes) of its involvement in this capitalist world-economy.

The essential elements of a capitalist world-economy include the creation of a single world division of labor, production for profit in this world-market, capital accumulation for expanded reproduction as a key mode of maximizing profit in the long run, emergence of three zones of economic activity (core, semiperiphery; and periphery) with not merely unequal exchange between them[1] but also persistent merchandise trade imbalances,[2] a multiplicity of state-structures (strongest in the core, weakest in the periphery), and the development over time of two principal world class-formations (a bourgeoisie and a proletariat) whose concrete manifestations are however complicated by the constant formation and reformation of a host of ethno-national groupings (Wallerstein, 1972, 1974a, 1975b). This historically unique combination of elements first crystallized in Europe in the sixteenth century (Wallerstein, 1974b), and the boundaries slowly expanded to include the entire world. This is why it could be thought of, quite misleadingly, as the "expansion of Europe" (when it was really the "expansion of the capitalist mode of production") and why it could lead to both Eurocentric and, by reaction, Afrocentric versions of modern African history.

Because the capitalist world-economy originated in one part of the globe and then expanded to include all parts, areas (such as Africa) not within the original boundaries were at one point in time outside the world-economy and at a later point in time incorporated into it. At the earlier point in time, to the extent that various African systems and the European world-economy were in trade contact one with the other, they were in each other's "external arena," and the trade was of a nature quite different from that which would subsequently occur between the African periphery and the European core of the capitalist world-economy. It is to this early period that we must first turn in order to clarify later developments.

Trade between external arenas is trade in "luxuries" (Wallerstein, 1974b). If it is not, if the trade becomes trade in essentials, the two arenas have become one, a single division of labor. "Luxury" may be defined in terms of consumption, as does Samir Amin: "In the strictest sense of the term, luxury goods are those for which the demand originates from the part of profit which is consumed" as opposed to demand coming from wages (1974).[3] Or it may be defined in terms of whether the products are themselves means of production, as does Piero Sraffa, luxury products being those *not* used in the production of others:

> Luxury products have no part in the determination of the system. Their role is purely passive. If an invention were to reduce by half the quantity of each of the means of production which are required to produce a unit of a "luxury" commodity of this type, the commodity itself would be halved in price, but there would be no further consequences. . . .
>
> What has just been said of the passive role of luxury goods can readily be extended to such "luxuries" as are merely used in their own reproduction either directly (e.g. race horses) or indirectly (e.g. ostriches and ostrich-eggs) or merely for the production of other luxuries (e.g. raw silk).
>
> The criterion is whether a commodity enters (no matter whether directly or indirectly) into the production of *all* commodities. [1972:6-7]

In terms of either of these definitions, the trade of various parts of Africa with various European traders prior to about 1750 falls in this category, especially if we bear in mind Amin's stricture about "the historically relative nature of the distinction between mass consumption goods and luxury goods" (1974).

Indeed the point that should be borne in mind is that the kind of trade the Portuguese launched in West Africa, in the Congo region, and in East Africa in the fifteenth and sixteenth centuries (and in which subsequently other European powers engaged) at first was essentially of the same nature, and involved essentially the same products, as the trans-Saharan trade that dates at least to the tenth century A.D. and the Indian Ocean trade that goes back further still (Alpers, 1973:111-113).

All of this trade prior to 1750 which involved various African states with partners outside of themselves was "long-distance trade" whose quantity varied on a market determined less by demand than by effective supply, that is, of products successfully transported from the point of production to the mart. As a consequence, production was not determined by variations in this demand but by the politico-technological ability of the long-distance traders to transport the material. The resulting trade involved no transfer of surplus, but could in fact be considered a mutual windfall.

Because this was so, this trade had very limited consequences for the social organization of the trading societies, except to strengthen somewhat the political machineries that guaranteed it. A stoppage in the trade, which occurred frequently over the centuries, had relatively few repercussions other than on the lives of the state officials and merchants directly living off the trade. The data on the nature of the trade between Europe and Africa from 1450 to 1750 has not yet been collected in a sufficiently systematic manner to verify this argument definitely, but I have presented previously some evidence that would support this interpretation (Wallerstein, 1973:7-9). What is important here is to suggest what may have happened around 1750 to have changed the situation.

In fact, as with all such situations, the change was not abrupt. It was the case that since about 1700, the export in slaves from West Africa began to increase in importance in response to a growing demand in the Caribbean area[4] and a relative diminution of interference with movement on the seas. In a recent calculation, Richard Bean located the shift in curve quite precisely:

> Both the price of slaves in Africa and the number of slaves doubled after the Peace of Ryswick in 1697. From then until the reductions in the trade following 1807, slaves were clearly the most important export of Africa. [1974:354-355]

Looked at more closely, decade by decade, we see that the export of slaves from Africa to the Western Hemisphere rises quantitatively until 1750, after which it remains at a high level until 1810.[5]

PHASE I: 1750-1900

Slave exports from Africa had certainly now ceased to be a "luxury" item from the point of view of the capitalist world-economy. They were, in Sraffa's terms, "entering into the production of all commodities." And the quantitative expansion of the trade was in turn having its effect on the social structures of the exporting regions. As has long been noted, the growth of the slave trade led to the expansion of such states as Dahomey and Oyo. Although, as Hopkins (1973:106) cautions us, "it would be mistaken to imply that the slave trade was a necessary condition for the formation of large, centralised states in West Africa,"[6] the point is that the initial impact of increased trade was by and large to strengthen the state structures in the exporting arena, a consequence typical of trade in the external arena.

But matters could not stop there precisely because Africa, or at least the coastal regions, were now being in fact "incorporated" into the world-economy and thereby becoming peripheralized.

It was about 1750 that the capitalist world-economy was emerging from the long-term relative contraction which it had been suffering since about 1620. This contraction had led to acute competition among those states that were in the core of the world-economy in 1620—the United Provinces, England, and France. This competition took the form of mercantilist closure for both England and France in order to strengthn their position against the United Provinces, which, as of 1620, was more efficient economically. One aspect of this mercantilism was the creation of closed imperial trade networks between the European metropoles, the Caribbean, and North America. The slow increase in economic activity that resulted accounted for the steady increase in importation of slaves after 1700.

But by 1750, the whole world-economy was in an upswing once again, and England and France were in the last stages of their struggle for economic (and political) hegemony in the world-economy. This world-economy could now sustain a considerably increased production of manufactures, provided one could rapidly augment primary production. There was thus a rush to expand. One obvious place was in the Caribbean. As a result:

> In the second half of the eighteenth century the French government offered bounties to slave ships leaving France for Africa, and made an additional payment for every slave they landed in the French West Indies. This concern is understandable when it is realised that . . . sugar was the most valuable commodity sent to France from over-seas. Sugar was also the largest single item imported into England in the eighteenth century [Hopkins, 1973:91]

Nor did Britain's growing military success vis-à-vis France in fact lessen French economic activity, at least at first:

> England's supremacy was the result of the relatively quick pace of her commercial expansion and was not brought about by an absolute decline in French commerce with West Africa. . . . Indeed, the tempo of French activity in West Africa actually increased after 1763, following Choiseul's efforts to develop Africa to compensate for the loss of Canada, and to free the French West Indies from dependence on British ships for supplies of slaves. [Hopkins, 1973:92][7]

The pressure to expand the geographic bounds of the capitalist world-economy began to be felt from 1750 on. One of the easiest ways to expand total primary production to feed the industries that were being established was to expand extensively, to include new areas of primary production, because this involves the windfall profits of labor and land priced below world market rates. Of course, in addition, primary producers already in existence sought to maintain and expand their production.

This double effort to expand led to a labor shortage within the world-economy and hence accounts for the need for more slaves. Thus there came to be a growing demand in Africa for slaves at the same time as there was a growing demand for the use of African land—and African labor on African land—for primary crop production.

At first, the prior demand took priority. It accorded with the existing mores and trade channels. And neither Britain nor France could take the chance that the other would surge ahead in such areas as sugar production in the West Indies. Furthermore, it was precisely the acuteness of their rivalry that strengthened the hand of slave-raiding states in West Africa like Ashanti.[8] The crucial aspect to note of such states is that they were engaged less in wars than in "raids," as Daaku insists, which were "made possible mainly by the introduction of firearms" (1968:136). Ashanti (and its analogues) thus became part of the periphery[9] of the capitalist world-economy not by *producing* slaves but by raiding them from areas outside this world-economy.

This kind of involvement of coastal West Africa made it impossible, however, to use these same areas as cash-crop producing areas. Daaku speaks of the failure of the Dutch attempt to create sugar, cotton, and indigo plantations in West Africa, explaining it thus:

It can be said that between the 17th and 18th centuries, West African interest was permanently subordinated to that of the West Indies and the Americas. This more than anything else must be the explanation for why the Europeans did not interest themselves in both the political and economic well being of West Africa, rather than the popularly accepted view that the African system of land tenure, their numerical superiority and the inhospitable climate debarred the Europeans from taking other interests apart from the commercial in affairs of Africa. [1968:138-139]

But it did not necessarily have to remain eternally true that both trade partners would be primarily served by the primacy of the slave trade. The situation did in fact change. As the British moved into clear hegemony in the world-economy, their priorities shifted, and their ability to make these priorities prevail increased. Furthermore, it now became profitable for some Africans to produce agricultural crops for this world-economy, as we shall see.

Thus the slave trade served as the cutting edge of the peripheralization of Africa in the period 1750-1900, but it was also incompatible with it, because the production of slaves is less profitable than cash-crop production, forcing slaves to be continuously drawn from outside the world-economy. Hence, we see a clear pattern of geographic dislocation. As the nineteenth century proceeded, the slave trade died out in West Africa and to a lesser extent in Angola, to be replaced by a slave trade based on the East African mainland, whose incorporation into the world-economy would not come about until the very end of the nineteenth century.

Let us trace the steps of this shift of locus. The abolition of the slave trade by Great Britain, the prospectively hegemonic world power, as Boahen points out:

> rendered illegal as much as nine-tenths of European trade with the coast of West Africa. A huge economic vacuum was thus created and the British hoped that it might be filled by the encouragement of the cultivation of exportable commodities such as white rice, indigo, cotton, coffee and palm oil. [1974:179] [10]

What served British interest, however, did not necessarily serve the interest of other actors in the world-economy. The slave-trading African states saw their principal source of wealth attacked and, in Boahen's words, "found abolition incomprehensible." He goes on to point out the *short-term* economic dilemmas of the African traders:

> Like other powerful rulers, the Asantehene now had the problem of the disposal of war captives. Though he strongly denied going to war simply to acquire slaves, he pointed out that one of the readiest ways of disposing of war captives who could not be absorbed locally was to sell them. At the time of abolition [1807] he had twenty thousand captives on his hands whom, he frankly confessed, he could not feed, adding that unless I kill or sell them, they will grow strong and kill my people. [1974:179]

Similarly, some European groups equally were dismayed by abolition. It was the weakness of Portugal's export position in the world-economy that explains why she "was clinging to the Atlantic slave-trade and to the institution of slavery in Brazil" (Rodney, 1968:62).

Neither slavery nor the slave-trade was abolished from one day to the next in the capitalist world-economy. Rather, there was a century-long disengagement from the use of slave labor, during which not only did many sectors of the world-economy resist this process, but its leading proponent, Great Britain, sacrificed logical consistency to the complex and contradictory economic needs of powerful internal forces. Eric Williams succinctly summarized the dilemma:

> The British West Indian planters pleaded that theirs was a free labour economy which deserved protection from slave grown products in Brazil and Cuba. Britain's textile industry was, however, completely dependent on the slave grown cotton of the Southern States of the United States of America. [1964:15] [11]

Nonetheless, the major thrust was toward abolition—in West Africa, in Angola, and in the Cape Colony, leaving East Africa relatively untouched until much later. And those hurt by this shift moved to minimize or recoup their losses.

In Angola, the Portuguese sought to replace revenue from the slave trade with increased taxation on the African population, increased customs duties, and the expansion of the area under Portuguese sovereignty, which then precisely ran into British opposition because both expansion and customs dues "would inevitably curtail the freedom of trade then enjoyed by British merchants" (Wheeler, 1971:54).

In the Cape, where, since 1716, slaves had been imported (Omer-Cooper, 1966b:347-348) from West Africa, Madagascar, and Mozambique, as well as from the East Indies (those who would come to be called the Cape Malays), the British administration undermined not merely the ethos but the economic basis of the Boer farm units:

> The price of slaves [in the Cape], driven up by the limitation of supply which resulted from the stopping of the slave trade in 1807, had risen too high for slaves to be used very extensively by frontier farmers operating on small capital. [Omer-Cooper, 1966a:369]

Eventually, this economic (and hence cultural and political) pressure on the Boers would culminate in the Great Trek of 1837 (Patterson, 1957, chap. 1; Davenport, 1969:287-297).

East Africa, by contrast, began to play in the nineteenth century the role that West Africa had played in the eighteenth. It remained largely outside the capitalist world-economy, the slave trade expanding steadily[12] and strengthening thereby slave-trading state structures on the mainland.[13] While the mainland areas came to be the external arenas of slave recruitment, the Indian Ocean islands (particularly Zanzibar, but also Madagascar, Reunion, and Mauritius) became peripheral areas of the world-economy, producing export crops for exchange with Europe and obtaining slaves from the mainland as workers.[14]

The abolition of the slave trade by Great Britain was most efficacious and had the greatest consequences in West Africa. Economic "substitutes" grew up: timber trade in coastal Sierra Leone, palm oil in the Niger Delta and Dahomey, groundnut oil in Gambia and Senegal. Thus, as Fyfe notes:

> The colonial economic relationship . . . was intensified. The volume of manufactured imports from the expanding factories of Europe increased steadily, pushing the frontier of import-export trading inland and bringing more peoples within the European trading sphere. [1974:47][15]

The growth of this trade began to affect the structure of production in West Africa. Some previous economic activities—blacksmithing, iron smelting, even the mining of iron—declined, "ruined by the competition of cheaper and purer iron bars imported from Europe," as well as by

> increasing quantities of cheap European imports of iron basins, matchets, knives, hoes, wire and other metal goods turned out by the expanding mass production techniques of the industrial revolution. [Flint, 1974:387]

Nor was African textile production better able to maintain its local market untouched. In the seventeenth and eighteenth centuries, the African producers had effectively resisted European intrusion because of product differentiation, but this began to change once the English mills began to mass produce cheap cotton cloth after the mid-eighteenth century (Flint, 1974:388-389). Nor, as Fyfe notes, were Africans able to establish new industries:

> Produce was exported in a raw state. No processing industries grew up; a few factories which were opened in Freetown in the 1840's for pressing groundnut oil soon closed. The French prohibited oil-processing in Senegal. [1974:47]

In short, West Africa was being peripheralized or, in the splendidly arrogant phraseology of the Sierra Leone Company, made to conform to "the true principles of Commerce," that is, "the export of British manufactures in return for African produce."[16]

Peripheralization is a corrosive process. Trade with an external arena requires strong partners—to guarantee its continuity (since presumably the internal economic needs of the systems that are trading are not dependent or less dependent on the continuity of the trade) and to minimize transaction costs when the intermittent trade occurs. But trade within a capitalist world-economy must be able to respond rapidly and accurately to the demands of the market, capitalist producers seeking to control the vagaries of the market by expanding vertical and horizontal integration to the degree the technology and political systems permit.

From the point of view of the dominant economic forces—that is, those with most capital, who were now located largely in Europe—the "strong" states of West Africa were potential competitors.[17] As peripheralization proceeded, the local bourgeoisies might come to utilize the local state structures to erect mercantilist barriers. Ideally what the core countries wanted was a direct channel to primary producers, an unencumbered economic alliance.

The political response of Africans in the first three-quarters of the nineteenth century was mixed. As already noted, slave-trading rulers were unhappy about abolition, but they sought to compensate in several ways: warfare with neighbors, which was in the end mutually destructive and contributed to the decline of these states; creation of export-crop estates using slave labor, which was often undermined by competition from peasant farmers producing for the export market more efficiently; creation of alliances between the state and small producers, which was difficult and did not succeed because of all the forces opposing such an alliance. A.G. Hopkins underlines the limits of the contradictions involved in these attempts to conserve the relatively strong state structures as peripheralization proceeded:

> The difficulties of the progressive rulers arose first from an internal conflict of interest stemming from a basic change in the structure of export-producing firms, and second from the fact that they were unable or unwilling to make the necessary adjustments in the time allowed by impatient and often unsympathetic foreigners. For a while it seemed that there was a chance of stabilizing the existing frontier between Europeans and Africans on the West Coast, but in the last quarter of the century the indigenous rulers were called upon to make concessions upon such matters as railways, internal tolls and slavery, which they judged, quite rightly, would undermine their independence. [1973:145]

One may view as essentially similar the source of the continuing latent tensions between the British and the strong states established by the Boers in southern Africa[18] and by the Omani Arabs in eastern Africa (John Flint, 1963).

Indeed, not only were the European countries faced with strong states with whom their interests increasingly diverged but some of the now flourishing African merchant classes were thinking of inspiring new ones, such as the Fanti Confederation.[19] Presented by James Africanus Horton to Lord Granville as a mode of relieving the imperial exchequer,[20] the proposal received an ambivalent and ultimately negative British response.[21] Furthermore, as the quantity of total export trade from Africa continued to expand steadily, if slowly,[22] there was growing competition in the coastal trading markets

> between European and African jurisdiction over the traders. In the mutually antagonistic methods of bringing sanctions to bear against thieves and debtors, in the struggle between the rough justice of the "palm oil ruffians" and the attempt to extend the power of colonial courts, in the sanctions of African boycott and European naval blockade lay a search for authority which transcended the search for trade. [Newbury, 1969:84][23]

As long as the capitalist world-economy lived under the smug and clear hegemonic control of Great Britain, roughly 1815-1873, the peripheralization of African coastal regions advanced slowly, like lava curling down a mountainside. But when the capitalist world-economy erupted into a major crisis of accumulation, whose onset was signaled by the market crash of 1873, the rules of the game suddenly changed. For one thing, Great Britain's hegemony was now openly challenged anew by France, her perennial rival; by Germany, sharply rising as Europe's new great political and economic power; and by her erstwhile junior partner, the United States.

What this meant for Africa was that the process of political decline would be suddenly accelerated as the European powers, first tentatively and then in a sudden onrush, undertook the "scramble for Africa," dividing up the continent (somewhat unevenly) and "pacifying" those who dared to resist.

Prior to partition, Britain dominated trade in Africa throughout the nineteenth century. But already in mid-century, the percentage was declining, even though it was still the leading commercial power. Newbury summarizes the situation on the west coast as follows:

> Expressed as a percentage, the United Kingdom share with British possessions on the Coast declined between the fifties and sixties to about half of their total trade, as German, French and American agents took advantage of the lack of restrictions at Bathurst, Freetown, Cape Coast and Lagos. . . . British trade with other parts of the coast (though still much greater than Britain's stake in her own West African colonies) also declined. [1969:79]

Furthermore, the value of the particular export products was declining. The boom in palm oil ended in 1861, caused by the expansion of worldwide commodity production, as competitive products from the U.S., Australia, and India come on the world market (Hopkins, 1973:133).

This is not the place to argue once more the immediate causes of partition. I will merely assert my view that in a contracting world market, France and Germany sought to seal off areas of this market from Britain by colonization, to which the only sensible response by Britain was to join the scramble (and indeed largely win it). Thus, one does not have to argue the economic importance of particular areas to explain colonization, for it was above all "preemptive colonization" (Wallerstein, 1970). G.N. Uzoigwe wrote:

Evidently those in Britain who cried for new markets had every reason to be alarmed. It can, of course, be argued that since the cry for new markets only became loud in the 1890's when Africa had practically been partitioned, it was a mere rationalization after the event. It must be pointed out however that those in authority were not unaware of Britain's economic difficulties in the 1880's. That this consideration may have driven them to participate in the greatest international share-out in world history cannot be ruled out. Rosebery's summary of the partition as pegging out claims for futurity explains a great deal about this. . . . Indeed Africa may have been partitioned in the 1880's but this was only on paper. The real partition took place in the 1890's with effective occupation. [1974:34]

Whatever the immediate explanation, there was indeed effective occupation. The slave trade finally ended throughout Africa.[24]

Phase I was the phase of "informal empire";[25] that is, those areas of Africa, mainly on the coast, that came to be incorporated into the capitalist world-economy as peripheral zones retained their local sovereign political institutions for the most part. It is not that sovereignty was never alienated by a core state. It is that the expense of direct political domination was avoided to the extent possible because it was seldom required to maintain the flow of commerce. Gallagher and Robinson seize the situation precisely when they say, "By informal means if possible or by formal annexations when necessary, British paramountcy was steadily upheld" (1970:145). By the end of the nineteenth century, however, all African sovereignty disappeared (except that of Liberia and Ethiopia). The way was open now for a second integration of Africa into the capitalist world-economy, which would occur in the twentieth century, one that would not only be more extensive but more intensive, as it would begin to reorganize the class structure.

PHASE II: 1900-1975

We have seen that the combination of the growing competition of British (and other European) merchants versus indigenous Africans and the growing challenge of German, French, and American industry to British world market hegemony together led to the dislocation of the balance that sustained "informal empire" and hence to the scramble for Africa.

The period 1873-1897 was a period of contraction in the capitalist world-economy (Schumpeter, 1939:321-325, 335-341, 356-366). When the phase of expansion occurred, notably during the period 1900-1913, there was an alteration in the world terms of trade in favor of agricultural exports (Lewis, 1952). In effect, there was a felt shortage in the supply of world raw materials, and hence it was eminently profitable to initiate new (or expanded) production of export crops in Africa. However, since these areas were now under direct European political control, the largest part of the profits of this expansion could be diverted into European hands either by direct ownership of the agricultural domains, by monopsonistic control of the purchasing of the product for export, by monopolistic control of transportation facilities, or by direct taxation. The direct benefits of colonization for Great Britain, presumably the reluctant dragon, have been argued by Richard Wolff:

> In terms of supplying food and raw materials imports, colonial administration meant for Britain ultimate control and hence a greater measure of security than would have obtained if France or Germany or another power had annexed the territories. Also, whatever the final destination of food and raw materials export from any colony, British political control almost always meant British predominance in the financing, insurance, and freight for the colony's exports, and hence British balance of payments advantages. Foreign political control could and frequently did deny Britain such predominance, regardless of the relative prices of the services provided by Britain and other countries. Finally, . . . colonial control enabled the British authorities to determine to a large extent the choice of foods and raw materials developed and exported from any colonial territory. Thus, it is reasonable to conclude that, in the absence of Britain's new empire, her security, her gains from invisible exports, and both the general mix and quantities of food and raw materials supplied to world markets would have been less favorable to her. [1974:23]

And nothing is said here of the advantage to individual settlers.

One of the reasons why, given a felt shortage in the world-economy of certain commodities, it is so eminently profitable to open up *new* areas for peripheral inclusion in the world-economy (as opposed to intensifying production in old areas) is the low cost of labor in terms of world market prices at a given era. There is a school of thought that sees these low wages as the marginal sales value of previously unutilized labor. Thus Szereszewski argues of the new cocoa industry in the Gold Coast in the period 1891-1911:

> [T]he first forest belt of the Gold Coast had a built-in capacity to increase its real output under certain stimuli which disturbed the equilibrium position of individual economic units. This resulted from the existence of unutilised labour potential and from the fact that labour services were the limiting factor over a wide range of activities: the economic units could react to the introduction of new commodities, to new price situations and to changes in transport conditions with increased flow of exportable output. . . . This was basically an *underemployment situation* in the sense that the resources of the economy—land and labour—were at the low level of *physical utilisation* determined by the preferences of the population for income and leisure and the available conversion rates between the two. [1965:84-85] [26]

In this theory, economically virgin land and labor await the plucking by world capitalism. In fact, this was not historically true for West Africa, which by the 1880s had "an internal exchange economy of some magnitude," as Marion Johnson points out in specific response to this explanation (1974:180). Still it might be argued that it was true for some of the land areas brought into cash-crop cultivation at that time. We would then retain the explanation of the profitability but look for *institutional* in addition to *market* factors to explain the emergence of this agricultural production for the world market.

One of the vital mechanisms involved in the utilization of this "surplus" labor force was the development of a transportation network which would keep the total cost of the product on the world market competitive,[27] and such "external economies" depended in turn on an active role of the colonial governments. Fieldhouse recognized this when he warned us against seeing colonial rule and informal empire as "merely points along the same spectrum, differing in degree rather than kind."

> The distinctive feature of an imperial economic system was that the metropolis could, within limits, create the formal framework for economic activity and in some degree determine the character of development. [1971:600]

To appreciate, then, the dynamics of the evolution, we must take into account that the colonial governments operated in a double context: they reflected the economic needs of the various metropolitan economic actors, as mediated through political pressures on the government (both in the metropole and directly on the colonial administrations), but as a substructure they had their own immediate needs to fulfill. What is striking in this early period of colonial rule is that the larger needs of metropolitan economic institutions for expanded cash-crop production in Africa coincided with the administrative needs of the colonial officials. Export production was needed to provide a tax base sufficient to cover the costs of administration. And export production provided an ideological reinforcement. It was seen as part of the "civilizing" process, as well as an alternative to the slave trade. Finally, as Barber notes:

> Mixed with these factors was a consideration of prudence. The *pax* in Africa, it was widely believed, depended on the provision of opportunities for Africans to earn money incomes. Otherwise, idleness among African men might well breed mischief and thereby expensive threats to the new order. [1964:301]

Moreover, the point is that in terms of income to those African producers who had already been related to the world market during the late nineteenth century, a period of slump, there was a rise in income from the improvement in world terms of trade. Hence, Hopkins is probably right when he says that "it helped to reconcile Africans to colonial rule, and so made the task of the new administrations much easier than it would otherwise have been" (1973:183).

Thus opportunities were created by the favorable world market, and both metropolitan economic interests and colonial administrators were interested in seizing the opportunities offered. The modes of possible response to these opportunities, in terms of the formal organization of the new agricultural enterprises, were varied. In fact, empirically Africa knew three such modes: African peasant farming, European concessions, and white settler farming.[28] Within limits, these modes corresponded to geographical areas: peasant farming in West Africa, concessions in Equatorial Africa, white settlers in the East, South, and North (although there were some pockets of peasant farming in these latter areas—most notably in Uganda).

Why were different modes employed? From the point of view of colonial administrators, the preferred mode was the one that was easiest in terms of its consequence for administration. Presumably African peasant farming usually fit this bill best. First of all, it required least disruption and dislocation of Africans and hence the least administrative machinery to enforce. Secondly, it represented a dispersal of economic power and hence minimized the growth of economic entities *within* the colony that could put forward political demands upon the administration. It was a path of least resistance.

Obviously, however, it required a situation where Africans could be tempted into cash-crop production with perhaps some technical assistance and a little judicious coercion. Thus, the more involved some local Africans had been previously in market-oriented activities, the more likely it was that there would be speedy response to market opportunities. This explains why the coastal and forest regions of West Africa were likely candidates for this mode.

The other factor, however, was the political strength of persons interested in an alternative mode of development. Thus, the question should be posed as follows: given that there might be said to be an initial administrative bias in favor of African peasant production, under what conditions do concessionary companies or white settlers displace the peasantry as the mode of development?

How do we explain, for example, that of the two major arenas of French colonization in black Africa—West Africa and Equatorial Africa—the latter developed a concessionary regime and the former did not?[29] Basically, it represented a competition between two French interest groups—those involved in large import-export firms and those seeking monopolistic concessions. The former were well established in West Africa as a result of the long commerce of the nineteenth century but were not similarly established in Equatorial Africa. This seemed to make the difference in who won out (Suret-Canale, 1964:37-39). In terms of securing production for the world-economy, the two systems both "worked." As Jean Suret-Canale put it:

> [I]n French West Africa, colonial trade *(la traite)* reigned under the auspices of "free trade"—and of the *de facto* monopoly of merchant houses. The exploitation of the "independent" African peasant occurred through the mediation of the market. . . .
>
> In French Equatorial Africa, colonial trade reigned via the channel of large colonial [chartered] companies, holding legal monopolies. On the surface, investments in agriculture, forestry, and mining were more significant if one believes the titles of the companies and the activities projected in their statutes.
>
> Actually, it was import and export that constituted their real activity, with this difference that the facade of free trade was more often replaced by pure and simple brutal plundering, the companies considering the men and the product of their labor as their property. [1964:39, 41]

A second important arena of concessionary development was the Congo Free State, which from 1885 to 1908 constituted a juridically "independent state" owned and personally governed by King Leopold II of Belgium. This bizarre political structure created a situation in which it was in the personal financial interest of the head of the colonial administration to invite in concessionary companies. Under the *régime domanial* the state appropriated all so-called "vacant land," which it then sold to willing buyers (Stengers, 1969:265-271). The concessionary companies that bought much of this land felt they had the right to exploit the African's labor for their own private profit, thereby reaping "unheard of profits" and creating "veritable hells-on-earth," wherein "the lot of the Africans was tragic" (Stengers, 1969:270-271).

As it turned out, the generic administrator's instinct against concessions as a mode of development was right, for concessions turned out to be a less profitable mode from the point of view of the world-economy as a whole. Between 1900 and 1920, "French West Africa appeared relatively prosperous, while French Equatorial Africa suffered bitter distress" (Coquery-Vidrovitch, 1969:193).[30] As for the Congo Free State, Merlier points out the other side of Leopold's financial advantage:

> These Leopoldian expropriations retained their speculative character. Thanks to the concessions, the companies speculated on the stock exchange but seldom exploited the land. Each expropriation enriched Leopold II and those close to him, the crooks who hung around the royal family and the offices of the companies: they rushed to divide up the concessions into smaller lots and resell them to less important companies or to settlers. Often the land consisted of vast swamps that could not be cultivated. . . . Except for some operations that involved simple gathering *(la cueillette)* undertaken in accessible areas, the granting of concessions did not often result in effective occupation of lands and forests. [1962:58]

It was thus as much because of their inefficiency as because of the cruelties associated with them that the Belgian government after 1908 sought to liquidate the Leopoldian concessions.[31]

If we now take the second alternative to peasant farming, the installation of white settlers, we discover that settlers came usually because they pressed to come, and frequently against the will or at least to the discomfort of the administrators. There were three main areas of white settlement: southern Africa, North Africa, and East Africa. Each deserves a brief word.

The origins of white farming in South Africa center on the fact that the Cape was a strategic way station on the world's sea routes, first for the Dutch, then for the British. When in the late nineteenth century, diamonds and gold were discovered, this led to still further white immigration and confirmed the role of South Africa as an area of white settlement, both in farming and in mining. It was in a sense, however, the white farming that protected politically the role of whites as the skilled personnel of the mining operations, as the later history of Zambia and Katanga was to prove.

It was the presence of white settlers in the Cape that explains why the British South Africa Company turned to white settlers to recoup its losses in its Rhodesian "concession" when the hopes of mineral wealth turned out to be fruitless and the African revolts posed a political threat.[32] This was ultimately to be enshrined in the self-government act of 1923, the critical political base for the unilateral declaration of independence of 1965.

In the German areas, settlers came because they pushed to come, and they encountered ambivalent responses from the administrators. In Southwest Africa, it was quite possibly only the transfer of power from Germany to South Africa after World War I that enabled the settlers to survive the growing hostility of the government.[33] As for German East Africa, its history involved a constant strain between the settlers and the Africans and an open hostility toward the settlers on the part of the most successful governor, Albrecht Rechenberg.[34] The oscillation of colonial administrative attitudes was to continue under the British

Mandate and result in an inability of the settlers to consolidate political power.[35]

If we turn to North Africa, we find that the French administration in Algeria did not start out in clear support of settlers. The so-called founder of French Algeria, General Bugeaud, was, in Charles-André Julien's phrase, "profoundly anti-settler." He was converted to "official and systematic colonization" only to counter the "private and anarchic colonization which had led to the massacre of Mitidja" (1964:231). Under the Second Empire, the administrators still were cool to settlers:

> This is because the Emperor preferred capitalist colonization, which did not require the intervention of the State, to family colonization and settlement which required administrative overseeing. The government, by favoring primarily large concessionaries, indicated disinterest in the fate [of the settlers] and refused to offer them assistance in case of difficulty. [Julien, 1964:403]

It is only in 1871 with the simultaneous defeat by Germany (and the impulses it created for compensatory outlets), the repression of the Paris Commune, and the putting down of the Kabyle uprising that white settlement politically won out in Algeria (and thus consequently in the latter part of the century in Tunisia and Morocco):

> The end of the war [of 1870-71] marked the opening, in effect, of the era of colonization triumphant. Reassured by the repression, proud of its vitality and spirit of its correctness and of its republican and civilizing vocation, the European population felt itself at last free to impose, on the country and the indigenous masses, a political, economic and social dominance that nothing could shake. [Julien, 1964:500]

In fact, it is only in Kenya that the colonial authorities seemed to have been committed from the outset to white settlers as a solution to the need for cash-crop production. It seems that the most likely source of this relative unusual position on the part of administrators, in striking contrast to British attitudes in neighboring Uganda, may have been the sense of British officials that the earlier disruption by slave trading combined with the absence of hierarchical states had created a situation in which Africans would not respond to cash-crop market opportunities.[36] Furthermore, the building of the railroad had established a high cost load for the administration, which required urgent measures to secure immediate income (Low, 1965:21-22).

Thus we have argued that the essential objective of the second phase of African incorporation into the capitalist world-economy was to create sufficient cash crops to meet world needs as defined at this stage and to sustain the political administrative costs that European powers had forced on each other. Where possible, this was done by using Africans as the farm managers (as well as the farm laborers), either in the form of small peasant holdings or, where the social structure was too centralized to permit this, as in parts of the West African savannah zones where the Muslim brotherhoods were strong, in the form of large networks coordinated by these religious structures monopolizing the marketing.[37] But where the African social structure was too disintegrated or the settlers too strong for historical reasons or where concessionary companies were in a position to be momentarily very persuasive in the metropole, other modes of social organization emerged. From the point of view of metropolitan capitalist interests as a whole, however, it is probably true to say that these alternative forms (concessions which had a short life, and white settlement which survived longer) were less desirable than African land ownership. And this fact would in part explain some of the unexpected alliances in the later era of "decolonization."

If the first segment (1900-1913) of this second phase was a moment of a very favorable market for Africa's products, the world balance of trade would shift against Africa subsequently, very markedly in the period between the two world wars, less so but still so in the period following World War II. The reasons for these unfavorable balances in the two latter periods were however different. Between the two wars, the world market was basically depressed for all primary products. After World War II, at least until 1965 or so, demand for Africa's exports was expanding, but this fact was more than counterbalanced by a marked increase in imports.

That the first period 1900-1913/1920 was exceptionally favorable to African income levels and saw consequently greater *structural* change than later periods is attested to around the continent. Ehrlich notes:

> It was Uganda's good fortune that, at the very time [1903-1913] that the [British] Administration was becoming concerned with the development of a viable export crop, world market conditions were uniquely favourable for such experiments. [1965:399]

In the case of South Africa, De Kiewiet marks the change as coming between 1890 and World War I:

> With a speed that even the United States could hardly match, thriving towns sprang up where there formerly had been a struggling village or simply the bare veld. Between 1891 and 1911 the urban population increased by more than 200 per cent. In New Zealand, Australia, and Canada industry, commerce and the movement of population were stimulated by rising prices and an increased demand for goods. But in South Africa these world conditions were spurred forward still more emphatically by diamonds, gold, railway building, and the expenditures of war and reconstruction. [1957:195] [38]

Szereszewski, whose discussion of structural change in Ghana between 1891 and 1911 we have already mentioned, explicitly notes how this period was different from the subsequent period:

> [T] he process of structural change lost its momentum after 1911, and after 50 years Ghana's economy retains a close affinity with 1911 Gold Coast, albeit at a level of roughly double per capita income. The pattern evolved between 1891 and 1911 almost froze for half a century. [1965:112]

Samir Amin, noting that one of the realities of colonial domination was the decline of the indigenous bourgeoisie, says that in Senegal the attempts of

French merchants to liquidate the indigenous bourgeoisie succeeded only after World War I when it lost its independent status and its members either became employees of European firms or, if younger sons, went into the civil service (1969:20-29).[39] Finally, Merlier argues that this economic transformation did not occur in the Belgian Congo before the 1920s, exceptionally because of the Leopoldian interlude (and presumably the outcome of its errors). "The colony of the Congo paid the price of its late conquest" (1962:74). Or, perhaps more relevantly, as Vellut indicates, the Leopoldian period was one in which the social basis for imperialist enterprise was unusual: it consisted of "speculators, military men seeking an escape from the mediocre boredom of Belgian garrisons" (1975:17), rather than the usual solid financial groups.

Leaving aside the perhaps special case of the Belgian Congo, how do we account for a slowdown in further structural change in the patterns of economic production after World War I? Very simply, it is that a pattern had been established which fitted within the parameters of the needs of the world-economy and which would be relatively stable until these parameters shifted.

The first half of the twentieth century is sometimes referred to as the "second industrial revolution," one based heavily on the automobile and petro-chemical industries. The worldwide spurt in the forces of production required an expansion in industrial facilities and in global production of raw materials and foodstuffs, as well as an expansion of consumption income to provide markets. As to be expected, these expansions did not proceed evenly, as is reflected in both shifting global terms of trade and shifting loci of world unemployment. Basically the world curve of raw material production rose more rapidly at first than the curve of industrial production. This was because there was a demand pull coming from profitable sectors of new industries and because expansion of raw material production required relatively little investment on the part of the entrepreneurs of this production (as we have seen in the case of Africa). This relatively more rapid rise of raw material production took place before World War I. The period between the two wars was one of relative stagnation (or slow upward movement) of both raw materials and industrial curves. The period from 1945 to 1965 was one in which the industrial curve rose *more* rapidly than the raw materials curve, although both went up.

It follows from this general pattern that what went on in Africa from 1919 to 1965 was an expansion of total output, especially after 1945, but always facing a weak world market.[40] The one exception to this is the period immediately following the Korean War when there was a very sudden increase in world demand, which quickly however evened out.

The consequent political economy of Africa was composed of four main elements:

(1) Most production was primary production, but primary production was itself divided into three zones. The first zone produced for the world market. Its size was limited by the weakness of this market, but its fluctuating needs governed the other two zones. The second zone essentially produced food crops

for workers in the first zone and in the allied urban zones and occupations. Both these zones added up to a small proportion of the total land area. The third zone produced manpower to export to the first zone (and to a very small extent to the second zone), sustaining itself largely on "subsistence" agriculture or pasturage.

The land of the first zone was controlled in different ways, as we have already seen: by white settler farmers, by companies (concessions), by African peasant farmers. The land of the second zone was controlled largely by Africans. The land of the third zone was controlled by the indigenous population, largely in the form of communal ownership.

(2) The manpower of the first zone (and even of the second zone) was largely migratory, which kept the cost of labor low in terms of world scales, a corollary of being in a weak world market for the products. As a consequence, the vast majority of Africans were "semiproletarians," persons who earned part of their life family income in wage labor (whether contractual or forced) and the other part of it in so-called subsistence production. Such a system optimized the possibility of shifting any burden of reduced relative world demand onto the direct producers rather than the owners of enterprise. Nonetheless, the steady expansion of absolute production involved a steady increase in "proletariani-zation," the increase in the number of workers who obtained virtually their entire life-income from wage-labor, as well as in "peasantization," the increase in the number of Africans who moved into ownership status in the second (and even the first) zone.

(3) The administrative bureaucracy that was required for such a system was small and relatively inexpensive. There were two main functions for the admin-istration. One was to construct the necessary economic infrastructure. This was done more or less on a cost basis. The taxes on African direct producers largely covered the costs of this infrastructure, but it brought in no profit as such. Needless to say, most of the owners of the first zone found this an admirable arrangement.[41]

The second function was to assure a proper *location* of African producers, getting them to move from one zone to the other as required. At first, force was widely used to get persons from the third to the first zone. Later, as the persons in the third zone became increasingly dependent on the cash economy, taxation or even temptation sufficed. In addition, workers in the third zone were often prevented from becoming owners in the first or second zones in order that they be available as wage workers (Arrighi, 1973). Finally, often the government intervened to force surplus workers back to the third zone.

Given the general lack of well-organized resistance in Africa, the bureaucracy needed to perform these two limited functions remained small until the rise of nationalist movements after the Second World War.

(4) The fourth aspect of the political economy was the slow growth of African middle classes. They remained few in number, given the limited urban and intermediary occupations for which they were required. Nonetheless, they

grew, and over time the contradictions between their strength and their limited political and economic opportunities accounted for the rise of nationalist movements. Once these movements began to link up with mass protest, the potential cost of colonial administration rose drastically, both the direct costs resulting from the need to expand the bureaucracy for purposes of control and the indirect costs of investment in infrastructure required for purposes of political appeasement.

This provided the major impetus for "decolonization." This story is now quite familiar, and we shall not repeat it.

The second phase of Africa's incorporation into the capitalist world-economy would be brought to an end by the accumulated contradictions both of the world-economy as a whole and of Africa's role within it. On the one hand, the expansion of total industrial capacity in the world-economy had by the mid-1960s significantly outdistanced both the expansion of raw material production and more importantly the expansion of effective demand, given the world distribution of income. This led to the beginning of the world economic downturn whose first serious signs were the world monetary crises circa 1967.

The fact that the expansion of total industrial capacity had led to a diminution of the relative share of the United States, as well as a lowered relative efficiency of U.S. production, meant the end of undisputed U.S. world economic hegemony; and there ensued the uncertain transition of the 1970s when at least five centers of structural power (the U.S., Western Europe, the U.S.S.R., China, and Japan) maneuvered for optimal advantage in the prospective realignment of forces.

The fact that raw material production had fallen relatively behind accounted for both the energy and the food crises. The energy crisis made possible the improved terms of trade for petroleum via the politics of OPEC, with similar organizations of producers of critical raw materials in prospect. The food crisis, combined with transitory climatological shifts, led to the widespread famine, in Africa and elsewhere.[42]

This sudden shift in the patterns of the world system accounted in large part for the sudden "decolonization" of Portuguese Africa, and the prospective decolonization of Zimbabwe and Namibia, thus completing a political process started in the 1950s, except for the case of South Africa. Phase two, that of colonialism, was passing into history.

PHASE III: 1975-

The third phase now starting will complete Africa's integration into the world-economy. In the coming 50 years this incorporation will take one of two forms: dependent development[43] or revolutionary transformation as part of a network of forces within the world-economy as a whole, which will further the transformation to a socialist world system.

I will merely sketch very briefly the factors at play. The capitalist world-economy will probably now see a phase of contraction and depression, during which there will be a slowdown of expansion of industrial productive capacity and a reallocation of world income to increase effective demand and recreate the conditions for a further significant expansion of overall world expansion of the forces of production, probably to begin again circa 1990. This will be accompanied by a political realignment to reflect the new socioeconomic hierarchy of the world system (Wallerstein, 1975a).

In the early period of contraction, semiperipheral areas of the world-economy will be in a relatively strong position. In Africa, this means areas with relative industrial and critical raw material strength: South Africa, Zaire, Nigeria, and possibly Algeria and Egypt. They will emerge as significant producers of industrial products not only for their home markets but for neighboring countries, and this increased income will represent part of the worldwide expansion of effective demand for the products of the core countries.

This same period will be one of acute suffering for truly peripheral areas, whose nonessential exports will find a very weak world market and whose internal food production may collapse further. They will bear the brunt of death from famine and major transfers of remaining populations from rural areas to bidonvilles. The corresponding political regimes will almost certainly be that of corrupt and repressive pretorians. The principal consequence for the social structure will be the disintegration of the third zone, the so-called subsistence sector, clearing the land areas of men and largely sounding the death knell for the concept of a semiproletarian labor force. The "reserve army of the unemployed" will thus become visible but also will have to be kept alive by some process of social redistribution of income.

The emptying out of the land areas will provide the space for an immense mechanization of African primary production, whether controlled by cooperatives, the state, multinational corporations, or some combinations thereof, permitting dramatic "development" of export crops when the new moment of world economic expansion begins.

The South African journal, *To the Point International,* caught the flavor of this prospect exactly in an article entitled "The Sahel: Today's disaster area . . . tomorrow's glorious garden?" (October 5, 1974, pp. 24-25). The article opened:

> Space-age farms, modern cattle ranches and lush market gardens in the middle of the Sahara. . . . This is no mirage. It is what experts from six of the world's most backward nations have conjured up for the future. Their idea is to roll back the desert and turn their drought-ravaged countries into a fertile green belt of productive crop land and pasture.

> The plan calls for giant dams to harness the Senegal and Niger rivers and provide power; advanced irrigation systems to water the dust bowls; and forest walls to check the southern march of the Sahara.

> It could eventually turn the rural subsistence economies of the west African nations of Chad, Mali, Mauritania, Niger, Senegal and Upper Volta into a vegetable garden for Europe and a vast beef belt.

But to have a chance to succeed, the plan would require millions of dollars, take years to accomplish and need a spectacular social and political revolution within the countries.

It is clear that one version or another of this "revolution" will occur, but in whose interests? This will depend on the outcome of the class struggles both internal to Africa and in the world system as a whole.

What the third phase of incorporation of Africa signals is the culmination of a long process of expansion of the geographic parameters of the capitalist world system, and the approximation in reality, *for the first time,* of the model of this system, as outlined by both the classical economists and Marx. It thus constitutes a vital *political* turning-point, as it finally threatens to remove the veils that have obscured the functioning of the capitalist system and thus have sustained it.

The elimination of the African (and other) subsistence sectors and the corollary full proletarianization of world labor must in the coming period intensify the political conflict caused by contradictory interests, unless the capitalist classes can discover some new artificial equivalent of the subsistence sector and its semiproletarian labor force. The substitute, if one be found, would bound to be more expensive and hence only partially preserve the system; but for the tenants of privilege, every extra few decades of survival are worth it.

NOTES

1. The now-classic exposition is Arghiri Emmanuel's *Unequal Exchange* (1972), a book that has given rise to a voluminous debate.

2. See the forthcoming article by André Gunder Frank, "Multilateral Merchandise Trade Imbalances and Uneven Economic Development." Frank sees these imbalances as an element different from unequal exchange, each significantly reinforcing and aggravating the other.

3. Amin is, however, talking of exchange within the capitalist world-economy, of the periphery exporting essential goods and importing luxuries. I am talking of exchange in which both sides are exchanging luxuries, or preciosities. As I put it previously, it is a form of exchange in which "each can export to the other what is in its system socially defined as worth little in return for the import of what in its system is defined as worth much" (Wallerstein, 1974a). Compare the similar expression of Edward Alpers: "trade from which each side believed itself to be profiting" (1973). Alpers, however, asserts this is the pattern of all Euro-African trade prior to "direct colonial rule," whereas I argue, as shall be seen, that a shift in pattern occurred earlier, circa 1750.

4. A.G. Hopkins (1973:90-91) said: "The eighteenth century was the golden age of prosperity for the West Indies, the time when the Islands became the chief suppliers of sugar to Europe. . . . [A]bout two-thirds of all the slaves shipped to the Caribbean worked on sugar plantations. . . . The expansion of sugar production was stimulated by a rise in demand in Europe following an increase in the consumption of tea and coffee; by a growth in the capacity of the sugar processing industry, which had caught up with supply by about the middle of the eighteenth century; and by government support, which underpinned the structure of Atlantic trade."

5. Philip D. Curtin (1969:222) notes, "In the mid-[eighteenth] century, [slave] exports from both [West Africa and Central and East Africa] reached a plateau of relative stability." See also his Figure 15 and Table 63.

6. Hopkins cites Benin, which developed without the slave trade, and the Niger Delta, where the trade did not lend itself to the creation of major states.

7. Of course, this increased effort by the French government, it could be argued, only brought the French slave trade back to the level it was at before 1763, and from which it fell because of military defeat. See, for example, Pierre H. Boulle (1972:106-107): "It was the slave trade, the fastest growing sector before the war, which suffered the most serious impact, dropping below prewar levels until the last years of the Ancien Régime. Indeed, the figures of the 1750's when Nantes' slavers carried from Africa an annual average of over 9000 Blacks for five years running, were never again equalled."

8. See Adu Boahen (1974:174, 178): "Finally, though the British had not abandoned their policy of Fante support, it is clear that their own position was so weakened by the turn of the nineteenth century, due mainly to the Seven Years' War, the American War of Independence and the Napoleonic Wars, that the policy could not be effectively enforced. . . . The final conquest of Fante by Asante produced a situation the British had done everything to prevent in the eighteenth century, the domination of the entire coastline by Asante."

9. Or perhaps they did not become peripheralized through the slave trade even to the limited extent suggested here. Dov Ronen makes the case that right up to the end of slave trading, it remained for Dahomey what I have called a trade in "luxuries," the exchange of a leftover accumulation (hence worthless in Dahomean terms) for European weapons and gifts. "It is suggested here, basically as an inference from a re-analysis of the role of the king, that the 'slave raids' were not carried out for the purpose of selling those captured but for the glorification and the aggrandizement of Dahomey (by means of sacrifice and absorption), the prime function of the king in his ritual role in the society. The surplus captives were exchanged for weapons and gifts, and were then sold as slaves by the European trade, quite possibly together with others that the latter, with his own men, had hunted. The weapons he gave the Dahomeans were used in the Annual Wars and the gifts redistributed to Dahomeans at the Annual Customs. Dahomey was not a slave-trading state and slaves were not a trading item in the Dahomean economy, but Dahomey was a society dominated by the ancestor cult and had an economy based on agriculture" (1971:13).

10. Boahen cites as evidence c.o. 267/24, Zachary Macauley to Lord Castlereagh, 6 May 1807.

11. At first, the British West Indian planters pressed for protection. Later they pressed to enforce abolition of the slave trade. In any case, the net effect of the ambivalence was to keep abolition an objective rather than a reality. See Christopher Fyfe (1974:44): "Despite the apparatus of enforcement the transatlantic slave trade went on undeterred. Large expanding markets for slaves opened in Brazil and Cuba, which were developed intensively for sugar production during the early nineteenth century. Supply met demand. . . . By the late 1830's it was estimated that the slave trade, far from being 'abolished,' had doubled since 1807."

12. See Curtin (1969), Tables 66 and 74 and Figure 18. Edward A. Alpers (1967:81) argues: "It is only in the last two decades of the eighteenth century, then, that the East African slave trade began to reach the proportions of the sixteenth century trade in West Africa. By 1810 the total East African trade was barely two-thirds of the average annual number of slaves exported from West Africa throughout the seventeenth century. It was not until after 1810 that the East African slave trade became anywhere near as voracious as the West African trade at its height in the eighteenth and first half of the nineteenth centuries."

13. Alpers (1969:246) notes: "There is, however, another aspect of the [East African] slave trade [in the 19th century] : not only did it uproot people, it also encouraged the growth of larger political units."

14. See the discussion of the consequences of these agricultural developments for the social structure of Zanzibar in J.M. Gray, "Zanzibar and the Coastal Belt, 1840-1884" (1963:217f.). The pattern of Indian Ocean trade changed as well, as explained by Alpers (forthcoming): "Gujarati textiles continued to dominate the East African market into the early decades of the nineteenth century, when first American and then British cottons seized the East African market while decimating the Indian cotton textile manufacturing industry. Although Gujarati merchants continued to play a vital role in East Africa after this time, they no longer operated as independent merchant capitalists, but as compradors for Western industrial capitalism."

15. See also George E. Brooks (1975:30): "Spurred by European and Eurafrican coastal

traders, African agriculturists responded [in the 1830s and 1840s] to the new marketing opportunities [for peanuts] with remarkable swiftness."

16. The latter phrase is that of Fyfe (1974:38-39). The former phrase is that of the Company, which Fyfe cites from Sierra Leone Studies, o.s., 1932, 18:42-77.

17. See J.E. Flint (1974:399): "The *laissez faire* attitude to trade seemed in fact to have worked itself out, the trade seemed stagnant, competition too fierce, and African middlemen too strong. Increasingly some of the British traders began to turn to ideas of monopoly as a way out of their difficulties. From this time forward there were constant negotiations among the more powerful Liverpool traders, designed to secure price-fixing arrangements whereby African middlemen could be presented with a united front."

18. Leonard Thompson (1971a:291) notes: "The growth of the diamond-mining industry in Griqualand West and the gold-mining industry in the Transvaal strengthened the previously tenuous arguments for territorial supremacy."

19. "Now flourishing" may give a wrong impression. They were flourishing in the sense of expanding in numbers in response to a widening world trade. But obviously many of these merchants were unsuccessful, which may have been one of the motivations behind the Fanti Confederation. Edward Reynolds (1975:114) argues: "Although the merchant community of the Gold Coast was in sympathy with the objectives of the Confederation, it is significant that most of the leaders and advisors of the movement were ambitious literate Africans who had failed to make good in trade and other employment."

20. Letter No. IX, to the Right Hon. Earl Granville, K.G., D.C.L., Secretary of State for the Colonies, on "The Fantee Confederation" from James Africanus B. Horton, *Letters on the Political Condition of the Gold Coast* (1870), reprinted in Henry S. Wilson (1969). The proposed Constitution of the Fanti Confederacy (1873) provided in Article 43 that "the officers of the Confederation shall render assistance as directed by the executive in carrying out the wishes of the British Government" (p. 218).

21. Governor Pope-Hennessy of Sierra Leone (under whom the Gold Coast then came) urged the British government to seize upon the desire for change of "every educated native at Cape Coast" as shown in support for the Fanti Confederation by "extending the system of Colonial Administration," which however he would have combined with "a certain amount of native self-government in the towns, and of judicial power by chiefs in the interior, in concert with District Magistrates" (Wilson, 1969:221-222). The ultimate frustration of Horton's plans is described by Christopher Fyfe (1972, chap. 5). Far from getting self-government, what the Fanti got was the proclamation by the British of a protectorate over the Gold Coast in 1874.

22. Colin W. Newbury (1969:77) noted: "Throughout the decades of the 'economic revolution' in the palm-oil and ground-nut trade there was an erratic upward progression in the value of exports between 1850 and 1880."

23. "By the end of the seventies, limited colonial enclaves and consular jurisdiction were no longer felt to be enough where relations with African rulers were concerned" (Newbury, 1969:94). The motives for the accelerating desire by local whites for political authority over Africans in South Africa after 1870 is described by Leonard Thompson (1971b:251): "Chiefdoms were undermined from within and overwhelmed from without. Resident missionaries were a revolutionary influence, because they condemned African customs and institutions. . . . Resident traders pushed the chiefdoms more tightly into the network of British commerce and created a demand for European manufactures and the money with which to buy them. White farmers infiltrated inside the frontiers of African chiefdoms, often starting by asking permission . . . , but usually ending by claiming proprietary rights over farms. Recruiters sought labourers for railway construction and for the diamond- and gold-mines. Speculators solicited all manner of industrial and mining concessions from chiefs."

24. See Richard Wolff (1974:33-35): "The change in British policy [in East Africa between 1873 and 1887] was first and foremost a response to closely interconnected phenomena: the commercial interests of private European companies in East Africa, which had increased rapidly, and the simultaneous activity there of the major European powers. . . .

"Facing this situation, the British government operating through Consul Kirk resorted to a strategy that had succeeded well for the previous half century. Put bluntly, the strategy

involved the activation of serious anti-slave trade campaigns as a means of establishing British economic and political hegemony in an area. . . .
"In the second stage [of the British campaign], from 1884 through the 1890's, the British finally subjected the slave trade to a systematic attack sufficient to stop it and to confront the traders with economic ruin. The coup de grâce followed, as Britain replaced both the Sultan and the Arab-Swahili aristocracy with the direct economy and political hegemony of the British colonial administration." Thus the last of the external arenas in Africa was being liquidated. Slavery had become definitely uneconomic.

25. The term is found in an essay by C.R. Fay in the Cambridge History of the British Empire, 1940, 2:399.

26. This argument is basically the same as that of Hla Myint, as Szereszewski recognizes (see p. 77, fn. 5), who argues that surplus land and labor is the basis of rapid development, thus applying Adam Smith's "vent-for-surplus" theory. See Myint's The Economics of the Developing Countries, London: Hutchinson, 1964, chap. 3.

27. See S. Daniel Neumark (1964:151-152): "The essential point is that, given an export demand the whole development of agricultural products in Africa prior to World War I has depended upon the provision of bulk transport, equally for plantation production and for peasant production which predominates in Africa. In West Africa, river transport made accessible forest zones along the Niger, the Gambia, the Congo, and other rivers. New areas were opened later by railways, which not only make the effectiveness of river transport, as in the case of the Niger, the Congo, and the Senegal, but also make the savannas available for commercial crops. Similarly, the opening of railway communications with the East Coast led to the expansion of cotton, coffee, and sisal production in East Africa, and to the production for export of tobacco, tea, and cotton in Nyassaland."

28. These correspond to the three categories used by Samir Amin (1973): Africa of the colonial economy (économie de traite), Africa of the concession-owning companies, Africa of the labor reserves.

29. For a very brief history of the policy of concessions, see Catherine Coquery-Vidrovitch (1969), especially pp. 186-194.

30. Coquery-Vidrovitch's figures for growth of imports and exports in French West Africa showed a 25-fold leap (1969:181).

31. Why this was not so easy is explained in Merlier (1962:59-61). See also Robert Harms (1975:77): "Recent research on events in the concession of Abir, the most notorious of the Congo concession companies, has revealed that attempts at reform in the concession area were notably unsuccessful, and that the rubber system in the Abir territory had already broken down by 1906, when serious debate on the Congo question was just beginning in Europe. The cause of this breakdown had little to do with the reform movement or international diplomacy; the concession had run out of rubber."

32. T.O. Ranger (1967:334-335) notes: "As far as [Cecil] Rhodes [the dominant figure in the British South Africa Company] was concerned, then, the [revolts in both Mashona-land and Matabeleland] in 1896 and 1897 merely decided him to move towards settler representation more rapidly. . . . Finally, of course, there was the reluctance of the British government to become in any way financially responsible for Rhodesia which powerfully induced them to accept any reasonable looking settlement negotiated between Rhodes and [Lord] Milner [British High Commissioner in South Africa]. As Milner reminded them in December 1897, if further native troubles were to bankrupt the Company it 'will throw an impecunious, undeveloped country bigger than France upon your hands'." How the settlers pushed the African peasantry out of the food-crop sector as well as is described in I.R. Phimister (1974).

33. Between 1911 and 1913 there were "a series of court cases in South-West Africa in which settlers were charged with the murder or manslaughter of Africans. . . . Although the trials were concerned with social tensions on the farms, they were taken by the whole of the settler population and the administration as representative test-cases. Thus, the two major groups of the German population in SWA were in open conflict; on the one side the settlers, the dependents, their defence counsel, their witnesses and jurymen; the farming press, and the whole of public opinion in Windhoek, on the other, the Civil Servants as judges and prosecutors, the police, and medical officers. The government intervened on behalf of the African victims and also called Africans as witnesses for the prosecution" (Bley, 1967:261).

34. Rechenberg's "private opposition to the settlers was never concealed. 'Any settlement by Europeans on a large scale,' he wrote, 'must lead to a conflict with the natives, which could only be settled in bloody fashion.' He never forgot the danger of rebellion. Further, he believed that the proper goal of German settlement was Eastern Europe" (Iliffe, 1969:131).

35. "The plantation sector, then, grew fairly slowly [in Tanganyika in the 1920s] and became really substantial only in the 1930's by which time . . . a rival African sector of cash crop production had emerged to balance it. Partly for this reason, the plantations never came to dominate the economy as did the European farms in Kenya" (Iliffe, 1971:14).

36. This is what Wolff suggests. He says (1974:135) that the British feared that Kenya in its "depressed economic conditions" faced only two alternatives: "to revert to an 'earlier, primitive' form of tribal, more or less subsistence economy or to implant non-African settlers in order to organize, invest in, and manage agricultural production of cash crops." As for the contrast of Uganda, Wolff argues (p. 177): "The geographic position of Uganda in the interior of the continent greatly reduced the economically damaging effects of the slave trade and its abolition. Furthermore, the relatively strictly structured and 'stable' Buganda Kingdom offered the attractive possibility of organizing African peasant agricultural production managed at middle and lower levels by Africans already accustomed to workable hierarchical relationships."

37. Amin points out (1973:191): "On the other hand, in the savannah, from Senegal through Northern Nigeria to Sudan, the Moslem brotherhoods permitted another type of colonial trading: the organization of production and export (groundnuts and cotton) in the context of vast areas subject to a theocratic political power—that of the Mourid brotherhoods of Senegal, the Sultanates of Nigeria and Ansar and Ashiqqa in the Sudan—which kept the form of a tribute—paying social formation, but was integrated into the international system because the surplus appropriated in the form of tribute levied on the village communities was itself marketed. It was the Egyptian colonization in Sudan which created the most advanced conditions for the development of this type of organization, which in that country tended towards a pure and simple *latifundium* system. The British merely gathered the fruits of this evolution. The new *latifundia*-owners, who after 1898 accepted the colonial administration, had cotton grown for the benefit of British industry. Powerful modern techniques (large-scale irrigation in the Gezira) were made available to them. But the second transformation of Islam in West Africa, after the colonial conquest, opened the way to the same kind of evolution, although less definite and slower."

38. Compare the discussion of the "mining revolution" of 1866-1918 offered by D. Hobart Houghton (1969). Figure 2 on page 18 of his essay shows how sharp the jump in exports were in the period of which we are speaking, doubling for example in the period 1906-1910 over the previous five years.

39. Hopkins (1973:204) does warn against exaggerating the decline of the African bourgeoisie on the grounds that "the European firms already dominated the trade of the main ports in the period 1850-1880," that the decline was relative but not absolute, that Africans went into forms of commerce other than export-import, "being astute enough to realize" where their comparative disadvantage lay. But none of this undoes the basic point that a mjaor structural change occurred at this point in time, what Hopkins calls "completing the open economy."

40. See for example this comment on the presumably relatively prosperous group of white settlers in Kenya (Van Zwanenberg, 1972:8-10): "In the period up to 1939 the European settlers were struggling to establish their estates on a firm economic and technical base. The settlers suffered from an almost permanent shortage of labour, inadequate finances, and a lack of sufficient technical knowledge and, as a result, the majority of estates were only able to use less than half the available land. . . . The whole plantation system had been rocked by the great depression. . . . In Kenya's case credit through the branches of the international banks was stopped for the duration of slump, while export prices dropped drastically [beginning in 1919]."

41. E.A. Brett (1973:87) captures the flavor of this situation splendidly: "Commitment [of the colonial administration in East Africa] to the 'managed economy' did not involve any ideological doubts about the right of private interests to exploit resources when they could so profitably without excessively raising the costs of everyone else. . . . What does emerge is the congruence between the interests of a bureaucracy committed to large-scale

centralized administrative structures for reasons of simplicity of management and economy and those of private producing and trading groups that needed to have services provided at the cheapest possible rate. . . . [Where there was conflict, it] was really about the relative advantages to different private interests of a state versus a private monopoly for the provision of essential services. In the cases detailed here the State solution was accepted because the most important of the capitalist groups were not prepared to pay subsidies to the incompetence or greed of others of their number."

42. The socioeconomic roots of the African famine are well discussed in Comité Information Sahel, *Qui se nourrit de la famine en Afrique?* Paris: Ed. Maspero, Cahiers Libres 292-293, 1974, and two articles in Review of African Political Economy, No. 1, 1974: Claude Meillassoux, "Development or Exploitation: Is the Sahel Famine Good Business?," pp. 27-33; Lionel Cliffe, "Feudalism, Capitalism and Famine in Ethiopia," pp. 34-40.

43. I am using the phrase of F.H. Cardoso and Enzo Faletto, which emphasizes the fact that increased dependency and increased development (in terms of increase in industrial capacity and more generally in the forces of production) may go hand in hand. See their *Dependencia y desarollo en América Latina*, Mexico: Siglo XXI, 1965.

REFERENCES

ALPERS, E. (1967). The East African slave trade (Historical Association of Tanzania Paper no. 3). Nairobi: East African Publishing House.

——— (1969). "The nineteenth century: Prelude to colonialism." In B.A. Ogot and J.A. Kieran (eds.), Zamani: A survey of East African history. Nairobi: East African Publishing House.

——— (1973). "Rethinking African economic history." Ufahumu, 3(winter).

——— (forthcoming). "Gujarati and the trade of East Africa, c. 1500-1800."

AMIN, S. (1969). Le monde des affaires sénégalais. Paris: Editions de Minuit.

——— (1973). "Underdevelopment and dependence in black Africa—Their historical origins and contemporary forms." Social and Economic Studies, 22(1).

——— (1974). "Accumulation and development: A theoretical model." Review of African Political Economy (no. 1).

ARRIGHI, G. (1973). "Labor supplies in historical perspective: A study of the proletarianization of the African peasantry in Rhodesia." Pp. 180-234 in G. Arrighi and J.S. Saul (eds.), Essays on the political economy of Africa. New York: Monthly Review Press.

BARBER, W.J. (1964). "The movement into the world economy." In M.J. Herskovits and M. Harwitz (eds.), Economic transition in Africa. Evanston, Ill.: Northwestern University Press.

BEAN, R. (1974). "A note on the relative importance of slaves and gold in West African exports." Journal of African History, 15(3).

BLEY, H. (1967). South-West Africa under German rule, 1894-1914. Evanston, Ill.: Northwestern University Press.

BOAHEN, A. (1974). "Politics in Ghana, 1800-1874." In J.F.A. Ajayi and M. Crowder (eds.), History of West Africa (vol. 2). London: Longmans.

BOULLE, P.H. (1972). "Slave trade, commercial organization and industrial growth in eighteenth-century Nantes." Revue française d'histoire d'outre-mer, 59(214, 1er trimestre).

BRETT, E.A. (1973). Colonialism and underdevelopment in East Africa. London: Heinemann.

BROOKS, G.E. (1975). "Peanuts and colonialization: Consequences of the commercialization of peanuts in West Africa, 1830-70." Journal of African History, 16(1).

COQUERY-VIDROVITCH, C. (1969). "French colonization in Africa to 1920: Administration and economic development." In L.H. Gann and P. Duignan (eds.), Colonialism in Africa, 1870-1960 (vol. 1). Cambridge: University Press.

CURTIN, P.D. (1969). The Atlantic slave trade: A census. Madison: University of Wisconsin Press.

DAAKU, K.Y. (1968). "The slave trade and African society." In T.O. Ranger (ed.), Emerging themes of African history. Nairobi: East African Publishing House.
DAVENPORT, T.R.H. (1969). "The consolidation of a new society: The Cape Colony." In M. Wilson and L. Thompson (eds.), The Oxford history of South Africa (vol. 1). New York: Oxford University Press.
DE KIEWIET, C.W. (1957). A history of South Africa: Social and economic. London: Oxford University Press.
EHRLICH, C. (1965). "The Uganda economy, 1903-1945." In V. Harlow and E.M. Chilver (eds.), History of East Africa (vol. 2). Oxford: Clarendon Press.
EMMANUEL, A. (1972). Unequal exchange. New York: Monthly Review Press.
FIELDHOUSE, D.K. (1971). "The economic exploitation of Africa: Some British and French comparisons." In P. Gifford and W.R. Lewis (eds.), France and Britain in Africa. New Haven, Conn.: Yale University Press.
FLINT, J.E. (1963). "The wider background to partition and colonial occupation." Pp. 350-390 in R. Oliver and G. Mathew (eds.), History of East Africa (vol. 1). Oxford: Clarendon Press.
——— (1974). "Economic change in West Africa in the nineteenth century." In J.F.A. Ajayi and M. Crowder (eds.), History of West Africa (vol. 2). London: Longmans.
FYFE, C. (1972). Africanus Horton. New York: Oxford University Press.
——— (1974). "Reform in West Africa: The abolition of the slave trade." In J.F.A. Ajayi and M. Crowder (eds.), History of West Africa (vol. 2). London: Longmans.
GALLAGHER, J., and ROBINSON, R. (1970). "The imperialism of free trade." In A.G.L. Shaw (ed.), Great Britain and the colonies. London: Methuen. This is a reprint which originally appeared in Economic History Review (2nd ser.), 1953, 6(1).
GRAY, J.M. (1963). "Zanzibar and the coastal belt, 1840-1884." In R. Oliver and G. Mathew (eds.), History of East Africa (vol. 1). Oxford: Clarendon Press.
HARMS, R. (1975). "The end of red rubber: A reassessment." Journal of African History, 16(1).
HOPKINS, A.G. (1973). An economic history of West Africa. London: Longmans.
HOUGHTON, D.H. (1969). "Economic development, 1865-1965." In M. Wilson and L. Thompson (eds.), The Oxford history of South Africa (vol. 2). New York: Oxford University Press.
ILIFFE, J. (1969). Tanganyika under German rule, 1905-1912. Cambridge: University Press.
——— (1971). Agricultural change in modern Tanganyika (Historical Association of Tanzania Paper no. 10). Nairobi: East African Publishing House.
JOHNSON, M. (1974). "Cotton imperialism in West Africa." African Affairs, 73(291).
JULIEN, C.-A. (1964). Histoire de l'Algérie contemporaine (vol. 1). Paris: Presses Universitaires de France.
LEWIS, W.A. (1952). "World production, prices and trade, 1870-1960." Manchester School of Economic and Social Studies, 20(1).
LOW, D.A. (1965). "British rule, 1895-1912." In V. Harlow and E.M. Chilver (eds.), History of East Africa (vol. 2). Oxford: Clarendon Press.
MERLIER, M. (1962). Le Congo de la colonisation belge à l'independence. Paris: Ed. Maspero.
NEUMARK, S.D. (1964). Foreign trade and economic development in Africa: A historical perspective. Stanford, Calif.: Food Research Institute.
NEWBURY, C.W. (1969). "Trade and authority in West Africa from 1850 to 1880." In L.H. Gann and P. Duignan (eds.), Colonialism in Africa, 1870-1960 (vol. 1). Cambridge: University Press.
OMER-COOPER, J.D. (1966a). "The Mfecane and the Great Trek." In J.C. Anene and G.N. Brown (eds.), Africa in the nineteenth and twentieth centuries. Ibadan: Ibadan University Press.
——— (1966b). "South Africa at the dawn of the nineteenth century." In J.C. Anene and G.N. Brown (eds.), Africa in the nineteenth and twentieth centuries. Ibadan: Ibadan University Press.
PATTERSON, S. (1957). The last trek. London: Routledge and Kegan Paul.
PHIMISTER, I.R. (1974). "Peasant production and underdevelopment in Southern Rhodesia, 1890-1914." African Affairs, 73:291.

RANGER, T.O. (1967). Revolt in Southern Rhodesia, 1896-97. Evanston, Ill.: North-western University Press.
REYNOLDS, E. (1975). "Economic imperialism: The case of the Gold Coast." Journal of Economic History, 35(1).
RODNEY, W. (1968). "European activity and African reaction in Angola." In T.O. Ranger (ed.), Aspects of Central African history. London: Heinemann.
RONEN, D. (1971). "On the African role in the trans-Atlantic slave trade in Dahomey." Cahiers d'études africaines, 11(1).
SCHUMPETER, J. (1939). Business cycles. New York: McGraw-Hill.
SRAFFA, P. (1972). Production of commodities by means of commodities. Cambridge: University Press.
STENGERS, J. (1969). "The Congo Free State and the Belgian Congo before 1914." In L.H. Gann and P. Guignan (eds.), Colonialization in Africa, 1870-1960 (vol. 1). Cambridge: University Press.
SURET-CANALE, J. (1964). Afrique noire occidentale et centrale (vol. 2). Paris: Edition Sociales.
SZERESZEWSKI, R. (1965). Structural changes in the economy of Ghana, 1891-1911. London: Weidenfeld and Nicholson.
THOMPSON, L. (1971a). "Great Britain and the Afrikaner republics, 1870-1899." In M. Wilson and L. Thompson (eds.), The Oxford history of South Africa (vol. 2). New York: Oxford University Press.
––– (1971b). "The subjection of the African chiefdoms, 1870-1898." In M. Wilson and L. Thompson (eds.), The Oxford history of South Africa (vol. 2). New York: Oxford University Press.
UZOIGWE, G.N. (1974). Britain and the conquest of Africa. Ann Arbor: University of Michigan Press.
VAN ZWANENBERG, R. (1972). The agricultural history of Kenya to 1939 (Historical Association of Kenya Paper no. 1). Nairobi: East African Publishing House.
VELLUT, J.-L. (1975). "Le Zaïre à la périphérie du capitalisme: quelques perspectives historiques." Unpublished paper delivered to the Canadian Association of African Studies, Toronto, February 19-22.
WALLERSTEIN, I. (1970). "The colonial era in Africa: Changes in social structure." In L.H. Gann and P. Guignan (eds.), Colonialism in Africa, 1870-1960 (vol. 2). Cambridge: University Press.
––– (1972). "Social conflict in post-independence black Africa: The concepts of race and status-group reconsidered." In E.Q. Campbell (ed.), Racial tensions and national identity. Nashville, Tenn.: Vanderbilt University Press.
––– (1973). "Africa in a capitalist world." Issue, 3(3).
––– (1974a). "The rise and future demise of the world capitalist system: Concepts for comparative analysis." Comparative Studies in Society and History, 16:387-415.
––– (1974b). The modern world-system: Capitalist agriculture and the origins of the European world-economy in the sixteenth century. New York: Academic Press.
––– (1975a). Old problems and new syntheses: The relation of revolutionary ideas and practices. Saskatoon: University of Saskatchewan Press.
––– (1975b). "Class-formation in the capitalist world-economy." Politics and Society, 5(3).
WHEELER, D.L. (1971). "Part one." In D.L. Wheeler and R. Pélissier (eds.), Angola. New York: Praeger.
WILLIAMS, E. (1964). British historians and the West Indies. Port-of-Spain, Trinidad: P.N.M. Publishing.
WILSON, H.S. (1969). Origins of West African nationalism. London: Macmillan.
WOLFF, R. (1974). The economies of colonialism: Britain and Kenya, 1870-93. New Haven, Conn.: Yale University Press.

2

POLARIZED ACCUMULATION AND THE THEORY OF ECONOMIC DEPENDENCE:
The Implications of South African Semi-Industrial Capitalism

PHILIP EHRENSAFT
Université du Québec à Montreal

Polarized accumulation as a mode of semi-industrial capitalism has arisen in two peripheral economies: South Africa and Brazil. This essay examines the South African experience as one instance of polarized accumulation and emphasizes the following issues: (1) the alleged tendency of peripheral capitalism to stagnate at a semi-industrial stage, this stage constituting the highest phase of dependence rather than an intermediate step toward "development"; (2) the comparative effectiveness of the bourgeoisies of the white Dominions within the British Empire in terms of mobilizing economic resources through their respective "national policies"; (3) the relation between apartheid and the accumulation of capital in South Africa, and whether there is, has been, or will be a contradiction between the former and the latter; (4) the question of whether direct investment necessarily introduces processes which lie beyond the control of ruling groups in semi-industrial capitalist societies and thus constitutes a qualitatively different experience than indirect investment.

The first section of this essay, "Types of Semi-Industrial Capitalism," begins by defining the precise sense in which the term "semi-industrial capitalism" is employed and suggests criteria useful for explicating variations among economies included within the rubric of this term. Next, "polarized accumulation" is defined and discussed as one possible route toward transcending the structural limits of semi-industrial capitalism. Readers broadly familiar with the literature on dependence or domination in the world economy (Ehrensaft, 1971; Amin, 1971; Latin American Perspectives, 1974) will recognize the questions and debates addressed in this quite compressed discussion. For readers less familiar with this literature, it will be necessary to briefly outline the origins, content, and problems of the theory of economic dependence before proceeding to the first section. Throughout the pages which follow, it should be kept in mind that two interrelated goals guide this essay: first, to interpret South Africa's economic history via the theory of dependence; secondly, to examine the implications of this history for a reformulation of the theory.

Contemporary analyses of economic dependence have their origins in two basic sources: the structuralist school of economics associated with the United Nations Economic Commission for Latin America (ECLA) and Paul Baran's reformulation of the Marxist theory of imperialism and the political economy of underdevelopment. The important writings of both the ECLA group and Baran first appeared during the 1950s and subsequently catalyzed a new understanding of the history and functions of Africa, Asia, and Latin America in world capitalism. First, let us turn to the lessons of structuralism.

From the late nineteenth century onwards, various Latin American societies experienced an industrialization through import-substitution, which intensified in pace and scope during World War II. The postwar years did not witness fulfillment of hopes that this industrialization represented intermediate processes which would carry Latin America from underdevelopment to development. Even where the industrial base had expanded to include a large capital goods sector, its market was largely restricted within national boundaries. Exports still consisted overwhelmingly of raw materials, industry was characterized by high costs and low efficiency, and the majority of the population seemed locked in conditions of low revenue, illiteracy, and low life expectancy. The ECLA group found that the orthodox economic theory prevailing in the United States and Europe was not only inadequate but inimical toward understanding the postwar economic problems of Latin America and gradually elaborated an alternative analysis:

> The structural approach to the problems of development, which is being generalized in Latin America, initially appeared in connection with theoretical studies trying to identify the primary causes of the inflationary disequilibrium (which results, as a rule, from the structural rigidities of supply inherent in underdeveloped economies) distinguishing them from the mechanisms of propagation of these disequilibria. Current attempts to control inflation by focusing only on the progagating mechanisms (inspired by the monetarist theory) constitute a classic example of sterile efforts towards modifying the behavior of economic agents without previous alterations in the structural parameters which condition that behavior. [Furtado, 1965:175]

Identification of structural parameters as the primary element in an analysis of underdevelopment led the ECLA group to examine the manner in which Latin American societies had been created and shaped by their role as raw material exporters in world trade during the past five centuries.

Structuralist analysis begins by looking at the world market which arose as the result of Europe's capitalist revolution and maritime expansion from the late fifteenth century onwards. Europe, and later the United States and Japan, emerged as the dynamic technological and financial *center* of world capitalism.

Latin America and, by inference, Africa and Asia, became incorporated into the world system as a dependent *periphery* supplying mineral and agricultural products which suited the needs of the dynamic center. Peripheral social structure was shaped by its role vis-à-vis the center. The periphery's resources were used in such a way that the major gains and accumulation of capital from international trade in primary products were reaped by the center or core nations. Vested minority interests associated with the conditioned social structure of the periphery benefited from the skewing of its resources while the masses remained in poverty.

Peripheral societies, then, are not in a transitional state from precapitalist structures toward capitalism, but rather constitute a particular and distinctive form of modern capitalism which developed pari passu and in direct relation to the needs of the core of the world economy. It is thus incorrect to speak of "modernizing" the periphery. Latin America, Asia, and Africa have been modernized for some centuries now, but in ways that have rendered them distinctive from and dependent upon the center. Using this historical perspective, the structuralists advanced explanations as to why industrialization in the periphery remained limited in extent and contained within domestic boundaries. Space limitations prevent us from delving further into the rich body of writings produced by the structuralists and offering a critique of their fundamental assumptions and propositions (see Ehrensaft, 1971:45-50). The most important lesson of structuralism for the purposes of this essay is the attention it drew to the distinct capitalist formations of center and periphery in the world economy, and the necessity to examine the role of a given peripheral territory from the moment of its initial integration into world capitalism if one is to understand its contemporary social system. Thus an analysis of the political economy of South Africa today must be based upon a knowledge of its successive peripheral capitalist roles from the mid-seventeenth century onwards and the manner in which these roles shaped its internal social structures.

Let us now turn to the second basic source of dependency theory, the writings of Paul Baran (1957, 1958). Baran noted the presence in what is now termed the periphery of a certain number of bourgeois elements engaged in activities akin to those of the eighteenth century capitalist middle classes of Great Britain who were to create the world's first industrial revolution. But the left would be mistaken, he argued, if it expected that peripheral protobourgeoisies could create a parallel capitalist transformation and would thus deserve the left's conditional and temporary support in struggles against foreign capital and "feudal" domestic elements. On the contrary, the internal configuration of vested interests in the periphery was such that the bourgeoisie was integrated with foreign capital and reactionary domestic elements in an economic and political amalgam which effectively blocked all possibilities of economic growth (1958:78, 80). The choice for the masses was socialism or stagnation. Specific aspects of Baran's argument now appear misconstrued, but, again, limitations of space prevent us from probling either these or the rich suggestiveness of his thinking.

Baran's central point, that the internal social configuration and international context of what is now termed peripheral capitalism are such that only a socialist revolution can lift the masses out of poverty, remained key in subsequent left thinking (and practice) with respect to dependence. This subsequent left analysis included, among other developments, a combination of Baran's view of the bourgeoisie with the center-periphery perspective of the structuralists. Andre Gunder Frank's crisp phrase, "the development of underdevelopment," best expresses this synthesis (1967). Underdevelopment is not a condition of being several centuries behind the kinds of transformations experienced by the capitalist center but a condition of satellitization forced upon the periphery since 1500 by this very center. Integration of a peripheral power structure, which benefits from satellitization, with corporate capital from the center results in structures which permit, at most, a limited degree of industrialization through import-substitution. Fundamental economic transformation is thus precluded within a peripheral capitalist mode of production. The choice for the masses, again, is stagnation or socialist revolution.

While Frank has been criticized on a variety of points (and has responded quite constructively to this criticism), the central contention of socialism or stagnation has rarely been questioned by left analysts of dependence. One concern of this essay is to look at the South African experience in comparative perspective (especially with Brazil) in order to ask whether there is at least a possibility that some peripheral societies might advance beyond stagnation within a capitalist mode of production. As the reader shall see below, we suggest that this possibility may exist and, if so, exists for some of the larger and more strategic units of the periphery. While socialism or stagnation may accurately describe a strong tendency in all peripheral capitalist societies, this formulation does not take account of the possibility of countervailing structures arising in some of them which might prove strong enough to overcome the basic tendency. We believe that the theory of dependence should be reformulated to account for this possibility, and the basis for this contention will be explicated in the following pages.

Before proceeding to the discussion of polarized accumulation as one possible mode of transcending the limits of semi-industrial capitalism, several final comments are in order. First, we have spoken of *the* theory of dependence. It would be more proper to speak of theories of dependence, given the various debates now raging in the analysis of center-periphery relations. Space limitations prevent us from presenting any more than the bare essentials shared by various schools of thought on dependency. Second, the "theory" of dependency is more properly termed a perspective than a theory. It will be some time yet before a sufficient number of studies have appeared which utilize the dependency perspective to analyze particular peripheral histories, common peripheral problems or processes, and various aspects of center-periphery relations (for example, patents) such that the raw material will exist to construct a systematic body of thought deserving the term "theory." It is hoped that this essay and the continuing research on South Africa's economic history which it represents will constitute one modest building block toward transforming a perspective into a theory. Finally, some writers object to the very term "dependence." For some, the term should be replaced by another which connotes the *domination* of metropolitan capital, in alliance with peripheral rulers, over the impoverished masses of the periphery and the necessity for socialist revolution to overcome this domination. For others, the term "dependence" is associated with schools of thought which foresee an ending of Africa's, Asia's, and Latin America's peripheral roles in the world system by means other than mobilization of the masses in class struggles. It seems to us that the term "dependence" has become so ingrained into discussions of center and periphery in the world system that there is now little likelihood of abandoning it. What is more important is to imbue the term with the proper content.

TYPES OF SEMI-INDUSTRIAL CAPITALISM

Semi-industrial capitalism is usually understood to mean a peripheral economy in which (1) industrialization through import-substitution has proceeded to the stage where a large part of the need for capital goods is met locally; (2) exports are predominantly primary products; manufactured exports flow largely to less industrialized parts of the periphery.[1] Semi-industrial capitalist societies may be broadly divided into two categories according to the nature of the labor force. These two cases may be termed the "classic" and "dominion" types of semi-industrial capitalism. South Africa and Brazil will both be seen to be combinations of the two types.

"Classic" semi-industrial capitalism possesses the following characteristics: (1) a large part of the labor force is engaged in agriculture and exhibits much "underemployment"; (2) the proportion of the labor force engaged in manufacturing remains small relative to the proportion so employed in the center; (3) a large proportion of the population has lumpen proletariat status. Mexico and India are prime examples of classic semi-industrial capitalism. Together, the three characteristics of the labor force which were just elaborated imply low purchasing power by the masses. Only a small proportion of the population has sufficient income to enter the market for consumer durables, which, because of higher capital-output ratios, usually generate more backward linkages to capital goods sectors than nondurables. Consequently, the process of industrialization through import-substitution does not create a market sufficient unto itself. A limited domestic market for industrial products, plus lack of export outlets, means stagnation.

"Dominion" semi-industrial capitalism prevails in temperate or semitemperate regions of the periphery which were sparsely settled by indigenous peoples previous to intensive waves of European settlement during the nineteenth and early twentieth centuries. This category includes Canada, Australia, New Zealand, Argentina, and Uruguay. In contrast to the classic case, agriculture is capital-intensive and utilizes a high level of technology. While agricultural exports constitute an important element in foreign trade, only a small fraction of the labor force is engaged in direct production. Second, the proportions of the population engaged in manufacturing and dwelling in urban areas are similar to the ratios in metropolitan economies. Third, wage rates and the standard of living that these wages purchase are also within the range prevailing in the center (this statement holding true for Argentina and Uruguay only through World War II).

Within the context of the labor force described above, the dominion category exhibits an industrial structure typical of a dependent, peripheral economy. Industrialization proceeds through import-substitution behind protective tariffs; high ratios of oligopolization in key sectors combined with metropolitan techniques of production and capital-labor ratios imply that few firms produce at a sufficient quantity to achieve optimal economies of scale; a large fraction of manufacturing (as well as mining and finance) is conducted by branch plants of multinational corporations. The result is a relatively inefficient industrial sector which also incurs extra costs via transportation of imported industrial inputs; external payments to multinationals, such as licensing fees and transfer pricing; and barriers to exports imposed by transportation costs, tariffs, and export limitations imposed by home offices on peripheral branch plants. Given the combination of a typical dependent industrial structure with high mass purchasing power, a market sufficient unto itself is created, though one restricted within national boundaries. A relatively inelastic demand exists for imported industrial inputs; continued prosperity depends upon high levels of primary-product exports.

Primary-product exports should not be viewed ipso facto as a defining characteristic of the "development of underdevelopment." In agriculture and forest products, the question is not one of primary versus secondary production, but of the nature of the forces of production in agriculture and the kind of backward linkages generated to capital goods industries such as agricultural machinery and chemicals. It should not be forgotten that in the case of the peripheral economy which became the center of world capitalism, agricultural exports still constitute an important component of external trade. In the case of dominion semi-industrial capitalism, New Zealand has, until the present, remained abreast of metropolitan living standards by relying upon a predominantly agricultural export structure.[2]

Application of new prospecting techniques over extensive hinterland territories to yield successive discoveries of mineral deposits has been a crucial element in the Canadian and Australian instances of dominion semi-industrial capitalism. Again, the issue is not so much one of the degree of national processing of raw materials, though this is not to be discounted, as it is one of the degree of backward linkages established with capital goods (e.g., mining equipment and chemicals) or services with a high level of "human capital" (e.g., exploration teams). The long-term vulnerability of relying upon new discoveries of minerals to replace existing wasting assets as a source of foreign exchange is evident. If capital goods industries and "human-capital-intensive" service resources are generated through backward linkages from mining, a national economy may possess exports which can, partially at least, compensate for exhaustion of domestic minerals (e.g., the drill rig industry in the United States or mining equipment exports by South Africa).[3]

In short, integration of an economy as a primary-product exporter does not necessarily lead to the "development of underdevelopment." On the other hand, neither backward nor forward linkages from the mineral sector have approached the potential extent and depth socially feasible in the dominion category of semi-industrial capitalism (though the degree to which this potential is approached varies from country to country). Consequently, the present structure of a market sufficient unto itself but restricted to national boundaries and dependent upon primary-product exports is vulnerable in the long-run, despite current living standards in the metropolitan range.

Classic semi-industrial capitalism, then, tends toward stagnation due to low purchasing power by the masses, whereas dominion semi-industrial capitalism exhibits long-term vulnerability due to restriction of the industrial base to national boundaries and dependence upon raw material exports to import necessary industrial inputs. South Africa and Brazil represent hybrids of the two categories of semi-industrial capitalism. European settlers in the dominions killed off indigenous peoples or drove them into marginal territories. In South Africa, of course, indigenous peoples were integrated into the capitalist economy as a labor force. The precise nature of this integration of various phases of South Africa's economic history is spelled out below. Examining the population as a whole, one would classify South Africa's economy as classic semi-industrial capitalism. Disaggregating, one has a European population with a standard of living and occupational and residential distribution comparable to the dominions superimposed on non-European masses whose life-situation is comparable to their counterparts in the classic category. As we shall see in a moment, the kind of distribution of economic roles and standard of living which South Africa has achieved by an absolute correlation of race and class appears not to be a unique structure but is being broadly replicated in Brazil on the basis primarily of class.

Before turning to the formal characteristics of this broad replication, one should note that the definition of land as marginal in the dominions, and therefore suitable for indigenous survivors, was initially made according to agricultural criteria. These survivors are usually of little importance as a source of labor. New mineral discoveries, however, frequently turn areas previously defined as marginal into key regions of the twentieth century economy. Indigenous peoples are then pushed aside after pious pronouncements appropriate to post-World-War-II formal norms of humanity and handed perfunctory cash settlements (e.g., the James Bay hydroelectric project in Canada; see Davis and Zannis, 1974). Thus internal colonialism based upon seizure of indigenous territories continues to be a key element in dominion semi-industrial capitalism where mineral exports assume importance. South Africa's indigenous peoples experience the double exploitation of internal colonialism via mineral production and integration as a labor force of subreproductive wages. In the case of Brazil's vast Amazon basin, the military regime has returned to an earlier practice of outright slaughter of native peoples, the likes of which has not been witnessed since the settlement of the American West.

Until recently, the hybrid South African form of semi-industrial capitalism appeared to be the product of a unique historical experience. Looking at the Brazilian "economic miracle," however, one is struck by a number of parallels with the South African political economy. The two societies seem to share the following characteristics: (1) the national market for durables (which have higher capital-output ratios than nondurables) is increased by squeezing the real income of the masses and redistributing an already skewed income even more in favor of the upper and middle classes; (2) squeezing the masses requires an organizationally and technologically proficient military and police apparatus which has the support or acquiescence of the upper- and middle-income groups (roughly a fifth of the population) which pursues a policy of crushing all opposition to the state; (3) the state is strongly linked with metropolitan capital, largely in the form of direct investment by multinational corporations; these corporations dominate the durable and capital goods sectors; (4) the state is an active organizer of the accumulation of capital and operates with a long-term perspective toward strengthening the relative power and autonomy of the national economy in the world system; in particular, the state operates in conjunction with capital to increase the proportion of manufactured goods in total exports. These four characteristics together define a mode of semi-industrial capitalism which is termed "polarized accumulation."

There is a fifth characteristic present for Brazil and South Africa, which, however, may not be an essential element of polarized accumulation: sub-imperialism, one aspect of which is the opening up of export outlets in weaker surrounding societies and gaining concessions from the metropole with respect to market openings in return for services rendered. Another shared characteristic which is probably not necessary to polarized accumulation, but which raises interesting questions, is that Brazil is also a hybrid of the classic and dominion forms of semi-industrial capitalism.[4]

Polarized accumulation in South Africa and Brazil has been associated with average annual increases in Gross Domestic Product (GDP), which have been among the highest in the world economy during recent years. Second, in the face of a general downturn in the world economy, in both the center and the periphery, since 1968, these high rates have been exceptional and made South Africa and Brazil more attractive to multinational investors. The reasons for this countercyclical behavior in the South African economy will be outlined below. Third, both countries claim to be actively pursuing a policy of structural transformation of the economy as well as high rates of increase in GDP which will uttimately overcome the limits and vulnerabilities of semi-industrial capitalism. In other words, they expect to be counted among the core of central countries by the end of this century. It is to the advantage of both governments to exaggerate the degree and rate of this structural transformation, this exaggeration occurring in Brazil to the extent that Brazilian businessmen complain that falsified statistics hamper their planning operations. Surveying sections of the international financial press intended primarily for aiding concrete investment decisions rather than for general publicity purposes, however, one gains an impression that the basic claim may not be an impossible one. Polarized accumulation should be viewed as *one possible* path through which *some* semi-industrial capitalist economies *might* move beyond semi-industrialism while remaining within the capitalist orbit. For some societies, semi-industrial capitalism may not turn out to be a terminal state, the "highest stage of dependence."

South Africa and Brazil both possess relatively large populations and territories compared to surrounding societies, favorable endowments of resources in strong demand on the international market, and key military positions or functions. Where similar characteristics prevail, one would expect the possibility of the rise of semi-industrial capitalism and the creation of a strong state which would attempt to organize capital accumulation so as to overcome the limits of this mode of production. Such a strong state does not mean that polarized accumulation will necessarily emerge. Iran's oil revenues, for. example, may enable her to avoid the first defining characteristic of polarized accumulation listed above—that is, forced negative redistribution of income away from the masses. Second, the conjunction of large size, favorable resource endowment, and strategic military value occurs in two other national societies in sub-Saharan Africa: Nigeria and Zaire. It is far from certain that a sufficiently organized regime will emerge in either society which would be capable of overseeing the creation of semi-industrial capitalism, much less moving beyond the limits of this mode of production. The mineral revenues of both Nigeria and Zaire may, in the long run, provide not much more than windfall gains.

Neither is a repressive state operating in the context of semi-industrial capitalism equivalent to polarized accumulation. There is probably not room for more than one instance of polarized accumulation in a given region of the periphery. First, metropolitan capital is faced with the decline of American hegemony and with increasing competition between core countries, combined with a decreasing ability to exercise direct military intervention in the periphery. Policing capitalism is increasingly delegated to subimperial units, and metropolitan capital is unlikely to see the need for backing the rise of more than one major subimperial unit and regional export base for manufactures per region. Second, one needs a fairly large population if the minority market enriched by squeezing masses already at low standards is to have sufficient purchasing power to support a more complex industrial structure. Third, one needs a favorable resource base endowment to support the import of capital goods required by the industrial structure. Only a few semi-industrial economies combine these three characteristics. The likely result is a repressive state operating with a semi-industrial capitalism unable to move beyond its limits. In other words, the Chilean military regime may become as proficient at torture as the Brazilians, but polarized accumulation is probably beyond its grasp.

SOUTH AFRICA'S ECONOMIC HISTORY

In 1716, Captain D.P. de Chavonnes, an official of the *Vereenigde Nederlandsche Ge-Octroyeerde Ost-Indische Compagnie* (VOC) at the Cape, put forward a point of view concerning the relative advantages of African versus European labor that has been one of the constant themes in the debate over economic history and policy in South Africa:

> He argued that though white labour appeared more expensive than slave labour, in the long run it was not, as two Europeans could do as much as three slaves. While money spent buying slaves was "dead money," which left the country permanently and burdened the country districts with debt, the wages of white labourers would circulate within the colony. Employing whites would increase consumption, revenue, and the potential military force. Moreover, a larger white population might stimulate greater subdivision and better land use, and provide the inducement to find new means of subsistence. [Wilson and Thompson, 1969, 1:200]

Two and one-half centuries later, we find a similar echo in Arghiri Emmanuel's unequal exchange:

> Out of Britain's five former colonies of settlement—the United States, Canada, Australia, New Zealand, and the Cape—the first four have become the richest countries in the world, with a national per capita income of $3000 or $4000 annually. The fifth, South Africa, has remained a semi-developed country, with a national income of about $500 per capita, about as poor as Greece or Argentina. Yet the natural resources of South Africa are not less considerable than those of North America and certainly are more so than those of Australia and New Zealand. All five were colonized by the same men of the same northern stock, tough and fearless [sic]. The climate of South Africa is no less healthy than those of the other four. Finally, all five were connected with the same source of capital, London, and belonged to the same commonwealth of nations and the same mercantile and financial networks. One factor alone was different, namely, what happened to the indigenous population. Whereas in the other four colonies the total extermination of the natives was undertaken, in South Africa the colonists confined themselves to relegating them to the ghettos of apartheid. The result is that in the first four countries wages have reached very high levels, while in South Africa, despite the selective wages enjoyed by the white workers, the average wage level has remained relatively very low, hardly any higher than in the underdeveloped countries, and below that of the Balkans, Portugal, and Spain.

> Let us suppose that tomorrow the South African whites were to exterminate the Bantus instead of employing them at low wages, and replace them with white settlers receiving high wages. There would certainly occur, insofar as this operation were carried out more or less brusquely, upheavals, bankruptcies, frictions of conversion and adjustment, a transition period of great difficulty; but the ultimate result would be a leap forward by South Africa, which would soon catch up with the more developed countries. This is a frightful thought, I know, but it fits the reality of the capitalist system. [Emmanuel, 1972:124-125]

As a first response to Emmanuel's contentions, which are as wrong as they are frightening, let us step back a century and a half to the Voortrekkers' linguistic distinction between *mense* (people) and *skepsels* (creatures). The latter were not cattle but all nonwhites. If the mense were little lower than the angels, whites' relations with Africans and mulattoes were little higher than animal husbandry. Skepsels were natural resources along with land, water, and livestock. They could be exterminated or incorporated, used in a manner such that replacement through reproduction could or could not take place, according to the Voortrekkers conceptions of their self-interest and their power to enforce the policy they considered most desirable. The question was never one of the greatest aggregate growth for the territory and thus the highest product per capita, but rather the highest revenue per mense.

The goal for South Africa's whites, with the exception of big capital, has not been to maximize per capita national income for the population as a whole, but for whites. One could argue that this is a typical example of the development of underdevelopment, in which a privileged minority limits the structural transformation in a way that maximizes its average income but lowers aggregate output and thus average income for the population as a whole.[5] This does not seem to be the case when one examines South Africa's economic history from the perspective of polarized accumulation as a mode of semi-industrial capitalism. The color bar and the particular path of industrialization through import substitution in South Africa were frequently enforced against the opposition of big capital. Forced negative income redistribution and the kind of internal market that was created most likely increased long-run aggregate income, returns to capital, and per capita white income beyond what they would have been without apartheid up until the present time—though this may not hold in the future. Furthermore, it is unlikely that high long-run returns to either white capital or white labor could have attained present levels without the color bar. White labor forced large white capital, despite the latter's opposition, to act in its own best interests.

Viewed from the perspective of polarized accumulation, South Africa's economic history up to 1948 may be divided into four periods: (1) the refreshment station phase, 1652 until 1820-1821; (2) the agrarian staple export phase, 1821-1867; (3) the era of mining capital hegemony, 1867-1924, in which big capital acted as a class in itself; and (4) the white coalition phase, 1924-1948, in which the foundations of state capitalism were established and big capital began to act as a class for itself. Following these four phases is the fifth and current phase, the period of Afrikaner state capitalism, when big capital acting as a class for itself united to organize and elaborate the trends initiated in phase four into polarized accumulation. We shall now proceed to a brief examination of the four earlier phases.

Refreshment Station Phase, 1652 to 1820-1821

The economy during this period centered on the area immediately surrounding Capetown, supplying passing ships with products of arable agriculture and pastoral agriculture in the hinterland and, to a lesser extent, supplying trading ships with animal products plus a range of high-weight-per-value exports to Europe, none of which assumed great economic importance. Within the empire established by Dutch mercantilist capitalism during the seventeenth and eighteenth centuries, the Cape was not meant to be a colony of settlement. The purpose was to establish a colony of limited population which would provide food and w.:ter to ships plying the route between Europe and Asia. Use of Africans as slaves arose at an early date in Cape agriculture. De Kiewit argued:

> Slavery was developed at the Cape by circumstance rather than by necessity. For want of great staples and intensive use of the soil a true slave economy, like that of the sugar islands, could not develop. There were few compelling reasons and no climatic reasons why the Dutch and the Huguenots could not have remained a truly white society. But the Cape lay between the two great slave-trading coasts of the world. From its rapacious sister company in the West Indies the Dutch East India Company has learned to tolerate slavery. The conscience of French and English captains did not shrink from helping to pay for the Cape's expensive meat by trafficking in slaves. [1941:21]

It seems to me that the opposite was true: slavery of Africans was used by necessity rather than circumstance, in the sense that this mode of labor control proved optimal in the context of the Cape's role in the eighteenth-century world capitalist economy. Cape slavery and the mode of labor control in the alleged subsistence economy of trekboer pastoralists in the hinterland was as linked to and conditioned by mercantilist capitalism as was Eastern Europe's second feudalism, Caribbean plantations, or New England fishing.

Arable agriculture was limited to a short distance surrounding Capetown. Given a lack of rivers for transport, low-value-per-weight food commodities were carried by oxcart. This slow and expensive means of transport restricted any distance from port at which agriculture was economically viable. The Cape also constitutes one of the world's unique vegetation regions (Darlington, 1965:108-110; Good, 1964:139, 207). Its semitemperate climate is characterized by relatively low annual precipitation, most of which is concentrated within a few months. There is also much year-to-year variability. The resultant vegetation is typified by the South African succulents now cherished by gardeners in many parts of the world. It was difficult to introduce European grains and vegetables into this climate, a difficulty compounded by local pests and diseases which often ravished newly introduced plant species. Grain production costs were high, and thus Cape grain was not attractive to passing ships even when available in good years. Cape wine was not attractive in quality or price. It was only in market vegetables that the Cape's location yielded an advantage to passing ships.

The market was largely limited to passing ships. Abundant supplies in good agricultural years or a decline in shipping could lead to drastic price declines. Export possibilities were limited. Within the confines of this narrow market, increases in the productivity of arable agriculture would not find a profitable outlet. White labor to perform agricultural labor would have been quite expensive. Even if one grants that whites would have been more productive than blacks, it is doubtful that the productivity of white manual labor in eighteenth century agriculture would have been so much higher than that of African slaves similarly employed as to compensate for far higher costs per man in a sharply limited market. Given the availability of both white and black labor, slavery and similar modes of employing non-Europeans was most likely optimal for the situation.

Pastoral agriculture, far from being the haven for the trekboers' semisubsistence existence, provided the colony's most valuable and stable products (Neumark, 1957). The trekboer supplied live animals, fresh meat, butter, and fat to passing ships. If demand for these products declined in a particular year, animals could be kept until better times on the veld, with no cost to the trekboer but his own labor (in contrast to the perishable products of arable agriculture). Hunting and trade with Africans also provided the trekboer with high-value-per-weight commodities which could be easily transported with his animals over long distances to the coast: ivory, ostrich eggs and feathers, and wild animal skins. Although the trekboers' continuing demand for coffee, tea, sugar, Bibles, ironmongery, and certain items of clothing were an inducement not to retreat from market exchange, there were far more powerful forces which impelled them to stay in the market: without rifles, gunpowder, and iron for wagon construction, their extensive pastoral agriculture would not have been possible. Territorial claims had to be established and maintained. Without muskets, circling wagon trains, and swift commando attacks by horseback, the trekboer could not have maintained his territorial claims against numerically superior African opponents. Exchange in the existing capitalist market was not a sideline; it was the basis of the trekboer's way of life.

For the trekboer, African labor was also the most attractive option, especially if the labor came from subdued and incorporated indigenous groups. In the latter case, the trekboer not only got very cheap labor but cheap *skilled* labor. Semimigratory pastoralism in the interior depended upon resources and techniques adopted from indigenous peoples: long-horned cattle used as oxen, fat-tailed sheep for meat, and the African goat. It was from surrounding African societies that the trekboers received their initial lessons on how to cope with the local environment. Thus one observes a capitalist pastoral system taking over the territory and many of the techniques of a precapitalist pastoralism.[6] Under the circumstances, it made most sense to incorporate conquered African pastoralists as a labor force rather than to expel or exterminate them.

Both arable and pastoral agriculture in the Cape colony thus were part and parcel of the world capitalist system. Servile African labor was employed not out of chance circumstance and hardened cultural preferences, but from calculations of optimal advantages within the context of the Cape's role in world capitalism. That this mode of labor control continued to be employed, in adapted form, during later phases of South Africa's economic history was because it proved advantageous under new circumstances. While the process of erosion may be lengthy, it is rare that cultural practices conflicting with basic structural imperatives of a capitalist economy have much chance of survival.

Agrarian Staple Export Phase, 1821-1867

From the 1820s onwards, the recently introduced Merino sheep began to spread through the South African hinterland, providing the colony with its first major staple export to Europe.[7] By the 1860s, wool was providing three-fourths of the colony's export income. A contemporary account notes:

> The Australian colonies never made such large deliveries as the return for the year 1862 shows, for above 70,000,000 lbs. were received in London from that quarter during the twelve months against 49,209,655 lbs. in 1857, or five years before; the Cape Colony delivered close upon 19,000,000 in the former year against 17,767,222 lbs. in 1857; while India delivered 21,326,205 lbs. in 1862 against 19,370,741 lbs. in 1857. . . . The probability is, that Southern Africa will in a no very lengthened period of time, rival even Australia as a wool exporting country; and the softness of the fibre, being a quality of primary importance to manufacturers, will always command a good price for the Cape and Natal wool. [Houghton and Dagut, 1972:143]

Merino sheep were introduced to Australia and South Africa at approximately the same time. Why did Australia, which had similar climatic conditions to South Africa, forge ahead during the period under consideration?

Expansion of Australian sheep herds proceeded through lands sparsely inhabited by indigenous peoples. White settlers in South Africa, on the other hand, faced dense populations operating at a far higher level of social and military organization than the Australian aborigines. This meant that more effort had to be devoted to encroaching upon Africans' land and maintaining this seizure. Acquisition of land usually implied simultaneous acquisition of labor, given that conquered peoples were incorporated as a labor force rather than exterminated or expelled. The labor acquired was also relatively skilled for herding purposes, given that the conquered peoples were usually pastoralists. Nevertheless, although by the end of this period a thin band of Boer settlement had covered the best sheep grazing areas of the South African interior, this hold was far from secure.

Prior to the introduction of Merino sheep, the potential of South African pastoral capitalism was realized only in small part. A port serving as a refreshment station could absorb only a quite limited amount of livestock product sales. Wool exports meant that hitherto surplus land and labor could be applied for capitalist production and exchange, but this application was limited below its physical potential because of the presence of the Africans. The economy was caught in a true vicious circle: the hinterland could not be made physically secure for production without the introduction of a transportation infrastructure and military forces employing modern European technology, which in turn meant commitment of large amounts of metropolitan capital. But current levels of production and expected rates of expansion did not appear important enough to justify a large investment, especially when there were alternate wool suppliers such as Australia. South Africa's importance to Great Britain during the

1821-1867 period was still primarily as a site for strategic ports, despite the introduction of staple export production. The introduction of mining capital, besides creating new urban markets for meat, also was to make it worthwhile to the metropole to commit the capital and military forces necessary to secure the hinterland against the temerity of Africans defending themselves against white seizure of their land and labor. Mining capital thus introduced the degree and security of control necessary to realize the physical and economic potential of pastoral staple exports from South Africa.

By the end of our period, even at this limited extent of pastoral capitalist expansion, an incipient crisis in the land-to-population ratio began to evidence itself. The increase in agricultural production proceeded through what may be termed lateral expansion. Boer pastoral units used an extensive area of land per white person. As population increased, new units of similar size were created as the sons of Boer farmers occupied new land and appropriated new African labor. The wool export trade brought no fundamental change in technique or man-land ratios. By 1867, as noted above, the best sheep grazing lands had been occupied. Further increases in population would require the occupation of inferior lands, the fragmentation of existing units, or a drift from farming areas. The opportunities of the wool trade brought more prosperity to some farmers than others, and the more successful ones began to aggrandize property holdings. There was thus a greater degree of differentiation by wealth among Boer pastoralists during the wool export phase then prevailed in the refreshment station era. The incipient crisis in Boer pastoralism, combined with increased differentiation consequent upon the creation of the wool trade, subsequently functioned as a key element in the economic and political responses of Boer pastoralists to the incursion of mining capital. Finally, the wool export era became associated with an ethnic division of labor among whites in the staple trade. Most, but not all, pastoralists were Boer. Both urban middlemen and merchants circulating through the hinterland were usually British or of non-Dutch origin. The correlation between white ethnic status and economic function was not perfect, but it was very strong and of prime importance in Boer-British antagonisms.

Era of Mining Capital Hegemony, 1867-1924

We begin discussion of this new phase in South Africa's economic history with the proposition that its bourgeoisie, in comparison with its counterparts in other areas of dominion semi-industrial capitalism, has been more effective in instituting a "national policy." The term "national policy" refers narrowly to a bill passed by Canada's parliament in 1879 which switched the dominion's policy from revenue tariffs to protective tariffs in order to encourage industrialization through import-substitution. More broadly, the term refers to a whole complex of actions taken with the ostensible intention of transforming Canada from a colonial hewer of wood and drawer of water into an industrially diversified economy possessing the ability to perform as an economic and technological unit in the center of the world system. We further broaden this term to include similar complexes of actions taken in other instances of semi-industrial capitalism.[8] The comparative effectiveness of South Africa's bourgeoisie may be attributed primarily to two factors: the nature of the opposition, which rose to its own hegemony, and the forces of production in the staple export sector.

With respect to the first factor, the Anglo-Boer War and defeat of the white miners in the Rand Rebellion of 1922 were the two key events in establishing mining capital's hegemony over South African society during this period. But the creation of the mining sector, in combination with these two events, engendered social forces, and a political organization of these forces, which successfully challenged mining capital's absolute hegemony but not the basic tenets of capitalist production. As shall be seen in the next section, this successful challenge forced mining capital to employ broader and long-term strategies which ultimately resulted in a higher return to capital. During the 1867-1924 phase, one may say that the big capital that pursued narrow, short-term interests represented a class-in-itself. Subsequent opposition forced a self-transformation into a class-for-itself.

It is the second factor that is accountable for the South African bourgeoisie's relative effectiveness; that is, it is the forces of production in the staple export sector which are the central focus during the 1867-1924 phase. Diamonds and gold shifted the economic and technological centers of control for two major commodities to South Africa. Although cartels for both commodities could not function without central trading offices in London and other financial capitals, control of supplies and markets required that a major part of organizational efforts be centered in South Africa itself (see Hocking, 1973). This was not simply because a large fraction of the diamonds and most of capitalism's gold came from South Africa. The Sudbury Basin in Canada, for example, supplied most of the world's nickel during the twentieth century. But its close location to New York enabled American capitalists to direct the economics of nickel mining, to supply much of the mining equipment, and to develop new technology without having to locate operations physically in Canada (Main, 1955). Similar developments occurred in the pulp and paper industry. In the case of Australian mining, this dominion neither cornered a controlling proportion of any key mineral commodity nor encountered major kinds of new technological problems which would have facilitated on-the-spot creation of a mining equipment sector and an associated body of technical experts (Blainey, 1969). South African mining, on the other hand, did encounter such new problems. As a consequence, mining capital arrived British and became South African. In Canada and Australia, capital tended to stay American or British.

The occurrence of both gold and diamonds in deep subterranean veins presented late nineteenth century mining with technological problems which were best worked out locally. The location of extensive coal deposits in close proximity to the Rand further encouraged the rise of a mining equipment sector in South Africa as well as the creation of a chemical industry (especially for explosives) and the local development of scientific expertise. Certain import-substituting industries arose to meet the needs of the new labor force and populations concentrated around the mines even without the shelter of protective tariffs. Thus mining was not the enclave typically pictured when one speaks of such activities in the periphery. (To return to a point made earlier, integrating an economy into the world system as a primary-product exporter is not invariably and fully a mark of the "development of underdevelopment.") Deep-vein mining, with its high capital requirements, plus the very high value per weight of gold and diamonds (minor variations in supply can have major consequences for places) together encouraged concentration of capital (Hocking, 1973; Wilson, 1972:24-44). Given the importance of South African mining —especially gold mining—in the world economy, the concentration of capital enabled the territory's top capitalists to rub shoulders with the metropolitan bourgeoisie on a basis of relative equality and extract hard bargains.

The nature of gold's price-response to fluctuations in the world economy was later to provide an important tool in South Africa's national policy. During periods of expansion in the world economy, gold tends toward a steady price. World expansion is reflected in upward pressures on the costs of capital and labor. This induces mining capital to decrease costs through technological innovation and increases in the productivity of labor (we shall return to this point shortly when discussing the Rand Rebellion). Contraction of the world economy tends to be associated with an increased reliance on gold, which raises prices. For the economy as a whole, this compensates for price declines in agricultural and other mineral exports. When, on the other hand, gold prices decline, this is compensated by increases for other exports. This countercyclical behavior is known in South Africa as "the flywheel effect" and exhibits obvious advantages for meeting the inelastic capital import demands of industrialization through import-substitution.

Periods of world contraction also exert pressures toward technological innovation and cutting labor costs, despite higher gold prices. The subterranean veins contain low-grade ore, but there is considerable variation of quality within this general category. Mineshafts follow higher grade veins. Once a decision has been made to follow a certain deposit, the high cost of boring and supporting tunnels means that bypassed lower-grade veins have been permanently lost, given present technology. A rise in the price of gold nevertheless enables mining capital to exploit more veins of lower-grade ores. And the opportunities presented by higher prices put much pressure on mining capital to increase productivity even when costs were rising. (See Wilson, 1972:1-20.) We shall now turn to one route to increasing productivity, that of cutting labor costs, and the methods employed to do so before and after the Rand Rebellion.

Diamond mining instituted the system of employing nonresident Africans housed in closed and guarded compounds during their contracted months on the mines. That blacks and whites were employed at approximately the same ratio in numbers and remuneration as during previous phases of the South African economy had less to do with custom than calculations of current economic advantages. Intensive labor was necessary to dig diamonds from the faces of extensions off deep shafts. Unskilled African labor, renumerated at a socially defined (and enforced) level of subsistence far below that of Europeans, was far cheaper for such work, even though Africans had a somewhat lower productivity per man hour than European workers. The compound system was instituted less to control the labor supply than to control the smuggling of such a high-value-per-weight mineral, but the implications for assuring adequate labor at extremely low wages were quite clear.

The unskilled Africans who were used as the major labor force in gold mines were similarly confined to compounds, even though the smuggling factor was not as important in deep-vein gold mining. The reason was that, if African miners had been allowed to settle permanently near the mines, they would have had to be paid at a subsistence level enabling them to reproduce the next generation of workers. By keeping the African workers' families on reserves, where they could grow at least part of their own food and perhaps gain money through sale of agricultural goods or through other activities, mining capital could pay workers at subreproductive levels. By restricting reserves to a size inadequate to support the contained populations, a supply of African labor could be ensured. But a problem existed here in that mining capital was not the only employer of African labor. White farmers and other white businesses also depended upon African workers. Hence the steady cry from mining capital about shortages of labor. By going outside the Union of South Africa's territory to recruit workers (who came to the mines because of the necessity to pay taxes or their inability to gain as high a cash income at home, or for both reasons), mining capital solved its problem of competition with other white employers (Wilson, 1972:69-94, 133-139). Crowding Africans in the Union onto approximately 13% of the land, giving them short-term employment on the mines and subreproductive wages, and confining them to compounds where their lives and diets[9] could be closely controlled were integrated and essential components of South Africa's capital-intensive and price-sensitive gold-mining sector.

Skilled work on the Rand was performed by whites, which at first were British immigrants. They were later joined by a second wave of immigrants from central and eastern Europe, and then by a third wave of Afrikaners (Simons and Simons, 1969:271). The first two groups carried with them the socialist currents flowing through Europe, though socialist ideas were grafted onto a defense of the interests of white labor. Afrikaner miners reinforced this trend. Out of the amalgam of all these elements there arose the Rand Rebellion of 1922, its essential goals best expressed in the slogan: "Workers of the world unite and fight for a white South Africa!" As Africans gained experience in the mines, mining capital would see a natural advantage in upgrading their skills and substituting them for more expensive whites. Not surprisingly, white labor failed to perceive the felicity of this substitution and demanded formal, enforced bars on the upgrading of blacks. In response to post-World-War-I declines in gold prices, mining capital attempted such a substitution. White gold miners rebelled and were suppressed only by armed force. Mining capital, however, won the battle and lost the war. Labor's reaction to suppression of the Rand Rebellion led to a pact with Afrikaner nationalists which won the 1924 elections and permanently broke mining capital's absolute hegemony over the state. Among other consequences, it henceforth proved impossible for mining labor to substitute black labor for white without the latter's explicit compliance (which was seldom granted).

Finally, we turn to the other element of the 1924 coalition that broke mining capital's absolute hegemony: Afrikaner nationalism. Until the advent of mining capital, it was far from certain that the various Afrikaans-speaking groups of what was to become the Union of South Africa would achieve a significant degree of ethnic and political unity. Nor was this achievement certain during the first decades of mining. Politics and societies in both the republics was fissiparous. Afrikaners in the Cape and Natal were divided among themselves as to how they should relate to the British and the two Boer republics (see Thompson, 1971:301-313). The Anglo-Boer War of 1899-1902 began the transformation of potential into actual unity. For the moment, let us examine the basis of potential unity.

By the 1870s, the geographic limits on the trekboers' extensive pastoral agriculture had been or were fast being reached in the South African hinterland. Large fractions of the land in some regions were coming under the control of speculators, and some pastoralists, both Boer and British, were enlarging their holdings in order to seize opportunities offered by wool; the result was either fragmentation of holdings or displacement from the land. Mining and associated urban complexes opened new opportunities. First, the new markets for food and, somewhat later, the railways that reached these markets, opened up the hinterland to commercial arable agriculture for the first time. Since arable agriculture is less extensive than pastoralism, this could absorb some of the surplus population. Some of the displaced Afrikaner population found employment in the new sectors while others formed an urban lumpen proletariat or continued to linger in a marginal existence on holdings that were either too small to support viable pastoralism or were unsuitable for arable agriculture for the urban market. The geographical limits of Boer pastoralism, combined with widening involvement in the new structures created by mining capitalism, were slowly but inexorably forcing a redefinition of Afrikaner society.

The Anglo-Boer War transformed Afrikaners' self-definition above and beyond existing tendencies. The presence of 300,000 British troops, the extensive razing of farmlands to starve out resistance, and the establishment of internment camps for a large proportion of the Afrikaans-speaking population created an intense desire to prevent the erosion of Afrikanerdom's existence after military defeat (the war itself created the concept of Afrikanerdom). Whereas the French-Canadian rebellion against British colonialism in 1837 had left the defeated population with the same set of socioeconomic relations as

before arms were raised, the Anglo-Boer War so compressed existing transformational trends as to constitute the sharpest of historical breaks. It would be
mistaken to view the rulers of the Boer republics as pastoral relics of mercantilist
capitalism which had to be swept away to meet the expanding needs of British
mining capital. A primary contributing factor to the war in fact was British
fears that the Boer republics might be quite capable of providing the necessary
infrastructure, but might do so with rival imperialist powers to the exclusion of
Great Britain. The war, however, brusquely and brutally transformed the Afrikaans-speaking masses from a pastoral capitalism into a twentieth-century
European political economy. They were not British Europeans, however, but
German Europeans with the equivalent of the eastern European's concepts of
lebensraum and Slav labor permanently at their disposition. What had been lost
on the battlefield would eventually be more than regained through the ballot
box and state capitalism.

White Coalition Phase, 1924-1948

The key planks of the platform advanced by the coalition of Afrikaner
nationalism and unionized white labor carried the 1924 elections. Both elements
in the coalition feared that gold and other minerals were wasting assets which
would be exhausted for the benefit of one fraction of the white population, big
capital. Instead, the coalition wanted to see these assets utilized for the benefit
of the white population as a whole. This goal implied that resources from the
export sector should be used to support industrialization through import-
substitution. For the nationalists, this was an important short-term measure
necessary to solve the "poor white" problem, the poor whites being mainly
Afrikaners suffering a lumpen existence either in cities or the hinterland. Both
elements of the coalition shared the long-term goal of creating an industrial
sector which would provide alternative employment and a vehicle for permanent
growth when the mines ran down.[10]

As remarked earlier, there was already some degree of industrialization
through import-substitution before 1924 without protective tariffs or state
infant-industry subsidies.[11] Active state encouragement, however, accelerated
existing trends and widened the scope of industrialization beyond what would
have been the case without political pressure on big capital to invest locally and
government aid in various forms (see Houghton, 1973:118-122). The ultimate
result was that big capital attained a broader and larger base for accumulation
than would have been likely if pre-1924 investment strategies had been continued, despite initial distaste for measures pressured upon the bourgeoisie by
the pact government. With time, big capital recognized that its own self-interest
would be furthered by industrialization through import-substitution. The most
important international corporation of big capital, Anglo-American, transformed
itself from a mining corporation joined with industries closely related to mining
needs into a conglomerate operating in multiple spheres (by the 1950s, Anglo-
American was involved in such activities as fruit farming, real estate, brick and

tile making, ranching, breakfast foods, fertilizers, chemicals, ceramics, and cold storage; see Hocking, 1973:273). Other fractions of mining and finance capital followed similar routes.

The previously mentioned countercyclical behavior of gold enabled industrialization to continue at a fast clip during the 1930s despite the Great Depression. By the beginning of World War II, the poor white problem had been more or less eliminated. We propose that this industrialization process was further hastened by unintended consequences of the color bar. After the 1924 election, it was clear that capital would not be able to lower labor costs simply by substituting blacks for whites since the blacks had now acquired experience and skills. Furthermore, as remarked above, white labor would demand and attain a large share of the gains of economic growth. By holding the real wage rate of non-Europeans at a constant rate, or by decreasing the rate, capital could maintain the high return on investment prevailing before it was forced to grant a better bargain to whites. Consequently, national income became more concentrated in favor of the white population, which constituted approximately one-fifth of the total. (The manner in which such negative redistribution of national income creates a minority market with a greater ability to purchase consumer goods with higher capital-output ratios, thus exerting greater transformational effects on the economy as a whole, has been spelled out by Serra, 1973, for Brazil.) South Africa constituted the first case of this process in the periphery. There is no evidence that the various white coalitions that governed South Africa between 1924 and 1948 conceived that negative redistribution would have these consequences or perceived what the effects would be once the process was in motion. White capital and white labor acted in particular ways to promote narrow interests; only later did the actions assume broader but unintended consequences. We shall return to this point in the next section.

Industrialization and enforcement of the color bar were joined by a third important element in the pact government's plank: the establishment of state capitalism in the guise of corporations financed by and formally joined to the state. Some of the corporations engaged in direct production as well as infrastructure activities and finance, while others—the cooperative movements—were vigorously encouraged by government support (Philips, 1974). The prime example of South African state capitalism in action during this period was the foundation of a state corporation, ISCOR, which established a steel industry based on the territory's large iron ore and coal deposits. Three goals directed the functioning of state capitalism: (1) mobilization of capital in areas where private capital considered the situation unattractive for investment, but which promised significant long-run returns to the economy as a whole (ISCOR being one case); (2) provision for alternate routes of capitalist social mobility for Afrikaners, who had found themselves mostly excluded from the peaks of the economy by Anglo-South African capitalists; (3) creation of Afrikaner economic counterweights to the power of corporate capital under Anglo-South African dominance. Since the first goal furthered its interests, non-Afrikaner white labor was willing to accept all three components as part of the bargain struck in the 1924 coalition.

Although state capitalism provided a counterweight to the mining bourgeoisie and resulted in a broader, long-term utilization of export resources for economic transformation, the shifting coalitions of various South African governments ruling between 1924 and 1948 limited the effectiveness of this counterweight. Assumptions of state power by Afrikaner nationalists in 1948 provided a steady and disciplined organizational core for state capitalist planning. Nationalists continued the basic lines of state capitalism laid down during the coalition era, but organized these goals more systematically and ambitiously than was previously the case. Corporate capital, both Anglo-South African and multinational, henceforth had to bargain with a state that was both stronger and more precise in its goals.

In the process of dealing with a progressively stronger state which claimed to be acting in the interests of all parts of the white population, mining and finance capital in South Africa were forced to transform their strategies and roles beyond an initially narrow base. Over time, they began to conceive of themselves not solely as intermediaries between peripheral resources and the metropolitan economy but as the leaders of an increasingly diversified economy with independent abilities to participate and innovate in the world economy. In addition, their perceptions of self-interest broadened to include the totality of social forces within South Africa, thus imbuing the bourgeoisie with some ability to avoid events like the Anglo-Boer War or Rand Rebellion, where the battle was won and the war lost. In short, strong opposition pressured the South African bourgeoisie to act less as a class in itself and more as a class for itself.[12]

Canada had witnessed a situation where strong opposition to the colonial bourgeoisie failed to develop during the formative years of corporate capitalism. The bourgeoisie pursued its narrow interests as an intermediary between metropolitan capital and Canadian resources and markets with a vengeance, resulting in an economic structure which constitutes a polar case of dependent semi-industrial capitalism (Naylor, 1972); the culminating effect has been a situation in which the Canadian bourgeoisie's power base, finance capital, is now threatened by metropolitan penetration. Intermediate between the poles of South Africa and Canada is Australia. Its strong social democratic labor movement, which included an important racist component (based on excluding non-Europeans as immigrants), provided an opposition to Australian and British capital and forced broader strategies and the development of a less dependent economy than in the case of Canada (Fitzpatrick, 1949). In short, the lack of a strong opposition, but one which shares capitalist goals, is one of the bourgeoisie's worst dangers during the formative stages of corporate capitalism in the periphery. Such opposition seems necessary to force a self-transformation of the bourgeoisie into a class for itself, which thus acts in ways that both increase its own long-run gains and a structural diversification of the economy as a whole.

The Period of Afrikaner State Capitalism, 1948-Present

The nature of Afrikaner state capitalism and its integration with Anglo-South African and metropolitan capital has been spelled out elsewhere (Bunting, 1969:369-400; First, 1972). Here we shall concern ourselves with possible conflicts between the mode of labor control and income distribution characteristic of polarized accumulation in South Africa and the economy's future prospects. Agriculture, mining, and the industrial sector will be considered in turn.

Agriculture continues to play a key role in the economic transformation of South Africa in two respects: (1) its importance as a component of export earnings;[13] (2) its backward linkages to agricultural machinery and chemicals. South Africa's semitemperate climate and particular patterns of water distribution, pests, and diseases required the development of an indigenous agricultural science if productivity was to be increased.[14] Application of this science did not occur, by and large, until after 1948, when the results were rather dramatic:

> Most South Africans are unaware of the major agricultural revolution that has been taking place since 1945. . . . The revolution which has taken place since 1946 on the better white farms is the change from a situation where productivity of the land was being destroyed at an alarming rate to one where future productivity is being steadily built up. [Houghton, 1973:64]

> The socio-economic consequences of change in South African agriculture have been far-reaching. . . . Indeed from about 1945, the tax consultant became a more frequent presence on the farm than the White bywoner. [Horwitz, 1967:280-281]

Even with systematic application of agricultural science and capital-intensive cultivation, there exists a range of operations for many crops, especially harvesting of fruits, which are labor-intensive. The most highly technological agriculture in the world, that of the United States, is notoriously dependent upon the labor of a migratory subproletariat for harvesting fruits and vegetables. South Africa's blacks are employed at wages far lower than those of the U.S. subproletariat and are even more under the control of rural capitalists. Apartheid should thus give South Africa cost advantages over other high-technology, capital-intensive agricultural exporters on the world market.

Mining, despite its capital-intensive character, still requires many labor-intensive operations down in the shafts. There is thus a clear advantage to be gained from cheap African labor. This advantage holds not only for the price of labor, but its availability. Mining towns in the other former dominions of the British Empire are experiencing increasing difficulties in holding a stable work force, despite wages higher than those offered by industry. Indeed, South Africa is experiencing the same difficulties with its white miners (Wilson, 1972:117). Mining is dirty, dangerous work, and whites increasingly prefer alternative employment. Due to the rigid color bar, a shortage of white labor in South Africa's mines has real costs in terms of lost output, but these costs are less than would be entailed by attempts to force white workers to swallow unacceptable changes. The problem, at least at the moment, is one of marginal adjustment rather than fundamental conflicts between the needs of mineral production and the mode of labor control. Should the problem become more serious, it seems probable, though by no means certain, that the necessary marginal readjustments would be accomplished through social fictions such as job redefinition or increasing latitude to use "competent nonscheduled persons." This could be accomplished without changing the formal norms or basic structure of apartheid.

Mining in South Africa also raises another question, one concerning the relative bargaining power of peripheral states and multinational corporations. First, growing concern over possible shortages of various mineral supplies gives peripheral states with mineral deposits a stronger potential bargaining position than would have been the case a decade ago. Second, metropolitan capital in the post-OPEC era is increasingly nervous about the "stability" of host Third World countries and is displaying an increasing preference for investments, where possible, in the minerals of the old white dominions. Again, this presents these countries with a potential strengthening of bargaining position. There is a variability in actualizing this potential which follows from the contrasting effectiveness of their respective bourgeoisies, as discussed in the last section. Third, the decline of American hegemony over the world system since the late 1960s, coupled with the post-1968 decline in the world economy, has intensified intermetropolitan competition. This presents peripheral states with the potential ability to play upon such competition to increase their own advantages. Fourth, there is an increasing understanding of the strategies of manipulation utilized by multinationals, and thus a growing potential to counter such actions, if peripheral states are sufficiently strong.

With respect to this fourth factor, it has become more or less axiomatic in most literature on dependence that there is a fundamental difference between direct investment by multinationals and the indirect or portfolio investment characteristic of nineteenth century metropolitan capital in the periphery. There are two problems to be considered in terms of this posited difference. First, it probably underestimates the power of portfolio capital to direct the economies of peripheral societies. Host states and capitalists were frequently constrained to take options that would ensure the "confidence" of foreign bond and debenture holders (until World War I, this largely meant London banking circles). Options that preserved confidence were typically ones that kept the host state in a peripheral role. Great Britain's informal empire in nineteenth century Latin America, for example, was quite effectively exercised via indirect investment. British portfolio capital in the United States, however, had different consequences. Indirect investment, we suggest, could lead to either development or the development of underdevelopment, depending upon the economic context of the host society, especially the perceived interests of its ruling groups and their power to pursue these interests. That metropolitan capital inflows were in the portfolio or indirect form had limited importance in and of itself.

In a similar fashion, the possibility presents itself that certain peripheral societies might exhibit sufficient strength so that direct investment may lead to development rather than the development of underdevelopment. One expects that the Soviet and Chinese states are sufficiently strong to drive hard bargains of mutual benefit with the multinational corporations allowed to invest in these states. Is it impossible that some of the peripheral capitalist societies might at least approximate this relative astuteness and strength in bargaining power? Given the four factors which potentially strengthen its bargaining power vis-à-vis metropolitan capital, plus an organizational ability to actualize this potential via the kind of state created by the hegemony of Afrikaner nationalism, South Africa could probably drive increasingly hard bargains with metropolitan capital, at least in the mineral sector. One indicator of this increasing relative strength is South Africa's recent announcement that a state corporation will enter into a partnership of relative equality with German capital to exploit the territory's rich uranium ore reserves. (This may be contrasted with one of the most flagrant failures by a semi-industrialist capitalist bourgeoisie to actualize potential bargaining strengths: Canada is considering intensive use of its scarce hydroelectric power to enrich its limited deposits of uranium ore for large-scale shipments to France, which will then use it to fuel reactors to compete with Canada's own Candu reactor system that functions on *un*enriched uranium ore.) We advance the hypothesis that certain peripheral capitalist societies are likely not only to exploit various situations to enhance their potential bargaining strength vis-à-vis multinational corporations but also to use their own organizational capacity to actualize this potential in ways that elicit kinds and consequences of direct metropolitan investment that advance their relative position in the center-periphery hierarchy of the world system.

South Africa's international pariah status, however, hinders her from driving as hard a bargain with metropolitan capital as might be expected from a strong peripheral state with desired resources. To the degree that multinationals have stakes there, they may be expected to pressure home governments to resist effective actions by the UN or any other body against South Africa. Brazil, despite bad press on its systematic roundup and torture of even the mildest of opponents to the existing regime, does not face such restraints on its bargaining position. The regime claims to be directing and coordinating direct multinational investment, such that it will not have the consequences of dependency typical for host peripheral countries (O'Connor, 1970). Whether these claims will prove actual or not remains to be seen. It may turn out that multinationals investing in Brazil have been treated to a rich bonanza with typical effects, this being overlaid with a cover of bombastic rhetorical claims. On the other hand, objective changes in the world system may potentially operate in favor of certain peripheral states (such as South Africa, Brazil, and Iran) and may turn them into sufficiently strong states to seize the bargaining opportunities while remaining within the capitalist orbit, and one should be alert to this possibility.

It is now time to turn to the industrial sector in South Africa. If one assumes that the prevailing distribution of income continues and that major opportunities for industrialization through import-substitution will have been more or less seized during the coming two decades, then the rate of industrial expansion will depend upon white consumers' replacement of goods as they wear out, upon depreciation of capital equipment, upon introductions of new products and technologies aimed at the white market, and upon the natural increase of the white population (which is at the relatively low rate typical of the center) and net white immigration. This could be expected to yield a modest but sustained level of industrial expansion typical of the other former dominions of the British Empire. But this industrial base would remain dependent upon mineral exports to support import of capital inputs such that the economy exhibits a long-term vulnerability repugnant to Afrikaner state capitalism and big Anglo-South African capital. Second, lowering of the growth rate below the average prevailing over the last five decades would be most undesirable, though more acceptable than long-run vulnerability. The rate of accumulation in the industrial sector might be maintained through two interdependent options: export of manu-factured goods or widening the domestic market through changes in income distribution. The first option, of course, would lower reliance upon the export of wasting assets. Both together would offer the possibility of deepening the capital goods sector such that dependence on industrial inputs would be less-ened.

A highly skewed distribution of income, when combined with capital-intensive, high-technology processes, implies an industrial structure characterized by low volume, high prices, a high ratio of non-competitive profits to sales, and a low ratio of wages to sales. Prices are high due to two factors: first, the market is not large enough for capital-intensive techniques to achieve optimal economies of scale, and modern technology is such that capital-intensive techniques prove more profitable than alternative methods using a larger component of abundant, low-cost labor; second, the large quantity of capital required to initiate pro-duction leads to a situation where one or several companies administer prices in order to gain monopoly profits (see Mehrav, 1969). High prices, in turn, hinder purchases by domestic masses with sharply limited incomes and hinder sales on the competitive export market. However, much of the argument just advanced rests upon an assumption concerning economies of scale. Recent research in the United States casts strong doubts upon previous assumptions concerning economies of scale (see Blair, 1972:184-185). It is possible that the prosperous white market of South Africa already supports or is capable of supporting a quantity of production for at least some products where optimal scales are reached. Thus export prices might be competitive on the international market without resorting to either widening the domestic consumption base through income redistribution until an optimal scale is reached or supplying subsidies to exports until international sales raise production to an optimal level.

For at least some products, however, there would be advantages in widening domestic consumption. Here Brazil exhibits a marked advantage over South Africa in maintaining the high rates of growth characterizing polarized accumulation. In Brazil, it is conceivable that the military regime would be able to enforce income redistribution policies that gradually added successive, small increments of the population to the wealthy minority market while maintaining political control. In fact, this is its goal. South Africa, due to apartheid, would face formidable difficulties in permitting such increments, which would mean adding non-Europeans as an increasing proportion of the wealthy market. It is not inconceivable that what Heribert Adam terms South Africa's "pragmatic race oligarchy" (1971) might raise the standards of the Asian or mulatto populations as a source of such increments, or perhaps support the rise of an African middle class in the Bantustans. But such actions would be fraught with political risks for white domination, and backlash from whites would threaten the position of any government attempting such changes. Given this political factor, plus a situation where possibilities for import-substitution in the prosperous white market and poor non-European mass market are not yet exhausted (even, surprisingly, in a field like woolen textiles) and abundant resources in the mineral and agricultural sectors to finance alternative schemes of supporting manufactured exports, it seems unlikely that income redistribution will serve as a principal vehicle for maintaining South Africa's rate of industrial expansion.

Low wages and tight control of labor make South Africa attractive to multinational capital as a regional export center for manufactured goods, as in the case of Brazil. Although the state may drive tougher bargains than its counterpart in most other peripheral societies, its power is reliable and exercised in a context where "by law it is a treasonable offence, carrying a maximum penalty of death, to advocate foreign economic withdrawals from South Africa" (Africa Research Group, 1974:117). In comparison with Brazil, however, South Africa's small and highly profitable white market does not hold anything like the attraction of Brazil's huge market, thus lowering South Africa's relative ability to exact export concessions from multinational corporations and metropolitan governments. Apartheid, of course, creates strong barriers against acceptance of South Africa by its natural target area, the weaker peripheral societies of Africa. South Africa's current "outward looking" foreign policy may decrease some of this resistance, but it seems unlikely to do so to any major extent. The current economic situation does not exert serious pressures upon the South African regime to make anything beyond minor adjustments and largely symbolic actions in the system of apartheid in order to lower African resistance to its exports. It is more likely to turn to other alternatives in order to lessen the long-term vulnerability of its industrial dependence on primary-product exports.[15]

The more likely alternatives would appear to be the following: First, the state might develop high-technology exports for selected sectors which will be internationally competitive in and of themselves, such as military equipment, mining equipment, or nuclear energy processes. Second, the regime may use its scarce mineral resources to extract concessions from metropolitan governments concerning entry of South African manufactures, such as textiles, leather goods, or agricultural products. Third, export revenues could be used to support export industries until optimal scales are reached, at which point the low wages of nonwhites would yield competitive advantages and elimination of the need for subsidies. Trade flows for all three categories would be largely to the central countries of the world system, where there is far less resistance to South African goods than in the periphery. Finally, there is another strategy which could cut dependence on exports of wasting assets—namely, investment of capital gained from these exports to the central economies, capital which would eventually bring an inflow of capital returns. Anglo-American has already experienced the impulsion to expand its investments beyond South Africa or stagnate (see Hocking, 1973:403). Anton Rupert, leader of the foremost bloc of private Afrikaner capital, has parlayed Rembrandt Tobacco to a multinational status in food and tobacco sufficiently important to receive front-page coverage in *Business Week* (probably the most important capitalist periodical). Given the integration of state and capital, it is likely that such investments will yield return capital flows to South Africa rather than just staying abroad and that this pattern will be replicated by other capitalist groups in South Africa.[16]

CONCLUSION

This essay began by posing four problems which would receive emphasis in our examination of the South African experience. The first of these problems was the tendency of peripheral capitalism to stagnate at a semi-industrial stage. We suggested that the South African and Brazilian economies shared certain characteristics which combined to form a particular type of semi-industrial capitalism, polarized accumulation. Reasons were then advanced as to why polarized accumulation might represent one possible route toward transcending the structural limitations of semi-industrial capitalism while retaining a capitalist mode of production. The discussion of South Africa's economic history from 1924 until the present attempted to indicate the value of this reasoning by examining one of the two concrete cases of polarized accumulation. At the same time, this discussion addressed the fourth problem listed at the beginning of the essay—namely, whether direct investment necessarily introduces processes which lie beyond the control of ruling groups in semi-industrial capitalist societies and thus constitutes a qualitatively different experience than indirect investment. We suggested that certain stronger peripheral states will be able to drive increasingly hard bargains with multinational corporations. Indeed, a necessary part of creating an integration of state and capital in a peripheral society which evidences a possibility of overcoming the structural limitations of semi-industrial capitalism is just this capacity to strike tougher bargains. The form of investment, direct or indirect, is less important than the relative strengths of hosts and investors.

The comparative effectiveness of the bourgeoisies of the white dominions within the British Empire was the second listed problem. We suggested that the relative effectiveness of the South African bourgeoisie was due to the particular nature of the forces of production in the staple export sector and the strong opposition it faced during the formative phases of corporate capitalism. The fact that South Africa produced a large proportion of two major world commodities and that both commodities had very high values per weight engendered a considerable localization of mining capital. Furthermore, the new technological problems faced in diamond and gold mining encouraged the development of an autonomous capacity in science and engineering and also the creation of backward linkages to capital goods sectors such as mining machinery and chemicals. Thus mining in South Africa did not at all fit the typical enclave image of such activities in the periphery. Second, the coalition of white labor and Afrikaner nationalists forced mining capital to adopt a broader and longer-term investment strategy than would have been the case if the mining bourgeoisie had continued its nearly absolute hegemony. On a broader plane, this suggests that particular peripheral bourgeoisies, given their specific economic base and historical experiences, may exhibit a capacity to combine with a strong state and impel the economy beyond stagnation.

Finally, there is the problem of the relationship between apartheid and the accumulation of capital in South Africa. We advanced reasons as to why the mode of labor control characterized by white minority dominance over cheap black labor was optimal for the accumulation of capital through the successive phases of South Africa's economic history. In particular, negative redistribution of national income toward the white minority probably deepened the process of industrialization through import-substitution, due to the higher capital-output ratio of consumer durables. It seems to us that the present relationship between apartheid and the structural imperatives of the economy is one of minor readjustment rather than fundamental conflict. South Africa will certainly make serious efforts to penetrate African markets, but we doubt that failure to achieve this penetration would cripple the future accumulation of capital. Our discussion of the post-1948 economy outlined the alternatives to such penetration. It would thus be quite incorrect, in our view, to expect that economic needs would pressure the South African regime toward making serious changes in the present mode of labor control. The long-term vulnerability of apartheid seems not to reside in any structural imperatives of the economy but in military pressures which would stretch the organizational resources of its white population beyond viable limits.

NOTES

1. Manufactured exports, however, constitute a major fraction of exports in the case of India's semi-industrial capitalism. The nature of these manufactures leaves them as vulnerable as primary-product exports: light manufactures, such as textiles, use the older industrial technology of the metropolitan powers. Such products are vulnerable on the following counts: they are excluded by tariff barriers both in the center and in peripheral economies which use such light industry products as the first components of industrialization through

import substitution; they are undercut pricewise by sweatshop operations in other parts of the periphery which have still lower wages. Furthermore, it is likely that certain kinds of heavy industries which have a high labor and pollution content will be transferred to semi-industrial capitalist societies, while technologically sophisticated and less obviously polluting industries (such as those using nuclear power and complex hydrocarbons) will be kept in the center of the world capitalist system. Consequently, a definition of semi-industrial capitalism 25 years from now will likely focus on the character of industrial exports rather than primary-versus-secondary exports as a criterion.

2. It is an open research question as to whether the post-World War II economic decline of Argentina is due, in large part, to the lack of minerals to complement agricultural exports (as contrasted with the two other "wheat boom" areas of European settlement in the periphery, Canada and Australia) or whether a different integration of state, capital, and labor denied Argentina the ability to maintain rates of economic growth similar to Canada's and Australia's on the basis principally of agricultural exports.

3. One might also add that the technology of agriculture is highly dependent on wasting certain assets—petroleum and natural gas—not only for running agricultural machinery but for manufacturing fertilizers and pesticides, the latter two being largely responsible for increases of output per man hour or acre after World War II. However, alternative techniques are now being generated to maintain this high output without resorting to petrochemicals; thus dominion (and center) agriculture in the future may not involve wasting assets as mining does.

4. Waves of European immigrants were crucial in developing Brazil into the world's leading coffee producer and in developing the new urban-industrial activities which created semi-industrial capitalism. Sections of Brazil were densely inhabited by the descendants of earlier waves of European settlers and African slaves when the new nineteenth century immigrants arrived, indigenous peoples having succumbed in these areas several centuries earlier. Second, Brazil's class structure does not approach the absolutism of South Africa's apartheid system, though a degree of positive correlation exists. While great violence might not be done by considering Brazil an example of classic semi-industrial capitalism, one should observe the very important role of immigration in the evolution of Brazil's contemporary political economy and investigate possible relations between this immigration and the eventual capacity to create a state characteristic of polarized accumulation.

5. The argument can be further modified to read that, in the long run, this minority itself would achieve higher average income by introducing the requisite changes. But the higher posited long-term returns are heavily discounted by a high risk factor, leaving the real present expectation of introductory change lower than that of holding the fort.

6. This economy probably yielded the trekboer a quite respectable standard of living, given seventeenth and eighteenth century norms for the Western European masses. Although he might dwell in a wagon or crude house and wear rough-spun clothes, his nutritional level was likely to be above that of the Dutch urban masses (which he would most likely have been part of, given the surplus population on the land). He traveled widely in a healthful environment rather than being cramped in the dismal sansculotte quarters of an eighteenth century European city. The government was too far distant to be much of an effective force in his daily life. He could go about shooting animals or his social inferiors, which were still a preserve of the aristocracy in most of Europe. Competition with African groups for territory made life hazardous, but probably not much more so than walking the streets of proletarian quarters in London. All in all, I should much rather have been a trekboer than a textile worker during the first phase of the Industrial Revolution.

7. The years 1820-1821 are chosen as the dividing line between the two phases because of the combination of the recent entry of Merino sheep with two important short-term factors: (1) the arrival of approximately 4,000 British settlers, most of them initially going to the eastern Cape; (2) Napoleon's death in 1821, which led to the closing of the station on St. Helena Island and a consequent decline in shipping past the Cape, which in turn helped contribute to a five-year depression in the colony's economy.

8. Part of the inspiration for Canada's national policy came from the example of U.S. protectionism after the Civil War, but even more important were the ideas and policies of Germany's national school of economics (see Bliss, 1974). The term national policy thus carries with it resonances of measures adopted by "backward" states in both the center and the periphery that tried to "catch up" in the race for industrialization.

9. After an initial policy of giving African miners the cheapest possible nourishment, mining capital perceived that the poor diet was hampering the workers' productivity. Capital then switched strategies and systematically improved diets in order to get better results from African labor—while always keeping a careful eye, of course, on marginal costs and returns (see Wilson, 1972:96). All this may be fairly classified as more akin to scientific animal husbandry than considerations of the workers as human beings.

10. In Australia, workers also constituted an important social pressure toward industrialization. This was much less the case in Canada, where surplus labor could easily move a short distance to the expanding, labor-short economy. During most of the latter part of the nineteenth century, more persons left Canada for the United States than entered the colony as immigrants from Europe. Pressure for industrialization came mainly from the commercial bourgeoisie, which was to have important consequence for the kind of industrial base that arose.

11. The exceptions are some mildly protective tariffs for certain commodities in the Cape Colony before union.

12. For excellent analyses of this transformation during the early stages of corporate capitalism involving what was to become the world's principal bourgeoisie, that of the United States, see Kolko, 1963, and Weinstein, 1968.

13. From figures given in Houghton (1973:276), I would calculate that, in 1969, agriculturally related goods constituted at least 397.5 million Rands out of total exports amounting to 1,532.7 million Rands.

14. Both South Africa and Australia, which face unique and difficult geoclimactic contexts, have gone much further toward developing an autonomous capacity in agricultural science than has Canada, which has been able to easily borrow and adopt techniques from similar geoclimactic environments in the neighboring United States.

15. Expanding fractions of large Afrikaner capital, both private and state, are likely to increase the chances of pushing through changes. Especially important is the entry of Afrikaner capital into the gold mining sector. Certain *verkrampte* fractions of the Nationalist regime foresaw the implications of this development and opposed Afrikaner entry into gold mining lest Afrikanerdom be poisoned by Harry Oppenheimer's liberation. See Hocking, 1973:371-373.

16. That certain fractions of capital in a semi-industrial peripheral society go multinatioanl is no guarantee of transformational effects on the home economy. Canada's commercial banks, which have emerged as some of the most powerful units in international finance, transferred capital abroad in ways that deepened the development of underdevelopment in Canada. See Naylor, 1975.

REFERENCES

ADAM, H. (1971). Modernizing racial domination. Berkeley: University of California.
Africa Research Group (1971). Race to power: The struggle for southern Africa. New York: Anchor Books.
AMIN, S. (1971). L'accumulation à l'echelle mondiale. Paris: Editions Anthropos.
BARAN, P. (1957). The political economy of growth. New York: Monthly Review Press.
——— (1958). "On the political economy of backwardness." In A. Argawala and S. Singh (eds.), The economics of underdevelopment. New York: Oxford University Press.
BLAINEY, G. (1969). The rush that never ended. Victoria: Melbourne University Press.
BLAIR, J.M. (1972). Economic concentration. New York: Harcourt Brace Jovanovich.
BLISS, M. (1974). A living profit. Toronto: McClelland and Stewart.
BUNTING, B. (1969). The rise of the South African reich. Baltimore: Penguin Books.
DARLINGTON, P.J. (1965). The biogeography of the southern end of the world. Cambridge: Cambridge University Press.
DE KIEWIET, C.W. (1941). A history of South Africa: Social and economic. London: Oxford University Press.
EHRENSAFT, P. (1971). "Semi-industrial capitalism: The implications for social research in Africa." Africa Today, 18:40-67.
EMMANUEL, A. (1972). Unequal exchange. New York: Monthly Review Press.

FIRST, R. (1972). The South African connection. Harmondsworth, Eng.: Penguin.

FITZPATRICK, B. (1949). The British Empire in Australia. Victoria: Melbourne University Press.

FRANK, A.G. (1967). Capitalism and underdevelopment in Latin America. New York: Monthly Review Press.

FURTADO, C. (1965). "Development and stagnation in Latin America: A structuralist approach." Studies in Comparative International Development, 1(11).

GOOD, R. (1964). The geography of the flowering plants. New York: Wiley.

HOCKING, H. (1973). Oppenheimer and son. New York: McGraw-Hill.

HORWITZ, R. (1967). The political economy of South Africa. London: Weidenfield and Nicolson.

HOUGHTON, D.H. (1973). The South African economy (3rd ed.). Capetown: Oxford University Press.

HOUGHTON, D.H., and DAGUT, J. (eds., 1972). Source material on South African economy, 1860-1970 (2 vols.). New York: Oxford University Press.

KOLKO, G. (1963). The triumph of conservatism. Chicago: University of Chicago Press.

Latin America Perspectives (1974). Dependency theory (no. 1). Riverside, Calif.: Author.

MAIN, O.W. (1955). The Canadian nickel industry. Toronto: University of Toronto Press.

MERHAV, M. (1969). Technological dependence, monopoly and growth. London: Permagon Press.

NAYLOR, R.T. (1972). "The rise and decline of the third commercial empire of the St. Lawrence." In G. Teeple (ed.), Capitalism and the national question in Canada. Toronto: University of Toronto Press.

——— (1975). "Canada's international commercial expansion to 1914." Our Generation, 10(4):5-46.

NEUMARK, S.D. (1957). Economic influences on the South African frontier 1652-1836. Stanford: Stanford University Press.

O'CONNOR, J. (1970). "International corporations and economic underdevelopment." Science and Society, 34(1):42-60.

PHILLIPS, E. (1974). "State regulation and economic initiative: The South African case to 1960." International Journal of African Historical Studies, 7(2):227-254.

SERRA, J. (1973). "Brazilian economic miracle." In J. Petras (ed.), Latin America: From dependence to revolution. New York: Wiley.

SIMONS, H.J., and SIMONS, R.E. (1969). Class and colour in South Africa 1850-1960. Harmondsworth, Eng.: Penguin Books.

TAVARES, M.C., and SERRA, J. (1973). "Beyond stagnation: A discussion on the nature of recent developments in Brazil." In J. Petras (ed.), Latin America: From dependence to revolution. New York: Wiley.

THOMPSON, L. (1971). "Great Britain and the Afrikaner republics, 1870-1899." In M. Wilson and L. Thompson (eds.), Oxford history of South Africa (vol. 2). London: Oxford University Press.

WEINSTEIN, J. (1968). The corporate ideal in the liberal state. Boston: Beacon Press.

WILSON, F. (1972). Labour in the South African gold mines 1911-1969. Cambridge: Cambridge University Press.

WILSON, M., and THOMPSON, L. (eds., 1969). Oxford history of South Africa (2 vols.). London: Oxford University Press.

3

THE POLITICAL ECONOMY OF THE AFRICAN PEASANTRY AND MODES OF PRODUCTION

CATHERINE COQUERY-VIDROVITCH
Université de Paris VII

In the past, especially during the first half of the twentieth century, Western ethnographers tended to view "traditional" African societies from a static perspective, as changeless or motionless, geared to customs and subsistence village economies that were more or less fixed and had changed scarcely at all over past ages. African societies were contrasted with dynamic Western societies which obeyed the laws of the marketplace. In this view, Western socieites were the model, toward which Africans should strive.

This model is simplistic, as banal as it is inaccurate. Nevertheless, it remains so important in Western thought that it forces us to try to answer a number of questions. To what extent is it legitimate to refer to the precolonial world as "traditional"? More specifically, what accounts for the technological backwardness of African societies? How useful are the concepts of a "lineage" mode of production, a "tributary" mode, or even an "Asiatic" mode to describe these societies which seem to resist participating in the contemporary world economy?

THE MYTH OF THE "TRADITIONAL" SOCIETY

We will only mention in passing the quarrel, fortunately almost forgotten, but characteristic of the French school of Africanists, between "sociologists" and "historians." Not without justification at the time, the former group took the latter to task for its ethnocentrism. French historians, in particular, saw the Africans as people "without history" because they were without written records. A tenacious "Eurocentrism" thus permeated research in the field of traditional "colonial history." In fact, this way of thinking, which flourished in the wake of

NOTE: Translated from the French by Jeanne Mayo.

triumphant imperialism at the end of the nineteenth century and which corresponded to the prejeudices of white supremacists and advocates of Western culture, was not restricted to historians alone. Other kinds of social scientists —geographers, economists, technologists—committed the same error by giving priority to the study of industrialized societies, as did even ethnologists, who often acted as accomplices in colonization (Jaulin, 1971; Alexandre, 1971). However, following the lead of Marc Bloch ("Everything that a man says or writes, everything that he produces, everything he touches can and should reveal something about him," 1949:27), historians have, in our day, begun to prove that they are capable of constructing, out of the abundance of documents of diverse origin (oral, written, archeological, linguistic, sociological, and so on), a history that is free from an exclusively Western perspective.

Now no one doubts any longer that precolonial societies had a history. The multiplicity of events which occurred in these constantly changing political formations indicates the diversity of responses to the stimuli received. Whether they were organized states or not, hegemonies based on military power (Samory), on religion (the Mahdist state), or on commerce (Yao, Nyamwezi, Chokwe), the precolonial nineteenth century was an era of changes, some continuous, some sudden. In fact, these reputedly stable societies rarely enjoyed the lovely equilibrium presumed to have been disrupted by the impact of colonialism. West Africa, for example, had been seething with activty ever since the eighteenth century waves of Fulani conquest and well before the creation of units of resistance to European influence (El Hadj Omar, Ahmadu, Samory, Mamadu Lamine). The slave trade kingdoms, in serious crisis, had been forced to react to the dwindling of the slave trade by intensifying agriculture exports. The Congolese basin was the site of still more profound upheavals linked to commercial penetration. In such cases the revolution in production rocked the very foundations of the political structure. As for South Africa, the rise of the Zulus and their expansion had repercussions up into central Africa. How far back do we have to go to find the stability alleged to be "characteristic" of the precolonial period: before the Portuguese conquest, before the Islamic invasion, before the Bantu expansion? Each of these great turning points marked the reversal of long-term trends, within which a whole series of shorter cycles might in turn be identified, as, for example, the succession of Sudanic empires, or even such shorter cycles as the periods of recession (1724-1740, 1767-1782, 1795-1811, and so on) and the upswing of the slave-trade economy of Dahomey (Akinjogbin, 1967). In short, the static concept of "traditional" society cannot withstand the historian's analysis.

The group still most guilty of ethnocentrism is perhaps the economists who, whatever their ideological bent, are inclined to consider the laws of capitalist development as absolutes and to universalize the exceptional historical experience of England and Western Europe (Sachs, 1971:123). For example, the otherwise useful analysis of Bairoch (1963) seeks to discover the explanation of the backwardness of underdeveloped countries in the rise of the West in the nineteenth and twentieth centuries.

Bairoch asserts, based on Western experience, that an increase in per capita agricultural productivity is the key independent variable accounting for economic development. But we know that population expansion has meant at most a slight rise and often a lowering of per capita production in the Third World. Is the Third World's situation therefore without hope? When we use the historical pattern of Western development as the norm, we transform virtually all distinctive characteristics of underdeveloped countries into one long list of obstacles. Would it not make more sense to try to invent a new key independent variable, one responding to contemporary conditions—for example, the use of the enormous productive potential of the currently underemployed? (Guilliot-Lageat, 1964).

The same criticism of limited relevance to the contemporary Third World can be made of the model, constructed by the Marxists in the 1930s, of three "classical" stages of evolution derived from Western European history: slavery, feudalism, and capitalism. And just because Marx and Engels sketched a possible fourth mode, the "Asiatic mode of production," must we therefore apply it textually to the newly discovered world of Africa, when the concept was based on the historical experience of the Middle East and Southeast Asia? Suret-Canale (1964) attempted to do just this. He located the Asiatic modes of production in precolonial black Africa at the end of an evolution involving three phases: the *primitive* community; the intermediate *tribopatriarchal* segmentary society (the so-called "anarchic" or "stateless" society, in which the basic social unit is the extended family); and then the clearly differentiated *class* society, in which the emergence of privileged aristocracies seems to have led to creation of the state, over and above the village patriarchies.

The classical contrast between hierarchical and stateless societies tends to be delineated more sharply in black Africa than elsewhere. But G. Balandier (1967) has shown the political coexistence of apparently contradictory elements within all African societies, both the "hierarchical" and the "stateless." For in practice, there is a continuous gamut of forms, with no clear point of disjunction between two opposed models. To be sure, as the state organization became more centralized, it began more to use the concept of territorial power. But even in the most presumably "despotic" states (the medieval Sudanic kingdoms, the kingdom of the Kongo, Ashanti, Dahomey), the prestige of the sovereign (inaccurately identified by European observers as an "absolute monarch") never completely effaced tribopatriarchal authority. At most, the kingship took the form of a superimposed bureaucracy which nonetheless respected the structures of rural life. As for segmentary societies, they excluded neither the political authority of the lineage chiefs nor the complex economic forms required for long-distance trade. The segmented structure of the Bubangui, for example, did not prevent this group of large-scale commercial brokers from procuring men and products from very long distances.

If the various models turn out to be quite inadequate, it is because the structure and evolution of "precolonial" African societies were fundamentally unlike our Western ones. The nature of this specificity now needs to be elucidated.

EXCHANGE AND PRODUCTION

The most likely locus in which we can find an explanation for Africa's technological backwardness is her socioeconomic structures. It remains, however, to be seen whether this means primarily in the sphere of circulation, which many scholars have tended to emphasize, or in the sphere of production.

The Sphere of Exchange

Traditional exchanges in a market economy. One of the first to raise the question of African specificity was the team of anthropologists led by Bohannan and Dalton (1962). In a series of monographs, they endeavored to classify societies according to the degree of their adherence to a market economy, that is to say, an economy regulated by a system of prices governed by the law of supply and demand, independent of the place of the transaction. They defined three categories of societies that were implicitly considered to be at various stages toward integration into the world economy:

(1) Societies without a local marketplace.

(2) "Peripheral" market economies, in which, even in the marketplace, transactions are controlled by local customs rather than economic laws.

(3) Finally, societies more or less integrated into a market economy.

In point of fact, it is difficult to understand why the authors distinguish the first two categories in terms of the existence or nonexistence of a local marketplace. The two are really one—namely, that ordinarily covered by the loose expression "traditional societies"—and they contrast strikingly with the third type, defined precisely by the preponderance of the law of supply and demand. Nevertheless, the analysis is helpful in suggesting the complexity of traditional societies and the juxtaposition of many economic "centers" whose spheres of exchange remained strictly isolated one from another, in terms of both their modes and their objectives. The analysis does account for three spheres of exchange:

(1) The sphere regulated by the principle of *reciprocity,* in which trade in prestige goods (necklaces, bows, quality cloths) is a result of social obligation or gift giving, primarily involving obligations among relatives.

(2) The sphere of *redistribution,* in which members of a society were obliged to make a payment (in the form of tribute, forced labor, tax, and so on) to a superior authority. Within an "ostentatious" type of economy, the latter (whether he be king, chief, or priest) redistributed this largess among the community during festivals, each person receiving according to his social status. Examples are the "Annual Customs" in Dahomey, the funerals of Ashanti kings, the distribution of military weapons, and so on (Meillassoux, 1968).

(3) This system did not exclude a small sphere of *market economy,* in which foodstuffs and local crafts (pottery, arms, and so forth) could be traded over a wide area; but the existence of money, or the equivalent of money, varied from one region to another. Thus in Ethiopia, cattle were valued in Maria-Theresa thalers but were paid for in Ethiopian dollars or in kind. On the west coast, the slave trade had a whole series of moneys of account (bar, ounce, "package"), but agricultural trade used only barter or the exchange of cowries. The creation of a unified monetary system broke once and for all the imperviousness between the spheres, since money could then be used for dowries or by secret societies.

Up until then an object could not "transfer" from one sphere to another except by codified processes that authors Bohannan and Dalton called "conversions": an *institutionalized* conversion upward, as when a man, for one reason or another, came into possession of prestige goods and could therefore be admitted definitively into a higher social category; and a *conjunctural* conversion downward, as when a family, because of some unforeseen event (war, famine, epidemic) had to divest itself of its prestige goods, sell its treasures, give its slaves as hostages, or whatnot. The exceptional character of this operation was the fact that the "transfer" generally took place outside the society entirely.

The merit of this mode of classification is that it distinguished among "traditional" societies, which were no longer schematically grouped en bloc, as though they were homogeneous, in opposition to something called "modern" society, which is the essence of the concept of the "dual economy," as promoted by some economists. There does not exist a split between a traditional subsistence sector on the one hand and a market economy sector on the other, each impervious to the other. On the contrary, the traditional sector itself is "multicentered"; the market economy and notably the use of money is not a new phenomenon, even if it has long played only a minimal role in the peasant economy; and various external influences, which we have noted go far back in time in Africa, have forced an interaction between the two sectors. Ever since the Islamic intervention, the Portuguese penetration, and most especially the development of cash crops, the peasant, while continuing to live within his customary framework has had, in order to survive, to participate in a trade economy that has encouraged him to sell his harvest to buy not only foreign consumer goods but also basic foodstuffs that he himself gradually ceased to grow when it became increasingly unprofitable for him to do so.

However, as Rey and Dupré (1969) have noted, it remains insufficient to look for the evolution of a society only in an analysis of its exchange. Exchange, the most obvious manifestation of the network of relationships, reflects the internal organization of society, but it is the *result* of the organization of production rather than its *cause.* Claude Meillassoux (1960) goes much further than Bohannan and Dalton (1962) in endeavoring to account for the origins of the circulation of goods.

The lineage system. In discussing reciprocity and redistribution, Meillassoux (1960:38-67) explained that the absence of *economic* exchange between members of a community is due to the importance of kinship bonds and to the dependence of the individual producers or "youngmen" within a family community presided over by "elders." The transfer of objects operates according to a system of reciprocal obligations (prestations) linked to the social situation of the protagonists: reciprocal gifts among the elders, and the rendering of goods and services by the youngmen to the elders and the redistribution of goods and favors by the elders to the youngmen.

On what is the elders' authority based? Certainly not on force, since the elders are weaker, not only numerically but also physically; nor on the physical control of the means of production (tools and land) because of the rudimentary technology and the collective ownership of the land. Their prestige lies in the respect for knowledge (social knowledge—acquaintance with customs, with genealogy, with history), which is identified with age and reinforced by a series of techniques (magic, divination, cultural rites, and so on) that guarantee the elders exclusivity by means of barriers that are either institutional (initiation rites) or esoteric (sorcery, medicine).

The surest guarantee of the elders' authority over the youngmen is their control over pubescent families, not in their role as workers, but in their role as bearers of children. Hence the importance of the control over marriage by means of the institution of the dowry: in order to preserve their authority, the elders of neighboring groups form alliances and regulate the access to women via their exclusive right to certain goods produced by the community, which means in fact by the youngmen. This is the sphere of reciprocity in which goods are exchanged less for the sake of exchange than to assure, by the process of circulation, control by one of the parties over the progeny of a woman coming from the other party. The dowry, at least before it was contaminated by the market economy, especially from the nineteenth century on, reflected neither the purchase of women, nor even an exchange for a woman, but the necessities of social prestige that fixed the access to women at a level inaccessible to the youngmen.

The exhibition of goods was a manifestation of aristocratic prestige, and their ostentatious destruction was its perfect form. There was thus a disproportion, disturbing to Western observers preoccupied with profit, between the use value of goods, which was sometimes nil, and their social value. Treasures such as ivory were hoarded by the chiefs of the Congolese basin, without ever serving even a decorative purpose until the time that they were introduced, in the nineteenth century, into the market economy by European demand.

In a similar way, the redistribution of foodstuffs to the youngmen did not represent remuneration for their work, but the manifestation of the authority of the elders. To give was to show superiority; to accept without reciprocating was to be subordinate.

This model, elaborated on the basis of the precolonial Guro of the Ivory Coast (Meillassoux, 1965), presumes, however, a situation of economic insularity relatively exceptional in black Africa, even within lineage societies (that is, in societies in which the political power was largely identical with the organization of the family community). But this system does not rule out a hierarchy of lineages. The numerical growth of the collectivity, for example, might involve an extension of the control of the elders to larger groups, manifested by the possession of varying symbols of prestige, more numerous and more effective as one rose in the social hierarchy. An authority transmitted by primogeniture might lead to the preponderance of a senior lineage, all of whose members enjoy similar prerogatives, transforming the primitive relationship between elders and youngmen into a relationship between patrons and clients (as in Buganda). This is the beginning of the hierarchization of social classes whereby the dominant group continued to monopolize for their personal use the prestige goods which eventually included merchandise exchanged with the outside world.

Thus we can understand how these societies, even undergoing intense economic commercial relationships (like the slave-trading kingdoms), could have preserved their patriarchal structures for so long. The two systems coexisted in the same society, but situated in spheres apparently impervious to each other —that of local village subsistence on one side, and international (even transcontinental) commerce on the other.

"Archaic" economy? Karl Polanyi (1966) proposed an explanation of precolonial Dahomey based on this perspective, but, although fascinating, it was oversimplified. Like most historians, Polanyi was struck by the contrast between the political power of the sovereign and the weak economic integration of his kingdom. For the most part the peasant mass lived in rural subsistence communities, obedient but not very involved, activated only by the rare local markets that traded exclusively in foodstuffs for cash (in the form of cowries). But these transactions had no connection with the commercial trade which was controlled by the state and lay in the hands of an African "despot," the sole owner and, therefore, sole dealer in slaves supplied through annual raids on the outer edges of his kingdom. Hence long-distance trade only crossed over the country, never penetrated it, due to a unique institution, the port of trade (Whydah), which was carefully isolated from the rest of the kingdom and whose activity was ensured by the firmness of its economic administration, its political neutrality, and its transportation advantages.

This bureaucratized economy, in contrast to a market economy, explains the stability of prices, despite internal disorders and the frantic competition of various European nationals. The prices and local customs charges were determined by royal decree, based not on the law of supply and demand but on ecological and military factors—for example, the standard price of a slave, the calculated estimate of his defects, the selection of "packages" (that is, packages of goods exchanged for the slaves), which were codified and price-fixed. The relatively stable value of the cowrie lasted a century and a half (32,000 cowries to one ounce of gold) and was guaranteed right up to the colonial conquest by a state that regulated its use and avoided oversupply by authoritarian control over its import.

Thus, the sovereign's power was closely tied up with a specific economic formula: absolute control over a large state sector of trade not integrated into local trade and a massive exchange of products rather than true trade, since the king was not looking for profit so much as ways to obtain certain merchandise from far-off lands—weapons (basic to his power and his supply of slaves), textiles, alcohol, and various trade merchandise *(la pacotille)*. These were the wherewithal of his generosity at the annual procession of treasures of trade accumulated from generation to generation. The "Annual Customs" thus served as occasion for the periodic regrouping and redistribution of the riches of the kingdom.

Polanyi's analysis is fascinating. In particular, it explains the traditional economy's capacity for resistance, emphasized by Rey and Dupré (1969). The goods supplied by European capitalism, far from causing, ipso facto, the expansion of the market economy, were absorbed by the lineage economy and transformed into prestige goods and, as part of the trade between elders, took the place of locally produced goods (blacksmith crafts, raffia loincloths, and so on). Certainly, the problem was to absorb the growing surplus. This was done by excessive hoarding, which sometimes led to an increase in redistribution, but more often to ostentatious destruction. For if the aim of ostentation was to guarantee the social prestige of the chief, its effect was to sterilize a certain portion of the production by turning it toward unproductive ends unconnected to production or consumption (Meillassoux, 1968:759). The burial or coronation ceremonies were the most striking examples. The Bateke (Congo) chiefs kept a large quantity of red European cotton aside to be used at their funerals (Sautter, 1960:37). The body, mummified for two months, was wrapped in a thick layer of cloth which gave it the form of a cylinder. This burial package, which could attain enormous proportions, constituted a repeated drain on wealth, as did the sacred festival that accompanied the ceremony, requiring huge offerings by the household. This was also the function of the "Great Customs" festival celebrated in Dahomey on the occasion of the death of a king, and it was not just chance that at the beginning of the eighteenth century with the rise of the slave trade these grandiose ceremonies became annual (in the so-called Annual Customs) in honor of the ancestors. It was, to be sure, an occasion for the king to collect tribute, but even more to dazzle his assembled subjects for several weeks with the dynasty's wealth and bounty, either by the public sacrifice of hundreds of slaves (surely a slack period) or by the consumption of alcohol distributed in massive quantities, or the scattering of cowries and cloth by fistfuls from the top of the public platforms (Coquery-Vidrovitch, 1964). There is a striking parallel with the festivals in the kingdom of the Kongo at the height of its slave-trading activity. Certainly, such episodes stimulated the economic life of the country and encouraged intense trading activity so as to supply this "fair" with all sorts of products. But they also "regulated" production, making sure that the level did not exceed the needs of the court plus that needed for simple reproduction of the community (Randles, 1969:75-78).

The limits of the analysis. Polanyi's model, although clarifying, does not fully satisfy the historian. First of all, it is too schematic. One should not exaggerate the imperviousness of this ideal separation between two heterogeneous economic spheres, even in the special case of Dahomey, which typified, according to Polanyi, an "archaic" economy in transition from a "primitive" economy to a market economy. The works of Marian Johnson (1969) tend to prove that the cowrie was not so perfectly stable and that its variations in value closely reflected the fluctuations of the market. The royal "despotism" seems to have been contaminated unduly by a Western notion, and the royal "monopoly" over slave trading by no means excluded the existence of a small but essential class of rich merchants in Whydah who participated in political power and at the same time controlled the commercial organization. They were a buffer class, both serving the king and acting as contract agents with the peasant mass; and they provided a link between the two commercial networks in the country, internal and external. For a portion of the merchandise from long-distance trading found its way into local markets (Coquery-Vidrovitch, 1971).

Polanyi too hastily affirmed that only prepared foodstuffs (such as cassava and palm oil) were found in local markets. Certainly, the articles for sale, grouped by sections of the town, were generally of traditional workmanship (such as foodstuffs, cloth, jewelry, medicines, and fetishes). But the fact that the two elements could be found showed at least a connection to long-distance trading. On the one hand, there were African products from other regions: karité butter, millet, and sorghum from the North, pottery and woven goods from the East, gari (cassava flour), fish, and shrimps from the lagoons of the West. On the other hand, there were manufactured articles of European origin. There are reports of trade that went from station to station as far as the River Niger. Even if this trade never took on the proportions that it did in the Ashanti kingdom, and despite the ban in principle against foreign trade, the Europeans noted the ever-present Muslim merchants in the court at Abomey, who, since the eighteenth century, had been coming in large numbers from the North, and pushed down as far as Angola (Burton, 1949, 2:26). Perhaps, after the king's intervention in the nineteenth century, some of them stopped going beyond the southern limits of Mahi. But that did not stop merchandise from passing from market to market until, along with a certain number of slaves (fewer, however, than those brought in by conquest), it finally arrived at the coast.

In the opposite direction, European merchandise also followed a complex path, finally reaching the interior markets. Polanyi seems, on the basis of purely economic considerations (the low value of the transactions), to have underestimated the social importance of these marketplaces, which were, in fact, centers of very active trade. Traditionally everything was for sale in the marketplace, which was a crossroads, an occasion to bring together on a fixed day all locally produced products. Thus it remained traditional for the blacksmith and potter regularly to come and display their wares, sometimes, several miles from their homes, even if the buyer was their closest neighbor (Brasseur and Brasseur-

Marion, 1953:111-117). And this industriousness in the Dahomean population, clearly ready to engage in every kind of trade and furthermore to take advantage of the resources of the country, is in contrast to the picture of a passive peasant mass uninterested in long-distance trading.

Besides being over-simplified, Polanyi's model has the limits of every model: it offers a static image of a balanced society in which two parallel economic systems (the subsistence economy and the state trade) and two political authorities (the lineage chief and the territorial sovereign) coexisted. The historians know full well that in Africa, as elsewhere, the equilibrium was always unstable and exceptional. Whenever equilibrium did exist, it was only for brief periods. The Kongo kingdom rapidly became decadent, bankrupted by the trade by which it had made its fortune. In the nineteenth century, the Bateke from the Congolese plains clashed with the river-dwelling Bubangi, who wrenched from them control over long-distance trading in the Congo. Even the Dahomey slave trade fits into the schema only for a relatively short period of time—during the period when slave trading reigned supreme, from the middle of the eighteenth century onwards. Now this was no longer the case from the beginning of the nineteenth century, and especially after 1840. Parallel to the traffic in slaves, more and more intensely opposed by European humanitarians, there developed the trade in palm oil, then the trade in palmettos, which quickly took first place. This new activity was evidently integrated into the county, if only because the determined intervention by the peasant-producers assured a constant coming and going between the sphere of royal commerce and that of village subsistence.

We should not allow, however, this special example of a balanced model of a multicentered precolonial society to lead us astray. On the contrary, the coming together, within the same group, of contradictory elements (tribal structure and a lineage system based on subsistence, as opposed to a territorial organization with centralizing tendencies and a sometimes preponderant emphasis on long-distance trading) could only generate disequilibrium and conflict. As Meillassoux (1968:770) argues, the question comes down to the ways in which

> two coexistent modes of production, the sector of village subsistence production and the sector of royal slave production, reproduce themselves and relate to each other. The former, which is dominant economically and subordinate politically, is not permitted to expand beyond the limits of simple reproduction through royal control over the means of production and by means of legal limitations on labor. The latter sector reproduces itself independently of the former, because warfare leads to slaves as booty and also leads to the recruitment of warriors who in turn bring in more slaves. Nonetheless, this sector too is limited in its production by means of the destruction of "excess" slaves.

Certainly, by preserving one or the other of the two sectors of production, the authorities could delay the enlargement of the economic system upon which their power was based; hence there was a tendency to reinforce the social conservatism of the lineage traditions, to freeze the bureaucratic institutions of the state, and to neutralize the disruptive element personified by the merchants by not integrating them into the society. The Ashanti kingdom accepted them only in the form of foreign guilds and severely limited trade activities by its own subjects. Dahomey controlled the situation by creating the "port of trades," the operation of which was monopolized by a specialized individual, the Yovoghan or "chief of the whites."

But at the risk of falling into the already rejected model of a "traditional" society condemned to immobility, supposedly able only to reproduce itself, it is important to clarify how such a "despot," such a privileged group, even such a social class could, on different occasions, just about all over the continent, upset the system for its profit by imposing on the relatively unconcerned peasant mass its economic and political overlordship.

The Level of Production

If one considers these societies not only in the sphere of institutionalized exchange but also in that of production, it is evident that they are defined by a largely agricultural production and characterized by a low level of technology and a weak degree of specialization and exchange, within a social organization in which private ownership of land in particular does not exist.

The technological backwardness. To characterize the peculiarities of the African socioeconomic context, certain authors have emphasized, among the criteria outlined above, the low level of technology. The unquestionably prolonged backwardness in this area continues to intrigue historians. It is common knowledge that the African peasant, up to the twentieth century, used a very limited number of machines, even rudimentary ones. The basic instrument remained the hoe. In Casamance (southern Senegal), the gathering of rice continued to be done blade by blade. The fundamental tool of the plow, which had spread over the whole of the Eurasian continent, did not reach Africa south of the Sahara, even where the absence of the tsetse fly would have permitted animal traction. The wheel was never adopted, even though it seems to have crossed the Sahara at the beginning of history, both in the West (by the caravan route of Tassili N'Ajjer) and the East (through Ethiopia and the eastern Sudan) and even though iron metallurgy has been known in Africa since the beginning of our era (Meroë in Nubia; Nok civilization in Nigeria). They could therefore have neither animal nor human traction to harness wind or water power. While in the driest regions of the Eurasian continent the wheel played an important role in drawing water from wells, the black African limited himself to storing water (cisterns dug in the laterite of Gonja, northern Ghana, or in Salaga, "the town of a thousand wells"). With certain exceptions, he never solved the enormous problem of the distribution of water, as his counterpart did in the Middle East or even in the oases of the Sahara. (Even today gardening hardly goes beyond the immediate banks of the Niger River.)

Some authors (Goody, 1971) have wanted to make this technological backwardness the reason for the stagnation of black Africa. Without the wheel or the plow, the area cultivated by each man never increases; therefore, there is no demand for productivity, no possibility of accumulation of surplus to support an increased number of artisans or to bring about differentiations in income or style of life apart from the constraints of agriculture which would be manifested in urban and political development. Nor does there exist an incentive to abandon the extensive techniques of itinerant agriculture and thereby fix to the land a middle class of private entrepreneurs. The African peasant, caught in a vicious circle, has been condemned to underdevelopment because of a lack of techno-logical skill.

But this hypothesis only pushes back the problem: what is, in fact, the cause of this technological backwardness? Malowist (1966, 1967), in an attempt to reply to the problem, tried to compare the African peasant society with that of the medieval West: why did the Sudanic zone, in spite of the prosperity of the medieval "empires" (Ghana, Mali, and others) continue to stagnate while Poland began to "take off"? His answer is that Africa lacked comparable economic pressures; African peasants were assured of a prosperous existence without having to work very hard, unlike peasants in Central Europe, which was less rich in natural resources. Having to struggle intensively to survive produced a stimu-lating energy that increased the possibility of expanding productivity and changing traditional social structures. Paradoxically, the Western Sudan might have been condemned by its "barbaric prosperity."

In fact, the thesis only reiterates the older theory of Huntington (1915), which attributed the birth of the greatest civilizations to the influence of temperate climates beneficial to human energy, compared to the lethargic heat of the tropical zones. This is generally the argument of Toynbee (see a summary of his thesis in Somervell, 1960) who saw in civilizations a "response" to the "challenge" of the natural environment. Hopkins (1967), however, found sport in denouncing the persistent myth of the fertility of West Africa. The savanna zone described enthusiastically by an abundance of travelers who knew only the most prosperous trans-Saharan trade routes, along which they were especially well treated, is far from corresponding to this image. The soils are poor in organic matter, even where there are no laterite carapaces that must be broken up with the hoe in order to do any planting. The brevity and irregularity of the rains combined with a long and hot dry season always made the transition between the old and new harvest hard. The lack of salt, a biological necessity, forced the people to import it at great cost from the Sahara; and the handicap of continual troubles—raids from village to village, slave forays, the civil wars—just added to the food deficiencies, to the epidemics, to the famines that were a regular occurrence in the life of the agricultural community.

On the other hand, such an environment (without mentioning the still more oppressing constraints of the dense forest) might lead us all the more to think that the "response" was weak because the "challenge" was insurmountable. In reality, this type of speculation does not seem appropriate. It comes back to making technology the motor force to explain the single alternatives of stag-nation or development.

However, the poor level of production, the most evident sign of stagnation, is not necessarily the reason for the stagnation. We know, on the contrary, that African peasants were not ignorant of a whole range of agricultural techniques: intensive agricultural cultivation of home gardens; extensive cultivation remarkably adapted to the ecological conditions (abundant but not very fertile soil, irregular climate). There had always been a potential for agricultural surpluses. If the potential was not exploited, it was perhaps less because of a feeling of fatalism toward the natural environment or the ignorance of men than because of an economic choice resulting from the vector of social forces. When adopted, technological improvements served at best to allow each family not to produce three times more, but to work three times less for the same result. If productivity remained low, might it not be because of the structure of the demand and the absence of division of labor and specialization—that is to say, because the organization of the society as a whole did not accommodate itself to an enlarged production within the system? Without neglecting, for all that, the weight of the intervention of exogenous elements (Arab or European impact), it is important to dwell, first of all, on the role of each of those internal factors that contributed to the extraordinary capacity for resistance to innovation in a relatively balanced society.

It is at this level that the Marxist concept of mode of production becomes operational since it allows us to examine the socioeconomic system by analyzing both the *productive forces* (resources, work force, technological level) and the *social relations of production*—that is to say, the relationship between those who produce and those who control the means of production (ownership of land, relationships of youngmen to elders, patrons to clients, masters to slaves, and so on). We should here indicate one qualification: the notion of the mode of production should be understood to be a theoretical model. Concretely, societies do not produce it in this schematic form. Their organization reflects a complex arrangement of production, which is affected by diverse factors originating in the history of a particular group and which reveals the sometimes contradictory influences that it underwent and the original institutions that developed from it. At most, we can define a "dominant" mode of production within a given economic ensemble, which can be characterized also by aspects of another mode of production. Thus, we will attempt to define an "African mode of production," not necessarily thereby eliminating certain fundamental traits of the "Asiatic mode of production," nor the sometimes far from negligible elements suggesting a slave or even feudal type of production.

The subsistence village economy or the "lineage mode of production." The land being, by definition, the dominant element in an agrarian economy, the American economist Stephen Hymer (1970) perceived precisely in the egalitarian nature of the land tenure system the key to the relative stability of the system.

Each family constituted, in actual fact, an autonomous center of production and consumption, covering a wide range of activities: it supplied its own food, built housing, and made furniture, equipment, clothes; in short, it was a self-sufficient unit. At the village level, the cooperation between families was related to clearly defined activities, marked by ritual festivals: clearing the land, constructing huts, hunting, maintaining defense. A few persons were specialized in religious, political, or artisanal activities—*griots,* blacksmiths, and potters. But very few were full-time in these activities since, without a complete division of labor, each head of family had in the end to make sure that his group's subsistence was provided for. For this purpose, each member of the community received a portion of land, eliminating the possibility of there being a role for an inactive class living exclusively on revenue from ground rent.

The above is true at least for our model, which is the typical society located mainly in forest regions where the impediments to movement probably favored the breakup of lineages. There was much less of a tendency to egalitarianism in the Sudanic zone, where there was a hierarchy of "castes" in society (notably in the case of the *griots* and the blacksmiths), and where the social pyramid, from the feudal-style chief to the slave at the very bottom, reflected at least partially the legacy of Islam. An example is precolonial Senegal, where the beginnings of land appropriation were discernible (Deme, 1966).

Apart from this restriction, how is it possible to explain the absence of ground rent? The low density of population and its corollary, the relative abundance of land, have correctly been emphasized (Hymer, 1970). This does not mean that land was free in the sense that anybody could do whatever he wished with it. Rights over the land that was the property of the group were jealously guarded by social institutions. (This was the origin of the role of the "chief of the land," whose duty was to see to its balanced distribution.) Certain individuals—strangers or captives—could have access to land only as servants or slaves. But these restrictions were limited, and since eventually every individual was part of some community, very few were forced to work for others. This land tenure system seemed to be aimed at protecting the group against an artificial land shortage, thus preventing a privileged few from accumulating it all.

Moreover, such a system did not exclude, as we have seen, certain inequalities in the distribution of tasks: within the family the women and young males did most of the work, to the benefit of the old people who consumed the largest share. But as each man throughout his life passed from one age class to another, it balanced out in the end. Similarly, if there was exchange between villages, it was limited to locally produced goods. The markets therefore represented less an economic organ than a multifunctional institution—social, religious, and political. This was evident, for example, among the Mossi of Upper Volta (Skinner, in Bohannan and Dalton, 1962), or the Mawri of Niger (Piault, 1971). At fixed intervals (which varied according to the African week, generally between four and nine days), a large number of people united by social and political ties, came together in the market. It was the center of communications, as well as the occasion for exchanging goods and news and even, in certain societies, the meeting of sexes. The market also assured the bringing together and dissemination of information. It also had political advantages as a means of control vy the chiefs over the people who frequented it and the goods that were offered for sale (such as the kola markets in Sanaga or the cattle markets in Atebubu in the Ashanti zone). The political authority in return guaranteed peace in the market-place by exercising the function of both police and justice, and even a religious role whose ceremony guaranteed the maintenance of peace.

Under this ideal form, the system could be said to define an economy in which all the members, united by blood, language, and customs, participated in orderly production and distributed goods within the family or among families by means of reciprocity and redistribution (not including remunerated work) and in which economic institutions could not be differentiated from political and social institutions. Hymer (1970) suggested that this state of affairs was a legacy of the past when people were hunters; and he implied that this was a "democratic" type of social organization able to coordinate its activities under the direction of a chief, whose prime objective was to preserve the principle of balance, hence social equality, vital for the cohesion of the group. Whatever its origin, this egalitarian land-tenure system seems to have hindered economic progress, precisely because it forbade the concentration of wealth and power and hence, a differentiation into social classes based on the social division of labor.

Indeed, if there had been a dominant aristocracy (which, as elsewhere, would have emerged from a class of warriors) and if it had been able to appropriate authoritatively the land and thereby obtain most of its revenue, it would have encouraged the formation of an artisan sector to serve its needs while devoting the surplus skimmed off the land to buy food and other consumer goods (jewelry, cloth, and so on), and it would have reinforced the agricultural sector by calling upon peasants to feed the whole of the population, while reserving a portion of the revenue to intensify production (roads, irrigation systems, and other works of infrastructure). Thus a whole series of technological innovations would have been encouraged, accelerating in turn the division of labor and, consequently, aiding the maturation of a civilization in the Western sense of the term, comparable to that of India, China, Egypt, or the Near East—engaged in what the Marxists called "the Asiatic mode of production."

Long-distance trade. Long-distance trade was found sometimes in Africa, but it never drew on the agricultural sector. Indeed, the lineage mode of production, though dominant within African peasant societies, was seldom exclusive. Parallel to subsistence agriculture, there developed war and trade activities creating prosperity for vast political ensembles. From the medieval Sudanic empires or the Zimbabwe kingdom (the Monomotapa of the Portuguese explorers) to the modern formations that interest us more directly here, examples abound: the Lunda empire, the kingdoms of the Kongo and Dahomey, Buganda, the Mossi states, the Hausa principalities, the brokerage chiefdoms along the river of the Congo basin, the Zulu kingdom, and so on. It is from this consideration of the whole that we have tried to define elsewhere an "African mode of production," characterized precisely by the apparently contradictory coexistence of the subsistence village and long-distance, even transcontinental, trade (Coquery-

Vidrovitch, 1969 and 1972). This primacy of long-distance trade (the exclusively warlike Zulu kingdom being an exception) seems to us different from that of the classic "Asiatic mode of production" model. The latter presupposes villages based on collective production and bound to a "higher unit" in the form of a state capable of compelling the people to work. Behind this generalized slavery stood the top economic command of a despot who exploited these communities economically at the same time that he ruled them (Chesneaux, 1964). Nowhere in Africa (except perhaps in the massive constructions of the "Builders of Stone" in southern Africa, fourteenth to eighteenth centuries) do we find this generalized slavery which made the state an entrepreneur, capable, despite the low level of technology, of carrying out enormous public works—hydraulic (the irrigation systems of the river states of the Near and Middle East), military (the Great Wall of China), or prestigious (the Egyptian pyramids). In Africa, on the contrary, the aristocratic minority that sometimes emerged dominated and exploited the communities "without interfering directly in their conditions of productions" (Godelier, 1963). The taxes raised with the aid of the ruling classes by the sovereigns who here and there assumed power were hardly ever levied on the peasants since Africa was precisely the place where agriculture was least able to produce a surplus. Apparently no ruler, in order to live, even needed to take large quantities of food from the villages. At most he was content to organize for his own benefit the labor of his wives (in the case of Dahomey, for example) and "domestic slaves." This was not comparable to generalized slavery or the forced labor of the ancient world. It seems, in effect, that the slave mode of production (even though it became nowhere dominant) developed as the result of the contacts built up with the exterior world through long-distance trade, at first North African, and then especially Atlantic. Similarly, the pseudofeudal organization of the most hierarchical societies (such as the Wolof kingdoms) was relatively late. Up to then, the tributes levied by the best-organized despots (Benin, Dahomey, Ashanti, Lunda kingdoms) were intended less, as we have seen, to pay for services or to meet general finances than to be hoarded, immediately consumed, or even destroyed. In short, the prestations or other economic obligations had primarily the symbolic role of guaranteeing the social structures.

The African despot exploited less his own subjects than the neighboring tribes. It was from long-distance trade that the major part of the surplus came. There were two ways of procuring goods—through war and through trade. War was the characteristic form of "production" of the parasitic military states, such as the Mossi or Buganda kingdoms, in which the state machinery seemed to be an enterprise of external depredation in search of booty—slaves and cattle. War was for the army leaders and the bravest warriors, but it made possible the mobilization of the majority of the population for the two annual campaigns. Dahomey was another example of a society in which life was marked by expeditions launched each dry season toward the Ashanti in the West or the Yoruba cities in the East, in order to bring back the slaves required by the economy. A further example can be found in the Fulani states, the heirs to Uthman dan Fodio, who in the nineteenth century controlled the slave trade which involved all the Sudan (the Fulani *lamidata* or sultanates of the Ngaundere Plateau) or the sultanates of upper Ubangi and of Bahr-el-Ghazal. A final example is the cattle raiders (Masai against Kikuyu in Kenya; Ndebele against the Shona in Rhodesia; Nama against Herero in Southwest Africa).

Nevertheless, most long-distance trade proceeded peacefully between complementary zones. After the medieval Sudanic empires there were the Ashanti who exchanged the products of the forest (kola) for cotton goods coming from the North, or the broker tribes, called oftentimes "anarchistic" or "stateless," which even had they wished, did not have sufficient military resources to impose force. Such was the case with the Bubangi of the Congo, who obtained manioc from the Bateke or the Mbochi at ridiculously low prices and who at the Stanley Pool resold redwood, ivory, and slaves at five or six times, indeed perhaps ten times, the price they had paid upstream (Coquery-Vidrovitch, 1969:108).

In such cases, this exogeneous circulation was comparable to a form of production, but one that was immediate and obvious, and proved to be in fact, degenerate and depredatory, since the merchandise only crossed over the country (in the manner of Portugal in the era of the Great Discoveries), sterilizing instead of enriching, either by taking away living forces (the drain of the slave trade) or by hoarding. Thus among the Masai, the capitalization of heads of cattle excluded the possibility of profit, since the herd represented not an exploitable surplus, but the very essence of wealth (the richest man being the one who possessed the largest possible number of cattle). That is why the Masai persisted in raiding cattle, of which they had plenty, rather than other goods (foodstuff, for example) which they severely lacked. The system did not forbid, therefore, the accumulation of wealth, but its use was paralyzed by the socioeconomic organization.

An "African mode of production"? In Africa, as in the Orient, the socioeconomic structure was based on a tributary mode of production (a term that is less restrictive than the overly geographic expression "Asiatic mode of production"), in that there was a continuous contradiction between the community and the negation of the community by the state (Amin, 1973). But the particular feature of the African mode was that it was based upon the combination of a patriarchal agrarian economy with a low internal surplus and the exclusive ascendancy of one group over long-distance trade. The form of power at any given moment depended upon the nature of this group. If political authority was in the hands of the lineage chiefs at the subsistence village level, their preeminence was then uncontested. In the case of the Fang or the Bubangi, it was threatened only by the instability derived from the rivalry of small groups involved in the same trade.

If, on the other hand, in a more differentiated political system, a privileged class succeeded in controlling long-distance trade by means of a hereditary caste as the result of the beginning of an accumulation of capital, the regime expressed a more or less coherent synthesis of the tribopatriarchal system and a new kind of territorial ambition. The medieval Sudanic empires, for example, were characterized by the utilization of traditional animist structures by an Arabized aristocracy which controlled trade. The function of these empires was to control and exploit trade between the western Sudan and North Africa. Their goal was domination of others for profit, and this economic objective explained their political form.

The history of Dahomey reveals a different attempt to resolve similar internal contradictions. The kingdom grew up gradually by filling a political void left by the decline of the Aja traditional structure, which had been undermined by the slave trade. Superimposed on communal institutions was a new kind of territorial state, in which each subject was to serve the king as well as the patriarchal chief. The paradox was that the kingdom, which first developed in order to resist the corrosive influences of the slave trade, committed itself to an economic and administrative structure based upon the trade. This was the direction taken by Agadja (1708-1740), whose transition to slave trader was the source of the flowering of the regime in the nineteenth century (Akinjogbin, 1967).

Finally, a privileged group or a despot that lost control of long-distance trade eventually experienced a decline of political power. This was the case in the kingdom of the Kongo. As soon as the ruler lost control of trade with Europe, he also lost control of the outlying provinces. Chiefs on the coast—from Loango and Soyo north of the river's mouth to Angola in the south—profited by their distance from the capital to seize control of markets, with the aid of Portuguese merchants from Saõ Tomé. These peripheral coastal peoples gradually freed themselves from the domination of the empire in the interior. The vassals became the brokers, and from this trade they drew the strength which permitted them to compete with the authority they henceforth rejected (Randles, 1969:65-74, 129-148).

The examples presented do not in themselves establish a general law. In the present state of our knowledge, they represent simply an effort to explain the coexistence of contradictory political and economic elements. This coexistence was undoubtedly explained by the preference of the minorities in power to exploit their neighbors rather than their subjects. No African regime, no matter how despotic, felt the need to eliminate communal village structures within its borders, for the villages scarcely interfered with the process of exploitation. As long as the village transmitted its tribute to the chief of the district or of the province, it ran the life of the collectivity as it pleased. The leaders assured the worship of the clan's ancestors; the chief of the land allotted arable land to each family and to each generation; the women's groups set the rules for transactions on the local food markets. There was no need to supply the ruler with a contingent of plantation laborers or caravan porters, jobs generally performed by royal slaves seized in foreign countries. The most frequent obligations were limited to military service in the time of war or, as in Dahomey, to the selection of some girls for the harem or the "Amazon" corps, the elite female warriors of the king.

We could complete and add to this vision by the commentary of Terray (1973) on Goody's thesis (1968)—challenging but not always convincing. He tends, in effect, to see the ruling aristocracy's *internal* exploitation of the slaves as the motive and the driving force both to declare war and to pursue external trade. Once this is argued, he then introduces the idea of a *dominant* slave mode of production, which, given the present state of our knowledge, seems somewhat exaggerated.

The determining role of the external factors. Thus an essential element in the African stagnation seems clarified. It was the consequence of a socioeconomic organization based on a dualistic structure (subsistence agriculture and long-distance trade). If this stage was to be transcended, domination of the aristocracy over the rest of the population, up to then indirect (as shown above all by the exclusive possession of exotic goods), would have had to have been exercised directly. Now, in these peasant societies, direct influence necessarily meant the control of the major means of production: the land. This naturally would have produced the disappearance of the community-based economy.

In truth, once the process of state-building had begun, it is difficult to understand why this transcendence did not take place. Indirect domination ought to have brought about its corollary, direct domination, especially in the special case when military arms were among the goods reserved to the aristocracy. Their acquisition meant that the sovereign had the power thereby to control enrollment into the army, the payment of tribute, and, above all, work on plantations that would in turn produce an accumulation of exportable surplus.

To be sure, the social organization was a handicap, but whatever its importance, on which we have always insisted, it cannot be interpreted as an absolute barrier. Is not the history of all civilization that of continuous or sudden mutations of its own structures? Even if power was exercised more over men than over land, by controlling the women and the slaves, the guns and the horses, it was capable of grouping the peasant communities around a centralized state.

The solution to the problem seems to push us back once again. It is necessary to determine why the African social structures, already unfavorable to change in themselves, remained for the most part radically congealed.

It is because in the modern era they have not found from the outside the pressures to change which were already grievously lacking inside the system. To be sure, the medieval Arab influence favored, throughout the continent, the birth of commercial civilizations that ended by accumulating not insignificant wealth. But what they did not succeed in doing was to make the surplus productive. When, with the decline of the Muslim world, the quick profits from trade became uncertain, why did the changeover still not take place? Because it was at the very moment that the Portuguese intervention upset the socio-economic givens of the continent.

In the end, the analysis at the internal level of the dynamic forces or factors of stagnation in the African societies seems both illuminating and incomplete. It is necessary to begin now the debate on the role and impact of foreign intrusions: What were the transformations born out of the expansion of Islam? How was the internal evolution of the societies of the Atlantic affected by the slave trade or, more recently in the nineteenth century, by the introduction of cash-crop agriculture?

Even if, for example, recent works (Curtin, 1969) seem to establish that the demographic drain of the slave trade was quantitatively less important than had previously been supposed, the trade nonetheless had an immeasurable impact in two respects at least: the general development of a slave-based society (Terray, 1973; Meillassoux, 1974) and the localized rise of African royal political systems based on military supremacy (firearms) and on the export of slaves. We find here again what we referred to at the beginning of this paper. European pressure made the African mode of production turn into something else. As Rey and Dupré (1969) have noted, in no instance did the appearance of modern economic forms result from the direct, logical development from a nonmarket to a market economy, via the intermediary of the "peripheral market" and the simple interplay of the peaceful progression of the law of supply and demand (following the model suggested by Bohannan and Dalton, 1962). The real process of African history was that of the collision of two heterogeneous modes of production, capitalist and "African," and the overthrow of one by the other.

This new phase, which destroyed the African structures and abruptly stopped what was up to then a relatively coherent evolution, intervened quite late and flourished particularly in the twentieth century.

By assimilating elements from the West if necessary, African societies were doubtless no less capable than others of overcrowding their contradictions and reintegrating themselves into a new economic system without a fundamental shattering of their equilibrium. But the sudden intervention of economic imperialism caused them to move toward an adulterated system of the colonial or neocolonial type "in which capitalist relationships of production are closely linked to the more archaic forms of relationship, to the greater profit of the privileged" (Lacoste, 1965).

Only then, in fact, did this possibility of the evolution of the internal structures, already begun in certain instances, come into conflict with the flourishing of a defined economy, then entirely dominated by the colonial powers.

REFERENCES

AKINJOGBIN, I.A. (1967). Dahomey and its neighbours, 1708-1818. Cambridge: Cambridge University Press.
ALEXANDRE, P. (1971). "De l'ignorance de l'Afrique et de son bon usage: Notule autobiocritique." Cahiers d'Etudes Africaines, 12(43):450.
AMIN, S. (1973). Le développement inégal. Paris: Minuit.
BAIROCH, M. (1963). Révolution industrielle et sous-développement. Paris: SEDES.

BALANDIER, G. (1967). Anthropologie politique. Paris: Presses Universitaires de France. English edition: Political anthropology. London: Allen Lane, 1970.
BLOCH, M. (1949). Apologie pour l'histoire ou métier d'historien. Paris: Cahier des Annales.
DOHANNAN, P., and DALTON, G. (eds., 1962). Markets in Africa. Evanston, Ill.: Northwestern University Press.
BRASSEUR, G., and BRASSEUR-MARION, P. (1953). Porto-Novo et sa palmeraie. Dakar: IFAN.
BRUNTON, R.F. (1864). A mission to Gelele, King of Dahome. London.
CHESNEAUX, J. (1964). "Le mode de production africain: Quelques perspectives de recherches." La Pensée, 114:13-46.
COQUERY-VIDROVITCH, C. (1964). "La fête des coutumes au Dahomey: Historique et essai d'interprétation." Annales, 19(4):696-716.
--- (1968). Brazza et la prise de possession du Congo. Paris: Mouton.
--- (1969). "Recherches sur un mode de production africain." La Pensée, 144:3-20. English edition: "Research on an African mode of production." Pp. 33-51 in G.W. Johnson and M. Klein (eds.), Perspectives on the African past. Boston: Little, Brown, 1972.
--- (1971). "De la traite des esclaves à l'exportation de l'huile de palme et des palmistes au Dahomey, XIXe soiècle." Pp. 107-123 in C. Meillassoux (ed.), The development of indigenous trade and markets in West Africa. London: Oxford University Press.
CURTIN, P. (1969). The Atlantic slave trade: A census. Madison: University of Wisconsin Press.
DEME, K. (1966). "Les classes sociales dans le Sénégal précolonial." La Pensée, 130:11-31.
GODELIER, M. (1963). La notion de mode de production Asiatique et les schémas marxistes d'évolution des sociétés. Paris: Centre d'Etudes et de Recherches Marxistes.
GOODY, J. (1969). "Economy and feudalism in Africa." The Economic History Review, 22(3):393-405.
--- (1971). Technology, tradition and the state in Africa. London: Oxford University Press.
GUILLOT-LEGEAT, J. (1964). "Révolution industrielle et sous-développement." Annales 19(6):1195-1207.
HOPKINS, A.G. (1967). "The Western Sudan in the Middle Ages: Underdevelopment in the empires of the western Sudan." Past and Present, 37:149-156.
--- (1968). "Economic imperialism in West Africa: Lagos, 1880-1892." Economic History Review, 21(3):580-606.
HUNTINGTON, E. (1915). Civilization and climate. New Haven.
HYMER, S. (1970). "Economic forms in precolonial Ghana." Journal of Economic History, 20(1):33-50.
JAULIN, R. (1971). La mort Sara. Paris: Plon.
JOHNSON, M. (1966). "The ounce in 18th century West African trade." Journal of African History, 7(2):197-214.
LACOSTE, Y. (1965). Géographie du sous-développement. Paris: Presses Universitaires de France.
LEVI-STRAUSS, C. (1960). "L'anthropologie sociale devant l'histoire." Annales, 15(4):625-637.
MALOWIST, M. (1966). "The social and economic stability of the western Sudan in the Middle Ages." Past and Present, 22:3-15.
--- (1967). "Rejoinder." Past and Present, 37:157-162.
MEILLASSOUX, C. (1960). "Essai d'interprétation du phénomène économique dans les sociétés traditionnelles d'autosubsistance." Cahiers d'Etudes Africaines, 4:38-67.
--- (1965). Anthropologie économiques des Gouro de Côte d'Ivoire. Paris: Mouton.
--- (1968). "Ostentation, destruction, reporduction." Cahiers de l'I.S.E.A., Economies et Sociétés, 2(4):759-772.
--- (ed., 1971). The development of indigenous trade and markets in West Africa. London: Oxford University Press.
--- (ed., 1975). L'esclavage en Afrique précoloniale. Paris: Maspero.
PIAULT, M. (1971). "Cycles de marché et espaces sous-politiques." Pp. 285-302 in The development of indigenous trade and markets in West Africa. London: Oxford University Press.

POLANYI, K. (1966). Dahomey and the slave trade. Seattle: University of Washington Press.

RANDLES, W.G.L. (1966). L'ancien royaume du Congo des origines à la fin du XIXe sciècle. Paris: Mouton.

REY, P.-P., and DUPRE, G. (1969). "Réflexions sur la pertinence d'une théorie de l'histoire et des échanges." Cahiers Internationaux de Sociologie, 46:133-162. English version: in Economy and Society, 1973, 2(2):131-163.

SACHS, I. (1971). La découverte du Tiers-Monde. Paris: Flammarion.

SAUTTER, G. (1960). "La Plateau Congolais de Mbé." Cahiers d'Etudes Africaines, 1(2):5-48.

SOMERVELL, D.C. (1960). A study of history. Oxford: Oxford University Press.

SURET-CANALE, J. (1964). "Les sociétés traditionnelles en Afrique Noire et le concept de mode de production Asiatique." La Pensée, 117:19-42.

Sur le mode de production Asiatique (1969). Paris: Editions Sociales.

TERRAY, E. (1973). "Technologie, etat et tradition en Afrique." Annales, 28(5):1331-1338.

4

RURAL POLITICAL ECONOMY OF AFRICA

LIONEL CLIFFE
University of Zambia

The parlous state of African agriculture has been starkly revealed in the 1970s. The horror pictures of famine in the Sahel and Ethiopia are, however, just the more obvious symptoms of a general failure of food production. This vast, rich, relatively underpopulated continent has become a massive food importer, and its share in production of all crops has fallen, except for a few, high-priced, and usually plantation-grown items like tea, sugar, and coffee. The very success of commercial production has, though, increased dependence and also inequalities and has often been at the expense of food production. It has led, some argue, to famine in dry areas (Meillassoux, 1974) and to involution in fertile ones (Bernard, 1972).

The situation is familiar and well documented (Feldman and Lawrence, 1975), but as Beckford (1974:35) points out, "few writings tell us why underdeveloped agriculture remains underdeveloped." The most common and officially accepted explanations (see FAO, 1962, or De Wilde, 1967) see the roots of the problem in some legacy of backward "tradition," "collective values" (De Wilde, 1967:54), "social insurance" (Joy, 1970:182), gerontocracy or sexism (Dumont, 1965:49), or, more often (the various arguments are summarized by Gerschenberg, 1971), the effects of land tenure.

CAUSES OF AGRARIAN UNDERDEVELOPMENT

In contrast, the structuralist formulations such as Gunder Frank's (1967, 1972a, 1972b), see underdevelopment as due not to the absence of such individual property relations and the like, but to the very existence of the "capitalist colonial formation of the rural class structure and the mode of production." Recently several writers in Africa have sought to explain what one study refers to as the "roots of rural poverty" in terms of the "development of underdevelopment" (Palmer and Parsons, forthcoming).

But as another such analyst has suggested it is by no means obvious *why* "capitalism could revolutionise agriculture in Europe but it could not do the same in Africa" (Rodney, 1972:239). Indeed, Marx (1961b:34) himself expected that "capitalism first makes the production of commodities general, and then, by degrees, transforms all commodity production into capitalist production." And Lenin (1967:317) in fact argued that "agricultural capitalism in Russia is a big progressive force." In thus seeking to answer Rodney's question one might usefully make at the outset the distinction that Laclau (1971:37-38), in his critique of Frank, makes between "involvement in the world capitalist economy" and the "capitalist mode of production." This formulation makes it clear that what has to be explained is not simply why African agriculture is not developed but why it is not capitalist, in the latter sense.

The fact is that the world capitalist system itself feeds on a process of accumulation, but in this process it uses different areas, peoples, and classes in differing ways. Where the capitalist mode of production exists (that is, in the industrialized centers but also in the mines, plantations, and factories of the periphery), accumulation occurs through a process of "expanded reproduction." That is, at the end of each cycle of production the capital stock has been augmented by the appropriation of additional surplus value that was created through the capitalist production. However, the dynamic of the system has been sustained by an additional process, that of so-called "primitive accumulation." Indeed, the original development of capitalism was possible only on the basis of such a *prior* accumulation of commercial and finance capital, which was itself of necessity the product of precapitalist modes of production. Marx called it "not the result of the capitalist mode of production but its starting point" (1961a:712).

However, in further examining the role of primitive accumulation, Preobrazhensky (1965:88) suggests that it may not be confined to an initial, short transition:

> The transition of society from the petty-bourgeois system of production to the capitalist could not have been accomplished without preliminary accumulation at the expense of petty production, and would thereafter have proceeded at a snail's pace if *additional* accumulation at the expense of petty production had not continued alongside capitalist accumulation at the expense of the labour-power of the proletariat.

This assertion indicates how "underdevelopment," in the sense of an untransformed mode of petty, precapitalist agricultural production, can continue to exist; and it also begins to suggest *why* it persists: because it is *profitable* to certain interests and because its profitability provides a necessary boost to the basic motor that provides the dynamic to the capitalist system as a whole. Laclau (1971:36-37) takes the theoretical explanation further. He argues that if the law of the falling average rate of profit[1] was in fact operative in the metropolitan centers, say in the last century and first part of this, primitive accumulation in the colonies might well have presented a way out of the contradiction. Investment in the periphery—in agriculture specifically (he gives the example of the hacienda)—where the organic composition of capital was low and where superexploitation of the labor force was possible (because of extra-economic coercion), would yield "super profits." In his view the historical evidence is only suggestive, but he states that "if it could then be proved that investment in these sectors has played an important role in determining the rate of profit, it would follow that the expansion of industrial capitalism in the metropolitan countries necessarily depended on the maintenance of pre-capitalist modes of production in the peripheral areas."[2]

THE PATTERNS OF AFRICA'S RURAL PERIPHERIES

However useful these theoretical insights may be, to fully comprehend the reasons for the persistence of precapitalist agricultural production, we must examine the particular mechanisms of primitive accumulation that have operated in Africa. Preobrazhensky (1965:85-87), quoting from the first volume of *Capital,* does list several of the mechanisms through which this primitive accumulation takes place. He differentiates between the various *political* and the various *economic* means. The political means, operating especially through colonialism, includes taxes, seizure of land and livestock, conversion of conquered peoples to slaves, compulsion of peasants, conquest of trade routes, and state loans; such a list certainly corresponds very much to African colonial experience (see, for instance, Rodney, 1972). The economic means are accumulations by way of economic channels, in particular a market system of "unequal exchange" whose exact mechanisms have changed over time but which have involved basically the "exchange of quasi-equivalents, behind which was hidden the exchange of a smaller for a larger quantity of labour."

With the exception of "aid"—which is the contemporary form of state loans (still repayable mainly by petty producers) and, as such, one of the extra-economic means of accumulation described by Marx—the political means of extraction are mainly freatures of the colonial past. The different economic forms of compulsion that have operated and still operate in Africa will be examined in detail below, but here it is useful to note that in relation to agriculture it occurs in two ways, one direct and one indirect. First, especially in those areas that in French are called *"l'économie de traite"* (see Amin, 1974), petty producers, such as "the peasant and the craftsman, are exploited by capital partly in the same way as the workers are exploited who receive as wages, in the form of the market price of their labour-power, only part of the newly created product of their labour" (Preobrazhensky, 1965:94). Moreover, if Africa was to produce the primary products that are so exchanged, some modification (and not always destruction) was necessary in the indigenous modes of production, but these were modifications (examined below) that did not necessarily herald in the capitalist mode.

But a second pattern of production also occurred. In Africa, as in various parts of the non-European world, the expansion of capitalism from Europe through trade did lead to the creation or installation of forms of agriculture, mining, and, later, industrial production that clearly were in the capitalist mode. In the northern parts of North America, in the so-called "white dominions," and in southern Africa, there were settler farms, plantations, mines, and other enterprises which had owners of land and other means of production employing a labor force.[3] The basic condition which made such capitalist production possible was the availability of necessary "free labor," a fact which dictated the type of transformation of production and therefore of the whole social formation throughout these areas, but also in turn the limits to which capitalist production could be installed. Where it did occur, the "superprofitability" of capitalist production was assured not by the direct plundering of a precapitalist mode of production but by relying on a low organic composition of capital (that is, a proportionately smaller use of constant capital plant) and on excessively cheap labor power. This latter was achieved not simply in a quantitative sense by keeping wages "low" in absolute terms; for extraeconomic coercion was also used to push wages below their "value" (measured in terms of the socially accepted minimum to ensure the reproduction of the labor power). Whereas in a developed capitalist society labor uses its wages to *purchase* all those means of subsistence necessary for its own continuing reproduction, in a peripheral society some of the means of subsistence are provided by the family's own "subsistence" production. (These subsistence items may include some food and other basic needs, the care of the family, and provision for the worker's own retirement and recuperation.)

Side by side with the establishment of a capitalist mode, a contradictory set of forces operated against neighboring indigenous modes: on the one hand, their production of commodities for sale was held in check so as to eliminate any productive alternative to labor migration (see Arrighi, 1970, for an account of this process in Rhodesia); but, on the other hand, the tendency to destruction of the indigenous mode had to be halted before the point where it ceased to provide for the reproduction of the labor power itself. Thus the relationships of production, notably with respect to access to land and the division of labor within the family, were held back from the differentiation process which would have promoted rapid internal proletarianization, but at the same time the productive forces of this indigenous agriculture remained stunted in their development in order to promote an exodus of semiproletarianized labor. But in the absence of unpopulated areas either natural or genocidally enforced, capitalist production did not everywhere find or obtain a labor force separable even partially from any of the means of production. Hence the very definite limits of existing capitalist production in agriculture and hence also the development of another process whereby existing modes of production were restructured to serve the same basic purpose of primitive accumulation.

The kinds of restructuring that arose as a result of articulation with the capitalist mode will be explored below. But the range of crops produced was in a variety of ways modified so as to allow surplus to be extracted by commercial and financial capital through a mechanism of "unequal exchange." Without going into a detailed analysis (for this see Emmanuel, 1972), we can state that unequal exchange does not mean simply an adverse shift or a generally negative trend in the terms of trade of agricultural or other goods of primary producing countries. Whether the trend is adverse or favorable, it is only a relative movement. The notion is analogous to the relationship of capitalist and worker. Whatever the relative shifts in the wage share (in relation to the profit level) even if it is moving so as to benefit the workers, there is always an element of *exploitation* (the appropriation of some part of his labor time as surplus value). It denotes an implicitly and inherently unequal relationship. The values of goods exchanged internationally have this inbuilt inequality, in part because of differences in the organic composition of capital (the developed countries' level of skill and use of technology is much greater), but also because of differences in wage levels. Emmanuel (1972) gives most emphasis to the latter. Palloix (1970), on the other hand, advances the discussion by arguing that it is not simply some arbitrary difference in wages, some *extra* exploitation of the workers in underdeveloped countries, that is responsible for the nonequivalence of the value of the commodities exchanged. He argues that "simple labour is purely and simply underevaluated in relation to complex labour" and moreover that this is possible because of the persistence, though "under attack," of the precapitalist modes of production. The labor is "nonequivalent" because it is not just the labor-power of another, less productive sector but because it is that "of another order, in another mode of production."

This does indeed imply, as Preobrazhensky has stated (see above), that surplus is extracted from the peasant in like manner as from the worker, but not only in the sense that each is paid only a part of the value of his labor power. In the colonial situation *both* classes of producers were superexploited and were left "responsible for their own reproduction ... everywhere in Africa" (Meillassoux, 1973).

THE ARTICULATION OF MODES OF PRODUCTION

There were in fact variations on the two basic patterns of change in rural Africa: the imposition of a capitalist mode *de novo,* and the restructuring of precapitalist modes to meet the requirements of commodity production. Amin (1972) in fact refers to *three* different modes of exploitation, each characteristic of a separate region:

 −Africa of the colonial economy, or *l'économie de traite* (western)

 −Africa of the concession-owning companies (Congo, equatorial)

 −Africa of the labor reserves (southern, central)

Certainly such a regional classification does underline the fact, for instance, that the whole of southern Africa contains a hierarchical system of dependent modes of production, with not only the Bantustans but several of the surrounding "independent" countries providing a source of cheap labor (see, for instance, Wolpe, 1972). And this in turn explains the persistence of technologically backward, precapitalist agriculture. Mafeje (1973) has argued that the "compelling reality" of not only the southern and central but all the East African countries fits this conception of "labor reserve economies." However, in including Uganda under this heading, he brings out the fact that labor migration can be a crucial element in a social formation that is not dominated by foreign-owned estates or mines. Laborers from northern Uganda and from Rwanda, Burundi, and northern Tanzania come not to work on settler plantations but to work on the increasingly commercialized farms of Baganda planters of cotton and coffee. This latter case is in fact one among many examples of labor being drawn from more remote areas to work in export-producing areas and not just to work on settler farms and plantations. In Ivory Coast, southern Nigeria, and Ghana, migrants from the northern regions and from Upper Volta and Mali have provided the surplus labor power for the production of coffee and cocoa; in Senegal they have come to produce groundnuts. In Tanzania recently, seasonal migrants who used to work on the sisal plantations are now heading toward peasant cotton- and coffee-growing areas.

These several examples thus suggest that Amin's category of "labor reserves" should not be confined to a single region, for it is a pattern found in some areas scattered throughout the continent. Moreover, this phenomenon of labor migration from "reserves" in fact provides not one but three types of locality, each with its characteristic mode of production. There are the areas of capitalist agricultural production, usually "installed " but which themselves contain aspects of relationships that are feudal or servile (like the hacienda)—variations which are important for defining the character of the labor force. But the areas like those in Uganda where African farmers have brought in labor migrants are not examples of "installed" capitalism. These are areas that are clearly in transition toward a capitalist mode of production, and differentiation has proceeded apace. The crucial difference lies not in the racial character of the large farmers however, but in the path of their evolution. This has involved a process of restructuring the indigenous mode; it will continue to show features stemming from that mode, and the evolution will typically be of Lenin's "kulak" type where the polarization into the two basic classes is not immediate and where gradations of middle peasants as well as capitalist farmers and laborers will persist for a long period. The particular structure of the emerging social formation in these transformed cash crop areas will of course vary depending on whether the labor-power is supplied by migrants or by residents of the community. But in most respects the dynamics of both such kinds of cash crop area will be similar.

A third area with its characteristic pattern of change is found in the source areas which supply the labor power. Whether the residents go off elsewhere to serve native planters or settlers or plantations, these source areas will be among those where the transition to a capitalist mode of production will be held back, often by deliberate measures—for instance, by actually preventing cash-crop production, as in colonial Kenya or in regions of Tanzania (Wayne, 1973, 1975), or by manipulating price mechanisms to the country's disadvantage (Arrighi, 1970), or by defending African "tradition," as in the South. But just as it is important to recognize this tendency for involvement in the capitalist system in order to conserve and not simply to destroy, it must also be realized that the conservation is only partial. In the labor source areas, commercial *production* either in a capitalist or a simple commodity mode is precluded, but social relationships are qualitatively transformed by their involvement "at a distance" in the capitalist system. Various exchanges in the local society become mediated through the cash nexus; food is sold to pay taxes rather than stored; the barter system is eroded, and the opportunity is provided for someone with a little cash to buy up the surplus of his neighbors. Perhaps most importantly the exchange relationship which provided for the reproduction of the community, that of bridewealth, has been inflated and monetarized. But not only is there a change in kinship relations, which some (Terray, 1971; Sahlins, 1972) see as relationships of production anyway, but also the absence of younger men changes the domestic mode of production in other fundamental ways, vitally affecting the position of women (Young, forthcoming, provides an excellent case study).

Similar patterns occur in the peasant cash-crop areas, but there the commercialization and differentiation processes are intensified by the fact that there is commodity production. Labor-power as a commodity begins to appear; and, with population pressure, land itself, in prospect of yielding exchange-value, comes to be treated as a commodity, with a consequent erosion of customary rights of access to land and thus of traditional kin and other obligations.

Thus we are suggesting there are three main types of rural areas; each is cast in a different role by the colonial division of labor; and in each the requirements of the international system have typically set in train characteristic trends. They are:

—Areas containing an installed capitalist mode of production.

—Areas witnessing a kulak evolution to capitalist production.

—Areas of labor supply and blocked development.

In addition, some other categories can be isolated, which are perhaps less typical. In a few areas a feudal or semifeudal mode of production preceded colonialism, as in parts of Ethiopia or even the interlacustrine kingdoms of Lake Victoria, or in areas where such modes emerged as the particular form of the colonial mode, as "in the Moslem savannah country in Senegal, Nigeria and the Sudan" (Amin, 1974:364). In such areas if new opportunities for commercial production are provided, a transition along what Lenin termed "landlord-bourgeois" lines may occur. Thus in southern Ethiopia (see Stahl, 1974; Cliffe, 1974) the impact of subsidized mechanization and of market openings has sparked off a classic process of conversion of landlords to capitalist farmers "by the forcible expropriation of the people from the soil" and through the "robbery of the common lands, the usurpation of feudal and clan property" (Marx, 1961a:685).

The former kingdom of Buganda in Uganda offers another case of a preexisting mode of production that offered enhanced prospects for a transition to capitalist production. Whether the kingdom was in fact a feudal social formation by the nineteenth century is a matter of some debate, but a pattern of landlord ownership had emerged and it was related to office holding. Early British attempts to formalize this landlordism and use it as a platform for a transition to capitalist production on newly established estates were not successful. But from the beginning of this century cultivation of cash crops was expanded on the basis of hired (immigrant) labor, and after World War II some large commercial farmers did emerge. However, even in Buganda, where some of the preconditions for larger-scale production and for the emergence of a propertyless class of workers existed, capitalist production was "shanghaied." To quote Mafeje (1972:17), "bureaucratic fsscination with 'professional farmers' led neither to a qualitative change in agriculture nor to a release of new energies consonant with a capitalist revolution. . . . [It merely] added to the existing strata of parasitic elites." The farmers remained aloof from production; they educated their sons into the bureaucratic stratum, and thus the class did not reproduce itself. The workers remained "laboring tenants," and consequently production relations —"neither feudal, peasant or capitalistic but a peculiar amalgam of all three— [were] not a natural starting point for any particular form of development."

A similar possibility for the transition of a property-owning class into commercial farmers is also offered in various pastoral or semipastoral societies—a takeoff from what Sahlins (1972) calls "pastoral feudalism." The "property" crucial to social life was livestock and not land, the use of which was in fact freely available to members of the community. Ownership of this movable property was in many instances very unevenly divided—large herds of hundreds at one end of the scale, many families with none. In these circumstances the expansion of commercial opportunities does generate a particular set of capitalist production relations: the private alienation of land; the separation of owners of small herds or those with no cattle or only small stock (such as goats and sheep) from the means of production (grazing areas and water); and the exploitation of labor by the large herders, the latter not always on a full capitalistic basis, perhaps on some "clientship" basis (Spencer, 1973:40). These trends can, for instance, be seen in Botswana, where the buildup of export outlets for cattle on the basis of careful livestock disease control has set in train a virtual "land rush" as private ranches are carved out of "traditional" lands (Chambers and Feldman, 1972). But here again the process of the emergence of cattle barons, controlling water and running large herds, is leading to the impoverishment of those losing access to communal grazing and, as often as not, also causing the ravages of overgrazing, to the neglect of scientific range management.

An alternative pattern of capitalist development has occurred as a result of a "frontier" process (see Cliffe, 1972)—the more or less spontaneous settlement of new lands by indigenous farmers seeking to engage in commercial production. Feldman (1970), Awiti (1974), and Raikes (1975) describe how mechanized production of grain crops in certain areas of Tanzania has spread in this fashion and led to a capitalist mode of production largely uninhibited by any preexisting property relationships, if not by other social ties. Polly Hill's famous description (1970) of migrant cocoa farmers in southern Ghana provides another example of this frontier process. She calls them "capitalists" on the basis of their calculated concern with accumulation. However, the actual mode of production, though an "installed" one, has not from the outset been characterized by purely capitalist relationships. It was mediated by a modification of the property relations in the area of immigration, and by the differing kinship (and production) relationships in the two main areas of emigration. In one area where patrilineal property relations were the custom, farmers formed "companies" to migrate and buy land; farmers from another area brought in their matrilineal kin to settle a new family estate. However, this system has clearly also involved a transition toward capitalist relationships of production (even though halted for a while by crop disease and falling prices); farm laborers (migrants from another area) were usually employed after the initial clearing of land.

These examples, especially the last, emphasize the fact that contemporary rural social formations and the modes of production in which they are involved are not pure examples of the capitalist mode; but the stalled advance of capitalism does not mean, on the other hand, that the production relations are still in their pristine precapitalist mode. There has instead been a combination or complex of relationships, as a result of some synthesis of modes. All the various modes that we have mentioned—those characteristic of the labor supply areas, of petty, export commodity areas, of former feudal societies, and even of the frontier communities—may be distinct from *imposed* capitalist production; but they have to be understood as having combined characteristics. They represent not simply transformations from precapitalism to capitalism, but an interaction between the two. It is in this sense that one speaks of an approach which analyzes them in terms of an "articulation of modes of production."[5]

The object here is to develop a theory of transition and interaction which together with an understanding of particular precapitalist modes would allow a theoretical approach to the understanding of the history of Africa's social formations. Rey (1973) recognized that such a theoretical task had first to be attempted in order that his own study of the Comilog in the Congo (Brazzaville) should not be simply "in an archaelogical spirit." The analysis above has tried to indicate some of the major forms of such articulation in Africa. Rey's own analysis suggests that at the root of these several patterns three general stages in the transition can be identified. The first stage is that associated with primitive accumulation, which he argues was everywhere (except in the areas where capitalism developed endogenously) accompanied by an intervention into what was the closed system of precapitalist modes and which was not possible "without recourse to non-economic means." In the second stage, labor power for capitalist production in industry is assured but subsistence production persists; this stage corresponds "to the actual situation in most of the ex-colonial countries." His first analysis suggested that this would give way (under the influence of contradictions that would steadily mature as this articulated mode reproduced itself) to a third phase of full capitalist production in agriculture as a result of the "Kautskyist conception of the disappearance of small-scale agriculture in favour of large-scale capitalist agriculture." However, he later modified this conception. He reconfirmed that the domination of capitalism does eventually emerge from the maintenance of the small or medium-sized self-employed agricultural enterprises. But he asserted that the transitional form represents the "kulak" route to capitalism, since the peasants that are not driven off the land still become dependent on industrial and finance capital.

These conclusions do reflect much of the African experience presented here: a politically enforced incorporation without transformation, giving way subsequently to part conservation, part modification of peasant production, so that labor-power or peasant products would be available to capitalism (chiefly through economic mechanisms). The suggestion of a third phase, in which kulak and small agricultural capitalists are held in thrall by national and international capital, in turn implies that the class contradiction between the different strata of peasantry and industrial and financial capitalists is more basic than the differentiation among the peasantry. The validity of this phase of articulation and the nature of the class struggle associated with it can be attested by a brief review of contemporary developments in agriculture, especially the various measures that independent states have taken to confront the impasse of agricultural underdevelopment.

Basically there have been three kinds of policy measures invoked. First, most African countries have employed a variety of *technical* measures for improvement; they have promoted higher yielding seed, improved husbandry techniques (worked out in research stations and passed on through government extension services, cooperatives, crop-purchasers, or chemical companies), and sometimes insecticides and herbicides, fertilizers, and new implements, even mechanized ones. Almost universally these inputs—either because of the indivisible nature of the packages (see the extensive literature on the Green Revolution and mechanization cited in Feldman and Lawrence, 1975) or because of the class bias in the allocation-communication process—go to capitalist farmers or kulaks and are unavailable to poor peasants. Their acceptance by capitalists and kulaks often even depresses the relative position of the poorer strata. The technical inputs promote differentiation, but, because they are not joined by adequate fostering of creative skills, they seldom lead to a general technological transformation of farming. Many of the programs, notably mechanization, have consistently been shown as disastrously inappropriate.

A second component of some agrarian strategies has involved the deliberate restructuring of production relations. In a minority of countries, such as Kenya, Senegal, and Malawi, official thinking has been influenced by those who see the replacement of "traditional" by capitalist property relations as a necessary first step toward agricultural advance. A legalized land reform has granted individual titles to land. This has confirmed the emergence of a "gentry" in some areas, but even then the transition to capitalist production has stopped short. In Kenya, for instance, the original colonial notion of fostering a yeoman class which would employ a large landless class has in the practice been modified, and a large stratum of middle peasants has preserved itself apart from these two antagonistic classes. Moreover, in Kenya, the intended market in land, which would have allowed for the concentration of ownership, has been discouraged; the "benevolent" capitalist state has modified its land policy in order to slow down the emergence of landlessness and to defuse the middle peasants (see Wasserman, 1973). The whole policy represents a counterrevolutionary device.

In some of the countries of North Africa a different kind of land reform, to abolish or reduce landlordism, has likewise not yet succeeded in thoroughly establishing a capitalist mode or any alternative to it. In Egypt the political power of the landowners has persisted long enough for them recently to reverse many of the land distribution measures of the 1950s. In Tunisia, the attempt to establish a widespread cooperative pattern of production was abandoned in 1969 (Duvignard, 1970), while Algeria is just getting round to implementing a similar reform but on a smaller scale (Sutton, 1974). The reforms just announced by the military government in Ethiopia go much further in abolishing the political and economic base of the nobility, but it remains to be seen whether they will provide a basis for transforming production.

Elsewhere, governments have chosen a third kind of strategy which does not confront any feudal or kinship property relations directly,[6] but which seeks to transform agricultural production, if only in order to maintain the level of agricultural export earnings against declining terms of trade or in order to feed a rapidly expanding urban population. The mere offering of technical improvements within existing production relations seldom has sufficient effect on total production. In addition, the mechanisms through which governments seek to promote such improvement are themselves a product of capitalist production, and thus the agricultural bureaucracy, the credit facilities, the technological inputs—not to mention the foreign research institutes and the oil companies hawking chemicals—take on their characteristic forms. Moreover, even when state planning of rural development is disinterested, it is carried on in a context in which it is responding to many initiatives coming from the capitalist system as a whole: from the general trade balancing pressures of the International Monetary Fund and from certain kinds of technical advice offered by the FAO, the World Bank, and (as Cleaver, 1970, has shown in the case of the Green Revolution) the foundations closely tied to the multinationals, as well as the large monopolies that purchase produce. In circumstances thus dominated by large-scale monopoly capital, all the pressure is for the modification of the mode of production in such a way that it will fit these technical and institutional forms of outside capital.

The existing modes are not only qualitatively maladjusted in their property relationships (many precolonial distributive obligations still persist and curb accumulation) but also quantitatively maladjusted. The "pigmy property of the many" has still to be transformed into "the huge property of the few" (Marx, 1961a:762). Thus governments have tried a range of policies which variously seek to find a way round the existing peasant production, either by opening up new land in the form of "settlements," state farms, and cooperatives or (long after the end of colonialism) by inviting in the plantation companies (Lonrho and Tate and Lyle in sugar in the Sudan, East Africa, and Zambia; Brooke Bond in tea in Kenya and Swaziland), and even by inviting in a new generation of "settlers" (as in Zambia and Malawi), often in partnership with the state. Or governments have sought various institutional devices whereby capital can insert itself into peasant farming areas; these have included various cooperatives (comprising producers, renters of tractors, input purchasers, or marketers), "group" farms (Uganda) or "block" farms (Tanzania), farms bordering on plantations ("outgrower" farms), processing plants, or other development schemes. What all these efforts amount to, as Mafeje (1972:19) has remarked about one estate-farming scheme, is that "in the absence of a virile national bourgeoisie the government was proposing state capitalism as an alternative."

It is important here to recognize cooperatives and even programs labeled "socialist" for what they are. As Goussault (1973:281) has pointed out, various types of cooperatives were "used by colonial regimes as instruments for controlling production and the peasants . . . and the best way of orienting large numbers of small producers towards market production." And far from being any kind of legacy of "primitive communalism" or traditional socialism (see Cliffe, 1970), they are a vehicle for capitalist involvement. Even populist programs, like Tanzania's *ujamaa* policy, have in practice taken on a form in which collective production is virtually absent: the government has extended its control to new villages but left existing production intact under the various modes, its basic purpose being to impose state control in order to extract surplus (see Raikes, 1973).

Excessive authoritarian control seems in fact to be a feature of many agricultural schemes throughout Africa. The essence of such schemes is such as to require a significant bureaucracy as the bridge between outside capital and technology and the small producers; the staff runs the central services, maintains liaison with outside agencies, and controls the activities of members. This anyway means that such schemes are inevitably saddled with high costs —frequently itself a cause for failure—or they are at best a formula whereby any surplus is just absorbed by state institutions at one level or another. Equally inevitably, the authoritarianism inspires resentment, a lack of incentives, and hence low productivity. Thus settlement schemes in western Nigeria have depended on a "guidance and control system . . . which used mainly compulsory means." State farms in Ghana entailed an "extensive centralisation of bureau-cracy" (Nieländer, 1972), as "the headquarters [tried] to direct daily activities at the farm level" (Miracle and Seidman, 1968a:16). In Zambia and Tanzania settlements and regrouped (ujamaa) villages have likewise been dependent on bureaucratic management, and in both countries members of the schemes refer to themselves as "government servants." Blume (1971:220) concludes that "high capital cost" and an "authoritarian aspect" are also features of outgrower and other "agro-industrial development agencies" that he studied in Ivory Coast, Dahomey, Uganda, and Kenya.

Along with the bureaucratic control, even when designated cooperatives, such state vehicles for capitalism not unexpectedly reproduce some capitalist rela-tionships in production. In Rwanda the *paysannats* were supposedly egalitarian but were not in practice (Silvestre, 1974). In Zambia members of cooperatives have continued to hire labor, as do members of the Gezira scheme in the Sudan. In Tanzania today and in Nkrumah's Ghana (Miracle and Seidman, 1968b) producer cooperatives have often existed only in a "signpost" sense (Raikes, 1973) and have been mechanisms for kulak access to state-provided capital. Similarly in Senegal, "the institutionalisation of the government's [cooperative] agricultural development programme has worked conspicuously to the advantage of privileged elements in rural society, often permitting a more authoritarian pattern of local leadership" (O'Brien, 1971:264). But for all that schemes exhibit such capitalist features, their production record is almost universally one of failure. They have not proved to be vehicles for development. Samir Amin (1974:367) crisply and crushingly sums up "policies of cooperative rural development":

> Carried on everywhere in accordance with the same rather naive paternalistic princi-ples, based, no doubt, on the Utopian desire to see the whole countryside progress without inequality . . . these policies have neither prevented the plantation system [by which he means commercial production in general] from developing where it was possible nor caused any noticeable qualitative changes.

The networks of marketing and administrative bureaucracies, whether they operate through the enactment of liberal land laws or through cooperative or other interventions in production, represent the different ways that the post-colonial state extracts surplus from peasant producers. O'Brien (1971) and Williams (1973) spell out some of these different mechanisms of surplus extrac-tion in Senegal and Nigeria respectively. Von Freyhold (1974), in documenting the same basic process in "socialist" Tanzania characterizes the noncapitalist modes of production, which are still being dragged into the sphere of primitive accumulation, as "despotic"—a colonial or neocolonial form of oriented despot-ism, what Marx called the "Asiatic," and Amin (1974) the "tributary" mode, involving a new bureaucratic class which extracts tribute from producers.

CONCLUSIONS

Our argument has been basically that the continued existence in rural Africa of precapitalist elements in the social formation is at once the measure of the continent's underdevelopment and also its cause and its continually reproduced result. Moreover, the elements that do persist are not simply superstructural features, the legacy of customary attitudes, but are basic to the production process itself. The different modes of production may have been modified, restructured, torn apart even, but for the most part have not evolved into a capitalist form. The transformations that have occurred have stalled, essentially because the wider international system has wanted the societies to be a source of primitive accumulation, not of expanded reproduction. African rural societies have thus been structured so as to provide the required commodities—peasant products and labor power—below the price of their reproduction through the market. Hence the basic contradiction that besets rural Africa is this:

> While agriculture should provide the necessary surplus to feed the industrial sector and requires therefore the highest degree of productivity, its obsolete organisation is maintained as long as possible by capitalism as a means of cheap reproduction of the labour force. [Meillassoux, 1973:89]

Yet it might be argued that whatever short-run gains may result from a labor supply only semiproletarianized and from commercial capital's exploitation of peasant production through unequal exchange, industrial capital will eventually require a more thorough transformation. It must allow the development of a more skilled, permanent labor force, and it must let rural areas become an expanded internal market, once producers are separated from their means of production and have to purchase their own subsistence.

In the postcolonial period, import-substituting industrialization has in fact generated some further efforts at change (as we have seen), but it does not force the pace because of its own character. Based as it is on satisfying the existing market for nonessential consumption (and often dependent for its continued expansion on further income redistribution away from the poor), the strategy does not for the most part generate an imperative for a capitalist development in agriculture. Moreover, peasant agriculture is by and large not allowed to retain the surplus which could be the basis for its own accumulation or could be used as subsistence for its own expanding number of producers.

There is a final inhibition ensuring that the imperative for capitalist agriculture is at best fitful and partial: in its efforts to promote industry (a necessary condition for the expanding reproduction of the bureaucracy itself) the state becomes dependent on imported means of production.[7] The result is stagnation of industrial employment and a rapid increase in the impoverished, marginal population in the town, to the extent that the full proletarianization of the peasantry becomes fraught with dangers for the continued stability of the state. Hence the "back to the land" campaigns and the reluctance to enact individual property rights. For Africa—as for France, which has retained a peasantry for some two hundred years (see Gervais et al., 1970)—the artificial preservation of precapitalist modes is a crucial counterrevolutionary measure as well as one which allows primitive accumulation.

Our conclusion is that the forces of international capital acting in a variety of ways on rural Africa are not in the end capable of fully transforming Africa's forces or relations of production. But this provides rather the beginning not the end of an analysis. One must logically go on to ask the question still remaining: If external capital cannot bring about development, can rural social forces be their own instrument for change? An analysis along the preceding lines does begin to provide an answer to this revolutionary issue. However, it is not enough to isolate the factors that determine continued agrarian underdevelopment or that identify the (changing) roles of different peasantries within an international process of accumulation. Identification of the forces for change can only come from a class analysis of particular social formations, which would reveal region by region those strata whose interests are likely to steer them into support of (or opposition to) a particular alternative to the existing political economy. Such analysis can clearly not be offered in these final remarks and, in any event, would have to be made in the context of a particular political struggle. So far in Africa it has only been made in the context of a struggle for national liberation. Thus the strategy for struggle in Guinea Bissau was based on the analysis by Cabral (1969), which describes the differing precolonial social formations found in various parts of the country, and the way in which their different strata were tied into the colonial system of capitalism. Likewise, FRELIMO's successful struggle in Mozambique had been predicted on similar calculations (according to Dos Santos, 1973, and Saul, 1974).

Some academic analysts (Goussault, 1972; Billaz, 1973; Rey, 1973) have gone some way toward realizing that an analysis of modes of production can be a step toward identifying class forces which can bring about a transition that is not toward capitalism. What is of some interest here is that this more concrete type and level of analysis is in fact the one that needs to draw upon some understanding not simply of the nature of imperialism or the colonial forms in Africa but also of the varieties of precolonial formations. These indigenous modes require study not to provide a nationalist consciousness through a celebration of the African past; they require study because the specific, contemporary class formations that have emerged in particular areas as a consequence of stunted transition toward capitalism are a complex social *resultant;* they are as much a product of the precapitalist mode of production as of the capitalist. Indeed, our earlier examples of the different kinds of transition based on feudal, pastoral, or other modes suggested this characteristic of articulation with merchant capital:

> To what extent [commercial capital] brings about a dissolution of the old mode of production depends on its solidity and internal structure. And whither this process of dissolution will lead, in other words, what mode of production will replace the old, does not depend on commerce but on the character of the old mode of production itself. [Marx, 1962:326]

The full task of a political economy of Africa must then start with an analysis of the precapitalist modes. The theoretical discussions between those who identify a "domestic" mode of production (Sahlins, 1972), a "lineage" mode (Terray, 1972), a "tributary" (or Asiatic) mode (Amin, 1974), or even an "African" mode (Coquery-Vidrovitch, 1969; Varga, 1970) have advanced our conceptualizing of the problem. More studies to identify the makeup of particular historical formations is also required, but these need to be conceived not "in an archaelogical spirit" but as the prelude to understanding the dynamic of these societies in the contemporary period. But rather than end with the usual academic note of a call for more research, I would prefer to end with a recognition of the limits of academic understanding. This essay has sought to clarify the contradictions which generate the reproduction of underdevelopment in Africa, but such an analysis cannot itself lay bare the future prospects, for as Rey (1973:217) notes, "it is the protracted struggle of classes, and not the process of reproduction, which produces the condition of transition." The peasants of Mozambique and Guinea, like those in Indochina, have begun to indicate this potential for change in rural Africa.

NOTES

1. Laclau (1971:36-37) gives this summary of the theoretical model (basically that developed by Marx in volume 3 of *Capital*) on which the falling rate of profit is predicated: "The process of capital accumulation—which is the fundamental motor force of the ensemble of the capitalist system—depends on the rate of profit. Now the rate of profit is in its turn determined by the rate of surplus-value and the organic composition of capital. A rise in the organic composition of capital is a condition for capitalist expansion, since technological progress is what permits the reconstitution of the reserve army of labour and the maintenance of a low level of wages. But unless a rise in the organic composition of capital is linked to a more than proportional increase in the rate of surplus value, it will necessarily produce a decline in the rate of profit. This tendency is partially compensated by capital movements from industries with a high organic composition to those with a low organic composition; from this there emerges an average rate of profit which is always higher in value terms than the corresponding rate of profit in the technologically more advanced industries. Nevertheless, since a growing augmentation in the organic composition of the total capital is inherent in capitalist expansion, in the long term there can only be a permanent tendency for the rate of profit to decline.
"It will be seen that in this scheme—which describes precisely enough the dominant tendencies at work in a free competitive capitalism—what seems to be the key to a sustained process of accumulation is the expansion, in any sector of the system, of production units in which either low technology or super-exploitation of labour makes it possible to counteract the depressive effect on the rate of profit of the increasing organic composition of capital in the dynamic or advanced industries. Now the enterprises of the peripheral areas are in an ideal position to play this role."
2. Laclau's suggestion as to the possible role of this primitive accumulation in the colonies in raising the average rate of profit is in some ways analogous to Rosa Luxemburg's argument (1951:336) that "accumulation of capital, as an historical process, depends in every respect upon non-capitalist social strata and forms of social organisation" and that it is thus imperialist expansion that rescues the system from the contradictions involved in "realising" surplus value. However, she also simplistically concluded that the net result of this process is always "a battle of annihilation against every historical form of natural economy."

3. Of course, it is also true that in some instances where a mode of production was *installed* rather than an existing one "restructured," the new mode was not capitalist but "slave" (the American South, the West Indies) or even feudal (the hacienda system in Latin America or some of the settler farms in Africa which absorbed squatters who performed corvée labor).

4. Marx (1961a:581) described the "normal" circumstances of the reproduction of labor power thus: "the mechanism of capitalist production provides (for additional labour-power) beforehand, by converting the working class into a class dependent on wages, a class whose ordinary wages suffice, not only for its own maintenance, but for its increase."

5. For a discussion of this concept see "Sur l'articulation de modes de production," the first part of Rey (1973). For an attempt to use it as a tool in class analysis, see Cliffe (forthcoming).

6. Even without government intervention, there has been in many areas of peasant cash-crop farming a de facto evolution of rights—from matrilineal to patrilineal; from multiple to single heirs; from rights to usufruct to permanent rights of disposal (even if, in the first stage, clans or lineages retain the right to veto sales of land).

7. This dependence exists in agriculture too, where the Green Revolution is the classic case of technological dependence on monopoly capital.

REFERENCES

AMIN, S. (1972). "Underdevelopment and dependence in black Africa." Journal of Modern African Studies 10(4):503-524.
——— (1974). Accumulation on a world scale: A critique of the theory of underdevelopment. New York: Monthly Review Press.
ARRIGHI, G. (1970). "Labour supplies in historical perspective: A study of the proletarianization of the African peasantry in Rhodesia." Journal of Development Studies, 6(3):197-234.
AWITI, A. (1974). "Analysis of a rural village in Tanzania." African Red Family, 1(3/4):26-61.
BECKFORD, G.L. (1974). "Comparative rural systems: Development and underdevelopment." World Development, 2(6):35-43.
BERNARD, F.E. (1972). East of Mount Kenya: Meru agriculture in transition. Munich: Weltforum Verlag.
BILLAZ, R. (1973). "Technologies, emploi et stratégies de développement agraire, quelques réflections à partir d'expériences recentes." Tiers-Monde, 14(54):229-260.
BLUME, H. (1971). Organisational aspects of agro-industrial development agencies. Munich: Weltforum Verlag.
CABRAL, A. (1969). Revolution in Guinea. London: Stage One.
CLEAVER, H. (1970). "The contradictions of the Green Revolution." Monthly Review, 24(2):80-111.
CLIFFE, L. (1970). "Traditional Ujamaa and modern producer cooperatives in Tanzania." In C.G. Widstrand (ed.), Cooperatives and rural development in East Africa. New York: Africana Publishing.
——— (1972). "The policy of Ujamaa Vijijini and the class struggle in Tanzania." In L. Cliffe and J.S. Saul (eds.), Socialism in Tanzania (vol. 2). Nairobi: East African Publishing House.
——— (1974). "Feudalism, capitalism and the famine in Ethiopia." Review of African Political Economy, 1(August-November):34-40.
——— (forthcoming). "Rural class formation in East Africa."
CHAMBERS, R., and FELDMAN, D. (1972). Report on rural development. Gaborone: Government Printer.
COQUERY-VIDROVITCH, C. (1969). "Recherches sur un mode de production africaine." La Pensée, 144(April):61-78. English translation in M. Klein and G.W. Johnson (eds.), Perspectives on the African past. Boston: Little, Brown, 1972.
DE WILDE, J.C. (1967). Experiences with agricultural development in tropical Africa (vol. 1). Baltimore: Johns Hopkins Press, for the International Bank for Reconstruction and Development.

DOS SANTOS, M. (1973). "FRELIMO faces the future." African Communist, 55:25-53.
DUMONT, R. (1965). African agricultural development: Reflections on the major lines of advance and the barriers to progress. Addis Ababa: United Nations Economic Commission for Africa.
DUVIGNAUD, J. (1970). Change at Shebika: Report from a North African village. New York: Vintage.
EMMANUEL, A. (1972). Unequal exchange: A study of the imperialism of trade. London: New Left Books.
FELDMAN, D., and LAWRENCE, P. (1975). Global 2 project on the social and economic implications of large-scale introduction of new varieties of food grains: Africa report. Geneva: United Nations Research Institute for Social Development.
FELDMAN, R. (1970). "Custom and capitalism: A study of land tenure in Ismani, Tanzania" (Economic Research Bureau Paper). Dar es Salaam: University of Dar es Salaam.
Food and Agriculture Organization (1962). Report on the possibilities of African rural development in relation to economic and social growth. Rome: Author.
FRANK, A.G. (1967). Capitalism and underdevelopment in Latin America: Historical studies of Brazil and Chile. New York: Monthly Review Press.
——— (1972a). "Economic dependence, class structure and underdevelopment policy." In J. Cockcroft, A.G. Frank, and D.L. Johnson (eds.), Dependence and underdevelopment: Latin America's political economy. New York: Anchor.
——— (1972b). Lumpenbourgeoisie and lumpendevelopment. New York: Monthly Review Press.
GERSCHENBERG, I. (1971). "Customary land tenure as a constraint on agricultural development: A re-evaluation." East African Journal of Rural Development, 4(1):51-62.
GERVAIS, S.; SERVOLIN, P.; and WEIL, L. (1970). Une France sans paysans. Paris.
GOUSSAULT, Y. (1972). "Modes of production and development of agrarian units: Implications of present policies." Dakar: United Nations Institute for Economic Development and Planning.
——— (1973). "Stratifications sociales et coopération agricole." Tiers Monde, 14(54):281-294.
HILL, P. (1970). Migrant cocoa farmers of southern Ghana. Cambridge: Cambridge University Press.
JOY, L. (1970). "Strategy for economic development." In D. Seers and L. Joy (eds.), Development in a divided world. Harmondsworth: Penguin.
LACLAU, E. (1971). "Feudalism and capitalism in Latin America." New Left Review, 67(May/June):19-38.
LENIN, V.I. (1967). The development of capitalism in Russia. Moscow: Progress Publishers.
LUXEMBURG, R. (1951). The accumulation of capital. London: Routledge and Kegan Paul.
MAFEJE, A. (1972). "Agricultural revolution and the land question in Buganda" (Occasional Papers). The Hague: Institute of Social Studies.
——— (1973). "The fallacy of 'dual economies' revisited: A case for east, central and southern Africa." In R. Leys (ed.), Dualism and rural development in East Africa. Copenhagen: Institute for Development Research.
MARX, K. (1961-1963). Capital (3 vols.). Moscow: Foreign Languages Publishing House.
——— (1971). Critique of political economy. London: Lawrence and Wishart.
——— (1972). On colonialism: Articles from the New York Tribune and other writings. New York: International Publishers.
MEILLASSOUX, C. (1973). "The social organisation of the peasantry." Journal of Peasant Studies, 1(1):81-90.
——— (1974). "Development or exploitation—Is the Sahel famine good business?" Review of African Political Economy, 1(August-November):27-33.
MIRACLE, M., and SEIDMAN, A. (1968a). "State farms in Ghana." Madison, Wisc.: Land Tenure Center.
——— (1968b). "Agricultural cooperatives and quasi-cooperatives." Madison, Wisc.: Land Tenure Center.
NIELANDER, W. (1972). "Establishment of state farms and its implications for the 'traditional' sector of agriculture: Case study of Ghana." In Agrarian structures in a changing world. Heidelberg: Research Centre for International Agrarian Development.

O'BRIEN, D.B.C. (1971). "Cooperators and bureaucrats: Class formation in a Senegalese peasant society." Africa, 12(4):263-278.
PALLOIX, C. (1970). "La question de l'échange inégal; une critique de l'économie politique." L'Homme et la Société, 18(October-December):5-33. English translation in Bulletin of the Conference of Socialist Economists, 1972, 2(1):67-94.
PALMER, R., and PARSONS, N.Q. (forthcoming). The roots of rural poverty: Historical essays on the development of underdevelopment in central and southern Africa.
PREOBRAZHENSKY, E. (1965). The new economics. Oxford: Clarendon Press.
RAIKES, P. (1973). "Ujamaa Vijijini and rural socialist development" (Social Science Conference Paper). Dar es Salaam: Universities of East Africa.
––– (1975). "Wheat production and the development of capitalism in north Iraq." Dar es Salaam: Rural Development Research Committee.
REY, P.P. (1973). Les alliances de classes. Paris: Maspero.
RODNEY, W. (1972). How Europe underdeveloped Africa. London: Bogle-L'Ouverture.
Rural Development Research Committee (eds., 1975). Rural cooperation in Tanzania. Dar es Salaam: Tanzania Publishing House.
SAHLINS, M. (1972). Stone age economics. New York: Aldine-Atherton.
SAUL, J.S. (1974). "African peasants and revolution." Review of African Political Economy, 1(August-November):41-68.
SILVESTRE, V. (1974). "Différentiations socio-économiques dans une société à vocation égalitaire: Masaka dans le pays de L'Icyanya." Cahiers d'études africaines, 53:104-169.
SPENCER, P. (1973). Nomads in alliance: Symbiosis and growth among the Rendille and Samburu of Kenya. London: Oxford University Press.
STAHL, M. (1974). Ethiopia: Political contradictions in agricultural development. Stockholm: Raben and Sjögren.
SUTTON, K. (1974). "Agrarian reform in Algeria: The conversion of projects into action." Afrika Spectrum, 74(1):50-68.
TERRAY, E. (1972). Marxism and "primitive" societies. London: New Left Books.
VARGA, I. (1970). "African mode of production: A research hypothesis" (Social Science Conference Paper). Dar es Salaam: Universities of East Africa.
VON FREYHOLD, M. (1974). "The rise and fall of colonial modes of production" (Management Paper). Dar es Salaam: Institute of Finance.
WASSERMAN, G. (1974). "European settlers and Kenya colony: Thoughts on a conflicted affair." African Studies Review, 17(2):425-434.
WAYNE, J. (1973). "Some notes on the sociology of dependence: The underdevelopment of Kigoma region, Tanzania" (Social Science Conference Paper). Dar es Salaam: Universities of East Africa.
––– (1975). "The development of backwardness in Kigoma region." In Rural Development Research Committee (ed.), Rural cooperation in Tanzania. Dar es Salaam: Tanzania Publishing House.
WILLIAMS, G. (1973). "Class, politics and the state in Nigeria" (Politics Seminar Paper). London: Institute of Commonwealth Studies.
WOLPE, H. (1972). "From segregation to apartheid: Capitalism and cheap labour in South Africa." Economy and Society, 1(4):425-456.
YOUNG, S. (forthcoming). "Fertility and famine: Women's agricultural history in southern Mozambique."

5

TAKING THE PART OF PEASANTS:
Rural Development in Nigeria and Tanzania

GAVIN WILLIAMS
St. Peter's College, Oxford University

> We must study the farmer, not patronize him: we must assume that he knows his business better than we do, unless there is evidence to the contrary. [Hill, 1970:28]

> In the matter of production, the agricultural producers' cooperatives must achieve higher crop yields than the individual peasant and mutual-aid schemes. Output cannot be allowed to remain at the individual peasant or mutual-aid team level, for that would mean failure; what point, then, would there be in having cooperatives at all? [Mao, 1965:399]

> The question whether human thinking can pretend to objective truth is not a theoretical but a practical question. Man must prove the truth, i.e., the reality and power, the "this-sidedness" of his thinking in practice. [Marx, 1963:82]

Modernization and development represent the achievements of advanced, industrial societies and define the objectives of backward, nonindustrial societies. Modernization refers to the adoption of complex forms of social organization of production and administration. Development refers to the capacity of advanced technology to increase the productivity of labor. By contrast, "peasant" denotes cultural and technological backwardness. Peasants are assumed to lack initiative and innovation. They are unable to develop. They must be developed.

Peasants are expected to contribute to development by providing the resources for others to develop the urban industrial economy. Alternatively, they are required to give way to capitalist producers or state farms. Either alternative

AUTHOR'S NOTE: I am indebted to Sara Berry and to the members of the Political Economy Group, Durham, for debates which stimulated this paper and to Kay Frost and Philip Corrigan for comments on a previous draft. I am indebted to the Social Science Research Council and the University of Durham Research Fund for supporting my research in Nigeria and the United Kingdom. I am indebted to the farmers of Ibadan for teaching me about the "peasant problem."

requires the ruthless application of violence against peasant communities (Marx, 1974:671-715; Lenin, 1907:273-275; Moore, 1966). Peasants have fought to maintain their access to and management of their own resources. They have refused obstinately to concede their limited measure of autonomy to the plans for a future society devised by their betters. Modernization and development have been achieved only on the backs and over the dead bodies of peasants or by the liquidation of peasants as a class. The recalcitrance of peasants to outsiders' conceptions of progress and the peasants' place in it defines the peasants as backward and delineates the peasant problem.

DEVELOPING PEASANTS

Colonialism incorporated African producers into the capitalist world market and subjected them to the colonial state. Even in communities where the proportion of output sold on the market is small, cash income is needed to buy a wide range of essential goods, to meet aspirations for improved material well-being, to acquire the labor (of hired workers or a wife and children), to acquire oftentimes the land for agricultural production (Boesen, 1972:11), and to pay taxes to the state. African producers have established new crops and expanded the production of old crops in response to favorable terms of trade. Smallholder production of palm oil first developed in Nigeria at the beginning of the nineteenth century. At the end of the century, the introduction of the steam-ship, the railway, and the motor lorry led to a dramatic increase in cocoa and groundnut production. Administrative attempts to promote the cultivation of cotton for the British textile industry failed because peasants controlled production on their own land and got better returns for other crops. Schemes for plantations were rejected because African peasants had already developed export production; a few experiments with plantations in the Gold Coast were an abject failure. The promotion of colonial conceptions of good husbandry was limited to exhortation, until the postwar epidemic of swollen shoot disease in parts of Ghana and Nigeria (Hopkins, 1973).

In Tanganyika, the Germans sought to finance their colonial adventure by enforcing the production of cotton. which provoked the Maji-Maji rebellion. Plantations and settlers grew coffee, rubber, and sisal, with lasting success only in the case of the sisal plantations. The British restricted the expansion of settlers but sustained the sisal plantations. These drew their labor from poor areas of the country, but no attempt was made to develop alternative sources of income (Iliffe, 1969; Cliffe, 1972a).

In the absence of peasant development of export crops on the Ghanaian or Nigerian scale, the administration sought to encourage and regulate peasant production by coercion. Regulations variously sought to enforce crop acreages for cash crops on the one hand and food crops on the other, to counter soil erosion and plant and animal diseases, and to impose "improved" methods of husbandry on African farmers. The practices they recommended were usually inappropriate in local conditions and imposed undue burdens on peasants. Their enforcement created opportunities for extortion by government agents. Resistance to agricultural regulations was the major source of nationalist protest in the countryside. The success of rural resistance and of the nationalist movement discredited the authority of local chiefs, agricultural officers, and sanitary inspectors and inculcated a distrust of the purposes and advice of officialdom. By 1960, plantations and settler estates, occupying only 1% of the land were still responsible for half of Tanganyika's agricultural exports. In the 1960s, peasants expanded acreage and production of cash crops dramatically, more than doubling the production of all export crops, bar groundnuts, despite an overall decline in world prices. Only after the end of colonial rule and regulation did Tanzanian peasants emulate the expansion of output which took place under colonial rule in Nigeria.

The aim of the first Nigerian ventures in cooperative marketing, in 1907 and again in 1929, was to export cocoa independently of the foreign trading companies. Colonial policy in both Nigeria and Tanzania encouraged cooperation; in the 1920s the aim was to improve the cultivation and preparation of the cocoa crop; and in the 1930s the aim was to bring it under state control and displace local middlemen but without challenging the colonial companies' hold on the export-import trade. Statutory marketing boards extended state control over marketing and the appropriation of surplus value from the peasantry. African governments inherited the colonial apparatus for regulation of, and surplus appropriation from, peasant production.

In Nigeria, cooperatives were brought under statutory regulation in 1934. They competed with established African middlemen and sold their produce to expatriate companies. Statutory marketing was established to cope with wartime conditions and proved effective in subsidizing the British consumer and withholding a share of the price from the farmers. These revenues were then invested in low-yielding treasury bonds to help shore up the declining fortunes of the pound sterling. Since self-government, the marketing board revenues have been used to fund regional and state government activities, party campaigns, and the consumption and accumulation of money by the rich and powerful. They have never been used to protect farmers, who have had to bear the full brunt of fluctuations in world prices and the additional costs of government marketing and deductions, usually between 25 and 70% of the price realized on the world market (Olatunbosun and Olayide, 1971). Cooperatives market only a small percentage of the cocoa, and little of anything else. Marketing boards buy only from licensed agents, to whom they ensure monopolistic profits. In this way the state accumulates money at the expense of farmers and controls the distribution of the private profits derived from produce trading (Essang, 1970).

Farmers have resisted low producer prices by selling to smugglers, by reducing production even to the point of not harvesting cocoa beans already on the trees, and by direct confrontation in the *Agbekoya* rebellion (Beer, 1975; Beer and Williams, 1975). In 1973, the federal government of Nigeria responded to the threat of political disaffection and a fall in production by taking over the determination of prices from state governments (whose first concern had been to maintain their revenues), and it promised to set prices in accordance with trends in world prices and local production costs, with no trading surpluses in view (Nigeria, 1973). Increases in the price paid to the producer have not matched the high, if precarious, prices on the world market. The peasant farmer remains at the mercy of the state and the world market, which control the sale of his crop and the distribution of the surplus value appropriated from him.

In Kilimanjaro region, Tanganyika, African farmers were required to market their crops cooperatively in 1929. A government ordinance brought cooperatives under statutory regulation in 1932. In 1937 a fall in coffee prices led to opposition by the farmers to the union, which they regarded as a government institution rather than a self-help organization. The union was replaced by a statutory coffee-marketing board with the same monopoly powers, which sells the crop on behalf of the farmers. In the 1950s, cooperative unions were established in Bukoba, Sukumaland, and the southern highlands, where coffee, cotton, and tobacco are grown for export. The Lint and Seed Marketing Board was established to buy cotton in 1952; and in 1963 the National Agricultural Products Board was established to purchase a number of export and food crops, and cooperative societies were hastily assembled to act as its agents. All crop marketing, except at a local level, has thus been brought under state management in the guise of cooperative marketing arrangements (Widstrand, 1970).

Farmers throughout Tanzania rapidly became dissatisfied. They complained to a government commission of low purchase prices and high selling prices, of replacing the "exploitation of the former middlemen" with "another worse type of middlemen under the cloak of Co-operative societies, Unions and marketing boards," of corrupt, inefficient and undemocratic officials and committee men, of unfair grading, of delays in payment, of the use of deductions from the price of crops, and of the societies' markets as collecting centers for taxes and party dues; and they declared that "after having achieved *uhuru* in this country, we, the farmers, have been deprived of all blessings of *uhuru,* our incomes have been dwindling, and what is worse, we are continually being overtaxed." The government's response was to strengthen the administration of cooperative marketing by establishing a unified cooperative service and introducing government cooperative officers to supervise the primary societies (Tanzania, 1966; see also Saul, 1971). Farmers' alternatives to producing for low prices are to cease production or smuggle crops to neighboring countries.

Since the Second World War governments in both Tanzania and Nigeria have sought to transform agricultural production along lines which would give them more direct control over the producer and which depend, as industrial production depends, on external provisions of skills and technology.

In 1946 Mr. Samuel of the United Africa Company proposed to the Labour Government that the British and world shortage of vegetable fats could be solved only by mechanized clearing of land for, and production of, groundnuts. He wrote:

> The peasantry's principal occupation is, and must continue to be, subsistence farming, and there is consequently no reasonable expectation of any rapid or substantial growth of production from this, the main source of world oilseed production. Support is given to this view by the fact that the groundnut crop in Northern Nigeria . . . has not increased materially despite a constant and large increase in the population. [Wood, 1950:52-53]

By 1949, Nigerian groundnut production had increased by nearly a half, and some 250,000 tons of groundnuts were held up in heaps awaiting transport to the coast. Meanwhile, in Tanganyika, £35 million was being totally wasted by a state corporation, acting on the proposals of Britain's major trading and manufacturing company (Wood, 1950; Frankel, 1953:141-153).

Undeterred by this example, the Nigerian government proposed a new groundnut scheme, in which mechanized cultivation would be introduced by hiring men to clear the land and build villages on which they would in due course be established as settlers. It was proposed to establish 22,400 settlers on 672,000 acres. Less than 200 settlers were ever recruited, most of them unwillingly.

> The settlers were told where to live, in houses they did not like; where to farm, on land selected by European strangers and not from local experience; what to plant, and frequently with seed which they did not regard as good, and when to plant, on dates which were late owing to the ridging not being finished. They found themselves in trouble if they went away to see their families or to attend some festival. Some found themselves farming on worse land or farther away than others owing to the allocations made. One local Nupe remarked bitterly about all this that "it is better to die of hunger than to be a slave." [Baldwin, 1957:159-160]

The project was terminated in 1954 after a loss of £123,494.

Again, this failure did not deter governments in both Nigeria and Tanzania from attempting new experiments with settlers. In East Africa the colonial government responded to rural rebellion in Kenya as Stolypin responded to the Russian revolution of 1905 by trying to promote "a healthy, prosperous yeoman farmer class, firmly established on the land, appreciative of its fruits, jealous of its inherent wealth, and dedicated to maintaining the family unit" (Cliffe and Cunningham, 1973:134). In western Nigeria and Tanzania attempts were made to settle "unemployed school leavers" on the land. Schemes in Nigeria and Tanzania sought to establish or expand the production of cash crops, notably tobacco, under close supervision. All these schemes assumed that production had to be "transformed" by removing farmers from their "traditional, conservative environment" to places where they would be more amenable to the advice of export supervisors. By concentrating farmers in villages, they would be better organized for governments to supply them the investments and technical and social services necessary to rural modernization. Most schemes failed dismally. Initial investments and continuing overhead costs were high. Farmers regarded themselves as laborers working on government farms for low pay (Cliffe and Cunningham, 1973; Ruthenberg, 1968; Olatunbosun, 1967).

In established communities, governments sought to "improve" agriculture by concentrating resources on "master farmers" whose relative wealth, education, and political influence marked them out as "progressive" men, responsive to "capitalist" incentives, who would set an example to their backward "peasant" fellows. Lacking the same resources, "peasant" farmers could never be expected to emulate the improvements adopted by such a "capitalist" elite. In most cases, wealthier farmers did not cultivate any differently from their fellows. They were often townsmen, with a primary interest in trading or salaried employment and with close ties to local officials (Essang, 1970; Boesen, 1972:26; Gottlieb, 1972:28).

Both the "transformation" and "improvement" approaches treat farmers as obstacles to development. Development is to be brought from outside by the state and its experts. This belief persists in both Nigeria and Tanzania despite the evident failure of settlement schemes and despite the success of peasant producers since the nineteenth century in developing new crops, expanding production, and introducing significant and often complex innovations in the organizations of production (Hill, 1970; Berry, 1975b).

Initially, most independent African countries gave first priority to industrial development. But even in Nigeria, where oil has replaced export crops as a source of foreign exchange and government revenue, agriculture must provide markets for industry, markets for craftsmen and traders, employment for most of the population, and food for the towns, as well as offer a continuing source of prosperity when oil is exhausted. Tanzania, lacking the market to attract foreign investment, first recognized that "We have put too much emphasis on industries" (TANU, 1967:11). In 1973, the *Guidelines to the Third Nigerian Development Plan,* 1975-1980, also gave first place to agricultural development.

The Nigerian government's diagnosis of rural stagnation blames first "the inadequate supplies of agricultural inputs due to ineffective extension services" followed by the "inadequacy or lack of farm credit" and "the lack of market information with regard to current prices, absence of a grading system for products and ineffective storage facilities." Poor rural feeder roads only come fourth, followed by "shortages of manpower in key areas," with the central issue for peasant farmers—low prices—relegated to sixth place, ahead of land tenure problems, diseases, and, only at the end of the list, rural labor shortages. The major bottleneck in agriculture is assumed to be the provision of expert advice and services by the state rather than the deprivation of the resources and incentives with which peasant farmers can develop agriculture themselves (Nigeria, 1973:9).

The third plan "seeks to bring improved practices to farmers through a co-ordinated inputs package approach closely supervised by trained officials" (Nigeria, 1973:12). The burden of state marketing will be extended from export crops to food crops. Alongside the "improvement" of peasant farming by state direction, the government plans the "transformation" of farming on large-scale settlements:

It will be the policy of the Federal Government to acquire large areas of suitable land to be leased out on uniform terms to farmers as in the case of industrial estates. It will be much easier to provide extension services, agricultural inputs, etc. on such "Agricultural Estates." [Nigeria, 1973:14]

The plan proposes to establish 3.6 million acres of cereals, 1.5 million acres of root crops, and 845,000 acres of tree crops. This presupposes state direction of production, rather than encouragement of peasant initiative which cannot be adapted to such precise and ambitious planning targets. This will be attempted by direct state participation in production and by settlements. Capitalist farmers will be subsidized by credit schemes, and cooperatives will be formed as an instrument of state policy, through which agricultural inputs will be allocated to the favored, and marketing of food crops brought under state control (*The Times*, March 4, 1975).

Nigeria thus plans to develop agriculture by encouraging capitalist and state farming and imposing state direction on peasant farmers, despite the repeated failures of these measures to promote production in the past. The state then enables private capitalists to acquire the money for their commercial activities and personal consumption. General Gowon's 1974 budget speech proudly announced that the Nigerian Agricultural Bank had given its first loan of £2.5 million to the Co-operation Union of the North Eastern State. It also granted £640,000 to 12 individual farmers (*Daily Times*, April 2, 1974). Suffice it to suggest that the North Eastern state lacks a long tradition of cooperation and that private capitalist farming has not hitherto been used to assimilating investments on the scale proposed. It may be more profitable to divert credit on this scale to more lucrative commercial purposes. The promotion of capitalist agriculture will not displace peasant farming as the source of rural development, but will deprive it of the resources it needs. Since it proceeds from false premises, the strategy of capitalist development will produce only a parody of itself.

The Arusha Declaration (TANU, 1967) promised a brave new world of socialism and self-reliance. Development would not be based on money, industry, and foreign aid, none of which were forthcoming. The emphasis would be on agriculture, the people, the policy of socialism and self-reliance, and good leadership. Government and party leaders were prohibited from shareholdings and directorships and from receiving more than one salary and house rents. Thus, political and bureaucratic office would not be used to create an indigenous class of urban capitalists. *Socialism and Rural Development* (Nyerere, 1969) applied these principles to agriculture. It assumed that the expansion of commodity production might "get a good statistical increase in the national wealth of Tanzania," but only by creating capitalist farmers employing "a rural proletariat depending on the decisions of other men for their existence and subject in consequence to all the subservience, social and economic inequality and insecurity, which such a position involves." Only through cooperation could producers adopt modern methods, take full advantage of the government's services, and cooperate with their fellow citizens. Farmers would be persuaded of the benefits of cooperation by experience and example. Unlike the settlement schemes, the new *ujamaa* villages would have to rely mainly on their own resources. Under socialist leadership, socialist policies of self-reliance would develop agriculture, without the emergence of a rural capitalist class.

The model for the ujamaa strategy was the communal settlements, which had begun around 1960 in the Ruvuma region, where young men established new communities to open up land for settlement. Although numerous spontaneous initiatives failed in Tanzania in this period, several Ruvuma communities survived and established the Ruvuma Development Association to coordinate their activities of the communities and to organize the provisions of schooling, marketing, services, and milling. The Ruvuma example depended on specific circumstances which could not simply be reproduced elsewhere, particularly by party and government officials. Communal organization of labor opened up new land for cultivation without expensive private investment in hired labor and mechanical equipment, as in many other parts of Africa. (See Hill, 1963.) The communal spirit in which the enterprise was launched was thus supported by the achievement of clear material benefits. In its early years, the Ruvuma settlements could call on the assistance of foreign sympathizers. But, more crucially, the settlements were built on the initiative of local people and out of their own experience. Once ujamaa was declared to be the cornerstone of government development strategy, its application became the task of government and party officials. Within two years of the Arusha Declaration, the Ruvuma Development Association was closed down, and TANU and the government took over direct responsibility for these villages (Cliffe and Cunningham, 1973).

Elsewhere, meetings were held, and regional commissioners announced to the farmers plans for the establishment of new settlements and the movement of people to new land and into planned villages. The various forms and purposes of the settlement and villagization policies of the early sixties were perpetuated under a new name, but under the same management (Raikes, 1975). The only difference was in the encouragement of a communal plot, alongside individual plots. In West Lake region, people without adequate employment or land were "encouraged and convinced" to join new settlements (Musoke, 1971). In Handeni, force was used to move the poor and scattered populations of the eastern area to large villages, to make it easier to provide services (Freyhold, 1973). In Rufiji, after floods in 1962 and 1968, the government set up new villages, away from the flood plains, along the roads, in large settlements; one has 16,000 people, many of them away from fertile land (Angwazi and Ndulu, 1973). Elsewhere, the old resettlement schemes were simply renamed "ujamaa villages," with no more change than possibly nominal provision for communal production (Raikes, 1975).

Rural resistance led Nyerere to denounce the use of force in 1968 (Nyerere, 1973). Coercion was either denied or attributed to the enthusiasm of local officials. But it is not clear how else they were to induce peasants to establish ujamaa villages in the absence of any clear evidence to the peasants that they would benefit materially from them. In 1969 Nyerere switched from the stick to the carrot. Regional development funds and routine expenditures for schools and services were provided to people who agreed to constitute themselves into ujamaa villages. Coordination was imposed in 1970 by sending out "Presidential Planning Teams" to the villages to draw up lists of production targets and government aids for the village. Villagers formally agreed to plans and even to the establishment of communal plots, but they did so in order to pacify bureaucrats and gain access to land, credit, machines, schools, and services, without any intention of meeting the plans or committing much of their time to communal plots (Coulson, 1975).

Under the label of ujamaa the World Bank extended schemes of supervised production of tobacco and tea so as to meet the requirements of capitalist companies rather than to ensure the best return to the farmer for his labor. (See Feldman, 1969; Moody, 1972.) Schemes of this nature continued to meet a measure of "success"—on these criteria. Lacking such "power levers," the government found that the spread of ujamaa villages elsewhere was slow and failed to increase production.

For their part peasants learned the lessons of ujamaa. Communal production was a waste of honest labor. Returns from communal plots had usually been derisory or nonexistent (Angwazi and Ndulu, 1973; Boesen, 1972:37). Peasants learned again to distrust the purposes and good sense of government and to view any talk ·of cooperation and socialism with suspicion and even downright hostility.

Up to this point, ujamaa settlements and villages were few and far between and mainly in poor and sparsely populated areas. In 1970, the Second National Development Plan promised a "frontal" approach which would extend ujamaa across the whole country. The problem was how to achieve this in the absence of peasant enthusiasm. Several Marxists argued that Nyerere's "voluntaristic" policy failed to take account of class differentiation within rural communities. Capitalist farmers and rich peasants stood to lose both from the creation of alternative opportunities for their labor force and from the expropriation of their land for communal production. The party should win the support of the middle and especially the poor peasants, who alone stand to gain from socialist cooperation by the promotion of rural class struggle and the politicization of middle and poor peasants by socialist cadres (Cliffe, 1972c, 1972-1973:95; Awiti, 1972).

It has been assumed that the major source of rural social differentiation is the spread of commodity relations and the emergence of rural capitalists and proletarians out of the peasantry. This ignores the major class divisions between the peasants on the one hand and the state and its beneficiaries on the other. The major source of differentiation within rural communities lies in the relation of rich peasants to the bureaucracy, through which they can control access to material resources and political influence within rural society. Conflict within rural communities is the result of peasant hostility to the local allies of an oppressive government. When richer peasants found government staffs expecting them too to move to villages and waste their time on communal production, they tended to speak out for their communities against the government. In this way government measures against the peasants in Tanzania reinforced the solidarity of all peasants against outside interference (Freyhold, 1973).

Mobilization of the peasants requires the encouragement of cultural revolution against the government itself. TANU's *Mwongozo* Guidelines (1973a) appeared to move toward such a strategy. The party was to "lead the masses" and "guide all activities of the masses." Development was declared to mean the people's "control of their *own* affairs" and required that "the people must participate in considering, planning and implementing their development plans." Leaders and experts were not to usurp the people's right to decide.

However, the government's own policy followed the dictates of bureaucratic practice rather than Leninist theory or Maoist exhortation. Farmers in the poor central region of Dodom and southern region of Mtwara were moved into new villages. An attempt by the regional commissioner, Dr. Kleruu, to confront the capitalist maize farmers established in Ismani led a farmer to shoot him on Christmas day, 1971. The government responded to this challenge by a retreat to colonial practice. At Iringa, *Siasi ni kilimo* (TANU, 1973b) enunciated government policy. As in the Nigerian Guidelines, the problem was stated to be the lack of fertilizers and other inputs, the failure to observe "the basic rules of good husbandry," and the difficulties of small-scale farming. The solution was to apply the rules—rules imposed with lack of regard for local conditions and resources and with marked lack of success by the colonial government. Herders were ominously warned to "abandon practices and customs which if continued will hamper advancement of skill and effort in agriculture." (See Raikes, 1975.) Since "small farmsteads and hand implements cannot be expected to bring about modern development, . . . it is our responsibility to hasten to join the Ujamaa villages so as to be able to till bigger farms and use modern techniques" (TANU, 1973b:14). Government is to provide services, inputs, and experts and political education to farmers. Party members are to encourage farmers to adopt better agricultural practices.

Frustrated by the lack of peasant enthusiasm for forming villages or settlements or producing communally, ujamaa turned into a program of compulsory villagization, without any element of communal production. Houses have been destroyed to prevent peasants from returning to their homes, and peasants have been moved to villages with unfinished houses and no running water. No organized resistance appears to have developed, but there have been reports of mysterious fires, protests by individuals, and attacks on local militia recruited to implement the policy (Raikes, 1975; Coulson, 1975).

Production of food crops has been severely disrupted during a period of serious drought and soaring import prices. By 1974 the country's foreign exchange reserves were virtually exhausted, and the president warned that the country simply could not pay for any food imports in 1975. Colonial laws requiring minimum acreage of food and cash crops have been reimposed. In a desperate attempt to press peasants to increase output, beer drinking has been banned, and rural markets closed during the week. In some areas, identity cards are issued showing whether or not farmers have cultivated their required acreages and have permission to travel outside their villages (Raikes, 1975; Coulson, 1975). *The Guardian* (May 20, 1975) reported that the U.S. government was trying to find an American agricultural corporation to go into partnership with the Tanzanian government to produce rice and maize in southwest Tanzania. The Tanzanians have promised 30,000 acres for rice and 50,000 acres for maize, a management contract guaranteeing a set fee, whether or not the venture makes money, and arrangements for the original investment to be repaid in less than five years. Even the groundnut project did not offer as much.

The strategy of ujamaa aimed to prevent the development of privileged capitalist classes in the urban and rural areas and to end dependence on foreign corporations by vesting control of industry and marketing in the state and by developing cooperative production in agriculture. It has become a program for herding people unwillingly into "development villages," imposing futile colonial regulations, handing land and profits to U.S. agribusiness, recruiting farmers to produce tobacco on a scheme sponsored by the World Bank, and begging the United States for food aid. It proceeded from the assumption that the benefits of cooperative production are self-evident and need only be demonstrated to the peasants. Since these promises could not be validated in practice, cooperation could only be implemented by bureaucratic direction. Bureaucrats, however, require sustenance from the workers and peasants they direct. They have an interest in extending the country's resources. They inherited from the colonial era attitudes which defined them as the bearers of expertise and defined opposition to their plans as evidence of peasant ignorance and backwardness. (See Raikes, 1975; Freyhold, 1973.) When the party no longer speaks for the people against bureaucratic oppression, it becomes a servant of that bureaucracy, whose task is to persuade, cajole, and bully the people to adapt to the commands of the state. Tanzania's "socialist" development strategy, like Nigeria's capitalist strategy, proceeded from false premises. Thus it too produced a parody of itself.

PEASANT ECONOMICS

Despite the great difference in their ideologies and policies, both the Nigerian and the Tanzanian states have defined peasants as a problem. They share the assumption of capitalist and socialist economists who identify progress with the replacement of peasant production by capitalist or state forms of production, characterized by the application of advanced technology and increasing division of labor within the productive enterprise.

One view of the peasant problem defines the peasant as "traditional man." Peasants are allegedly bound by tradition, suspicious of individual betterment, and confined by a lack of imagination and resistance to innovation. They have limited wants or are just plain lazy. They prefer to defend a traditional way of life rather than adapt to market incentives. From the "formal" viewpoint of neoclassical economics, such conduct leads to a suboptimal allocation of resources, which should therefore be removed from the control of peasants and placed in more responsible hands. (See Ruthenberg, 1968.)

By contrast, Jones (1960) defines the rural producer in Africa as "economic man"—that is, as "rational man." Rural producers are redefined as "capitalists," whose decisions are assumed to be based on a utilitarian calculation of the relative costs and returns to allocating scarce resources to alternative ends. Thus Hill (1970:21-29; cf. Berry, 1975a) argues that Ghanaian cocoa farmers are "rural capitalists" in that "they have always regarded cocoa gorwing as a business." They have bought land according to commercial criteria, have mobilized savings and credit, have reinvested part of their profits in the acquisition of new land, have financed public facilities such as roads, and have taken a long-term view in deciding on investments. Jones (1960:133) argues that, since rural producers will adjust supply to match changes in price, their own well-being, along with the well-being of everyone else, will be secured if the economy is not "state directed," but rather is "economically free," so that "all members of the society are assured equal access to markets, to resources, and to knowledge." This may be a satisfactory theorem in the imaginary world of general equilibrium theory. In the real world, it only legitimates the subordination of the peasant to the unfree and unequal relations of the capitalist world market.

Both schools of thought identify progress with the adoption of the rationality characteristic of capitalist profit-making. The only question between them is whether African farmers are "traditional peasants" who must be reformed or replaced or whether they are budding "capitalist farmers" who only need to be integrated into "the market" for all to be well.

Chayanov (1966) contrasted the social organization of peasant production with capitalist production. In capitalist enterprises, the producer does not own the means of production, but is employed as wage labor. The worker is free from servile obligation. He has neither land nor tools with which to meet his needs and is forced to seek employment (Marx, 1874:174). Peasant agriculture is conducted ideally by the family labor unit, working its own land with its own equipment. Since the producer does not pay either himself or his family a wage, we cannot apply the capitalist category of net profit to the operation of the farm. The peasant is unable to treat the family farm as an enterprise "for reinvestment and business, looking on the land as commodity and capital" (Redfield, 1956:18-19). The farm is rather his source of livelihood.

"Peasants" are defined by their relation to overlord, market, and state. The "peasant economy" cannot therefore be analyzed as a self-sufficient "natural economy," independently of its relation to commodity exchange.

In "feudal" society, peasant production meets the demands of the landlord for tribute in labor or kind and meets the subsistence needs of the family.

Landlords may exchange the proceeds of tribute in a market and may even come to commute it for payments in cash, thus adapting "feudal" claims to the requirements of commodity exchange. Alternatively, peasants may free themselves from servile obligation and organize production for the market themselves. Lenin analyzed these two adaptions to commodity production as representing two alternative transitions to capitalist production: "the Prussian path," in which the "feudal" Junkers became capitalists, and the "American path," in which peasants themselves became capitalists. Peasant production is "subordinated to the market." This creates within the peasantry:

> all those contradictions which are inherent in every commodity economy and every order of capitalism: competition, the struggle for economic independence, the grabbing of land (purchasable and rentable), the concentration of production in the hands of the proletariat, their exploitation by a minority through the medium of merchant's capital and the hiring of farm labourers. [Lenin, 1969:175]

Peasants are differentiated into a "rural bourgeoisie or . . . well-to-do peasantry," from among whom "a class of capitalist farmers is created," and a "rural proletariat . . . of *allotment-holding wage-workers.*" A precarious "middle peasantry" is progressively eliminated by the advance of commodity relations and the consequent differentiation of the peasantry. Differentiation is retarded by the perpetuation of such features of precapitalist economies as "bondage, usury, labour-service, etc." The elimination of the landlord economy in favor of peasant landholding leads to the more rapid development of the forces of production and of capitalist social relations in the countryside (Lenin, 1969:175-190).

For both Lenin and the Bolsheviks on the one hand and Stolypin and the tsarist state on the other, this

> general picture of the dynamics of peasant society . . . was firmly established as a piece of self-evident knowledge, i.e., it had become part of the prevailing ideology not only in the normative but also in the cognitive sense. [Shanin, 1971:222-223; 1972:1]

Lenin's revolutionary achievements have established the self-evident correctness of these propositions for subsequent Marxists. Thus Cliffe (forthcoming) suggests that the above quotation from Lenin "seems admirably to sum up the kind of changes whose occurrence among the Tanzanian peasantries we have been trying to document." Nyerere (1969:343-344) argues that scarcity of land, in the absence of socialist intervention, must lead to the creation of "a farmer's class and a labourer's class."

Commodity production by family farms is thus interpreted as one of the ways in which capitalist production assimilates precapitalist modes of production to itself, by identifying inequality and wage employment as features of the transition from the peasant economy to capitalist production, rather than as features of the peasant economy per se (Lenin, 1969:71-92).

Numerous studies in different societies have established varied but significant inequalities among peasants in access to the whole range of sources of income.

Wealthier farmers not only own more land than others, but usually command more family labor and more and better tools with which to cultivate it. They are more likely to employ hired labor and can do so at lower average costs than poorer farmers. Their farm production is better organized and is more likely to take place at the best time of year. They grow more food crops per family member or per working man than others and are more likely to diversify production into one or more lucrative cash crops. They are more likely than others to purchase land or to rent land, and they do so on better terms than poorer farmers. Income inequalities from nonfarm employment—trading, money-lending, manufactures, and salaries—are usually even greater than inequalities from agricultural production. Wealthier farmers can market their crop more cheaply and expeditiously and may be in a position to store grain for profitable resale to the less fortunate. They are likely to be recognized by the authorities and by other farmers as the proper representatives of their communities, and they have far greater access than others to credit, extension services, sprays, and fertilizers. (See Lenin, 1969:138-143; Hill, 1970:152; Galetti, 1956:145, 151-153, 285, 459; Essang, 1970; Gottlieb, 1972:24; Boesen, 1972; Madsen, 1972; Thoden van Velzen, 1973.) The extent of differentiation is greatest in areas of land abundance, where settlement has been more recent. In such areas, the cultivation of land may be initiated by capitalist farmers who can finance the opening of large tracts of land with machines and hired labor (Lenin, 1969:142; Awiti, 1972).

Inequalities are not sufficient evidence for the fundamentally capitalist tendencies of the development of the peasant economy. Class relations, not inequality as such, define production as capitalist. Classifications based on the extent of landholdings are inevitably somewhat arbitrary, even when they are controlled for size of family household and labor force. Consequently, they tend to reflect the conclusion that the researcher wishes to establish rather than distinctions among modes of production and relations among distinct classes. Lenin (1969:72, 77, 132-135) and Awiti (1972:17, 25) both reduce the number of "middle peasants" by assigning to the categories of "poor peasants" and "rich peasants" or "capitalist farmers" some producers whose activities are clearly similar to those of "middle peasants" rather than the "allotment-holding wage workers" and "capitalist farmers" with whom they are identified at either extreme. Shanin (1972:170-174) and Gottlieb (1972) present evidence which shows that in Russia and Tanzania the "middle peasants" made up the vast majority of peasant households. As Lenin (1969:69) himself declared, "only in proportion as [labor power] is transformed into a commodity does capitalism embrace the entire production of the country."

With the expansion of commodity production, and the availability of opportunities for wage employment outside the peasant household, labor-time itself acquires a cash value. Conventional arrangements for the mobilization of labor break down, and neighbors and strangers are employed for wages to supplement family labor. For their part, the employees may supplement the products and incomes from their own farms by wage employment. Thus we are no longer dealing with Chayanov's ideal peasant-farm, from which the very principle of wage labor is excluded. Nor are we dealing with Marx's and Weber's free wage capitalism in which the producer has no access to his own means of production. (See Lenin, 1969:181.)

Employment for wages, both within and outside the rural economy, may provide a source of cash income and of savings which are then reinvested in the establishment of peasant holdings. Migrant workers may be able to earn cash incomes in periods when their labor is not required on their home farms (Feldman, 1969:109; Berry, 1975b). Migrant cocoa farmers in Western Nigeria finance the purchase of land and the hiring of labor to establish their own farms with savings from wage employment on others' farms (Berry, 1975b). Boesen (1972), and Madsen (1972) show how, during a specific period in their life cycle, young men are faced with demands for cash income to pay both for daily necessities and for such investments as a dowry (the main means of acquiring farm labor) and the land on which to establish their own cash crops. Young men who have completed periods of apprenticeship as craftsmen earn wages to purchase the equipment necessary for their business. Thus the use of wage labor does not necessarily presuppose the existence of a landless proletariat or even of allotment-holders tied for a lifetime to wage employment because of the lack of other sources of income. Aggregate figures for Russia, before and after the Revolution, as well as for contemporary Tanzania, reveal few proletarians outside plantations and state farms. This is not incompatible with periods of wage employment by peasants, especially younger men (Lenin, 1969:160. Shanin, 1972:170-171; Gottlieb, 1972). Wage employment, like inequality, may be integrated into peasant production rather than become a feature of the "self-evident" transition from peasant to capitalist farming. The "self-evident" nature of this transition stems from the identification of the "forces of production" with "technology" (Cliffe, forthcoming; see also Li, 1973). It is assumed that larger units of production can take advantage of economies of scale over a range which extends beyond the size of the largest peasant landholdings. This enables wealthier farmers to take advantage of advanced technology and of a more complex division of labor in the organization of production. For this reason, "efficient" capitalist producers are assumed to be able to displace "backward" peasants, and the reorganization of production along cooperative lines is assumed to offer unquestionable advantages to peasant producers (Lenin, 1969:140; Nyerere, 1969:345; Tanzania, 1969:26; Nigeria, 1973).

Undoubtedly there are cumulative advantages accruing to the better-off in a rural economy as in any other. As we have already seen, wealthier farmers have greater access on more favorable terms to the whole range of productive resources than do the rural poor. They apply these resources more effectively and market their products on more favorable terms. There are also evident advantages in cooperation in certain productive activities. The opening up of new land for settlement demands either the employment of machines and hired labor by capitalist farmers or the cooperation of settlers in clearing land and establishing settlements. Cooperative labor can build roads and other public facilities. Cooperation may offer economies of scale in storage, marketing, and access to public resources. The range over which such economies exist will vary for each activity (Feldman and Feldman, 1969).

Nevertheless, peasants survive the development of capitalism and the expansion of commodity relations because of their ability to deliver goods to consumers at lower prices than capitalists. They have adapted production to take advantage of new opportunities and to integrate changes into the peasant economy. Peasants benefit from their knowledge of the local environment. They are able to combine the production of different crops with symbiotic ecological features and complementary requirements for labor and other inputs. They are knowledgeable about the availability and relative costs, including opportunity costs, of local resources and can adapt decisions to the requirements of particular farms and localities. Labor is provided by family members at no marginal cost, except in additional drudgery to the household, and by temporary employment of hired labor for peak periods (Chayanov, 1966; Jones, 1960).

Innovations can be integrated into existing patterns of production. Existing social institutions can be used to acquire cash funds, labor, and land and to regulate the provision of these resources (Berry, 1975a, 1975b). The introduction of new crops and methods may be combined with older, tried methods for the production of subsistence crops, thus enabling farmers to experiment with new possibilities while ensuring their own security (Ruthenberg, 1968:245, 331-332, 344; Madsen, 1972:38; Feldman, 1969:105-106). Unlike wage earners who rely on their employers to provide their means of subsistence, peasants must save out of their income and invest that saving in order to sustain their own source of livelihood. Thus contrary to the prejudices of many economists, peasant producers have high marginal and average rates of savings. (See Galetti, 1956:471-475, 595-597; Upton, 1967:42; Okurume, 1969:91-92; Warriner, 1939:163.)

The management of capitalist and state farms and of state schemes for settlements and cooperative cultivation incurs high costs for items which are not required by peasant households or met more cheaply within them. High salaries are paid to officials, managers, and technicians, and the wages are paid in advance of the sale of the product of labor. Settlers on state schemes are paid a subsistence allowance to tide them over until the first, or even subsequent, harvests. The provision of housing and of social facilities, often the major incentive to settlers, is a further prior charge on the future income of the enterprise. Outsiders have all too often misunderstood local conditions and sought to apply rules and examples without due regard for the advice of peasants, the availability and complementarity of local resources, and the burden of labor on the prospective returns to innovation. It is not financed out of earnings, as in peasant communities. (See Wood, 1950; Frankel, 1953; Baldwin, 1957; Olatunbosun, 1967; Wells, 1967; Laurent, 1968; Ruthenberg, 1968; Cliffe and Cunningham, 1973; Raikes, 1975.)

Mechanized inputs, whose superior yields are held to justify more authoritarian forms of labor organization, are often too costly to justify the improved
returns they bring, if any. Equipment, spare parts, and repairs must be paid for;
skilled workers must be employed to operate and maintain machines; and
complementary inputs of unskilled labor must be employed to prepare land for
plowing and to weed plowed lands (Wood, 1950; Frankel, 1953; Baldwin, 1957).
Other costs may include the exclusion of intercropping of other crops, the
expense of fertilizers to maintain soil fertility, and the loss of both topsoil and
the cover for the land. Capitalist farmers tend to treat the land as a source of
profit, which can be reinvested in other activities, so that they may have less
incentive than peasants to maintain soil fertility (Awiti, 1972; see also Warriner,
1939:149-150). Wage earners do not share the peasant's commitment to his
work since they do not own the product. Peasants regard state-managed settlements and cooperatives as "government farms" and consider work on these
schemes as work for the government, and subsistence allowances to settlers as
low wages (Baldwin, 1957; Freyhold, 1973).

Peasants have initiated a variety of cooperative activities. These have usually
been undertaken for specific tasks, over specific periods, to supplement household production or to develop resources for household use. Communal systems
for allocating resources have been widely used, but as a means of regulating
access to resources among individual households. Plans for cooperative labor
flounder when no clear relation can be established between an individual's
earnings and the effort and efficiency of his work (Hill, 1963; Feldman, 1969).

Cooperation imposed from above has rarely recouped its administrative costs
in increased output. In some cases, the more powerful members of a community
have turned it to private advantage. It has rarely enhanced the well-being of its
members. Usually it has subjected peasants to outside direction and confirmed
peasant suspicion of state plans. Peasants resist outsiders' plans to change the
countryside not out of an obtuse conservatism, but because of a clear and
comprehensible preference for a way of life which allows them the freedom to
manage their own resources. They will not welcome schemes for cooperation
without clear evidence that the schemes will bring material benefits and improve
their way of life, rather than destroy it.

Studies of social mobility (Chayanov, 1966; Shanin, 1971, 1972; Hill, 1970;
Berry, 1975a; Boesen, 1972) within and between generations in peasant communities have revealed tendencies which counteract "short-term spirals of
relative affluence or poverty" (Hill, 1970:152) and contain peasant social
differentiation within the broad parameters of an unequal peasant society.

Accumulations of wealth in one generation are rarely passed on to the next in
the form of large landholdings. A wealthy farmer tends to have several wives and
many sons, none of whom inherit the whole of his property or household
including the ability to command and organize the labor of its members. While
larger households tend to divide, smaller households may merge (Shanin, 1971,
1972; Hill, 1970; Berry, 1975a). Extreme poverty within rural communities is

attributed to the individual misfortunes to which poor people are always vulnerable. Lack of family labor is the most common circumstance cited in a Russian study and a Nigerian study. This in turn may be occasioned by illness or natural disasters. The downward spiral into extreme poverty involves the isolation of the individual from a household—and by the same token the extinction of the household (Shanin, 1972:172; Hill, 1970:147).

The size of peasant households tends through division, merger, and extinction to regress to the modal size. This is not just a product of rules of inheritance and the imperative of cultural tradition. It reflects the limited advantages of expansion of scale beyond the means of the peasant household, which do not outweigh the benefits of an equitable division of household resources that is essential to cooperation in developing the household economy.

The process of merger and division also depends on the relative advantages of employment, income, and profit in the urban economy relative to farming. Poor farmers will migrate to seek opportunities elsewhere if either land or wage employment is available. Wealthier men will seek to educate their children to give them access to the benefits of salaried employment or will establish themselves or their children in trade. Both salaried employment and trading offer opportunities for monopolistic advantages to those who can get access to formal education at a relatively high level or can corner trading opportunities. Such advantages can only be established in farming if peasant farmers can be forcibly excluded from access to the land. State taxes and spending tend to transfer resources and thus opportunities out of the rural into the urban areas. Thus rich peasants may not pass on protocapitalist farming enterprises to their sons, but they can pass on access to education and to commerical opportunities, so that their sons can become bureaucrats and urban entrepreneurs. Capitalist farming can only be introduced to develop new areas of cultivation, often at the cost of pastoralists and the expansion of peasant cultivation, or by measures to eliminate peasant competition. Socialist programs for the proletarian management of agricultural estates require expropriation of peasants or landlords and the exclusion of peasants from the seizure of landed estates. (See Lenin, Collected Works, 13:430-431.) It may be easier to leave the business of agricultural production in peasant hands, and exploit them rather than overcome peasant resistance.

Both capitalist and socialist development strategies require peasants to provide the resources necessary for the development of the urban, industrial economy (Helleiner, 1966:140; Preobrazhenskii, 1965). Peasant households control and manage their means of production, thus allowing them a measure of autonomy vis-à-vis other classes. This autonomy must be broken down if peasant production is to be adapted to the requirements of urban, industrial capital formation and state development planning. Peasants must be made dependent on external markets and power-holders for access to the resources which come to be necessary to their way of life, or they must be coerced into organizing production to meet external requirements.

The surplus value of peasant labor can be appropriated by control of the exchange relations through which the value of the product is realized. Peasants can limit the rate of exploitation to the extent that they can switch production from one crop to another and from production for exchange to direct consumption, and they can seek out alternative buyers and sellers of commodities. State marketing monopolies allow the state to determine the rate of exploitation according to its own priorities. State monopolies reflect an authoritarian belief in the virtues of state regulation of commerce and production and state direction of resources and opportunities—a belief common to colonial administrators and their successors and shared with the bureaucrats of tsarist Russia and Stalin and his successors. State monopolies have been used as instruments for exploiting peasants, just as the tsarists used the imposition of redemption payments and Stalin used the machine tractor stations to tax peasants. State control can be enforced on corporate communities more effectively than on isolated farmers. In tsarist Russia the redemption payments were exacted from communes; Stalin collectivized the farmers to enforce grain procurement on villages. In Tanzania, peasants have been resettled into villages so that the state can provide amenities, impose taxes, and supervise production more easily. But it lacks instruments for enforcing the compulsory delivery of crop quotas (Raikes, 1975). Conformity with official priorities and directives and provisions of economic plans can be imposed more easily when the state controls access to land, irrigation, and other resources necessary to production. Hence the continued attractions to bureaucrats, despite repeated disasters, of settlement schemes where farmers are dependent on the state for their livelihood, isolated from their communities, and subordinated to the supervision and control of officials. Coercion needs to be supplemented by incentives. Incentives are relative and may depend on the state's ability to limit alternative sources of income (Ruthenberg, 1968:347-352). The model for all subsequent settlement schemes, the Gezira, depends on management's monopoly of irrigated land to enforce the delivery of cotton from tenants (Barnett, 1975).

Capitalist and socialist strategies of so-called "primitive accumulation" either displace peasant producers to make way for capitalist or state farms or impose institutions to force peasant agriculture to deliver its tribute to the powers of advanced mechanical, social, and military technology. The underdevelopment of peasant production is the condition for the development of capitalist and state production, in the interests of the state and its beneficiaries rather than the livelihood of the people.

PEASANT POLITICS

The first priority of the colonial state was to establish itself as the ultimate source of legitimate power and to remove any rulers who failed to give it full recognition. The state ruled through local intermediaries. In return for their loyalty and the carrying out of administrative tasks the government supported them, not only in exercising authority, but in their claim to land rights, political jurisdiction, and favors for themselves and their clients (Beer and Williams, 1975; Iliffe, 1969).

When government policy shifted toward institutional reform and economic development, colonial rulers and their successors used the "progressive" elements, identified by their education, wealth, and outlook to promote "modernization" among their communities. Officials formed an alliance with local community leaders based on control of access to the resources within their respective arenas: on the one hand, there was access to the patronage, credit, office, and plain graft of public institutions (including the state, the cooperatives, and the party), and, on the other hand, there was access to land, ready cash, and influence among the community (Essang, 1970; Beer and Williams, 1975; Thoden van Velzen, 1973).

Peasants will normally adapt to the realities of institutional power and public status. Their opposition to unpopular officials and resentment toward local notables may take such forms as witchcraft accusations or campaigns for the removal of particular individuals from office, with the support of their rivals among the local elite. Objectionable state directives are met by various strategies, from sullen obedience and a formal show of cooperation to dumb insolence.

Peasants have resisted the exactions of the state, landlords, and capitalist farmers when such exactions have threatened to deprive them of the resources necessary to maintain their way of life, especially by denying them access to land and by imposing excessive and arbitrary taxation. "Middle" peasants control their own means of production and form the backbone of peasant society. They are most committed to the conservation of the peasant way of life and are the most militant in its defense. (See Alavi, 1965; Wolf, 1969; Beer and Williams, 1975.) In Africa, rural communities have resisted their subordination to the administration of the colonial state, and they have resisted state measures that force them into cash-crop cultivation, enforce labor service, and coerce them into wage employment. Successive Nigerian risings have opposed extortionate exactions by state agents and the extension of taxation in periods of worsening terms of trade for rural producers. Tanzanians and Nigerians resisted the imposition of agricultural regulations by colonial authorities. Peasant hostility was directed against government agents, notably court officials, agricultural officers, and the ubiquitous sanitary inspectors and against government institutions, courts, offices, even railways and schools. They also attacked local rulers, who were seen to support their masters rather than speak for their people, and they have attacked their local allies, usually wealthier farmers and traders (Post, 1972; Beer, 1975; Beer and Williams, 1975; Iliffe, 1969).

Conflicts within peasant communities did not arise out of the internal differentiation of peasant society. They arose out of the primary contradiction between peasants and the state, and the resistance of peasants to state exactions which threatened their way of life. Local rulers, traders, and wealthy farmers were attacked and even killed because in such conflicts they were loyal ultimately to their protectors, the state, rather than to their own communities.

Peasants resistance has been able to redress specific grievances, such as excessive taxation or agricultural regulations. Peasants have not ended their dependence on external markets and subordination to the state, but they have imposed limitations on their own exploitation. Nor have peasants ended the domination of rural communities by a "bloc" of officials, traders, and farmers or intervened effectively in the routine process of resource allocation, except as clients of influential patrons (Beer, 1975).

Peasants have not usually sought to transform their society either along lines of their own choosing or on the lines willed for them by socialist intellectuals. They have sought to defend their gains within the frontiers of peasant society, but have not acted of their own accord to seize state power and thus control the instrument of their own exploitation. This is not because of their lack of imagination or their inability to acquire an appropriate political consciousness. It stems from two sources. First, peasants lack any clear evidence that a transformation of their way of life along capitalist or socialist lines will ensure their security, improve their well-being, and extend their independence—and they find considerable evidence to the contrary. Second, not only do they lack the resources necessary to conquer the state; they even lack the means of gaining access to its administration. In particular, African peasants lack access to the literate culture through which the contemporary state is administered and legitimated. They do not command the technology with which industrial production, together with many of the exchange and marketing activities necessary to the prosperity of the rural economy, are carried out. They do not wish to withdraw from the market economy and bring into being a vision of a precapitalist community. They therefore remain committed to the institutions which are the means of their exploitation and oppression.

Peasants will stand up for themselves when they are forced to reject external domination and to unite with an urban revolutionary movement which is forced to rely on the peasants for the prosecution of the revolutionary struggle. As Cabral (1969:70) directed his comrades in Guinea:

> Always bear in mind that the people are not fighting for ideas, for the things in anyone's head. They are fighting to win material benefits, to live better, and in peace, to see their lives go forward, to guarantee the future of their children.

Mao Tse-tung (1974:61-83) argued that the development of heavy industry as the leading sector of the economy can only be built on an agricultural foundation. He argued for increasing investment in agriculture and light industry, lightening of the burden of agricultural taxation, and establishment of favorable prices for agricultural in relation to industrial goods. The development of agriculture and light industry provides markets for heavy industry and also accumulates investment funds for heavy industry more rapidly than heavy industry itself. But most importantly, agriculture and light industry produce the daily necessities of the people's livelihood, which is essential if the creative and productive abilities of the people are to be mobilized to increase production. The development of agricultural production is not achieved by the development of the technical forces of production in urban industry and the donation of technical improvements to agriculture. Rather, the development of peasant production is a condition for the development of industrial production. The economy needs to "walk on two legs." But the leg of agriculture cannot support the leg of industry until policies are no longer defined for peasants by their betters, and when peasants stand up for themselves.

Cabral (1969) recognized that revolutionary victory may give the "petty bourgeoisie" control of the institutions of state power which they alone are capable of directing, thus ending their reliance on the masses. Hence the need to avoid taking over the institutions of a centralized colonial state, with its capital, presidential palace, concentrated ministries, and authoritarian change of command. In economic policy, the priority must be given to raising food production. This cannot be achieved by state direction of peasant producers, but only by encouraging peasant initiative based on their own experience and improving their own material well-being, and defending their own gains against the demands even of the revolutionary state.

REFERENCES

ALAVI, H. (1965). "Peasants and revolution." Socialist Register.
ANGWAZI, J., and NDULU, B. (1973). "An evaluation of ujamaa villages in the Rufiji." Paper presented to the East African Universities Annual Social Sciences Conference.
AWITI, A. (1972). "Class struggle in the rural society of Tanzania." Maji-Maji, 7:1-39.
BALDWIN, K.D.S. (1957). The Niger agricultural project. Oxford: Blackwell.
BARNETT, A. (1975). "The Gezira scheme: Production of cotton and the reproduction of underdevelopment." In I. Oxaal, T. Barnett, and D. Booth (eds.), Beyond the sociology of development. London: Routledge and Kegan Paul.
BEER, C.E.F. (1975). The politics of peasant groups in Western Nigeria. Ibadan: Ibadan University Press.
BEER, C.E.F., and WILLIAMS, G. (1975). "The politics of the Ibadan peasantry." African Review, 5.
BERRY, S.S. (1975a). "Export growth, entrepreneurship and class formation in rural western Nigeria." In R.E. Dummett and L. Brainherd (eds.), Problems of rural development. Leiden: E.J. Brill.
——— (1975b). Cocoa, custom and socio-economic change in rural western Nigeria. Oxford: Clarendon Press.
BOESEN, J. (1972). Development and class structure in a smallholder society and the potential of ujamaa. Copenhagen: Institute for Development Research.
CABRAL, A. (1969). Revolution in Guinea. London: Stage 1.
CHAYANOV, A.V. (1966). The theory of peasant economy (D. Thorner et al., trans.). Homewood, Ill.: R.D. Irwin.
CLIFFE, L. (1972a). "Nationalism and the reaction to enforced agricultural change in Tanganyika during the colonial period." In L. Cliffe and J.S. Saul (eds.), Socialism in Tanzania (2 vols.). Nairobi: East African Publishing House.
——— (1972b). "Planning rural development." Development and Change, 3(3):78-98.
——— (1972c). "The policy of ujamaa vijijini and the class struggle in Tanzania." In L. Cliffe and J.S. Saul (eds.), Socialism in Tanzania (2 vols.). Nairobi: East African Publishing House.
——— (forthcoming). "The method of political economy and socialist practice in rural Tanzania."
CLIFFE, L., and CUNNINGHAM, G.L. (1973). "Ideology, organisation and the settlement experience in Tanzania." In L. Cliffe and J.S. Saul (eds.), Socialism in Tanzania (2 vols.). Nairobi: East African Publishing House.

COULSON, A. (1975). "The evolution of rural policies in Tanzania." Review of African Political Economy, 3:53-58.

ESSANG, S.M. (1970). "The distribution of earnings in the cocoa economy of western Nigeria." Unpublished Ph.D. thesis, Michigan State University.

FELDMAN, D. (1969). "The economics of ideology." In C. Leys (ed.), Politics and change in developing countries. London: Cambridge University Press.

FELDMAN, D., and FELDMAN, R. (1969). Co-operation and the production environment (No. 69:12). Dar es Salaam: Economic Research Bureau.

FRANKEL, S.H. (1953). The economic impact on underdeveloped societies. London: Oxford University Press.

FREYHOLD, M. von (1973). "Government staff and ujamaa villages." Paper presented to the East African Universities Annual Social Science Conference.

GALETTI, R., et al. (1956). Nigerian cocoa farmers. London: Oxford University Press.

GOTTLIEB, M. (1972). "The extent and character of differentiation in Tanzanian agriculture and rural society, 1967-1969." Paper presented to the East African Universities Social Sciences Conference.

HELLEINER, G.K. (1966). Peasant agriculture, growth and economic development in Nigeria. Homewood, Ill.: R.D. Irwin.

HILL, P. (1963). Migrant cocoa farmers of southern Ghana. London: Cambridge University Press.

––– (1970). Studies in rural capitalism. London: Cambridge University Press.

HOPKINS, A.G. (1973). An economic history of West Africa. London: Longmans.

ILIFFE, J. (1969). "Tanzania under German and British rule." In L. Cliffe and J.S. Saul (eds.), Socialism in Tanzania (2 vols.). Nairobi: East African Publishing House.

JONES, W.O. (1960). "Economic man in Africa." Food Research Institute Studies, 1:107-134.

LAURENT, C.K. (1968). Investment in Nigerian tree crops. East Lansing and Ibadan: C.S.N.R.D. 18.

LENIN, V.I. (1907). "Preface" to the second edition of Lenin.

––– (1960-1970). Collected works (45 vols.). Moscow: Progress Publishers.

––– (1969). The development of capitalism in Russia. New York: Beekman Publishers.

LI CHENG (1973). "Theory of productive forces." Peking Review, 30(November 11-15).

MADSEN, B.S. (1972). A preliminary report on socio-economic patterns in an urbanised rural area and the response to planned development. Copenhagen: Institute for Development Research.

MAO TSE-TUNG (1965). Selected readings. Peking: Foreign Languages Press.

––– (1974). Mao Tse Tung unrehearsed (ed. S. Schram). Harmondsworth: Penguin.

MARX, K. (1963). Selected writings in sociology and social philosophy. Harmondsworth: Penguin.

––– (1969). Selected works (3 vols.). Moscow: Progress Publishers.

––– (1974). Capital. London: Lawrence and Wishart.

MOODY, T. (1972). Mapinduzi Majani: The Bukoba tea scheme. Copenhagen: Institute for Development Studies.

MOORE, B. (1966). Social origins of dictatorship and democracy. Boston: Beacon Press.

MUSOKE, I.K.S. (1971). "Building socialism in Bukoba." In J.E. Proctor (ed.), Building ujamaa villages in Tanzania. Dar es Salaam: Tanzania Publishing House.

Nigeria (1973). Guidelines for the third national development plan, 1975-80. Lagos: Government Printer.

NYERERE, J.K. (1969). Freedom and socialism. Nairobi: Oxford University Press.

––– (1973). Freedom and development. Nairobi: Oxford University Press.

OKURUME, G.E. (1969). The food crop economy in Nigerian agricultural policy. East Lansing and Ibadan: C.S.N.R.D. 31.

OLATUNBOSUN, D. (1967). Nigerian farm settlements and school leaver's farms. East Lansing and Ibadan: C.S.N.R.D. 9.

OLATUNBOSUN, D., and OLAYIDE, S.O. (1971). Effects of the marketing boards on the output and income of primary producers. Ibadan: N.I.S.E.R. International Conference on the Marketing Board System.

POST, K.W.J. (1972). " 'Peasantisation' and rural political movements in western Nigeria." Archives Européenes de Sociologie, 13(2):223-254.

PREOBRAZHENSKII, E.A. (1965). The new economics (B. Pierce, trans.). Oxford: Clarendon Press.
RAIKES, P. (1975). "Ujamaa vijijini and rural socialist development." Review of African Political Economy, 3:33-52.
REDFIELD, R. (1956). Peasant society and culture. Chicago: University of Chicago Press.
RUTHENBERG, H. (1968). Smallholder farming and smallholder development in Tanzania. Munich: Weltforum Verlag.
SAUL, J.S. (1971). "Marketing co-operatives in a developing country." in L. Cliffe and J.S. Saul (eds.), Socialism in Tanzania (2 vols.). Nairobi: East African Publishing House.
SHANIN, T. (1971). "Socio-economic mobility and the rural history of Russia, 1905-30." Soviet Studies, 23(2):222-235.
——— (1972). The awkward class. Oxford: Clarendon Press.
TANU (1967). The Arusha declaration. Dar es Salaam: Government Printers.
——— (1973a). Guidelines on guarding, consolidating and advancing the revolution of Tanzania and of Africa. In C.G. Widstrand (ed.), Tre dokument fran Tanzania. Uppsala: Nordiska Afrikan Institutet.
——— (1973b). "Siasi ni kilimo." In C.G. Widstrand (ed.), Tre dokument fran Tanzania. Uppsala: Nordiska Afrikan Institutet.
Tanzania (1966). Report of the presidential special committee of enquiry into the co-operative movement and marketing boards. Dar es Salaam: Government Printers.
——— (1969). Five year development plan, 1969-74. Dar es Salaam: Government Printers.
THODEN VAN VELZEN, H. (1973). "Staff, kulaks and peasants." In L. Cliffe and J.S. Saul (eds.), Socialism in Tanzania (2 vols.). Nairobi: East African Publishing House.
UPTON, M. (1967). Agriculture in south western Nigeria. University of Reading Department of Agricultural Economics.
WARRINER, D. (1939). The economics of peasant farming. Oxford: Oxford University Press.
WELLS, J.C. (1967). Government agricultural investment in Nigeria. Ann Arbor and Ibadan: University of Michigan and N.I.S.E.R.
WIDSTRAND, C.G. (1970). Co-operative and rural development in East Africa. Uppsala: Institute of African Studies.
WILLIAMS, G. (ed., 1975). Nigeria: economy and society. London: Rex Collings.
WOLF, E.R. (1969). "On peasant rebellions." International Social Science Journal, 21:286-293.
WOOD, A. (1950). The groundnut affair. London: Bodley Head.

6

FROM PEASANTS TO WORKERS IN AFRICA

ROBIN COHEN
University of Birmingham

The very title of this chapter will surely provoke dissent from those who consider that the social categories employed are misleading or inappropriate in the African context. "Peasants" is a term resisted by scholars who associate its etymology with medieval Europe and its contemporary usage with Latin America and Asia, but who prefer, in Africa, to use "tribesmen," "rural cultivators," "small farmers," and the like. "Workers" is a more neutral term, since in itself it implies little organization or consciousness. The denotations "proletariat" or "working class" do of course imply both these elements, but they also imply a higher degree of social differentiation along economic lines than many scholars would at present be prepared to accord to the African situation. I do not myself hesitate to use such terminology, because I wish to lay emphasis on two pitfalls which, I believe, the conservative position on this matter pays scant heed to. One is the tendency to place concepts in an historical deep freeze, embalmed around a particular historical conjuncture. conditioned by an image of an ideal or pure form of the social object. A purist position can take no account of a changing context within which a previous identification of a social category finds a new expression. Ours is not, of course, a totally similar expression but one which is close enough to draw illustrative and meaningful comparisons—comparisons which may indeed serve to illumine the parameters both of the new and of the older contexts. The second pitfall in a purist position is an incapacity to comprehend the processual character involved in all social change. Thus categories are rejected out of hand because they fail to conform in every respect, or in what are deemed essential respects. to an idealized reconstruction in the mind of the scholar. The charge of ethnocentricity often directed against those who would wish to employ general sociological concepts, particularly Marxian ones, in their appraisal of African data can in fact more accurately be leveled against those who wish to isolate European or North American experiences from the mainstream of common social processes. The origins of Africanist scholarship are rooted in a pursuit of the exotic folklore of peoples previously unknown to Western experience, and this tradition is still conventionally manifested in a constant insistence on the situationally specific and unique feature of African data.

The perspective adopted here is deliberately general and macroscopic. It focuses on two interrelated social processes—those of peasantization and proletarianization—processes that take different forms, but that are common to all societies, with the exception only of the most isolated and small-scale units (which, in any case, are fast disappearing from the face of the earth). The process of peasantization refers essentially to the widening and depersonalization of market relations consequent to the introduction of a pervasive cash economy and a colonial state (see Post, 1973). But the close connection that I shall seek to establish between the processes of peasantization and proletarianization suggests that there are more general dynamic forces (specified, for the moment, simply as the introduction and spread of capitalist social relations) which set *both* processes in train more or less simultaneously. The problem under review is thus conceived not as a continuum from an original condition of "peasanthood" to one which contains a fully fledged proletariat, but, on the contrary, as a dynamic form of social change impelled partly from internal factors, but largely from homonomic external factors which propel each ongoing chain of processes. The "chains" of proletarianization and peasantization—like breeding chains in a nuclear reactor—proceed at differential rates, with differing degrees of intensity and completeness and with a greater or lesser level of internal differentiation. Proletarianization is, however, imminent in peasantization in that the former represents a branch or side chain originating in the displacement and undermining of precapitalist modes of production (see Gutkind, 1974:5).

Further amplification of the notions just outlined is provided below: here I wish merely to note the continuing elements of interconnectedness between the two major chains, seen, for example in the development of a small rural proletariat and, par excellence, in the persistence of migrant labor even in the areas of the most intensive capitalist development like the South African gold mines.

THE EMERGENCE OF WAGE LABOR

The creation of a stable wage-labor force in Africa is essentially a product of white settlement and the establishment of European colonial administrations. Yet, as Sandbrook and Cohen have argued (1975), the organized expropriation of labor power had also been widespread in indigenous societies. Various forms of chattel and domestic slavery existed in many precolonial states; customary family labor was common, while itinerant groups of workers, like the *aro* age groups of Yorubaland or the *ankofone* of Sierra Leone, engaged in house building or heavy farming on an essentially contractual basis (International Labour Office, 1962:65-66). In contemporary Senegal certainly, and perhaps elsewhere too, this type of labor survives in the following form. A group of young men tour the farms of the wealthier peasants when heavy brush needs to be cleared, the land tilled, seeds sown, or the crop harvested. In earlier days the toilers would be content with a generous feast provided by the farmers, plus perhaps a token payment in cash or kind. Nowadays the laborers are hired in advance, the cost of their transport met and an agreed payment made. In essence, this was a localized relationship that became both more structured and more institutionalized as the mode of payment moved in harmony with shifts in the means of exchange. Equally, however, with the introduction of a pervasive cash economy, large movements of seasonal labor over vast distances became common—for example, in groundnut farming in West Africa. Here again piecework payments (plus shelter and food) developed as a norm, but this time between employer and employees with no interpersonal or consanguinial relationship.

Within precolonial cities, craft traditions and guilds were well established, most of them involving the use of apprentice labor. In Liberia too, the Americo-Liberian settlers used "apprentices" as cheap farm labor. In 1887 it was estimated that every Americo-Liberian had six to eight youths in service, while the president of the republic alone employed 120 "apprentices."

In short, the idea of precolonial African societies comprising a set of autarchic communities, "primitive communalist" if you will, is very misleading. Nonetheless, the colonial administrators in the early years of colonial rule found it difficult to displace surplus labor and to recruit sufficient laborers with the qualities they wanted and at the price they were willing to pay. Of course some colonial authorities did not attempt to introduce a free labor market and developed instead brutal policies of forced labor (notoriously so in German South West Africa, Oubangi-Shari, and the Belgium Congo). The French did not abolish *prestation,* a labor tax which compelled adult males to work for a number of days a year, until 1946; while the British, although far less culpable in this respect, nonetheless used unfree labor in the production of essential war supplies, like Nigerian tin, during the Second World War.

Where the buying and selling of labor did take place, administrators (Governors McCallam and Lugard of Lagos are examples) were wont to complain about the supposed idleness and cost of African labor, particularly in comparison to Indian labor. As a consequence, several schemes were either contemplated or undertaken to introduce farm labor from outside the continent. The Indian indentured laborers on the Natal sugar plantations were the largest group of imported laborers, but Chinese constituted 27% of the labor force in the South African gold mines in 1905, while small groups of workers from the Caribbean were also contracted, particularly for work on the railways. Neither forced labor nor recruitment from abroad could, however, meet the demand for labor in the long term. Africans therefore had to be induced by force or persuasion to sell their own labor power. Conquest and the dispossession of land rights, notably in Kenya, southern Africa, and the Rhodesias, began the process; the imposition of hut and poll taxes more generally completed it.

The chains of proletarianization and peasantization are rooted essentially in these policies. Those Africans who remained on the land gradually became incorporated into the remains of the old mercantilist system and then, later, the world capitalist system. In some places African farmers were initially able to successfully respond to the new commercial opportunities and wider internal markets that were opened up by white settlement: African farmers around the Witwatersrand area, for example, took the lion's share of food production in the nineteenth century supplied to the white uitlanders, until they were forced out by political discrimination. But, for the most part, incorporation into the world capitalist market produced a set of "greenhouse" economies. Regional mono-cultures, determined by the needs of the colonial system became common; production was oriented to the external market; and the appropriation of the surplus (in the form of export dues and the difference between the local price paid and the price commanded on the world market) was controlled by the colonial authorities and foreign enterprises. The process by which the com-mercialization of agriculture took place concentrated both agricultural pro-duction on a limited number of products and disrupted the capacity of indige-nous economies to absorb labor.

It was the creation of a landless group of rural dwellers, a group who also could no longer meet the cash demands of the colonial administration, who provided the making of an embryonic proletariat. A continuous and stable labor supply nonetheless remained a problem for the colonial state until the 1930s, for one major reason—colonial governments refused to pay unskilled laborers at a sufficiently attractive rate. Virtually from their inception, government wage rates in British West Africa remained unchanged until the late thirties, while in South Africa real wages in agriculture and in the mines actually fell from 1890 to 1970, when agitation by black miners finally forced an increase. The failure to recruit unskilled labor up to the 1930s had little or nothing to do with the Africans' unfamiliarity with wage labor or their lack of commitment: rather, the conditions and type of work offered and the rate of remuneration were the major disincentives involved.

Colonial administrators cared little for such realities. First, they wanted labor on the cheap, and they considered often that they were offering a "just" wage. Second, many administrators operated with the now discredited theory of a backward-bending supply curve of labor—that is, the notion that demand and consumption patterns were inelastic and that the supply of labor would dry up if income targets were reached too early. Third, in some places where labor was being employed in the production of export crops—for example, palm oil—administrators did not want to divert agricultural labor by making government labor in the towns too attractive a prospect. Problems of labor recruitment only disappeared in the 1930s due to the effects of the worldwide depression. As

Elliot Berg argues, "The depression of the 1930's marked the turning point. It radically changed conditions in the labour market; with the prices of primary products sinking to new lows, the volume of wage employment contracted sharply. Perhaps for the first time in most African countries, there were more men offering themselves for wage employment than there were jobs to be had" (Berg, 1965:412).

By the 1930s the chains of proletarianization and peasantization were considerably advanced. Within the cities of colonial Africa, a stabilized proletariat came into existence—particularly on public works programs, in the mines, in the building of roads and railways, and in the development of harbor and port facilities. Other than unskilled "general" labor, as it was called, colonial governments had additional manpower needs in accord with their *etatist* character. Soldiers, clerks, court stenographers, sanitary inspectors, policemen, and messengers all serviced this need for local manpower to prop up the *pax colonica*. But before discussing the forms of social consciousness, identity, and organization which grew up among such workers, we shall follow the chain of peasantization for a while longer.

MIGRANT LABOR

A circular movement of migrant labor is involved, as numbers of the labor force shifted off the land (initially in response to the repressive policies of the colonial and white settler regime and later also in response to the "pull" factors of the city) to join the chain of proletarianization. Many of course did so only seasonally, or for temporary contracts, but over the years the rate of return to the rural areas declined. The reasons for this are manifold, but three factors may be suggested. First, though this process is still far from complete, production in the rural areas shifted slowly out of the hands of the community into individual peasant proprietorship. Second, employment opportunities in the cities opened up as industry and administration expanded. Expansion rarely was sufficient to meet job demands, but social aspirations deriving partly from the expansion of education remained high and many unemployed workers prefer to stay in the towns. Finally, the degree of impoverishment which became common in many African rural economies meant that a return to the land was in any case unfeasible for most migrants.

The contemporary patterns of in-migration to the cities are clear. Demographers have noted an upward shift in the median age of town dwellers, while many scholars have commented on the huge and growing pool of unemployed or casually employed labor in the cities and the associated growth of shantytowns and slum conditions. Such an outcome was, as is argued below, entirely consistent with the policies of labor recruitment inaugurated in the colonial period. But leaving aside this general issue for the moment, the trends of city growth noted above all suggest that the pattern of short-term migration is seriously in decay.

Only in southern Africa does an efficient and institutionalized use of migrant labor survive, and this too is showing signs of strain, particularly in response to recent political events on the subcontinent. A few comments on this situation may be appropriate. When the Chinese mine laborers were deported after the Boer War by the Liberal Government in Britain, the gold mines relied extensively on a system of private recruiting, often done by unscrupulous, so-called "black-birder" agents. Gradually, the mining companies combined to form a recruiting agency themselves. As the supply of suitably pliant and cheap labor from the immediate area decreased, the recruiters extended their range—into present-day Mozambique, Malawi, Lesotho, and Botswana and often further afield. It is quite fallacious to see the system of contract labor to the South African gold fields as an anachronistic survival of a precapitalist mode of production. On the contrary, it was designed and carried out precisely according to the needs of a highly capitalized extractive industry of the type involved. (That the use of migrants is not simply a survival of an anachronistic mode may incidentally be seen in Western Europe, where the very exemplars of European capitalism, Germany and Switzerland, rely considerably on migrant labor from Turkey, Italy, and other poorer areas of southern Europe). In its most intensive form in southern Africa, aircraft are chartered to the areas of supply, a medical inspection is carried out, and recruits are batched and labeled with names and destinations attached to their wrists. On arrival at the Witwatersrand, they are lectured in a common denominator patois on matters of safety, mining terminology, and so on and are housed in single-sex compounds. The latest version of this, outside Johannesburg, comprises a modern set of high-rise buildings, with strategically located gates, electronically controlled from a defensible strongpoint and capable of being brought into operation if unrest reaches alarming proportions. The "compound" architecture is San Quentin penitentiary rather than tradi-tional African. As mentioned earlier, however, this system is becoming subject to some strain as the home governments of the laborers concerned (Malawi, Botswana, and Lesotho notably) have become increasingly involved in the conditions of employment of their nationals. The government of Mozambique (which prior to 1974 supplied over one-quarter of the recruits) may also take measures to cut down on the number of recruits from its northern territories. The mining companies, aided by the huge rise in the price of gold, may be able to withstand this pressure on their labor supply and have shown an increasing willingness to pay higher wages in order to stabilize a locally recruited labor force. Large investments in research and development of labor saving devices and operations have recently been announced.

The owners of the South African gold mines, if not the South African government, are now firm converts to a policy of labor stabilization and urban residence that the Belgian Congolese authorities adopted 40 years ago. Though the Belgians have often been praised for their progressive policies on this issue, in point of fact the devastation that was wrought on the rural populations during the pacification period was so great that the Belgians were left with little alternative but to provide the means of subsistence around the areas of employment. In other parts of Africa, migrant labor was a useful source of labor supply, and its use left the rural areas just sufficiently viable to support the reproduction of labor power and the minimal welfare needs of returning laborers.

The political economy of the colonial period thus hinged on the following features: (a) a peripheral or ribbon development of capitalist enterprises around the loci of administration; (b) an appropriation of surplus agricultural wealth by the metropole at the points of distribution and marketing. The ideal situation, from the point of view of the metropole and its agents, was one in which agricultural production remained sufficiently virile to produce an exportable primary product and absorb returning migrants, but not so viable that it threatened the supply of cheap unskilled labor. Such a delicate balance was impossible to achieve and may indeed be considered one of the central contradictions of the colonial political economy. Migrant labor represented a possible resolution of this contradiction but one that was incapable of solving the ultimately incompatible ends of the colonial state. The tendency is for migrant labor, as an organized system of recruitment, to be on the decline, as the reserve army of the proletariat created by colonialism increasingly prefers a precarious existence in the towns and cities to an impoverished existence in the rural areas. Some consequences of this shift in population are explored below.

THE RURAL PROLETARIAT

Before turning to the main chain of proletarianization, a few comments on the process of rural proletarianization are in order. This element was, of course, a large one in the Caribbean, Malaysia, and parts of Latin America, where plantation economies were common. In Africa, extensive experiments with plantation agriculture were, however, for the most part unsuccessful (Hopkins, 1973:211-212). Some exceptions to this overall failure should nonetheless be noted. The use of indentured Indian labor on the Natal sugar plantations has been mentioned. In Liberia, rubber plantations of one million acres, leased for 99 years by the Firestone Rubber Company became operative in 1926. Employment of rural workers was also considerable in the Tanzanian sisal plantations, until adverse world prices for the crop forced the closure of many plantations. A considerable problem of rural unemployment has resulted. Lastly, in the Ivory Coast the local plantation interests were sufficiently important to produce a political party (the PDCI) organized to represent their interests. More recently, French commercial interests in the Ivory Coast have begun to grow citrus destined for the French market on a large scale.

Despite the absence of large numbers of plantation workers in Africa there has recently been a largely undocumented growth of a rural labor force working wholly or largely for wages. In Kenya, for example, the indigenous takeover of the so-called white highlands after independence did not foster a return to smaller units of production. If anything, the commercialization of agriculture, often undertaken by Kenyans prominent in business and industry, has produced a further stage in the growth of capitalist social relations—namely, an absentee landlord, employing an on-the-site manager who in turn supervises the farm labor. This pattern is as yet fairly rare in Africa, at least on a large farm basis, though several observers have noted that senior civil servants in West African countries are shifting their investable capital from speculative urban property to land and poultry farming. In more general terms, the degree of social differentiation already present in the countryside has been carefully explored by Polly Hill (1965, 1972). Though hostile to the concept of peasantization (she prefers instead to talk of "farmers" and "rural capitalists") her work is outstanding in shattering, to use one of her own phrases, "the myth of the amorphous peasantry." While peasant proprietorship is, in my view, becoming the dominant agricultural mode of production, at the same time the term "peasant" may conceal the vast differences in wealth, incomes, and power in the countryside. Many of the richer peasants and farmers are fast moving into the position of becoming small employers of rural labor, and it is in this area, rather than in plantations that rural proletarianization will grow.

THE UNSKILLED URBAN WORKER

While the development of rural proletarianization and differentiation has as yet merited little attention from radical scholars, the growth and characteristics of the urban worker have been more extensively commented on. Basically, a common theme in this area has been to move away from the self-interested concerns of white administrators in the problems of labor productivity, recruitment, and supply and toward an actor-directed perspective of a group groping for self-expression and the creation of a corporate identity.

Once the labor history of the continent is approached in this manner—from below rather than from above—case after case of action undertaken to defend class interests appears. Workers, in other words, are seen as active agents in the creation of their own group solidarity, consciousness, and action. As E.M. Thompson remarked of the English working class, the African working class "made itself as much as it was made."

Here I can do no more than indicate some of the lines of recent research pursued. Some authors have concentrated on describing early manifestations of strike action. Railwaymen and dockers were usually at the forefront of such events, but Hopkins (1966) has described the case of the Lagos strike of 1897, when PWD workers were the major element involved. (See also Conway, 1968; Hughes and Cohen, 1971; and chapters by Iliffe, Turner, and Allen in Sandbrook and Cohen, 1975.) More often than not, strikes in the early years of colonial rule were short-lived affairs generated in the heat of the moment; and, though frequently involving large numbers of workers across several occupational ranges, they left little in the way of an organizational imprint. The degree to which the workers concerned were aware of their class position, in itself and in relation to the dominant authority and the class structures of the colonial period, cannot easily be discerned. For the most part the degree of class consciousness involved has simply been inferred from the nature of class action, but Gutkind (1974) has forcibly argued that even in the pre-Second World War period, there is sufficient evidence in workers' petitions and in the observations of colonial officers to argue that a working-class consciousness had emerged. Naturally, an argument along such lines should not be overstated. The social universe that was comprehended was often the workplace for a localized employer-employee relationship; rarely did workers express, in the early period of colonial rule, a national, let along an international, solidarity. Other mitigating factors included a fairly sharp division of status between the unskilled workers and the members of a more respectable white-collar salariat, and the persistence in many areas of ethnic forms of identity and interaction. Where, in rare cases, the employer was an indigenous private entrepreneur, patron-client links reinforced ethnic ties and damaged the capacity of workers to organize along class lines.

The degree to which ethnicity replaced or undercut forms of social interaction based on class lines is still a contentious issue, and one which cannot fully be explored here. Suffice to say that the new studies of labor history referred to are unanimous in showing that the work relationship was a far more determinate experience than a picture of African societies divided rigidly along ethnic lines of competition can possibly allow for. For the sociologists and social anthropologists working on the copperbelt (for example, see Epstein, 1958), the diversity of the social worlds that African workers entered into and came from could be encompassed in a set of alternating models of social interaction. Basically, the theory proposed was that a worker shifted or changed his identity as new social fields or networks were encountered. But a working-class identity could shift back into ethnic forms of consciousness once the stimuli or environment of industrial employment had been removed. The theory in its cruder forms was far too mechanistic and in point of fact rested on an ideal-typical model of the circular flow of migrant labor from, and back to, the rural areas. But as Epstein recognized, insofar as industrial employment assumed a permanent character both in the lifetime of any one individual and as an irremovable mode of production, the forms of social consciousness and organization that grew up had to move more or less in harness with the changing economic realities.

The chain of proletarianization has been discussed in relation to the growth of class consciousness and in relation to class action. The third necessary component is that of organization. It is clear that strike action has to have a degree of organization behind it, but it is less clear that workers were able prior to 1945 to organize bodies—that is, trade unions—to defend or promote their interests in a sustained fashion. Though it has been customary to argue that an organizational hiatus existed in most African countries prior to 1945, this view has to be somewhat modified. In Nigeria and Ghana, an examination of archival and newspaper evidence reveals the existence of many worker organizations, some of them, to be sure, being moribund or ineffective for much of their existence (Hughes and Cohen, 1971; Cohen, 1973). In South Africa the Industrial and Commercial Union, organized in the interwar period, mobilized large numbers of African workers until its demise.

After 1945, the pace of proletarianization was considerably advanced. Absolute numbers of workers who were engaged in full-time employment increased considerably, while the struggles that workers were engaged in to increase their pay or ameliorate the conditions of their employment became enmeshed in a more general anticolonial movement. There is considerable controversy in the literature as to how involved the trade unions were in the nationalist movements or the degre to which they were able to maintain an organizational independence apart from the elite-controlled political parties. Such questions are only of interest in this context in two respects. First, insofar as the unions were able to mobilize a popular base in the postwar period outside the confines of their membership, this base was not a sufficiently strong one to challenge the basis of legitimacy that the parties laid claim to. Proletarianization had not in other words proceeded so totally as to allow the proletariat to act as the "general representatives" of the society at large. Second, and this is the other side of the coin, the trade unions had just sufficient organizational coherence and popularity not to be ignored by the nationalist politicians.

In a sense, the period from 1945 until the independence of most black African territories was one in which a temporary and often fitful class alliance was forged between the indigenous bourgeoisies and the organized working class. This cooperation rarely penetrated to levels below that of formalized structures (parties and unions) that organized each class, except on occasions like election days and rallies when the politicians needed a suitable display of mass support or acquiescence to use in their negotiations with the colonial authorities and in their construction of a neocolonial state. Nonetheless a substratum of worker radicalism, particularly at the rank-and-file level, survived throughout this period and was to dramatically resurrect itself in the postcolonial period.

MANAGERS, PROFESSIONALS, AND BUREAUCRATS

Lest anyone be misled into thinking that all those who sell their labor power in African societies can be considered as part of an exploited working class, some comments can be made on those in the higher echelons of salaried employment.

In this category I include members of the civil service in senior staff positions, those who work in private industry or public corporations on the managerial side and those, like government doctors and university lecturers, who are employed on the public purse (I exclude professionals like lawyers and private doctors who work on an individual contractual basis). Though not normally discussed in descriptions of African labor issues, this group does merit some comment in its own right, for three reasons. First, civil servants, in particular, are often well organized, especially in Francophone African countries. In Dahomey, for example, civil servants were able to effect upward salary increases during successive military and civilian regimes which amounted at one point to two-thirds of the national budget. Second, the salariat are often in a situation where their skills can be bought or sold internationally. Their reference groups tend, therefore, to be located outside the countries they live in. (Nigerian university lecturers, for example, went out on strike in 1973 and used United Kingdom university pay scales in pursuit of their demands.) If successful, such pay claims serve to further widen the normally high wage differentials. They may then produce a demonstration effect downwards in the form of a felt sense of relative deprivation by other workers in the society, a deprivation that it may not be easy to satisfy within the framework of a postcolonial state. Third, the social and political role of the group identified can be seen as parasitical on other segments of the society and instrumental in serving the ends of neoimperialism either as direct employees of the state or as auxiliaries of the external estate (the foreign powers and interests that dominate most African countries and are located at the metropole). The group concerned are often trained in metropolitan institutions imbued with Western tastes and prejudices, or in local institutions heavily penetrated by the influences of the external estate. They are, in short, a true labor aristocracy, a term which has been misleadingly applied (Arrighi and Saul, 1973) to all workers engaged in selling their labor power above the level of what they call a semiproletarianized peasantry. I would myself resist such a blanket dismissal of the African working class (but, for a modified position, see Saul in Sandbrook and Cohen, 1975). On the other hand, there is no doubt that there does exist a reactionary element in the top echelons of those in employment, who are so close to the occupiers of the seats of power that they are virtually indistinguishable from them.

OTHER URBAN MIGRANTS

If a common thread of organizational endeavor, class consciousness, and class action can be traced throughout the colonial period in the case of wage laborers, the same cannot be said for other dispossessed segments of the urban social structure. Once the chains of proletarianization and peasantization became fully operative, many Africans migrating to the cities found themselves either without employment of any kind or in a situation in which what few opportunities existed were incommensurate with their aspirations or job expectations. Some accommodated themselves to a socially disapproved existence as pimps, touts, prostitutes, or thieves, living often at the margins of subsistence or preying, like parasites, at what few pickings a capital city of an impoverished country can offer. Others swelled the ranks of those who staff the industries, small trades, and services that blanket the landscape of any African city. Workshops run by masters and apprentices cover every possible small-scale need—from photography to the making of farmers' machetes, the making of low-cost furniture, or tire-retreading. This sector of the urban economy, described often nowadays as the "informal sector," in fact accounts for a considerable degree of urban employment. Several writers, notably Keith Hart (1973), have demonstrated how useful and important the informal sector is to the national economy. It is a sector which operates without government subsidies, tax concessions, low-interest loans, or other incentives that governments have provided primarily to attract foreign capital and industrial investment. It also provides on-the-job training in a wide range of skills for a minimal cost. But while a good deal can be said for the economic advantages that derive from the operation of a healthy informal sector, it is worth remembering that the conditions of employment can be extremely harsh. For three or four years apprentices are bound to their masters in a condition resembling that of servitude. A space on the workshop floor is living accommodation, and pocket money barely covers the means of survival, while the eldorado to the apprentice, namely a workshop of his own, is difficult to finance and may indeed never materialize. The exploitative character of the work relationship in such a context can rarely be personalized, for the master himself, in a buyers' market for his goods, usually ekes out a precarious existence and has to turn away more young migrants than he can employ.

Finally, there exist a group of genuinely unemployed workers, "job applicants" by self-description, but in fact a lumpen proletariat proper. The origins of this group go back to the contradiction in the colonial political economy that was outlined earlier. As Gutkind (1974:17, 22) puts it:

> Recruitment policies were designed to create a readily available labour reservoir, yet the consequences resulting from policies establishing a stabilised labour force were thought to be undesirable economically and especially politically.

> [And later] administrators . . . needed cheap and readily available labour. . . . However, they were reluctant to support the establishment of a stable, urban, resident labour force by means of good wages and adequate urban facilities.

The consequences of this ambivalence were already observable in colonial times. The most dramatic growth of an urban lumpen proletariat occurred, not without coincidence, in the areas of white settlement—where land-grabbing and the breakup of rural, particularly pastoral, economies had occurred most ruthlessly. In Kenya, influx control measures in the form of the notorious *kipande* (work certificate) provided much of the incendiary material that fueled the Mau Mau rebellion. The pass system in South Africa, indeed the whole construction of apartheid as a systematic ideology, can also be considered as an attempt to meet the dilemma that white settlement and conquest generated. For the white South African regime to turn back the flow of urban migrants, let alone resettle those who have been urbanized for generations, it has to revitalize rural economies which previous white regimes systematically succeeded in underdeveloping and emasculating. Yet the chains of proletarianization and forced peasantization have gone too far to be reversed, even assuming that the South African government had the ability and the white electorate the willingness to countenance the massive redistribution of resources that would be necessary to achieve such an objective.

For the bulk of African countries the measures employed in colonial Kenya or white Africa to arrest migration to the cities are politically unfeasible. The growing numbers of shantytown dwellers and unemployed workers represent a formidable, and probably intractable, social problem. To what degree they represent a political threat is a moot point. I am myself inclined to the view that the degree of normlessness and disorientation manifested in this group, its incapacity, in contrast to the working class, to evince a collective consciousness and organization, and the possibility that its loyalties can be bought by repressive agents mean that the lumpen proletariat, acting alone, is a minimal political threat to the ruling classes in African societies. On the other hand, Worsley (1972) has argued that the very opprobrium that attaches to the lumpen proletariat in traditional Marxist writings itself conditions the view that they are incapable of revolutionary action. He maintains that the subproletariat (the term he prefers) can indeed be mobilized provided that there is a degree of revolutionary leadership and organization.

Where a certain degree of consensus is emerging is in the view that it may be possible to effect a degree of political collaboration across several segments of the urban poor—the unskilled wage laborers, the unemployed, those employed in the informal sector, petty traders, and the like. Some descriptive evidence of such links having been forged in the past are provided in descriptions of strike action in Sekondi-Takoradi in 1961 and in Lagos in 1971 (see chapters by Jeffries and Peace in Sandbrook and Cohen, 1975). What they represent in essence is a form of urban populism, not the manipulative "Peronist" brand orchestrated from above, but rather the evolution of a set of demands and grievances common to the urban dispossessed, but articulated by its most active elements.

If this scenario does indeed lay bare an outline of the shape of political opposition to the postcolonial state, it is likely that the working class will be instrumental in constructing such a combination of forces and may indeed play a leading role in challenging the present-day rulers, military and civilian, of African states. However, one should end on a cautionary note. With the exception of those countries where liberation movements have succeeded in spreading political consciousness to the humblest rural dweller, there is little evidence as yet to suggest that urban protest, however radical in rhetoric, has been able to channel rural discontent into a national political form. And without liberation from the rural indebtedness and wretchedness produced by the satellitization of the agricultural economy during the colonial period, a revolution led by urban workers can only be both partial and incomplete.

REFERENCES

ARRIGHI, G., and SAUL, J.S. (1973). Essays on the political economy of Africa. New York: Monthly Review Press.

BERG, E.J. (1965). "The development of a labor force in sub-Saharan Africa." Economic Development and Cultural Change, 13:394-412.

COHEN, R. (1973). "The making of a West African working class." Paper presented at the Conference of the Canadian African Studies Association, Halifax.

CONWAY, H.E. (1968). "Labour protest activity in Sierra Leone." Labour History, 15:49-63.

EPSTEIN, A.L. (1958). Politics in an urban African community. Manchester: Manchester University Press.

GUTKIND, P.C.W. (1974). The emergent African urban proletariat (Occasional Papers, No. 8. Centre for Developing Areas Studies). Montreal: McGill University.

HART, K. (1973). "Informal income opportunities and urban employment in Ghana." Journal of Modern African Studies, 11:61-89.

HILL, P. (1965). The Gold Coast farmer. London: OUP.

––– (1972). Studies in rural capitalism in Africa. Cambridge: Cambridge University Press.

HOPKINS, A.G. (1960). "The Lagos strike of 1897: An exploration in Nigerian labour history." Past and Present, 35.

––– (1973). An economic history of West Africa. London: Longmans.

HUGHES, A., and COHEN, R. (1971). "Towards the emergence of a Nigerian working class: The social identity of the Lagos labour force, 1897-1939" (Occasional Paper, Series D, No. 7, Faculty of Commerce and Social Science). Birmingham: University of Birmingham.

International Labour Office (1962). African labour survey. Geneva: Author.

POST, K. (1973). "Peasantisation and rural political movements in western Africa." Archives Européennes de Sociologie, 3(2):223-254.

SANDBROOK, R., and COHEN, R. (eds., 1975). The development of an African working class: Studies in class formation and class action. London: Longmans.

WORSLEY, P. (1972). "Fanon and the lumpenproletariat." In R. Miliband and J. Saville (eds.), The socialist register. London: Merlin Press.

7

THE EVOLUTION OF THE CLASS STRUCTURE IN AFRICA

BERNARD MAGUBANE

University of Connecticut

> The "tribe" of today no longer sets the limits—politically, economically or geographi-
> cally—on the society of which it constitutes but a part. It has been incorporated, often
> involuntarily, into states and empires within which it normally occupies a subordinate
> position; and its resources in land and labor have, to one degree or another, been
> affected by and linked in a number of ways to the money economy of the modern
> state and world market. It is, in short, impinged upon by external forces which are
> beyond its power to control and which in most cases constitute significant factors in
> shaping its present structure and future development. [D. Barnett, 1973:2]

The analytical problem of studying the evolution of the class structure in Africa,
given its long history of incorporation into the world system, is indeed immense.
And the issue is not made easier by the fact that most of Africa today is
independent from formal colonial rule. The recognition of the methodological
problems is not new in social anthropology. Redfield (1960:114) asked:

> How, in describing the little community, are we to include the fact that it is a
> community within communities, a whole within other wholes? . . . What forms of
> thought are available to us for conceiving and describing a whole that is both
> enclosed within other wholes and is also in some part permeated by them?

But having posed these questions, Redfield did not begin to answer them.
Most studies of class and class structure focus on the local area and appear to
avoid or be incapable of focusing on the crucial issue of the world system and
the consequent structural relations it necessitates. The problem here is to achieve
nothing less than a coherent understanding of the making of the modern world
and the unique development of capitalism as a global economic system.

Historical incorporation of distinct societies under capitalism proceeds by
means of conquest, domination, and enslavement of alien peoples, followed by
the socioeconomic restructuring of the dominated society in order to install new

AUTHOR'S NOTE: I wish to express my thanks to Professor J.C. Faris for his fine
suggestions and to the Research Foundation, University of Connecticut, for typing the final
copy. Needless to say, all mistakes are mine.

forms of production or exploit the former productive activities. The fundamental objective of this restructuring is to bind the incorporated society into the
expansionist world economy as part of its productive system. This is commonly
followed by the diffusion of the colonizer's cultural tradition.

By means of what concept is it possible to understand the social relationships
noted above? By what concept can we answer the questions raised by Redfield?
More generally, by means of what concepts is it possible to think of the
determination of a subordinate structure by a dominant structure?

The concept of "colonial capitalist mode of production" (CCMP) is most
useful in the analysis of particular, concrete, historical realities of incorporation.
In defining such a productive mode one must define the exact form and content
of the articulation and combination of various modes of production that are
subsumed by capitalism under the special conditions of colonialism. Insofar as
the capitalist mode of production dominates the precapitalist modes and subjects their manpower to its need and the logic of its own mode of functioning,
i.e., integrates them more or less in the mechanism of its own reproduction, then
we have a class situation. But there are fewer concepts in the social science
vocabulary which have been so subject to distortion and disputation as the
concept of class. Central to Marx's studies of political economy, the concept of
class has remained a politically and intellectually suspect one. The reasons for
this are not hard to find; the concept of class addresses itself to the most
fundamental aspects of contemporary human life—the distribution of resources
in society and the power relations which are implied by this distribution. It is
thus necessary to show how the concept of class will be used in this paper.

In society there are a great many distinctions between individuals; for
example, there are differences in terms of nationality, social status, age, sex,
occupation, education, and income. All these lead to the social grading of the
population and may produce various categories of social strata. In contemporary
bourgeois sociology, "class" is viewed as a descriptive category of social stratification subject to empirical specification in concrete societies. This accounts for
the plethora of criteria used in class analysis, for there are as many points of
view concerning the way in which groups should be divided and classified as
there are discrete societies and criteria to classify them.

In classical sociology, the social scientist understood that class relationships
could not be studied apart from the study of political economy. Today the
confusion arises partly because of ideological rejection of the concept of class
and also because the economic, sociological, and political dimensions of society
are split up and parceled out among the different academic interests devoted to
them. Thus one has "classes" in the economic sense, the sociological sense, and
the political sense and in the sense of the distribution of status and prestige. This
division helps to discourage consideration of the nature of the economic system
in any terms other than that of its ideological separateness. Thus, the overall
class structure is lost in the absorption with detail. The bourgeois sociologists
have trivialized class as simply one aspect of a graded system of social stratifi-

cation as understood by individuals. The criteria for differentiation between strata are quantitative, not qualitative, people at the top having simply more of the valued resources. How does one distinguish between significant and insignificant distinctions? In the model that does not investigate the political economy, the salient aspects of class division—e.g., exploitation, class struggle, and revolution—are excluded. Superficial empiricism substitutes for the study of the underlying nonempirical structural reality.

This raises the question of the levels of abstraction on which the problem of classes and class structure in Africa is to be studied. We can study the class structure in Africa through the abstract-deductive method. Or we can practice with Marx the method of "successive approximations," which consists in moving from the more abstract to the more concrete in a step-by-step fashion, removing simplifying assumptions at successive stages of the investigation so that theory may take account of and explain an ever wider range of actual phenomena (Sweezy, 1942:1).

Social classes are not a given with which certain societies are blessed and which other, more retarded societies lack. Social classes describe the *relations* between producers and those in control of their production. The question of whether social classes exist or do not exist (or did or did not exist) in Africa can be answered only on the basis of a truly scientific method of studying economic and social development. That is, the determination of fundamental classes in society is not a task of empirical observation, but one for theoretical investigation of the relations of production that are the foundation of society. As Marx put it:

> The first question to be answered is this: What constitutes a class? and the reply to this follows naturally from the reply to another question namely: What makes wage laborers, capitalists and landlords constitute three great classes? [Quoted in Dos Santos, 1970:172]

In other words, the question of whether these or those classes exist turns out to be an analysis of the mode of production. We can therefore resolve the contradiction between the general law of class formation and the concrete forms in which it appears. As a theoretical postulate the theory of class involves "the relations or modes of relations conditioning the possibilities of interaction among men, given a determinate mode of production" (Dos Santos, 1970:181). Cabral (1969:77) agrees with this formulation of the problem and writes:

> Those who affirm—in our case correctly—that the motive force of history is the class struggle would certainly agree to a revision of this affirmation to make it more precise and give it an even wider field of application if they had a better knowledge of the essential characteristics of certain colonized peoples, that is to say peoples dominated by imperialism. In fact in the general evolution of humanity and each of the peoples of which it is composed, classes appear neither as a generalized and simultaneous phenomenon throughout the totality of these groups, nor as a finished, perfect, uniform and spontaneous whole. *The definition of classes within one or several human groups is a fundamental consequence of the progressive development of the productive forces and of the characteristics of the wealth produced by the*

group or usurped from others. That is to say that the socio-economic phenomenon "class" is created and develops as a function of at least two essential and inter-dependent variables–the level of productive forces and the pattern of ownership of the means of production. [Emphasis added.]

In the last few years a number of studies have appeared, such as those by Kuper and Smith (1969), which have focused the problem on "new" analysis of African reality. Kuper and Smith attempt to refute the fundamental concepts of Marxist class analysis of postcolonial Africa. They offer in the place of class analysis the notion of social and/or cultural pluralism.

Obviously the bourgeois social scientists who have disputed the relevance of class analysis in Africa ignore the colonial political economy and the classes it created. The current vogue of cultural and/or social pluralism is a typical way in which prefabricated models are imposed on African reality. Cultural and/or social pluralism by concentrating on cultural differences conveniently blocks out the possibility of a comprehensive historical inquiry into the actual grounds of why cultural differences assume the importance they have in a colonial situation.

The bourgeois social scientist sought to resolve the contradiction between the general law of class formation and the concrete forms in which it manifested itself not by seeking to find the mediating elements, but by directly adopting the concrete to the abstract. Since this did not work, they either denied the law or faced an insoluable contradiction.

If there is a uniquely "bourgeois view" of African society, it is the one that is advanced by Van den Berghe (1965) in his essay, "Toward a Sociology of Africa." He defines the characteristics of African societies in terms of their ethnic, linguistic, and cultural cleavages. In typical style Van den Berghe (pp. 78-79) describes pluralism as:

characterized by relative absence of value consensus; the relative rigidity and clarity of group definition; the relative pressure of conflict, or at least of lack of integration and complementarity between various parts of the social system, the segmentary and specific character of relationships and the relative existence of sheer institutional duplication . . . between the various segments of society.

The main criticism against the concept of pluralism (social or cultural) is that it turns the immediate into an absolute, since it cannot show its relations with the modes of being or the conditions that determine it. That is, "empiricist science, by overvaluing the datum as compared with determination, replaces the totality by the aspects or forms in which it appears" (Dos Santos, 1970:180). It tends thereby to confuse the essence of society with its outward appearance. The criticism offered by Cohen (1972:234) of "cultural pluralism" hits its major weaknesses. He writes:

Tendentially and essentially, . . . "cultural pluralism" leads to either a simplification or obfuscation of other forms of social conflict, for example "class conflict," which may be linked to, but is also distinct from, ethnic conflict. The cultural determinism of the pluralist has also led to a distinct uncertainty in the spelling out of the precise conditions under which relationships of dominance and disability as between ethnic or racial groups are modified or overturned. To undertake this task a much wider analysis of the relations of production and consumption within a given social matrix must be undertaken. These relations . . . may exist as coterminous with, as an adjunct of, or in contradiction to the relations between cultural groups.

The lack or avoidance of class analysis has also been raised in a recent article (Kitching, 1972). According to this writer, the situation is not helped by African political leaders who write and speak nostalgically about the communal past that characterized precapitalist and/or traditional African societies.

It is not the major purpose of this paper to pursue abstractly the argument against the social pluralist or why class analysis is conspicuous by its avoidance. With no claim to originality I shall, through a few selected societies (as sources of empirical reference), show the development of classes in colonial and post-colonial Africa as part of the world-system (see Wallerstein, 1974). It is my belief that only a profound knowledge of the socioeconomic and political history of individual countries, particularly the level of social development in the precolonial and colonial periods, can furnish the researcher with the necessary initial material to make a correct judgment of whether or not the Marxist class analysis is applicable to the present African conditions.

Clearly classes in modern Africa are not determined by the nation-state. In this new configuration—following incorporation into the world-economy—certain structural characteristics developed as a reflection of the higher order into which the African societies had been incorporated. That is, whatever classes developed after its incorporation were not reflective of an autonomous economy, but were auxiliary to the world class structure. Developing within the framework of the colonial capitalist mode of production, the class structure of most African countries today is a distorted and truncated version of the class structure of the ruling center.

In this paper I adopt a Marxian framework of the analysis of social classes in colonial and postcolonial Africa. I am assuming the progressive dominance of the capitalist mode of production throughout the colonial and postcolonial period. This should not be taken as an attempt to ignore the existence of the precapitalist class structures in most of Africa. But as will be discussed below, the experiences of slaving, conquest, colonialism, and imperialism are the historical reality most relevant to understanding class structure in Africa today.

PRECAPITALIST CLASS FORMATION AND STRUCTURE

The conditions under which Africans produced and exchanged their means of sustenance have varied from country to country and within each country from generation to generation. In the traditional village community with its communal ownership of land—which most of modern rural Africa still has in some form or other—a fairly equal distribution of products was a matter of course. The changes in the forms of production and distribution in certain societies gave rise to the division of society into different strata.

The communal mode of production is one of the oldest systems of social relations in Africa. Typically, it was characterized by an extremely low level of productive forces and no production of surplus. Under the "primitive" mode of production man was helpless before nature, and this explains the collective forms of labor and communalistic social relations implied in the collective ownership of the land and the egalitarian forms of distribution of products. Primitive and/or communalistic relations of this type were and are still characteristic of certain parts of Africa even though the continent was incorporated into the orbit of the evolving capitalist system (see Maquet, 1972:113).

The absence of private property in land, which has enamored many African socialists, did not mean that Africa prior to the incorporation into the world capitalist system was an eldorado of egalitarianism. In many societies class division had emerged which expressed itself in the inequality in property relations that arose among peasants; it expressed itself in the emergence of a traditional aristocracy that concentrated in its hands large herds. There were already in existence large detachments of armed men headed by military commanders. Rodney (1972:53) writes:

> In the period of transition, while African societies retained many features that were undisputably communal, it also accepted the principle that some families or clans or lineages were destined to rule and others were not. This was true not only of cultivators but of pastoralists as well. In fact, livestock become unevenly distributed much more than land; and those families with the largest herds became socially and politically dominant.

It was, however, the common access to land that was the mainstay of African communalism. The African village settlements were based on arrangements in which each family had usufruct of the lands which they cultivated or on which they grazed their animals or on which they hunted or gathered. Particular phases of this or that evolution were the main interest of ethnologists.

In the collection of essays, *African Political Systems* (1940), Fortes and Evans-Pritchard made a distinction between acephalous societies, which did not have duly constituted centralized political authority, and societies with centralized authority structures, that is, primitive "states." It was shown that in the former, the acephalous or "stateless" societies, political power was organized, or rather political functions were discharged, within the framework of segmentary lineage systems, i.e., a plexus of relationships between (and within) corporate kin groups organized at various levels. In such societies, all "roles," including political and economic roles, appeared in the form of kinship roles (see Alavi, 1973:33). But to the extent that social division of labor developed and society was divided into classes, the state appeared and its nature was defined.

> In societies with centralized authority, the primitive "states," however, another set of "roles" overlays the network of kinship organization, *viz.*, kings, administrators and judges. Such societies displayed unique distribution of wealth and power. One might, therefore, expect cleavages between groups in such societies. [Alavi, 1973:33]

The concept of "stateless" societies, therefore, describes those people who had no machinery of governmental coercion and no concept of a political unit wider than the family or the village. According to Rodney (1972:56):

Generally speaking, one can consider the stateless societies as among the older forms of socio-political organization in Africa, while the large states represented an evolution away from communalism—sometimes to the point of feudalism.

The reconstruction of African societies prior to their incorporation into the world capitalist system reveals uneven development. The existing division (classes) were incompletely crystalized, and changes were in most cases very slow. Even the stratified societies exhibited minimal internal mechanisms for radical social transformation. Either conflicts were locally resolved or they led to the hiving-off and creation of parallel entities with little difference from the original society. Certainly Gluckman (1964:31) fails to understand all the dynamics operating when he writes:

> Rich there were and the poor suffered greater shortages of food; but the main interest of the rich lay in building up bands of followers by giving them land for which they had no other use, and feeding them from surplus stocks of cattle and grain. There are no complicating conflicts arising from clashes of economic interests between classes.

To sum up: Prior to the advent of imperialism there were in Africa certain societies with no state machinery but there also existed societies that had developed to a point where social classes appeared and where governmental functions were reserved for a minority who exercised power in an exclusive way. There existed class conflicts. It is simply that in Africa, unlike Europe, these could be relieved instead of having to be resolved by qualitative transformation. Feudal and slave-based modes of production existed widely and were taken advantage of and subsumed by the evolving capitalist system.

THE ADVENT OF CAPITALISM IN EUROPE AND ITS EFFECT ON AFRICA

The incorporation of Africa into the evolving world capitalist mode of production extends beyond the period of formal colonialism. Long before Africa was divided among European powers at the Berlin Conference in 1884, African slavery constituted the most important form of trade between Europe and Africa, but this has always been underestimated as a source of finance capital growth (see Williams, 1974).

The African slave trade lasted for about three centuries from 1550 to 1850. Its devastation was felt by African societies from the middle of the seventeenth century to after its termination. There have been innumerable arguments about the effects of the slave trade on the African economic development. However, there is no question that it led to direct dismemberment of Africa in the nineteenth century.

The striking consequence of the slave trade was on two aspects of African political economy. Africa, it is estimated, lost between 12 and 50 million ablebodied souls. From 1650 to 1900 Europe's population grew by over 600%, that of Asia by over 300%, and that of Africa by only 20%. Today Africa has but one-twelfth of the world's population; prior to the slave trade it had about one-fifth the world's total. The destruction of African political economies and the loss of Africa's men and women ("who are the human agents from whom inventiveness springs") distorted its political and economic evolution. The pattern of arrested development was accentuated by colonization. Commenting on the development of capitalism in the eighteenth century, Dubois (1965:58) wrote:

> It was the Negro slave who made the sugar colonies the most precious colonies ever recorded in the annals of imperialism. Experts called them "the fundamental prop and support" of the Empire. The British Empire in the 18th century was a magnificent superstructure of American commerce and naval power on an African foundation.

Throughout the eighteenth and for the first half of the nineteenth century, the exploitation of Africa and African labor continued to be the source for the accumulation of capital that was reinvested in Western Europe and America. The slave trade was thus the first incorporation of Africa's labor force into the world economy.

THE ADVENT OF IMPERIALISM

The third quarter of the nineteenth century saw the superseding of competitive capitalism by monopoly capitalism. The most salient aspects of imperialism were the transformation and the socioeconomic restructuring of African societies by colonially imposed capitalist development. The export of capital influenced and greatly accelerated the development of capitalism in those countries to which it was exported. Lenin summed up imperialism as follows (1968:233):

> Imperialism is capitalism at that stage of development at which the dominance of monopolies and finance capital has established itself; in which the export of capital has acquired pronounced importance, in which the division of the world among the international trusts has begun, in which the division of all territories of the globe among the biggest capitalist powers has been completed.

Lenin goes on to say that, "The thing to be noted . . . is that imperialism represents a special stage in the development of capitalism." This definition of imperialism sees it as a specific organization of capitalist production on a world scale embracing all the salient characteristics including the class structure. In the introduction to Bukharin's *Imperialism and the World Economy* (1972:11) Lenin wrote:

> The typical ruler of the world became finance capital, a power that is peculiarly mobile and flexible, peculiarly intertwined at home and internationally, peculiarly devoid of individuality and divorced from the immediate processes of production, peculiarly easy to concentrate, a power that has already made peculiarly large strides on the road of concentration, so that literally several hundred billionaires and millionaires hold in their hands the fate of the whole world.

The study of classes and class formation in Africa under imperialistic capitalism is extremely complex and difficult. Worsley (1964:374) points out:

> Social theory has utterly failed to grapple with the outstanding feature of the last hundred years—the emergence of a world system of social relations, a new and higher level of development in human organization. The only serious systematic intellectual treatment of this change in levels so far has been Lenin's *Imperialism*.

In studying the evolution of Africa's class structure under imperialism, one must study the activities and structure of British, French, Belgian, Portuguese, and American finance capital in Africa: the specific forms of the reorganization of African labor power to serve imperialist enterprises; and the development of secondary forms of capitalist enterprises, controlled in some parts of Africa by Asian and Eurasian minorities and in other cases by the indigenous petty bourgeoisie serving, after independence, in competition with (as well as agents of) imperialist capital. That is, the study of classes should involve the study of how the bourgeoisie makes the country dependent on the town and those countries lagging in economic development "dependent on the civilized ones, nations of peasants on the nations of bourgeois, the East on the West" (Marx, 1968:39).

This raises further the methodological question of the level of abstraction on which the problem of classes is to be studied. So complicated is the subject and so numerous are its empirical variants that a single paper can only offer tentative suggestions. Lenin (1964:33) writes that:

> Infinitely diverse combinations and elements of this or that type of capitalist evolution are possible and only hopeless pedants could set about solving the peculiar and complex problems merely by quoting this or that opinion of Marx about a different historical epoch.

The attempt to study the class structure in Africa is a risky undertaking indeed. These general observations will not be entirely adequate for any particular region or country. However, they do apply at a general level.

The historical specificity of imperialism in Africa lay in the fact that, although it integrates Africa within the world capitalist economy, it did not create in Africa a wholly capitalist social milieu. "Capitalism, and especially imperialism, combined development and underdevelopment, the rapid growth of some nations with the retarded growth of others, not by making all produce under the same capitalist conditions of production, but precisely by maintaining varying degrees of pre-capitalist or semi-capitalist relations of production in most colonial and semi-colonial countries" (Mandel, 1972:96).

The analysis of the distinctive features of Africa's integration into the world-economy is fundamental for the study and specific features of its class structure. If the capitalist mode of production was to develop, it was essential for imperialism to do more than deprive the African subsistence producer of the means of production; those who had lost their livelihood had to be forcibly enrolled in the production process *as* laborers. The evolution of the Africans' social structure subjected to total colonial domination profoundly altered the whole class problem. Colonial oppression and exploitation impoverished all strata of African society without creating social divisions typical of the mature capitalist countries.

We can sum up the expansion of capitalism in its imperialistic phase: it took place (a) through the export of mature capital, (b) by the creation of overseas markets, and (c) through the creation of peasantries and proletariats as well as a dependent petty bourgeoisie. In its imperialistic phase, capitalism brought populations with precapitalist relations of production and exchange into productive relationships with international capitalist organizations, but it maintained and strengthened to the utmost the differences between the various societies brought under its ambit.

In the study of classes, therefore, our objective is to develop a theoretical understanding of certain definite conditions which do not exist in a pure form or empirically; such a definition is a prerequisite to an explanation of the class reality in Africa. At the highest level of generality there is the structural and specific nature of capitalist production: What is the relation between the scientific, logical analysis of capitalism, which creates the capitalist class and the working class, and the real historical process of the origin and development of capitalism in its imperialistic phase in Africa? Is there a structural similarity between the English peasants forced off the land (who then provided a pool of labor for the factories) and African peasants similarly forced temporarily or permanently to labor in mines and plantations? While the movement of African peasants comes at a later time in history, and while many African peasants have come to play a different version of the proletarian role, structurally they stand in the same relationship to capital as English workers, then and now (see Friedmann and Wayne, 1974:40). In Africa today there exists a predominant capitalist mode of production which modifies and subordinates to itself the elements of precolonial relations of production.

It follows therefore that it is impossible to talk about the class structure of specific countries without a prior understanding of the workings of imperialism and monopoly capitalism. In a sense, we must have a theory of the elephant before we can criticize the partial view of the blind men. The introduction of capitalism within the framework of the colonial system of imperialism had a deforming effect on the evolution of Africa's class structure. The exploitation of African raw materials by foreign capital and techniques meant that the emergence of social classes was different from, and perhaps more complex than, what existed in Western Europe.

The decisiveness of colonialism and imperialism, though short in duration, is seen in the fact that it usurped from the African societies their productive forces. Thus, the most serious blow suffered by the African people under colonial rule was to be removed from history and from their communities. As Cabral puts it (1973:41-42):

> The principal characteristic, common to every kind of imperialist domination, is the negation of the *historical process* of the dominated people by means of violently

usurping the free operation of the process of development of the *productive forces*. Now, in any given society, the level of development of the productive forces and the system for social utilization of these forces (the ownership system) determine the *mode of production*. In our opinion, the mode of production whose contradictions are manifested with more or less intensity through the class struggle, is the principal factor in the history of any human group, the level of the productive forces being the tone and permanent driving power in history.

How the Africans experienced the negation of their historical process and the distortion of their classes is described by Rodney (1972:246):

> To be specific, it must be noted that colonialism crushed by force the surviving feudal states of North Africa; that the French wiped out the large Muslim states of the Western Sudan, as well as Dahomey and kingdoms in Madagascar; the British eliminated Egypt, the Mahdist Sudan, Asante, Benin, the Yoruba kingdoms, Swaziland, Matabeleland, the Lozi and the East African Lake kingdoms as great states. It should further be noted that a multiplicity of smaller and growing states were removed from the face of Africa by the Belgians, Portuguese, British, French, Germans, Spaniards, and Italians. Finally, those that appeared to survive were nothing but puppet creations. For instance, the Sultan of Morocco retained nominal existence under colonial rule which started in 1912; and the same applied to the Bey of Tunis; but Morocco and Tunisia were just as much under the power of French colonial administrators as neighbouring Algeria, where the feudal rulers were removed altogether.

The colonial situation manifested itself in different dimensions—political, economic, sociological, and psychological. Politically, colonialism "is a system of rule which assumes the right of one people to impose their will upon another. This situation inevitably leads to a situation of dominance and dependency which . . . systematically subordinates those governed by it to the imported culture in social, economic and political life" (Brett, 1973:vii).

The violent penetration and rupture of traditional precapitalist societies and the subjugation of their economic life to the profit impulse of the Western bourgeoisie constitute the fundamental class reality of modern Africa. As a result of the colonial situation, the peoples of Africa found their resources and their land developed and exploited (by their labor power) not for them, but for the capitalist classes of Europe. They found that the effective capacity for political decision making over their own destiny had largely been taken from their hands. They found that the colonial situation had produced vast changes in the network of their social relationships: there were primary industrialization, the growth of towns, the development of an urbanized and proletarianized population; there was the transformation of subsistence economies to a cash-crop economy; there grew new forms of social differentiation based on education and religious affiliation—that is, there emerged a new system of social stratification. Of course, the colonial situation affected different African colonies, or even peoples in the same country, differently. But the genesis of colonial capitalism constitutes the contextural base line from which we must study the current class structure in Africa. The analysis of the class structure of the various regions should be based on the mode of generation of the surplus from the African workers and the transfer of the surplus to the metropolis and among the various recipients in the colony itself. That is, classes are objectified at the level of concrete analysis of a specific mode of production. Classes are the personification of the central economic categories of a given system of production. They are the expression of the central contradictions of a given mode of production in terms of the structural relations between producers and controllers of production.

Samir Amin (1974:76) divides Africa under colonial rule into three macroregions: the Africa of the colonial economy; the Africa of the concession companies; and the Africa of the labor reserves. He explains that this division is based on the effects of the colonial period on the history of Africa. The definition of the colonial political economy makes it clear how the most fundamental class divisions in Africa were created. It was during the colonial period, for instance, that the inequitable economic relations between certain African countries and white settler countries began. And in the structure of the colonial political economy we find out why the basic means of production in most African countries still belong to foreign capital.

The sociological consequences of the colonial capitalist mode of production —or CCMP—were remarkable. An industrial economy based on narrowly limited kinds of economic activity—the extraction of minerals and agricultural products—bypassed the development of an internal market and an articulated commercial economy. As a result, "classes were formed not through an historical process of material and cultural evolution within the society, but were created by decree to serve a distant imperial metropolis." Expropriations, taxation, corvées, and paternalist control were conscious instruments of policy that created the needed labor force (Murray, 1962:121).

The principal classes during the colonial era were those whose interrelations determined the essence of the CCMP. Brett's discussion (1973:284) of the crucial differences between the class structure in the metropolitan countries and the class structure in the colonies is very important and should be quoted at length:

> Capitalism had evolved organically in the areas of origin, but it was injected into the colonial world from the outside and, where necessary, imposed upon unwilling populations there at the point of a gun. The process of organic evolution, for example in Britain, produced an indigenous capitalist class which was securely rooted in the social structure and culture and which, whatever its limits, had necessarily to rely upon internal sources of support to legitimate and defend its claims to social predominance. The dominance of this class in European society was subjected to intense opposition both from the old feudal order and from the emergent working class, but its claims to represent at least one significant tendency within the national culture could never be entirely rejected. But external dominance in the Third World meant that the commanding heights of the new economy and administration were occupied by expatriate groups from the beginning; expatriate groups, moreover, with access to resources derived from their metropolitan base which were far in excess of anything which indigenous groups could hope to acquire in the short run. The crucial question for the long-term development of the society as a whole therefore relates to

the effect of their dominance upon the emergence of indigenous social formations which might be capable of replacing them and establishing an autonomous base for the exercise of political and economic power.

Within the CCMP the main class contradictions were those between the metropolis and the various interest groups within a colony. In Africa, an understanding of the class structure must begin with an inquiry into the degree of exploitation of African resources and labor and must proceed to follow the surplus to its destination outside Africa—into the bank accounts of the world capitalist class who control the majority shares in huge multinational combines (see Rodney, 1972:167). Secondary "classes" emerged related to the economic sectors that survived or were retained from the previous mode of production or emerged to serve the colonial economy. That is, colonial rule deeply disrupted traditional social stratification and differentiation, creating not those typical of an indigenous process of capitalist development, but those typical and specific to the colonial situation. The CCMP incorporated or reconstructed traditional power structures; it also educated larger or smaller groups of professionals and minor employees to carry out functions that were either unattractive to or impossible for the members of the ruling "race" (see Waterman, 1969).

Colonial capitalism derived its ability to exploit African societies from the power of the colonial state on the one hand and the inability of members of the indigenous society to compete with the colonial order on the other as a result of the devastation of three hundred years of slavery and conquest. "Echoing the economic order," writes Waterman (1969), was "a political structure in which the ruling stratum was foreign and the [indigenous] inhabitants appeared in a descending order of subservience and dependence." According to Murray (1963:88):

> In certain areas, the customary authority of traditional chiefs was supplemented by political, economic and juridical powers conferred on them as instruments of indirect rule (Northern Nigeria, Buganda); elsewhere, as in most of the French African colonies, an administrative "chefferie" was created out of extremely heterogeneous elements (willing chiefs or their kinsmen where available; otherwise, ex-NCO's, junior clerks, even cooks and chauffeurs). French colonial policy, which, unlike the British, was a system of "direct administration," generally weakened chiefly power except in the more densely populated and politically articulated savannah regions (e.g., Mossi of the Volta, Djerma of the Niger, etc.). Secondly, the advance of African rural capitalism and commerce quickened after World War II in such areas as the southern Ivory Coast, Cameroun and Buganda. Social differentiation was consequently accentuated, and with it the movement of labour from the savannah to the plantations and forest zones.

Finally and most importantly, the greatest impact of the CCMP was on the level of the working class which produced the super profits in the plantations and mines. The colonial capitalist economy was narrowly focused; a narrow specialization, producing one or two technical commodities designed entirely for export, was imposed on each colony. Other colonies, (such as the Portuguese colonies of Mozambique and Angola and the British colonies of Nyasaland,

Basutoland, and Bechuanaland) served as labor reservoirs for farms and mines in other areas.

The creation of an abundant labor supply for the mines and farms and for construction of the infrastructure of roads, railways, ports, and so on, became critical. The imposition of hut taxes or the intensification of precapitalist forms of exploitation in the countryside made the poor peasants desperate for any additional source of income. This labor was hired through the system of migrant workers. The "temporary" migration of adult male labor to the mines and plantations has been described as unique. According to Jack Woddis (1960:82):

> First, it [was] a migration *almost overwhelmingly of adult males,* single men, or husbands unaccompanied by their wives and children, who have been left behind in the ruined countryside. Secondly, the migrants usually *[took] up employment for a strictly limited duration*—six months, a year, two years, but seldom longer. Thirdly, *the migration [was] repeated again and again in the life of the individual peasant-worker,* his career consisting of numerous short terms of employment alternating with periods at home in his village or the Reserve. Fourthly, whether he migrate[d] from the countryside to a town or mining area within the same territory, or whether it [was] a question of 'alien migration' across frontiers, it [was] on foot. Fifthly, it [was] frequently *connected with various forms of labor recruitment* which sometimes tend[ed] to be disguised forms of forced labor. *And sixthly, it [was] on such a scale and of such a character that it produce[d] a completely disproportioned population both in the towns and in the rural areas, aggravate[d] terribly the already acute agrarian crisis, and [led] to a total disharmony of the economy of the African territories most affected by it.* From the standpoint of labor it [had] three further results; the constant change of personnel in employment which [arose] from this system *[made] difficult the acquisition of labor skill, create[d] enormous difficulties for trade-union organization, and tend[ed] to depress wages.* [Emphasis in the original.]

Never in its history did capitalism rely on such an extensive use of migrant labor. What did it mean for the character of the African working class? We think of capitalism as a system of production in which capital implies wage labor, free labor, a labor market, and the sale of labor power. In classical capitalist societies the proletariat effected a complete break from the subsistence economy. In Africa, on the other hand, because of the traditional system of land tenure and because of the extractive nature of colonial capitalism, the integration of African peasants into the world capitalist system was marginal. It led to impoverishment without complete proletarianization (see Amin, 1974:59).

The incorporation of African peasants as migrant laborers into the capitalist economy led to some strange results. According to the nature of his labor, his hiring conditions, and mode of life and according to his class consciousness, the colonial worker in mines, cash crop farms, and so on was frequently engaged in "traditional" social relations and their limitations. The "dual" character of migrant laborers is described as follows by Basil Davidson (1966:202-203):

> In the same way that many "subsistence peasants" are found, on looking closer, to be well and truly wedged into a cash economy, so too are many urban wage earners still reliant to some extent on their family food-production in a more or less distant village. If you journey with African peasants going to town you may well be

encumbered and set about with their piles of baggage; what they are likely to be carrying is not clothing or adornment, however, but food of one sort or another. The reason for this carrying of food to town is not a simple love of frugal living. It is rather a dislike of starvation. It arises from the happy colonial custom of calculating the wages of the married urban African as though he were always a bachelor. As the East African Royal Commission of 1955 placidly but usefully explained, wage rates in the past had been set for migrant workers who came to town without their families. "Their wages were calculated on the needs of a single man," and yet, even though many men now had their families with them, "this has remained the basis on which wages are paid until the present day." These wages, not too surprisingly, the learned Commissioners found to be insufficient for African urban workers, "not only to feed, house, and clothe their families, but even for their own needs"; and they proceeded to quote from the 1954 report of a Committee on African Wages, in Kenya, which ought to go down in history as a classic statement about the realities of life under colonial "trusteeship." This Committee found that "approximately one half of the urban workers in Private Industry, and approximately one quarter of those in the Public Services, are in receipt of wages insufficient to provide for their basic, essential needs of health, decency, and working efficiency."

This extraordinary situation was based on a rationalization which assumed that the towns and commerce in these urban areas were for whites only. The dominant vision (especially by the British) was that African development was to be based on subsistence agriculture based on the village. This, it was assumed, would disturb their cultural pattern the least. The applications of this attitude on the formation and crystallization of the African working class are not hard to imagine.

The African migrant laborers were not allowed to break away completely from the "tribal" social environment. Depending on the uncertain demand for their labor in the mines and agro-industries, a great many workers were forced to engage in subsistence agriculture for part of the year and go to find employment in towns, plantations, or mines for another part of the year. The "partial" employment in wage labor hampered the formation of a full-fledged proletariat and caused intensive pauperization in the labor reserves—the countryside. Thus the term "wage worker" in Africa embraces a large group of various semiproletarian elements.

Because the conditions in which the African proletariat was born were determined by the socioeconomic needs of extractive capitalism and because the proletariat maintained in Africa periodical or permanent connection with the country, class consciousness remained underdeveloped. According to Zarine (1968:49):

These ties determine some aspects of its ideology, organizational level, and, in the long run now, the trend of the workers' movement. The proletariat's semi-peasant psychology hampers the development of its class-consciousness, the emergence and growth of its organizations and the dissemination of its ideology.

A study of the salient features of the colonial economy leads to the conclusion that the metropolitan bourgeoisie appropriates the labor power of the African peasantry. The mode of acquiring and the size of the surplus value extracted from the peasantry were determined by the manner in which the traditional economy was integrated into the CCMP, as in Latin America (see Frank, 1967). Where the monopolization of the means of production was "total"—for example, in the white settler regimes of southern Africa—there the proletarianization of the peasants was almost complete.

In 1954 the United Nations document, *Enlargement of the Exchange Economy in Tropical Africa,* identified three groups of African territories in tropical Africa that it distinguished in terms of the relative importance of production for a market or of wage employment in the commercialization of their indigenous agricultural economies:

> First were those territories in which cash-cropping [was] mainly for overseas markets and there [was] little or no export of labor: French West Africa, Gold Coast, Nigeria and Uganda. [Secondly, the] territories in which cash-cropping [was] combined with export of labor: Belgian Congo, French Equatorial Africa and Tanganyika; [and thirdly, the] territories in which substantial export of labor [was] combined with limited agricultural production, mainly for internal markets: Kenya, Northern Rhodesia and Southern Rhodesia. [Barnett, 1973:10]

The relation of the peasants to the CCMP was thus extremely complex. In each colony alongside the capitalist relations of production there continued to survive old elements of production. The interpenetration of modernity and traditional forms of labor power is the typical way in which the colonial capitalist mode of production commands the labor of the people it subordinates. The class conflict manifests itself as the conflict between those social classes (the colonizers) controlling the "modern" sector through their economic power and those subordinate classes (the colonized) exploited through traditional social relations which frustrate the development of a truly working class consciousness.

A correct definition of classes in the CCMP has tremendous significance, for it allows us to draw important practical conclusions regarding the nature of colonial capitalism. At the risk of being tedious, it is important to emphasize the fact that:

> The productive facilities for export from underdeveloped countries, which were so largely a result of foreign investment, never became a part of the internal economic structure of those underdeveloped countries themselves except in the purely geographical and physical sense. Economically speaking, they were really an outpost of the economies of more developed investing countries. The main secondary multiplier effects, which the textbooks tell us to expect from investments, took place not where the investment was physically or geographically located but (to the extent that the results of these investments returned directly home) where the investment came from. I would suggest that if the proper economic test of investment is the multiplier effect in the form of cumulative additions to income, employment, capital, technical knowledge, and growth of external economies, then a good deal of the investment in underdeveloped countries which we used to consider as "foreign" should in fact be considered as domestic investment on the part of the industrialized countries. [Singer, 1950:338-339]

Colonialism was, therefore, not merely a system of exploitation but one whose essential purpose was to repatriate the profits to the so-called "mother country." From the African viewpoint, that amounted to consistent expropriation of surplus produced by African labor out of African resources. It meant the development of Europe as part of the same dialectical process in which Africa was underdeveloped (Rodney, 1972:162). The satellite-metropolitan relationship affects and sets limits to the evolution of social classes in the satellite regions. It ensures that no independent bourgeoisie emerges and that the working class will remain as segments within peasant subsistence economies. Poulantzas (1974:148-149) puts it this way:

> The organization of class relations and State apparatuses in the dominated and dependent formation reproduces within itself the structure of the relation of domination characterizing the class[es] in power in the dominant social formation[s]. This domination corresponds to both indirect (through the position of the dominated formation in the imperialist chain) and direct (through direct investments) forms of exploitation of the popular masses of the dominated formations by the classes in power in the dominant formations. This exploitation is articulated with the exploitation they suffer at the hands of their own classes in power. Each phase of imperialism is marked by different forms of realisation of this domination and dependence.

That is, the structure of the political economy in Africa can only be understood in terms of the relation of various African countries to the international power structure and the social classes this power structure reproduced within the dominated formations. The links between African economies and the international markets are shaped by the local ruling classes that defer major decisions to the international ruling classes. External dependence was transformed at the achievement of independence into internal domination by the inheritors of the colonial estate.

The notion of the world ruling class located in the control of international corporations is no longer a fancy; it signifies the control of the world-economy by the rulers of the old capitalist countries. The world ruling class in Zurich, London, New York, Paris, and elsewhere, coordinates the interests of the various capitalist groups (see Magubane, 1974).

THE DEVELOPMENT OF CLASSES SINCE INDEPENDENCE

To understand the postcolonial developments, one must understand the nature of the colonial state. What was the social and economic condition of the state inherited from colonialism? Colonialism left postcolonial Africa with social structures which (combined with its new neocolonial status and severe internal problems) condemned these national entities to perpetual dependency and underdevelopment.

The class structure of postcolonial Africa was not just a matter of traditional division into bourgeoisie, proletariat, and peasantry, but also a matter of relations between those classes that were inheritors of the colonial state and imperialism. Cutting across the traditional divisions was the link between those classes in the former colonies who benefited from imperialism and those who suffered from it. The inheritors of the colonial state apparatus derived their power from imperialism.

"More or less consciously," writes Davidson (1966:206), "the British and the French were eager to hand their power to elites who would keep the African world safe for capitalism, above all for their own capitalism."

The achievement of national independence aggravated rather than resolved the class contradictions because some inheritors of the colonial estate further entrenched the full range of colonial privileges. Moreover, the achievement of independence confronted African governments with the extent of their misery. They were faced with social, economic, and cultural dislocations that had gone in some cases too far for the possibility of quick reintegration. Comparing the evolution of industrial capitalism in Europe and the ravages of the CCMP in Africa, Davidson (1969:277) writes:

> The first [industrialization] destroyed, but also, after its fashion, mightily rebuilt afresh; the second, having gone far to ruin what it found, could only leave for Africans the task of making a new society. No such new society came into being during the colonial period. Little was left behind but an utter chaos of ideas and social relationships. . . . When the principal colonizing powers eventually withdrew, everything of basic social meaning remained to be begun or rebuilt afresh.

At independence, the state in Africa lacked everything. The inherited economies could not produce enough grain to feed the population, enough shelter to house those who had assembled in urban slums, or enough schools to educate but one out of a hundred of its young population. The few who had escaped the bottleneck of colonial education enjoyed all the benefits of political independence. In the empire of scarcity, those who could make it reluctantly became spoiled. In the same essay, Davidson (1969:206) quotes a Nigerian economist who he says attacked "the system that pays a permanent secretary in the civil service £3,000 a year and his messenger boy £9 a month."

In politics, there were no durable political institutions, no democratic cultural traditions, no widely diffused social ideals, and no full sense of national identity. In this kingdom of deprivation, neither liberty, nor equality, nor fraternity were possible. There could be no equality where material goods were so scarce that only a fraction of a minority could possess them; there could be no democracy where lack of education created an elite. When deprivation and inequality are the destiny of an entire people, the development of classes tends to be distorted. The state becomes the sovereign source of social and economic development. According to Murray (1963:85):

> [A]fter independence, the state became a major economic force in the absence of an entrepreneurial class, occupying a key role in economic development. State functionaries . . . handle large contracts and negotiate the future of the country with representatives of overseas concerns: corruption and the enjoyment of unrecorded perquisites abound. The administrative services absorb the major part of budgetary allocations (60% in Dahomey) and state employment comes to symbolize all the attractions of the "advanced" sector in an under-developed country: grossly inflated salaries, lavish equipment, the amenities of urban, "civilized" living, Mercedes, "bardancing," alcoholism and the ten hour week (Abidjan, Yaoundé, Brazzaville, etc.). A new elite . . . acceded to these privileges, and the exercise of state functions is increasingly providing an institutional basis for the domination of "an administrative

bourgeoisie." Economic differentials are huge: only in the southern Ivory Coast and Cameroun is there a small class of planters capable of emulating the living standards of the new administrative elite. A deputy earns in 6 months (1½ of "work") the equivalent of 36 years' work by the average peasant. In Gabon (population: 450,000) a parliamentarian has a salary of F2,800 a year. Automobiles, "presents," luxury accommodation, seal their status.

The role of the state in capital formation was expressive of the fact that the African economies had not led to the development of an indigenous capitalist class capable of striving for hegemony in the state. The foreign capital that controls most of Africa's resources was already a highly developed form of capital, which had already held a privileged position in the colonizing country. That is, its articulation was to a system of international integration only, not national economic integration. The Ghanaian aluminum industry is a case in point. (See Green and Seidman, 1968.) The dependency on the foreign technology forces most African countries to continue utilizing capital-intensive techniques which enhance profits but do not develop the African economies. The foreign capital that was invested in Africa was capital with a particular greed for profits and one which was attempting to increase profits by brutal methods of exploitation.

The development of one-party states in Africa was thus an historical necessity. For some countries it became a means to break the stranglehold of foreign monopolies and to make a real effort to climb out of the vicious circle of underdevelopment; all existing resources had to be vigorously pooled. For other states, the one-party state was simply a means to preserve colonial interests undisturbed. The state gave the newly independent African countries power and freedom to maneuver vis-à-vis imperialist monopolies and opposing interest groups and nascent classes within the new state.

Any analysis of the social transformations of the class structure that have followed independence is complicated by the facts that we are dealing with a process at different stages of development in the various countries and we have a scarcity of detailed statistical and sociological data having a class perspective. Nevertheless, several studies have already been published on various African countries that have filled this lacuna and thus permit the construction of a tentative overall picture.

Except for Ghana, Guinea, Morocco, Sudan, and Tunisia, which achieved their independence in the mid-1950s, most of the African countries became independent in 1960 or (in East and Central Africa) at least by 1964. In examining the general trends of class formation and consolidation, one must keep in mind that these countries have, since independence, been following different sociopolitical orientations. Certain states are following a radical anti-imperialist restructuring of their economies, restricting private capitalist enterprise and instituting land reforms and rural development in the interest of the peasantry. Other countries, facing problems of socioeconomic development, have not interfered with the colonial structures or the capitalist mode of production.

The researcher who studies the postcolonial class structure of African societies is inevitably faced with a number of key questions: In each case, what is the relationship between the metropolitan (bourgeois) classes and the "political elite" that inherited the colonial state? What is the relationship between the political elite and the emerging working class? What is the relationship between town and country? To what extent has the peasantry been differentiated into various strata? To what extent is the process of proletarianization crystallizing a class of wage workers from the previous army of migrant laborers? To what extent is the political elite crystallizing into a class with vested interests in the ownership of the means of production?

A study of these and other aspects of postcolonial class formation is of primary importance in understanding the nature and the stages, the trends, and the political processes taking place in Africa today.

Let me begin with the statistical distribution of African workers in various categories of employment. According to the United Nations' *Survey of Economic Conditions in Africa, 1971,* the economically active population of postcolonial Africa is estimated at 135 million. The same report states that the ILO estimated that the number of unemployed exceeded 10 million, that is about 8% of the total labor force. In 23 African countries, persons working for hire accounted for about 19% of the labor force; the rest of the economically active population was self-employed or was unemployed. Of the 15 million persons working in wage labor, 8 million were in the Republic of Egypt and only 7 million in other African countries.

Fanon's theory is that the African proletariat, because its income is stable and generally higher than the peasants and because it is a small minority, enjoys a "privileged" position and therefore constitutes a point of support for the colonial and neocolonial system. The city-country dichotomy tends to emphasize the privileges enjoyed by the urban workers. President Kaunda of the Republic of Zambia (1969:28) expressed in a confused manner the rural-urban dilemma:

> Here in Zambia we face the danger of creating two nations within one. But not along capitalist patterns. The important division in our society is not that which exists between trade union labor on the one hand and managers or property owners on the other, but between the urban and rural areas. These are the two nations we are running the danger of creating, these are the two parts of our dualism: Urban and Rural and not so much between Labour and Employer.

That is certainly one side of the picture. But what about the people in the city slums? According to Romano Ledda (1967:573):

> Neo-colonialism builds cities (some of them impressive) that reflect the well-being of the upper classes and tries to make them islands of privilege. But economic stagnation and the agricultural crisis, the imbalance between development and underdevelopment inherent in the new colonial system limit the enjoyment of these privileges to an infinitesimal part of the urban population. The masses as always, are excluded, but with the difference that the contradictions of the system now take place directly under their noses and are thus more easily grasped.

The city in colonial and postcolonial Africa is a social form, a way of life predicated on a certain division of labor and a certain hierarchical ordering of activity which is broadly consistent with the class structure of the dominant mode of production. The city functions to stabilize the class structure. Hence, the postcolonial city in Africa has been the focus of the accumulated contradictions of colonial capitalism and its class conflict (see Harvey, 1973:203).

The development of colonial capitalism created the separation of the African peasantry into urban and commercial workers and agricultural workers. This led to the distinction between and opposition of town and country. Historically, the antithesis between town and country was a pivot of class conflict around which the whole economic history of society unfolded.

The colonial city in Africa also articulated the points of command in a global economy of great complexity. That economy is hierarchically ordered with local centers dominating local hinterlands, more important metropolitan centers dominating lesser centers, and urban points of command being ultimately subordinate to the central metropolitan command areas in North America and Western Europe. That is, a given metropolis may be placed in terms of its position in interlocking points of class command; its economic function is associated with its hierarchical level. The central analytical question concerns the attitude of the inheritors of the colonial estate to the inherited city.

Fanon (1963:32) argues, for example, that the town-country relationship within the colonial context exhibited colonial class inequality in its most brutal and stark reality. The urban class structure that results according to Fanon does not mask the economic inequalities:

> The originality of the colonial context is that economic reality, inequality and immense difference of ways of life never come to mask the human reality. When you examine at close quarters the colonial context, it is evident that what parcels out the world is to begin with the fact of belonging to or not belonging to a given race, a given species. In the colonies the economic substructure is also a superstructure.

The spatially defined inequality in Africa's urban areas was thus expressive of the colonial class structure. Spatial inequalities were brought into being by human action. As in Latin America, the leading towns of Africa—Dakar, Lagos, Nairobi, Dar es Salaam, Luanda, and so on—were not the creation of capitalist industrialization and inherent technical progress, but were rather the product of an export-directed colonial agriculture and mining, whose rents and profits found an urban outlet in consumption and speculation (see Murray, 1963:19).

The picture of the town structure in Portuguese Africa drawn in the following passage by Kamm (1974:73) was typical of most cities in colonial and post-colonial Africa.

> Luanda in Angola, Lourenço Marques and Beira in Mozambique are white man's cities—with downtowns of pleasant, Portuguese-style colonial houses of commerce of the last century, surrounded by the pompous public buildings of the authoritarian Government of Salazar Portugal and enveloped by the massive, shapeless concrete blocks of today's men of business. At the edges are housing developments for the "poor whites" and villas on tree-lined streets for those less poor. One wonders how

cities so seemingly small can have population figures as large as the 475,000 given for Luanda, 355,000 for Lourenço Marques and 114,000 for Beira. The answer lies beyond, in endless, warren-like shantytowns of surpassing wretchedness. There the African population lives, and there it becomes quite obvious that the population figures are, if anything, understated and, more likely, guesswork.

Shack next to shack, of the most disparate bits of wood, tin or anything else that will offer shade and shelter but uniform in their shabby inadequacy, are crowded into the plains of beaten dirt. It must have been savanna country before, with grass, bushes and some trees, but only at the edges do flashes of green relieve the dull barrenness now. The houses are arranged, if the word is not too strong for such unplanned mazes, to resemble the homesteads of families in the bush, with the shacks of the different members facing onto small patches of ground on which children play without toys and often without clothes and women cook over scraps of wood or charcoal.

The picture we have drawn so far of the transformation and social dynamics of colonial and postcolonial Africa has not dealt with the character of the African bourgeoisie. The nascent bourgeoisie of the first decade of independence has been well described by Fanon, who distinguished between the dynamic entrepreneurial bourgeoisie of nineteenth century Europe and the corrupt, enfeebled administrative bourgeoisie of postcolonial Africa.

Above, I referred to Davidson's observation that more or less consciously, the British and the French, when they were forced to relinquish their colonies were eager to hand their power to elites who would keep the African world safe for capitalism. Thus a policy was worked out to manufacture elites modeled for a middle-class solution. These elites were teachers, doctors, lawyers, ministers, and whatever remnants of the traditional elites that managed to salvage their credibility from the colonial phase. As a group, these elites had no autonomy of their own; they had no being without metropolitan backing which dominated the colonial economies. That is, their class position did not stem from the classical ownership of the means of production; they were rather class agents or allies of the foreign bourgeoisie.

The inheritors of the African political state constitute one of the most peculiar sociological phenomenon; their peculiarity lies in their unusual historical development and the nature of the state they inherited. Let me first deal with the problems they faced when they inherited the colonial state. According to Hamza Alavi (1972:60):

If the colony has a weak and underdeveloped indigenous bourgeoisie, it will be unable at the moment of independence to subordinate the relatively highly developed colonial State apparatus through which the Metropolitan power had exercised dominion over it.

A fundamental distinction can be made between former colonies which experienced "direct" rule and in which there was a large settler population (for example, Kenya, Zambia, and Rhodesia) and those colonial countries which experienced colonial exploitation under "indirect" rule, (for example, Nigeria and Ghana). In postcolonial states like Zambia and Kenya, the problem of the relationship between the state and the underlying economic structure is extremely complex. The control of the resources of the former colonies exercised by the metropolitan bourgeoisie (such as the control of copper by multinationals in Zambia and the Congo), and the presence of a sizable white settler population shackled and stunted the bourgeoisie which inherited the colonial state.

The French economist François Perroux (1961:43) stated the dilemma faced by the postcolonial bourgeoisie: "When a large firm sets up a concern in a small country, the concern is doubtless situated in the so-called 'national' territory of the smaller country. In reality, however, it belongs to the firm's own area." This confiscation of the economy condemned the postcolonial bourgeoisie to ex-treme difficulty. Alavi (1972:61) explains that the "essential problem about the state in postcolonial societies stems from the fact that it is not established by an ascendent native bourgeoisie but instead by a foreign imperialist bourgeoisie. At independence, however, the direct command of the latter over the colonial state is ended." He goes on to say, "But, by the same token, its influence over it is by no means brought to an end. The metropolitan bourgeoisie, now joined by other neo-colonial bourgeoisies, is present in the post colonial society. Together they constitute the powerful element in its class structure." Metropolitan capitalism having recruited often in the most cynical manner its local allies—allies which could only serve it and never challenge it because of the metropolitan grip on the postcolonial state's economy—could then recede from the scene.

In postcolonial Africa, the situation was complicated (as we shall see in the case of Ghana and Zambia) by the fact that there did not even exist in these societies a class that could be described as an African capitalist class or bour-geoisie. What we had, then, was a weak "middle class" which received political power because of its educational experience in colonial institutions. It exercised power with the political and economic help from the former metropolis (joined in most cases by the United States). Because of their comparative weakness, the inheritors of the colonial state in most cases have not been able to settle the underlying crisis of the structure in their own favor. On the contrary, with every effort they have made and continue to make in that direction, the conflict has sharpened (see Davidson, 1966:209) and in most cases led to military takeovers inspired from outside to preserve the imperialist grip on the local state.

The postcolonial situation has not been static by any means. Important changes and transformations of the whole economy and society, whose char-acters are consistent with the externally induced process of capitalist develop-ment, have led to the proliferation of new roles played by the African middle class. The Africanization policy of foreign firms and the inherited administrative structures has offered greater possibilities for Africans in professional careers and has also necessitated the extension of educational policies that foster a growing middle class. For the first time, Africans in some new categories of employment now command salaries that are relatively high compared to the salaries of the general population. This is partly because of the shortage of adequately qualified and trained personnel. In the policy of Africanization itself, which replaces expatriates by nationals, salary scales, once adjusted to metropolitan income levels, remain practically unchanged and thus further enhance the privileges of those Africans who have an educational qualification (see Szentes, 1971:273).

The social stratum of salaried elites, which is not the owner of the means of production, faces a cruel paradox. It cannot ensure its privileged material position so long as it serves foreign monopolies. How then do these privileged elites develop into independent ruling classes in their societies? According to Szentes, they cannot so long as they do not change the mode of production. He writes (1971:274):

> Social classes cannot exist without the characteristic production relations giving birth to them.... The formation of elites is not connected with the change of the character of production relations but only with some modification in them and a few transitory, temporarily effective factors. In the possession of state power this elite can undoubtedly influence the development of production relations, ... but the way it does also determines its own fate. Since the predominant relations of production in the backward economy inherited from colonialism are *de facto* capitalist relations which make even the surviving forms of precapitalist relations carry in them the tendency of capitalization, this elite will *either* fight against these relations or their expansion and further development. In the latter case its fate and role is clear and unambiguous enough: the elite itself will become part of the capitalist class, i.e., instead of an independent class, a source of the formation of the bourgeoisie.

The behavior and activities of the political elites in office show a great deal of ambivalence. Realizing the problems they face in competing with or supplanting the foreign monopolies that control the resources, they have opted for "socialistic" solutions. They have realized that the capitalist road has been hopelessly played out. The African political elites, in order to continue their control, have wanted to satisfy the great wave of popular awakening and demand for a different and better life and have embraced varieties of African socialism (see Mohan, 1966). This is the general situation which gave rise to the one-party state and the military takeovers (see below).

The political elite cleverly made use of the emasculated theory of socialism (in its various state manifestations), in order to appear as national leaders with a national purpose. In this process very feeble attempts were made to "nationalize" the commanding heights of the enclave economies, but the terms of "nationalization" only helped to stabilize foreign monopolies and frustrate the demands of the working class. Indeed, in the program of nationalizing 51% of the foreign monopolies, Kenya, for example, made the political elites loyal partners in an overall system which consciously or not, directly or indirectly, deprived the economy of the opportunity for true development, that is, "of any opportunity . . . for systematic change from one set of structures and relationships to another and more effective one, whether capitalist or not" (Davidson, 1974:10).

The political elites, remaining as they do within structures totally subjected to an external system and without prospects of growing into a class capable of creating and operating a system of local capitalism, find themselves unable to hold their ground. The capitalist-oriented regimes face popular discontent and upheaval, which often lead to sudden coups d'etat by one or another section of the ruling groups experiencing internal dissension (see Davidson, 1966:216).

The recent military coups must be seen within this framework. A political elite, faced with the prospect of a serious political and economic crisis, is pushed aside by the military, which can act as a shield for the nascent bourgeoisie and foreign interests until the former grows strong enough to impose its political and cultural hegemony. The conclusion is inevitable that military takeovers are a necessary outcome of neocolonialism and petty bourgeois rule in neocolonized countries. It is an inevitable result of the type of economic and social relations of dependency and in terms of this paper, of the compromised position of the local "ruler" classes—classes with the apparatus of political power, but without the economic foundations for true class rule.

SOME CONCLUSIONS

We can now attempt some overall observations regarding the evolution of the class structure in modern Africa. From what we have said above it is quite obvious that the class structure of modern Africa has to be studied on several interdependent levels of analysis. Africa in the last three hundred years has not existed in isolation. Its peoples have been tied in certain definite and more or less stable relations with the capitalist world. The evolution of the class structure has been determined by the character and form of these relations.

The historical incorporation of Africa and its precapitalist systems into the evolving capitalist mode of production produced extremely complex systems of class relations. The system was characterized by economic and political structures in which the possessing and ruling stratum was foreign and the Africans appeared in descending order of subservience and dependence. To study the class structure of modern Africa requires the study of the determinate mode of production—the CCMP. In any given region or country, social classes appear that complement the colonial relations of production. The empirical study of classes in any country has a definite meaning only when the class structure is located within a framework in which the control of the means of production is properly understood. As Szentes (1971:264) puts it:

> The distortion of the social structure, the extent of the survival of precapitalistic formations and their location, function and role in the social structure may vary from one underdeveloped country to another, depending on *what historical periods these remnants can be traced back to,* i.e., at what level of their historical development these societies were originally affected by the penetration of foreign capitalism, and, on the other hand, *what changes these remnants have undergone* as a result of external influences and the adjustment to a changed, heterogeneous environment. Thus it is due also to the original, i.e., the precolonial, differences in their development that the remnants of the most different periods of primitive, slave and feudal society can be found in the countries of Africa, Asia and Latin America.

Hence, the analysis of the CCMP will explain "the specific coexistence of foreign monopoly capital and the precapitalistic formations which are of a *diametrically opposed nature* and [will also explain] the formation of a distorted, heterogeneous social structure" (Szentes, 1971:264).

My purpose in this paper was to discuss in general terms the evolution of the class structure in Africa and to locate the fundamental determinants of the class structure in the analysis of the CCMP. Some scholars, especially because of the colonial context, have suggested that the concept of class does not describe the reality of modern Africa, but that the concept of social and cultural pluralism is more appropriate for the analysis of the African social structures. Some others have asserted that more adequate would be the concept of elite in the sense of a group possessing power.

Let me resolve the question of elites first. It does not seem that the concept of elite and that of class are mutually exclusive; the former refers to groups exercising power at a particular time and the latter to an economic relationship. I agree with Szentes (1971:274) that a social structure of a composition similar to elites (the so-called middle class and intelligentsia) also exists in the developed (European) class societies. "Its social position and rule and its relation to the basic classes, . . . are fairly clear and well defined; its character is determined by the prevailing class relations. It is merely a supplementary appendix to the basic classes. It may constitute a communication channel between them and even a source of supply for them, but cannot develop into an independent class."

It is obvious, therefore, that in the present conditions of Africa, an elite as a group which is not the owner of the means of production is a transitory formation whose hold on the state is extremely tenuous, as the recent military coups have demonstrated. The concept of elite cannot be a substitute for the concept of class.

Finally, and even more importantly, the theories of "social and/or cultural pluralism" are intended to obfuscate the role of class relations in colonial and postcolonial Africa. These theories absolutize the natural differences existing between people and promote them to an "eternal law of nature." As a theory of conflict, social and/or cultural pluralism was deliberately proposed to deal with the Marxian theory of class in such a manner as to deny the threatened social change which general acceptance of the Marxian theory would generate (see Harvey, 1973:125). That is;

> The Marxist theory was clearly dangerous in that it appeared to provide the key to understanding capitalist production from the position of those *not* in control of the means of production. Consequently, the categories, concepts, relationships and methods which had the potential to form a new paradigm were an enormous threat to the power structure of the capitalist world. [Harvey, 1973:126-127]

The theory of class in Africa, whose basic principles and evolution we have been setting out in this essay, should be used with an understanding of the specific conditions of time and place, the level of historical features of development of this or that country in Africa. These conditions are highly diverse because the impact of colonialism was not simultaneous or uniform. Therefore, it is methodologically unsound to look to a theory for cut-and-dried solutions for each individual case. The application of a theory to concrete conditions is a creative process. It requires the use of "sociological imagination." In contrast to the study of the superficial aspects of social life, the concept of class focuses attention on the various planes, contradictions, possibilities of analysis of human exploitation, and the possibility of liberation.

The social structure of African society, viewed in detail, presents a fairly complex kaleidoscope. Alongside the interethnic distinctions there have arisen important interclass distinctions. Alongside of modern evils, a whole series of inherited evils oppress the African people, arising from the passive survival of antiquated modes of production, frozen in time by capitalism with its inevitable train of social and political anachronisms (see Marx, 1967:9).

REFERENCES

ALAVI, H. (1972). "The post colonial state." New Left Review, 74(July-August):59-82.
——— (1973). "Peasant classes and primodial loyalties." Journal of Peasant Studies, 1(1):23-62.
ALLEN, V.L. (1972). "The meaning of the working class in Africa." Journal of Modern African Studies, 10(2):169-189.
AMIN, S. (1974). "Modes of production and social formations." UFAHAMU, 4(3):57-85.
BARNETT, D. (1973). Peasant types and revolutionary potential in colonial Africa (pamphlet). Richmond: LSM Press.
BRETT, E.A. (1973). Colonialism and underdevelopment in East Africa: The politics of economic change 1919-1939. New York: Nok Publishers.
BUKHARIN, N.I. (1972). Imperialism and the world economy. London: Merlin Press.
CABRAL, A. (1969). Revolution in Guinea. London: Stage I.
——— (1973). Return to the source. New York: Africa Information Service.
COHEN, R. (1972). "Classes in Africa: Analytical problems and prospectives." The Socialist Register, 1972. London: Merlin Press.
DANILOVA, L. (1971). "Controversial problems in the theory of precapitalist societies." Soviet Anthropology and Archaeology 9(4):269-328.
DAVIDSON, B. (1966). "The outlook for Africa." The Socialist Register, 1966. London: Merlin Press.
——— (1969). Africa in history: Themes and outlines. New York: Macmillan.
——— (1974). Can Africa survive? Arguments against growth without development. Boston: Little, Brown.
DOS SANTOS, T. (1970). "The concept of social classes." Science and Society, (summer): 166-193.
DU BOIS, W.E. (1965). The world and Africa: An inquiry into the part which Africa has played in world history. New York: International Publishers.
ELLIOT, C. (1968). "The Zambian economy." East African Journal 5(12):11-16.
ENGELS, F. (1939). Anti-Duhring. New York: International Publishers.
FANON, F. (1963). The wretched of the earth. New York: Grave Press.
FARIS, J. (1975). "Social evolution, population, and production." In S. Polgard (ed.), Population, ecology, and social evolution. The Hague: Mouton.
FRIEDMAN, H., and WAYNE, J. (1967). "Functionalism and dependency: Replacing old orthodoxies with new." Paper presented to the Eighth World Congress of Sociology, Toronto.
GENOUD, R. (1969). Nationalism and economic development in Ghana. New York: Praeger.
GLUCKMAN, M. (1964). Custom and conflict in Africa. New York: Barnes and Noble.
GREEN, R.H., and SEIDMAN, A. (1968). Unity or poverty? The economics of Pan Africanism. Baltimore: Penguin.

HALL, R. (1965). Zambia. New York: Praeger.
HARVEY, D. (1973). Social justice and the city. Baltimore: Johns Hopkins University Press.
KAMM, H. (1974). "Portugal's absurd empire." New York Times Magazine (August 8):8-9, 56-62.
KAUNDA, K. (1968). Zambia's guideline for the next decade. Lusaka, Zambia: Government Printer.
KITCHING, G.N. (1972). "The concept of class in the study of Africa." African Review, 2(3):327-350.
KUPER, L., and SMITH, M.G. (1969). Pluralism in Africa. Los Angeles: University of California Press.
LEDDA, R. (1967). "Social classes and political struggle in Africa." International Socialist Journal, 22(August):560-580.
LENIN, V.I. (1964). The development of capitalism in Russia. Moscow: Progress Publishers.
––– (1968). Selected works. Moscow: Progress Publishers.
MAGUBANE, B. (1974). "Imperialism and the character of class structure in southern Africa." Paper presented to the Eighth World Congress of Sociology, Toronto.
MAGUBANE, B., and O'BRIEN, J. (1972). "The political economy of migrant labor: A critique of conventional wisdom, or a case study in the functions of functionalism." Critical Anthropology, 11(2):88-103.
MANDEL, E. (1972). "The driving force of imperialism in our era." In Spheres of influence in the age of imperialism. Nottingham: Spokesman Books.
MAQUET, J. (1972). Civilizations of black Africa. New York: Oxford University Press.
MARX, K. (1963). The poverty of philosophy. New York: International Publishers.
––– (1967). Capital (Vol. 1). New York: International Publishers.
––– (1968). "The Communist manifesto." Selected works. Moscow: Progress Publishers.
––– (1972). The Grundrisse. New York: Harper and Row.
––– (1975). Wage-labour and capital. New York: International Publishers.
MEILLASSOUX, C. (1972). "From reproduction to production." Economy and Society, 1:93-105.
MOHAN, J. (1966). "Varieties of African socialism." The Socialist Register, 1966. London: Merlin Press.
MURRAY, R. (1962). "Colonial Congo." New Left Review, 17(winter):120-123.
––– (1963). "Agronomy and society." New Left Review, 19(March-April):85-90.
NICOLAUS, M. (1970). "The theory of the labor aristocracy." Monthly Review, 21(April): 91-102.
PERROUX, F. (1961). "Large firm–small nation." Presence Africaine, (38):36-51.
POULANTZAS, N. (1974). "Internationalization of capitalist relations and the nation state." Economy and Society, 3(2):147-179.
REDFIELD, R. (1960). The little community. Chicago: University of Chicago Press.
REY, P.-P. (1971). Colonialisme, néo-colonialisme et transition au capitalisme: Exemple de la "camilog" au Congo-Brazzaville. Paris: Maspero.
RIBEIRO, D. (1972). The Americans and civilization. New York: Dutton.
RODNEY, W. (1972). How Europe underdeveloped Africa. London: Bogle-L'Ouverture.
SINGER, H. (1950). "The distribution of gains between interest and borrowing countries." Pp. 336-350 in G. Dalton (eds.), Economic development and social change. New York: Natural History Press.
SWEEZY, P. (1942). The theory of capitalist development. New York: Monthly Review Press.
SZENTES, T. (1971). The political economy of underdevelopment. Budapest: Akademiai Kiado.
TERRAY, E. (1972). "Historical materialism and segmentary lineage based societies." In E. Terray (ed.), Marxism and primitive societies. New York: Monthly Review Press.
VAN DEN BERGHE, P.L. (1965). "Toward a sociology of Africa." In Africa: Social problems of change and conflict. San Francisco: Chandler.
WALLERSTEIN, I. (1974). The modern world-system: Capitalist agriculture and the origins of the European world-economy in the sixteenth century. New York: Academic Press.
WATERMAN, P. (1969). "Stratification in colonial and post colonial Africa." MS Center for African Studies, Birmingham University, November.

WILLIAMS, E. (1944). Capitalism and slavery. London: Andre Deutsch.
WODDIS, J. (1960). Africa: The roots of revolt. London: Lawrence and Wisehart.
WORSELY, P. (1964). "Democracy from the top." Pp. 370-390 in I.L. Horovitz (ed.), New sociology: Essays in social science and social theory in honor of C. Wright Mills. New York: Oxford University Press.
ZAKINE, D. (1968). "Classes and class struggle in developing countries." International Affairs, (4):47-55.

8

THE CONGRUENCE OF POLITICAL ECONOMIES AND IDEOLOGIES IN AFRICA

CLAUDE AKE

University of Dar es Salaam
and Carleton University

The assumption that ideologies are autonomous has led to false issues and considerable confusion. This assumption lies behind the debate as to whether Third World countries should adopt one-party systems or multiparty systems—a useless debate which rests on the erroneous presumption that ideological apparatuses such as party systems can be freely chosen and freely discarded. The assumption also lies behind the misleading notion that development is to a considerable extent simply a matter of choosing the right ideological framework. Finally the assumption lies behind what I may call the personalistic view of history, which is so misleading. By the personalistic view of history I mean the tendency to think that we can account for a country's historical development by the fact that it happened to have particular types of leaders who happened to do particular types of things and to hold particular types of ideas.

Ideas and ideologies are not autonomous but derivative. As Mannheim shows, men do not think alone; they think with and against one another as members of groups. Thinking is an integral part of the struggle of existence—the struggle to maintain the world in a desired state of being. This struggle expresses the objective contradictions of the real world. Our ideologies are essentially manifestations of our objective position in the struggle. In this paper, I try to show how objective forces shape the ideologies of African countries and how the ideologies of these countries are congruent with their economies.

THE COLONIAL ECONOMY

The Ideology of the Colonizers

The colonial economy is a useful point at which to begin this analysis. Although the colonial economy was an extension of Western capitalism or, at any rate, an effect of its development, it differed quite substantially from the capitalist economies of the West. The African colonial economies were based on explicit rejection of the notion of consumer sovereignty and frank acceptance of the necessity of authoritative allocation of work and of rewards.

These were not arbitrary modifications. They were imposed by the logic of colonialism. To begin with, the drive for colonies was dictated by the need to avoid wasteful competition and to secure sources of raw materials which could be completely monopolized. Since colonialism was such a massive pillage of the human and natural resources of the colonized peoples, aggression and hostility permeated, vitiated, and indeed defined the relationship between colonizer and colonized. Without coercion the equilibrium of the colonial system would have been destroyed. In the colonial economy, force became the key instrument of the profit motive. Force was used to allocate roles, force was used to insure the supply of labor, and force was used to extract and allocate the economic surplus.

The colonial political system was necessarily as unilateral as the colonial economic system. Consumer sovereignty could not be denied in the economic sphere and tolerated in the political sphere, because to allow it in the political sphere would trigger an irresistible pressure for allowing it in the economic sphere.

The logic of colonial relations and the concrete interests inherent in these relations determine the dominant ideology of the colonial system. It is customary to make much of the differences between the colonial practices and ideologies of the Portuguese, Belgians, French, Germans, English, Italians, and Spaniards. We have been sufficiently impressed by these distinctions that we now talk about enlightened colonizers and unenlightened ones, those who took seriously their *mission civilisatrice* and those who merely exploited. The fact of the matter is that colonialism is an objective relation which is the same everywhere. And the colonial relation demands, indeed imposes, a particular political system and particular ideologies congruent with its objective character. Thus, all colonizers used essentially the same ideology. They all developed very similar justification for colonialism from the same premises, namely that colonialism was beneficial to the colonized in the fundamental sense of improving the quality of their lives. Colonialism became not self-seeking, not exploitation, but salvation. The very terminology that the colonizers used to describe colonialism reflected the substance of their ideology. Thus they described the colonies as "protectorates," implying that the colonial power was really fiduciary and that its raison d'etat was protection of the colonies. The British often preferred to think of colonialism as a "mandate" to help backward peoples, the French and Portuguese and Belgians as a civilizing mission or "tutelage."

This characterization of colonialism not only had the effect of making it look like generosity instead of rapacity; it also enabled the colonizers to develop some defense against the charge that colonialism was racist or that colonization entailed treating the colonized peoples as subhuman. For this characterization of colonialism presupposed the possibility of civilizing the colonized people and hence their potential for cultural existence. Of course, one could not pretend that the colonized were civilized or equal to everyone else. Existing realities could not be ignored. The colonized had to be treated in a manner commensurate with their stage of development as men, and this unfortunately meant limiting their participation and their claims in the community of civilized men temporarily. However, the important thing was that the obstacles in the way of their development were removable, and colonialism ensured their removal. So with uncanny ingenuity, the colonizers were able to reconcile racism with the proclamation of the equality of all men.

The ideology of the colonized complemented the political economy of colonialism very well. It justified the system in terms of its benefits to the exploited without in any way compelling any mitigation of the harshness and the brutality of the exploitation. Every assault on the colonized person could be defended as a necessary concession to the realities of his state of development. In the meantime, the assault on his way of life and on his dignity became the very tool for creating these very "realities." In other words, the systematic brutalization of the colonized became the very instrument for reducing him to a subhuman existence, the condition of existence in which he would have to be in order to deserve colonization. Thus, somehow, the more inhuman the practice of colonialism, the more plausible its ideology.

The Ideology of Nationalism

We have looked at one side of the coin. We have seen the congruence between the ideology of the colonizers and their objective interests. We must now look at the other side of the colonial relation—the colonized. What is the relation of the thinking of the nationalist leaders to their objective situation and what are the implications of this relation?

To answer this question we must begin by noting the link between the nationalist movement and the contradictions of the colonial economy. One major source of contradiction was the economy's supply of labor. The colonizers needed labor to carry out the exploitation of the colony: roads and railways had to be built, a bureaucratic network had to be established, men were needed to gather the raw materials and to prepare them for export, and domestic servants were needed for commodious living. The colonial economy had to obtain labor from a subject population that was not in a monetary economy. The supply of labor could not be left to the usual market mechanism. Coercion had to be used. People were simply rounded up and compelled to work, or a money tax was imposed in order to compel people to enter the money economy. These measures deepened the antipathies between the colonizer and the colonized. The bitterness aroused by such massive coercion was deepened all the more because the system of compulsory labor greatly disrupted the traditional social structures. This was a neat dilemma: the colonial economy could not get the labor it needed without exacerbating the centrifugal forces that threatened to destroy it.

Virtually every policy which the colonizers devised to facilitate their economic exploitation recreated the same contradictions. Consider the education policy. Some basic education was necessary to ensure an adequate supply of labor. The colonizers wisely limited education to what was absolutely basic; hence higher education was undeveloped. They offered the most elementary liberal education with a heavy religious bias. A minimum of technical and scientific education was offered because colonial domination owed much to the spell of the colonizer's technological and scientific superiority. Religious education was emphasized because it was considered an excellent vehicle for indoctrinating the colonized into a cult of subservience. This educational program carried its own contradictions. To begin with, education, however basic, carried with it the threat of penetration into the colonizer's world, and the more the mystery of his power was penetrated, the more its spell was weakened. The concentration on liberal education may have protected the colonizer's monopoly of science and technology, but that was small consolation given the fact that liberal education led to the discovery of Western liberal ideas and to the development of political consciousness and the skills needed for political effectiveness. Liberal education generated an indigenous leadership and equipped its members with a common language. It helped create the conditions for eradicating colonialism.

The colonizer's quest for economies of scale led to similar contradictions. The search for economies of scale led to the geographical concentration of economic activities and subsequently to the concentration of the wretched victims of colonialism. They were concentrated geographically, subjected to a common life style, and given a new common consciousness. To make colonialism more profitable, this army of laborers was denied any welfare scheme. Eventually they called on their own ingenuity by setting up an elaborate and sophisticated network of tribal and "secondary" associations. These associations provided scholarships, loans, and succor for orphans, widows, the aged, and the unemployed. They became an invisible government. More importantly, they provided the nationalist movements with leadership training and a ready-made network of political organizations to build on. Those who are familiar with the contemporary history of Africa know that most of the nationalist parties in Africa grew from these associations.

We have seen how the colonial situation had a latent tendency to evolve toward its own dialectical negation. We have seen how the contradictions of the situation created the nationalist movements and their leadership. The leaders of the nationalist movements had fundamental common interests. They derived status from their proximity to the colonizer's culture. They had a vested interest in adhering to the colonizer's value system and in preserving some of their links to the colonizer's economy. They had an interest in keeping the nationalist revolution limited, to ensure the preservation of privilege. They were the ones who would benefit most from the displacement of the colonial regime, for they would inherit economic and political power. Let us look at how the nationalist leaders acted and how they thought in order to see whether they were thinking as a group in response to the interest inherent in their historical situation.

To begin with, let us look at their political stance. The political stance and the political style of both the colonizers and the nationalist leaders were rigidly defined by the colonial situation. As has been pointed out, the relation between colonizer and colonized was one permeated by profound antagonism. The capitalism of colonialism, which was booty capitalism, did not offer much scope for compromise. The single issue of booty capitalism was simply the possibility of its maintenance. And this issue resolved itself into the balance of power between colonizer and colonized. In the political sphere there was the same brutal simplicity. The colonizers could not maintain or expect to maintain their presence and their exploitation by the consent of their victims. It was clear that whatever else they may have done to maintain their presence, force was ultimately the basis of their claim. So, in the final analysis, the question of the survival of the colonial polity was a question of the maintenance of a balance of power which favored the colonizers. The colonizers were under pressure to monopolize power and to render the colonized powerless. One could not be a colonizer and a democrat at the same time. If the colonizers allowed popular participation in government, colonialism would automatically end. However much the colonizer might profess his commitment to democracy and thus to the political development of his victims, the primary goal of his politics was the exclusion of the subject population from power—though not necessarily from token participation. For their part, the leaders of the nationalist movements found that they too were obliged to take an uncompromising political stance. They had to make an exclusive claim to government in the name of the people and to deny the colonizers any claim at all to government. If they had simply sought to share power or to ameliorate their political status or to stand for more enlightened and more effective government, they would have implicitly legitimated the colonial regime. Therein lies the brutal simplicity of colonial politics: one exclusive claim to power against another. The politics aptly complemented the economic relation.

The leaders of nationalist movements used essentially the same ideology to support their struggle. Let us examine the major characteristics of this ideology. One aspect of this ideology was the rehabilitation of the self-respect of the colonized people. All the nationalist leaders, including the ones who were the most impregnated with the colonial mentality, engaged in such rehabilitation. The objective necessity of this element in the ideology of the nationalists is fairly obvious. The colonizers faced the problem of justifying the plunder of their victims' resources and their assault on their victims' way of life. When all the equivocations are done away with, their defense amounted to the claim that their victims were somewhat less than human—hence the whole point of the civilizing mission was to make them human. Colonial politics then set out to make their victims what they would have had to be like to deserve the treatment they got. Hence the systematic humiliation and the denigration of their culture and history. The maintenance of colonialism depended very much on the ability of the colonizer to make his claim to superiority plausible and on the acquiescence of the colonized in their representation as inferior. The people could not be mobilized into colonial politics and they could not effectively wage war against colonialism so long as they were burdened by a sense of inferiority. In these circumstances the ideologies of anticolonialism had to reflect the necessity of restoring the self-respect of the colonized. This rehabilitation of self-respect took several forms: the refutation of the arguments and writings which the colonizers had used to denigrate the history and culture of their victims, the glorification of the history and culture of Africa, and the assertion of the uniqueness and vitality of the African mind and African institutions—as, for instance, Negritude, the African personality, and African socialism. We find these themes in such writings as Senghor's *African Socialism,* Kenyatta's *Facing Mount Kenya,* Azikiwe's *Renascent Africa,* and Nkrumah's *I Speak of Freedom.*

The second component of the nationalist ideology was the denigration of colonial rule. There is a sense in which this component was merely an aspect of the restoration of the self-respect of the colonized. But it was more than this. It was necessary to reveal the evil of colonialism in its totality and enormity in order to fight it most effectively. So, without exception, the nationalist leaders tore at the mystifications of colonialism and tried to show how it had vitiated and impoverished its victims.

The third component of the nationalist ideology was the assertion of self-determination. There is no need to show the objective necessity of this component. Colonialism being what it is, to oppose colonialism in anything other than a trivial sense is to assert the right of self-determination. The demand for self-determination was inherent in the basic contradiction of the colonial situation.

The fourth component of the ideology of the nationalist leadership was the doctrine of liberal democracy. The leaders of the nationalist movements in Africa were liberal democrats. This seems somewhat surprising because liberal democracy was the ideology of the colonizers, whose culture the nationalist movement was supposed to be rejecting wholesale. It is surprising also because liberal democracy was the political correlate of capitalism, and the colonization of Africa was a logical outcome of West European capitalism. But if we look at the situation and the interests of the leaders of the nationalist movements in Africa, their resort to the doctrine of liberal democracy is natural, indeed inevitable. The choice of this doctrine was due to its accessibility and utility. The compelling reason for the adoption of the liberal ideology was its utility. First, it was useful for mobilizing liberal opinion in the metropolitan countries. It was most effective to make their appeal to Western liberals in terms of values and doctrines they understood and accepted. Second, it was the ideological correlate of the capitalist relations of production which the nationalist leaders intended to retain and which they have retained. Finally and most importantly, liberal ideology was the classic tool for coping with the fundamental contradiction of all bourgeois revolutions. This contradiction is as follows. On the one hand, the bourgeoisie has to appeal to the principle of self-determination in order to gain mass support to defeat feudalists (as in the case of the French and English revolutions) or imperialists (as in the case of the American Revolution and the Asian and African nationalist revolutions). On the other hand, class interests, especially as concretized in the relations of production, had to be defended. And this meant that popular sovereignty could not be allowed. For popular sovereignty or substantive democracy could not be allowed without eventually undermining the capitalist mode of production. Those who are familiar with the classic statements of the ideology of liberal democracy such as Locke's *Second Treatise on Government,* Mill's *Essay on Liberty,* Bentham's *Representative Government,* Hobbes's *Leviathan,* Rousseau's *Social Contract,* and *The Declaration of the Rights of Man and of the Citizen* are familiar with the way that liberal democracy has met this dilemma. The African nationalist leaders simply adapted the solution they found in these theories to their situation. They harped on the necessity of self-determination and on the virtues of democracy, equality, and the dignity of man. But these brave words were perfectly safe because in the colonial situation the substantive issue was alien rule and the substantive conception of self-determination would inevitably amount to overthrow of alien rule. So they could talk about self-determination without any commitments to democracy, equality, or the dignity of man. That they did not take these ideas seriously was soon apparent from their performance as the leaders of the new indigenous governments. However, they had already betrayed their indifference to these ideals even before independence by their very vagueness and by their unconcern for the political consequences of the capitalist mode of production.

These are the four themes which constitute the core of the political ideology of African leaders. There is no African nationalist leader whose political ideology was not built on one or more of those four themes. We have seen that, in developing their political ideologies, African nationalist leaders were simply responding logically to the realities of their existence. They thought as a group at least in the sense that their thinking was fundamentally the same and congruent with the similarities of their objective situation.

THE POSTCOLONIAL ERA

The performance of the nationalist leaders who inherited power gives us further illustration of the existential determination of thought and propensity to action. When political independence came, the interests of the nationalist leaders who inherited power changed somewhat. And their ideas and dispositions to action changed correspondingly. The change from being an oppositional group to one of being the government was full of perils as well as exciting possibilities. Authority had to be consolidated. The appetite for participation and better welfare which the nationalist leaders had excited had to be satisfied. The oppositional political orientation which the nationalist struggle had produced had to be changed. With the common enemy no longer formally in power, the problem of integration loomed large.

These problems quickly revealed the contradictions within the newly independent society, particularly the contradiction between the new rulers and the masses. Consider the politicization of the masses and the pressure for democratic participation which the nationalist struggle had created. If the new rulers had chosen to allow democracy in substance as opposed to appearance, they would have had to abolish the capitalist relations of production which they had inherited, for such relations of production are diametrically opposed to substantive democracy. So the choice was one of denying the demand for participation or changing the relations of production. Consider the question of the demand for material improvement of the masses. Colonial exploitation, neocolonialism, and other factors prevented the economies of the newly independent states from immediately generating goods and services of the magnitude to satisfy the expectations of material improvement of the people. So in the short run, the road to significant betterment of the material conditions of the masses really depended on the abolition of exploitative economic relations and on redistribution of resources. It is clear that the new rulers could not meet the pressure for participation or the demand for welfare in a manner compatible with the maintenance of existing relations of production and their privileges. And insofar as they could not solve these two problems, they were in no position to solve the problems of authority and integration.

The new rulers reacted in much the same way to these problems. And their reaction was all that could reasonably be expected of anyone in their situation. They decided to maintain the exploitative relations and a stratification system that they dominated. They decided to firmly discourage demands for redistribution of wealth and for mass participation. Having made these commitments, they were obliged to use coercion to solve the problems of authority and integration. The manifestations of these commitments were the same all over Africa. All over Africa the masses were deprived of effective political participation; they are allowed—sometimes compelled—to vote in elections, but their participation has been inconsequential. Elections have become a redundant formality all over Africa. Dissident groups, counter-elites and progressives are intimidated, incarcerated, or murdered. Worker's movements are deprived of all autonomy and effectiveness.

These are the realities that have now led to a hasty revision of the ideology of the nationalist leaders presently in power. If we compare the speeches and writings of the nationalist leaders before independence and after, we find that they all revised their ideologies along the following lines: First, their ideology now proclaims the end of internal ideological conflict. It is argued that the problems facing the nation are clear, that everyone should apply himself to the task. In effect, the leaders of Africa are reducing politics to administration insofar as questions are no longer to be asked regarding the overriding goals of society and the legitimacy of the existing political and economic order. Second, emphasis has shifted from liberty to order. They argue that order (in effect, conformism) is necessary for maximum effectiveness in dealing with the problems of development. Order has to be maintained to discourage the numerous enemies who have designs on the independence of the new state. The institutionalized disorder so characteristic of Western politics is absolutely contrary to the African tradition. The African tradition of unanimity has to be rehabilitated because it is a more efficient and more civilized way of conducting public affairs. This argument becomes generalized as an argument against dissent, interest articulation, and democratic participation and also as a defense of the monolithic political structure that is being created. Third, the significance of independence is redefined to conceal the poor performance and self-interested behavior of the ruling elite. Since they are unwilling to change existing relations of production and to redistribute available resources in a radically egalitarian direction and since constraints on their economies have ruled out any rapid increase of the economic surplus in the short run, they could not expect to increase the material well-being of the masses as expected. So they now argue that the immediate significance of independence is hard work, not self-indulgence. Legitimate expectations of the material betterment of the masses are now represented as naive or subversive or as reprehensible hedonism. The fourth characteristic of the postindependence ideologies is the emphasis on unity. This characteristic does not represent any change of trend because the preindependence ideology had also stressed unity. In both the preindependence and the postindependence eras the stress on unity has served the same purpose, namely to cover the contradictions in the society. In the postindependence era, the rulers have used the idea of unity in a manner that is blatantly self-serving.

In the period of the nationalist struggle, unity was associated with justice. In fact, the struggle for justice was the rationale of unity. The victims of colonialism needed to unite in order to combat their exploitation. The link between justice and unity, however, has become more tenuous in the postindependence period. African leaders are now calling for unity without reference to the justice of the relevant order. Indeed, they do not even tolerate questions concerning the justice of the existing order. At the same time, the injustice of the status quo has emerged in clear relief as the problems of the postindependence era reveal and deepen the contradictions between the leaders and the masses. To sum up, the salient features of the postindependence ideology of the nationalist leaders are the same features which have dominated all ideologies associated with the establishment and consolidation of the dictatorship of the bourgeoisie. The remarkable thing about the behavior and thought of African leaders is the absence of surprises.

A PROBLEM FOR THE THESIS

I have been arguing my thesis regarding the congruence of ideologies and political economies by showing how the African leaders facing rather similar situations have acted and thought alike. I want to consider a criticism of this view. The criticism goes like this: the argument that African leaders have thought and acted in roughly the same way is not supported by the evidence. African leaders are clearly divisible into progressive and conservatives. There are leaders such as Nyerere and Sékou Touré whose orientation is now unequivocally socialist. And there are those like Kenyatta, Houphuët-Boigny, Senghor, Mobutu, and Bongo whose preference is decidedly capitalist development.

The objection is understandable. But the difference is more apparent than real. First of all, let us note the fundamental institutional developments in all African countries, progressive and reactionary. To begin with, in all African countries, the leaders have held tenaciously to power. Change of government is brought about only by force. The second development is that the political systems of Africa have become uniformly monolithic. Power has become centralized, and opposition to those in power is illegitimate. Third, all African countries are now de facto one-party systems in which the masses have been effectively depoliticized, in the sense that their political participation has been reduced to choices which are totally inconsequential.

I take it that the first two developments are indisputable, so I will not dwell on them. The third one is no less true, but it is less obvious perhaps. So I shall continue this point. For a start, this development follows from the first two. Given the determination to monopolize power and the institutionalization of monolithic political systems, the masses cannot very well be given any power. Political participation must necessarily be one that would guarantee the survival of the existing leadership and power structure and the institutions by which they exercise power. But such a guarantee is not possible unless mass participation is trivialized to the point of being a formal confirmation of the status quo. The issue of the depoliticization of the masses has become blurred by the abstract debate about the possibility of democracy within the one-party state. Some people—usually liberals and reactionaries—maintain that single-party systems cannot be democratic, and some—usually progressives—argue that single party states are the more democratic. For our present purpose, the issue is not what can be, but what is. In other words, the question is not whether or not the one-party state can be democratic, but whether the one-party systems existing in Africa are in fact democratic. Clearly the answer is that they are not. There are two conditions that have to be met before they can be called democratic. The first is that the top party positions should be effectively elective. But there is no African country in which this is the case. In all the African single-party systems, the top leadership positions are effectively cooptive and only formally elective. The second condition is that party elections should be free in the sense that any party member can offer himself as a candidate for office and also in the related sense that members of the party should be free to choose between the candidates who offer themselves for elective office. There is no country in Africa where this condition is met. The party leadership handpicks candidates at every level. The absence of these two conditions amounts to disenfranchisement of the masses. Political developments in postcolonial Africa amount to the usual story of bourgeois revolutions being followed by the dictatorship of the bourgeoisie. If we turn from the political to the economic front, we find the same similarity between progressive and reactionary countries in those areas where the labels "progressive" and "reactionary" should indicate great differences. All African countries still maintain their customary dependence on the West, although every one of them has taken some modest step toward the diversification of dependence by building some bridges with the East-bloc countries. Perhaps it is unfair and misleading to make too much of the point, given the difficulties of disengagement from the old colonial ties.

Let us turn to another point. All African countries, even the most obviously capitalist, such as Nigeria, Zaire, Ivory Coast, and Senegal, have very large public sectors which are getting larger in every case. This type of economy was a legacy of colonialism which could not be maintained without statism. It is precisely such statism and its associated dominance of the public sector that makes the struggle to power in Africa so bitter. It means that, all over Africa, the state has become the major and sometimes the only owner of industry; the control of the machinery of the state is the key to wealth. In such circumstances the premium of political power becomes very high. The trend all over Africa has been an ever greater increase in the role of the state in the economy. The pressures for this development are the same all over Africa. One such pressure is the buying back of the country in the process of decolonization. The buying back has been done by the state, which alone has the requisite resources. Finally and most importantly, it is safer and perhaps cheaper for the rulers to extract the surplus by control rather than by ownership of the means of production. Nationalization and other measures for increasing the role of the public sector in the economy are necessary for the less visible form of exploitation, namely, exploitation by control.

This brings me to the third area where one would expect great differences between the progressive and reactionary countries, namely, the economic exploitation of the masses. On this score, the differences are marginal. The material well-being of the masses has not improved to any significant degree anywhere in Africa. To all appearances, their economic exploitation is unmitigated. Some countries appear to have drastically reduced the exploitation of the masses because of their populist rhetoric and because of some superficial egalitarian measures that have been adopted. But the masses continue to bear all the burdens of development and to supply the means for catering to the appetites of an unproductive ruling class. The gap between the incomes and the standard of living of the bourgeoisie and the masses is scandalously wide in every African country.

These considerations indicate that the differences between the African countries that are usually classified as progressive and those that are classified as reactionary are more apparent than real. That is not to say that there are no differences. The conspicuous difference is that the progressive countries prefer to take a socialist stance. Whatever the seriousness of the socialist stance, it is nevertheless a matter of interest and some significance that some African leaders and some African countries prefer to cultivate a progressive or socialist image. Why do some African countries prefer to cultivate this image?

This question appears to raise a serious difficulty for my thesis about the existential determination of ideology in Africa. It would seem that if, as we argue, the objective forces in Africa are essentially identical, then it is hard to explain why some countries will prefer the appearance of a particular ideological complexion while others prefer another. For if the thoughts we have and the images we seek to project are merely epiphenomenal, African leaders should seek to project the same image.

The answer to this is that far from contradicting the thesis, the difference in question corroborates it. It corroborates it in the sense that the difference is not due to caprice or choice; it is determined by objective conditions. The difference reflects social forces that are at work all over Africa but that are for the moment more potent in the African countries that we call "progressive." Every prognostication indicates that these social forces are likely to become stronger in the "reactionary" countries so that the difference in ideological posture will be obliterated. All African countries are under two very strongly related revolutionary pressures. These pressures are (1) desperate poverty and (2) the consciousness of the burden of poverty and the injustice of economic inequality.

Africa has been reduced to desperate poverty and is likely to remain so for quite a while. There is no need to trot out the statistics of Africa's crushing poverty. It is only necessary to remind ourselves that there is no relief in sight because the problems of underdevelopment have been accentuated in many ways. There is the Arab oil embargo, which has wiped out the reserves of several African countries and brought some of them to the brink of bankruptcy. There is the burden of debt. The cost of servicing debts is roughly equivalent to 25% of Africa's total exports. There is the drain of capital, due to Africa's dependency. There is the burden of natural disasters, such as the drought that has devastated Senegal, Chad, Mauritania, Niger, Upper Volta, Mali, Dahomey, and the northern areas of Nigeria, Ethiopia, and Somalia. Finally, there is the parasitism of the African bourgeoisie, which appears to have settled for extracting surpluses by sheer coercion instead of developing the forces of production.

The African masses are now acutely conscious of the burden of poverty and the unfairness of economic inequality. The new consciousness is due to two factors. First, the masses were mobilized into politics during the nationalist struggle by appeal to their impoverishment by colonialism and to the disparities between their own material well-being and that of their exploiters. Second, the penetration of Africa by the West filled Africans with a longing for affluence and Western consumer goods. This exposure has made the poverty of the African commoner all the more difficult to bear.

The extreme poverty and the consciousness of it are very strong revolutionary pressures. They keep expectations upwardly mobile, all the while breeding misery and resentment. They breed desperation and fill the rulers with fear of being swept away by violence. More to the point, the extreme poverty and consciousness of deprivation imply that the struggle for the surplus becomes particularly grim. There is so little surplus to appropriate, and everyone is passionately seeking this meager surplus. Both the have-nots and the haves act desperately, the former to overcome their deprivation and the latter to preserve their favored station.

This is the reality that Africa's rulers face. How do they respond to it? One theoretical possibility would be for them to become thoroughgoing socialist revolutionaries, to give up all their privileges and to universalize the proletarian condition. If they did this, they would no longer be exploiters or the focus of resentment. And they would be able to channel the energy of the masses to develop the forces of production. As was to be expected, they have not chosen to liquidate themselves as a class. Nevertheless, their existence as a dominant class remains precarious, rendered so by the real and potential revolutionary pressures of their wretchedly poor subjects. To survive, they have to contain these pressures.

They do this by punishing with the utmost ruthlessness all nonconformist behavior, particularly behavior that challenges property rights and behavior that allegedly undermines the legitimacy of the rulers. The evidence is overwhelming. There is no country in Africa that does not impose unspeakably harsh punishment—sometimes up to a decade in prison—for petty theft. There is no African country which is not freely using state power to imprison, banish, or murder political dissenters. What is happening in Africa is a reflection not of the uniqueness of the character of Africans, but rather of social forces which have the same effect wherever they occur. In all very poor countries where the rulers maintain exploitative relations and where the struggle for the surplus is very grim, the established order can be maintained only by ruthless coercion verging on fascism.

But the survival of a regime in conditions of intense competition for a meager surplus demands not only force, but also—perhaps most importantly—the rendering of privilege and exploitation by the rulers invisible. The present rulers of Africa are becoming increasingly aware of this point, and they are taking steps to conceal their privileges and their exploitation. Now the objective situation of the masses is such that the ideas that dominate and orient their struggle are equality and the elimination of exploitation. If the leaders are to conceal their exploitation, they cannot do so by opposing these ideas. On the contrary, they have to embrace them and appear to be their champions; they have to make some substantive concession to these ideas. This is part of the reason why all African leaders are so vociferous about the "improvement of the lot of our people." That is why even obscenely capitalist Nigeria is zealous about nationalization, a planned economy, and income redistribution. That explains why even Senghor has become a philosopher of socialism (though of course he has tortured that concept beyond all recognition). Kenya's *Sessional Paper No. 10,* Uganda's *Common Man's Charter,* Kaunda's humanism—all these are attempts to create a progressive image, to maintain power by what I may call defensive radicalism.

It must be stressed that whether or not the rulers of a country engage in defensive radicalism is something that is determined by the objective conditions of the country in question. As a rule, all countries subject to the revolutionary pressures we have described will necessarily engage in defensive radicalism to maintain the existing order. By extension, all African countries engage in defensive radicalism, although there is a difference in degree. It is largely the differences in the degree of defensive radicalism that have led us to the classification of African countries as progressive or reactionary.

The differences in the degree of defensive radicalism are in turn a function of the strength of the revolutionary pressures generated by poverty, the consciousness of the burden of poverty, and the resentment of inequality. Given the same level of consciousness, these pressures will be inversely proportional to the size of the surplus. If that is the case, we can predict that the poorest countries in Africa will display a stronger propensity to engage in defensive radicalism. Conversely, we would expect that, for any given country, the propensity to engage in defensive radicalism will increase in those periods when its economic prospects become particularly bleak; this will be especially true if the deterioration of its economy is protracted.

Defensive radicalism is a progressive force. Paradoxically, while it allows the bourgeoisie to buy time, it develops the consciousness of the people, reveals the contradictions of the social order, and intensifies the class struggle. It develops the consciousness of the masses because the rulers' objective interest demands that their defensive radicalism be given the maximum visibility. The process of giving it this visibility necessarily entails the propagation of the values and the ideology of the class enemies of the regime. The regime achieves the requisite visibility by propagating ideas and creating expectations which contradict its raison d'etat. Defensive radicalism reveals the contradictions of the social order by creating expectations which cannot be satisfied in the context of the existing order. It intensifies the class struggle by developing the consciousness of the masses and by revealing the contradictions of the system. Defensive radicalism has a dynamic all its own. To purchase legitimacy by defensive radicalism is to establish a new criterion of regime performance and legitimacy which becomes a constraint on the regime. It becomes a constraint because defensive radicalism is even more self-defeating when it is not plausible, that is to say, not plausible in relation to regime performances. So when a regime is obliged to undertake defensive radicalism, it will in all probability become increasingly progressive. At least one African country has been impelled by defensive radicalism to the brink of socialism. It would appear that Africa's movement in a progressive direction depends not on the development of the forces of production and the increase of the surplus, but on the lack of such development.

9

EXTERNAL INFLUENCES AND SUBIMPERIALISM IN FRANCOPHONE WEST AFRICA

P-KIVEN TUNTENG
Vanier College and University of Ottawa

The retreat of colonial powers from most of Africa has tended to create the impression that imperialism remains only as an aberrant exception in a few areas of the continent. In its classical form—that is, overt domination of another people or territory by a more powerful state—the evidence for persistent imperialism may not be great. But if we shift our concern from the form and concentrate on realities, the argument that imperialism has taken on other dimensions in the continent becomes very convincing. What we are suggesting is that the withdrawal of European powers to the background need not be viewed as synonymous with the elimination of inequality and its resulting injustices. From this perspective, the agent is less an accurate measure of the existence of imperialism than the effects. In other words, it is not sufficient to limit analysis of imperialism to those situations in which foreign powers and other racial groups enjoy an evidently dominant position in a territory. Imperialism can be practiced *within* racial groups as well as within states.

To some degree, this suggests a more fruitful strategy in the study of African politics. It is no longer sufficient, if it ever was, to portray developments in Africa along racial lines: that is, whites being the evil oppressors, with blacks as the suffering oppressed. In many cases, economic interests have made these racial distinctions irrelevant. There is increasing evidence that injustices meted out by blacks to their racial brethren may in some instances make white rule look rather benevolent. Nor can we argue, even in a place like South Africa, that the conflict is solely racial and that the advent of black majority rule will

AUTHOR'S NOTE: This paper is part of a broader study on the impact of Franco-African relations on development strategies in French-speaking Africa. The research has been supported by a grant from the Graduate Institute of International Studies, Geneva, within the context of its assistance program to the Institute of International Relations, Yaounde.

automatically eliminate injustices in the country. Why, for instance, have blacks fought with the Portuguese and Rhodesian armies against their own racial liberation movements? Further still, why have some whites identified with liberation movements in what amounts to a rejection of their racial domination in certain parts of Africa? Such questions cannot be answered meaningfully if racial distinctions are used as the parameters for analysis. The pattern of economic interests and the resulting linkages—internal and external—must be analyzed in order to derive more fruitful generalizations.

The phenomenon of subimperialism is not limited to French-speaking West Africa but is evident throughout the continent in areas where more privileged states seek to exercise influence over their less endowed neighbors. The efforts of President Sese Seko Mobutu of Zaire could be viewed as a case in point. Yet because of their obvious limitations, African states can only aspire to the role of subimperialists to the degree enjoyed by the major overseas centers of economic power—Paris, London, New York, and the like. It is within this context that French-speaking West Africa assumes a special importance. Perhaps more than elsewhere on the continent, the role of a foreign power is pervasive in the local rivalry for domination in this region. The rivalry between Senegal and the Ivory Coast for hegemony can only be understood within the overall framework of France's efforts to maintain its dominant position in all of French-speaking Africa. This is not to suggest that inequality within the region and in some states must be attributed solely to French machinations. Rather, it is merely to emphasize that the discussion would assume added clarity if conducted within the broader framework of French interaction with, and intervention in, the region.

In view of this dependent relationship, this study will begin with an examination of the impact of France on the development of inequality in Francophone West Africa, the rivalry between the two major regional powers, and, finally, the impact of these factors on domestic justice and prospects for future development in the region.

A FRAMEWORK FOR DEPENDENCY

It is true that, given the evolution of the Western economic system, African states will for the foreseeable future remain dependent on the major metropolitan centers. But the relationship between France and its former colonies has gone further than this, by reinforcing and legitimizing this dependency. The various accords signed by France and its African colonies on the eve of their independence provided the juridical framework for this patron-client relationship. (See N'Dongo, 1972; Corbett, 1972:49-84; Tunteng, 1974.)

The interest shown in the recent revisions of these accords seems to have been out of proportion to their real significance. After more than a decade of legal independence, it is hardly significant that these states should demand the correction of abnormalities and explicit limits on their sovereignty, such as revocation of the provision that the French ambassador be automatically the dean of the diplomatic corps in the 14 African states that had previously conceded this arrangement (Corbett, 1972:62). Demands by some states that this situation be rectified have readily been granted by the French largely because such minor adjustments would not radically alter the overall system of Franco-African relations. To guarantee the preservation of the larger interests, the French are likely to continue making such tactical adjustments in the face of mounting, though limited, African pressures.

However, in the substantive areas of financial and economic arrangements, the situation will for the foreseeable future remain unchanged, barring drastic innovations in the manner that Africans have tended to perceive *la présence française*. Although the major portion of Franco-African relations is governed by detailed bilateral accords between France and each of the states, their economies are grouped together by two regional central banks which jointly regulate their monetary arrangements with the French treasury. The Banque Centrale des Etats de l'Afrique de l'Ouest (BCEAO) controls the currencies of Senegal, Ivory Coast, Upper Volta, Dahomey, and Niger. Mauritania left the franc zone in 1972 to establish its own currency. Mali concluded a special arrangement with France in 1967, whereby the Mali franc came to enjoy the separate guarantee of the French treasury. Although not directly linked to the BCEAO, Mali is subject thus to the same monetary constraints from Paris as are its West African neighbors. For the same purpose, the Banque Centrale des Etats de l'Afrique Equatoriale et du Cameroun (BCEAEC) controls the currencies of Congo, Gabon, Central African Republic, Chad, and Cameroon. Only since the domestic changes of May 1972 has the Malagasy Republic established its own currency, the Malagasy franc. It should be noted that each of the regional banks covers an area similar to the old federations of French West Africa and French Equatorial Africa, which facilitated French control prior to independence.

These monetary arrangements have been viewed with mixed feelings. Apologists for French hegemony argue that they are evidence of France's benevolence as manifested by its readiness to provide monetary stability and guarantee the otherwise worthless currencies of some of these countries. Opponents argue that the surrender of these states to monetary control from France in effect deprives them of the right to exercise an essential component of their sovereignty. Whatever the merits of each of these arguments, one noticeable result of this control from Paris is that movements in the exchange rate of the French franc, as occurred in late 1969 and early 1974, automatically affect the currencies of these states. In other words, they can neither revalue nor devalue their currencies independently. These changes come automatically and to some extent unpredictably with shifts in the French franc on the world currency market.

While the currencies of these states are regulated by multilateral central banks, their international financial transactions are governed by bilateral agreements with France. Each state maintains a separate account with the French treasury, which regulates and controls the state's financial transactions with countries that are outside the franc zone. The foreign exchange reserves of these countries must be deposited in the French treasury. While these reserves are estimated individually for each state, they "cannot be drawn upon beyond a certain margin of credit governed in each case by a bilateral agreement with the French government. Local monetary policy, exchange control and duty policy . . . must operate within the framework of this central allocation by the French" (Nkrumah, 1965:226). It could be argued that all this is a worthy price to pay for monetary stability, but the limits which such an arrangement imposes on the exercise of sovereignty should not be ignored.

Demands for modifications in these arrangements have been met partly by the monetary reforms signed in the treaties of November 23, 1972, for the BCEAEC and November 14, 1973, for the BCEAO. The major innovation brought about by these reforms has been the increase in African membership and a corresponding reduction in French membership on the management boards. This amounts to no more than shifting faces in the boardrooms. The substantive and more troublesome policies—such as free transfer of currencies within the franc zone, fixed guarantee of the exchange rate between all CFA francs and the French franc, and of course the ubiquitous control of the French treasury—remain unchanged (see Aliburt, 1974:4-5). The inclination toward the perpetuation of the status quo is unmistakable.

That, however, is characteristic of Franco-African relations. In the spirit of these relations, nothing is ever permitted to disturb the pattern of tranquility, the illusion of harmonious change, and the ever-present spirit of *coopération franco-africaine.* Perhaps to satisfy the increasingly vocal demands by opposition forces for changes in the agreements with France, or to misdirect a suspicious outside world, some partisans have dramatized the changes contained in recent reforms to a degree that is far out of proportion. One sympathetic observer boldly asserted that the reforms had revealed a strengthening of solidarity among African states "in each of the regions, and their willingness to maintain their monetary cooperation with France, *while at the same time asserting their sovereignty*" (emphasis added; Aliburt, 1974:5). This conclusion is difficult to sustain. What happened in effect, was that economic necessity had compelled these states to extend their dependence on France.

The global accounting and secret nature of some key aspects of Franco-African relations makes it difficult to determine the extent to which the net flow benefits needy African states. Under the confusing and seemingly generous category of French aid, the list of items includes subsidies to French businessmen and enterprises, salaries of French military and civilian personnel, loans for purchases of French equipment and machinery, subsidies or gifts intended to sustain politically reliable persons in positions of power, and so on. That French aid is directed more at helping French firms and nationals than the indigenous African population cannot be doubted. As Kwame Nkrumah suggested (1965:17), it constitutes "a levy on French taxpayers for the benefit of French individuals and firms." But more importantly, it is now generally conceded that

France receives more through invisible and indirect flows from Francophone states than the latter gain from what appears on the surface to be generous French aid. As one critical Senegalese suggested in reference to the French presence in his country, "The French are here because of the economic interests of French investors and in order to protect them. French aid is not disinterested —France gives nothing free" (O'Brien, 1972:178). This reality is easily concealed by eye-catching appearances of French generosity.

Yet it is precisely these appearances that have justified the privileged position given to France and hence served to reinforce France's hegemony in the region. In other words, governmental suspicions about foreign involvement in questionable economic activities seem to disappear when the foreigners in question are Frenchmen. This attitude is predicated on the apparent belief that whatever the French do must by necessity be relatively disinterested. As a result, and without many constraints, French authorities at home and abroad determine the conditions of launching economic projects in Francophone African states. In effect, "they set the rules for competition and reserve the right to place obstacles in the paths of their nearest competitors, both African and non-African" (Bretton, 1973:77). The ability of Africans to rise into top positions in government and industry or to develop local business ventures is frequently limited in order to accommodate French interests.

THE DEVELOPMENT OF DEPENDENCY

The significance of French involvement in the analysis of subimperialism in Francophone West Africa is vividly illustrated by the changing roles of Senegal and the Ivory Coast, or more specifically of Dakar and Abidjan. During the period of direct French rule, two federations, French West Africa and French Equatorial Africa, not only facilitated French domination and exploitation, but equally, they hastened the emergence of Dakar and Brazzaville, the regional capitals, into greater prominence. Yet, in terms of resources and natural wealth, Senegal and the Congo were not necessarily the most endowed. With its mineral resources, Gabon was of course more economically endowed than the Congo in central Africa; and with its forest and plantation resources, the Ivory Coast enjoyed a position much superior in economic terms to that of Senegal. But to the extent that these federations facilitated French rule, they were retained, with Dakar and Brazzaville enjoying a privileged position as the capital cities. Ivorian and Gabonese wealth thus supported the development of Dakar and Brazzaville, something which the French perpetuated for their own interests.

But the rapid change in events with De Gaulle's ascendancy to the French presidency in 1958 drastically altered the political situation and made the perpetuation of both federations unnecessary. If the colonies were to become independent, as the post-1958 referendum demands for varying degrees of autonomy intimated, it was not in the French interest to develop two large units that might be difficult to control. Thus in 1959, these federations were dismantled. The major effect of this change was to make it easier for the French to direct and control the individually weak and nonviable states. In the same manner that the present states are dependent on France, the two federations were not permitted to evolve their own development strategies. Whenever the individual territories encountered financial difficulties, the French immediately offered stopgap curative measures. Inevitably, they were inclined to look to France rather than to each other for any form of future uplift. As William Foltz (1965:39) has succinctly put it: "This situation could hardly encourage the development of a sense of economic interdependence within the federation itself." Development could thus not be conceived in isolation from the paternal hand of the French government.

Unlike the militantly nationalist Sékou Touré, Léopold Senghor's quest for autonomy from France was rather unusual. Perhaps the black man most assimilated into French culture, he was initially an ardent advocate of African federations, which he felt could at a later stage link themselves vertically with France. Although his enthusiasm for federation subsided after his own bitter experience in the Mali Federation, his approach contrasted sharply with that of Félix Houphouët-Boigny, whose preference was for direct union between France and the individual African territories. In a revealing justification of dependence on France, Houphouët-Boigny told Nkrumah, shortly after Ghana's independence, that he had chosen the alternative of a "Franco-African Community based on equality and fraternity. France's enlightened self-interest, but especially its keen sense of humanity, have led it to seek with us, actively and sincerely, the achievement of a new community" (Woronoff, 1972:12; see also Houphouët-Boigny, 1957). Such a revelation suggests another proposition: That Houphouët-Boigny had become mentally dependent on the French, something much more difficult to eradicate than mere physical dependency.

Nor was Houphouët-Boigny alone in his belief that dependency on France was necessary for any form of local development. The uncertain candidacy of Dahomey as a member of the Mali Federation, which would in any case be short-lived, was resolved when the then Dahomean Premier Sourou-Migan Apithy decided that security could be found in following the French stand, which was to discourage such regional efforts. After a quick trip to Paris, Apithy stressed the importance of French "good will" to Dahomeans "at this stage of our economic development" (Foltz, 1965:111-112). That sealed once and for all any consideration of participation in the Mali Federation.

While dependent on France, these states are not enthusiastic to see French assistance directed to non-Francophone African states. In a sense, they claim a monopoly on French generosity. Senghor has long been a leading advocate of close ties with France, but in 1974 he expressed displeasure about the declining volume of technical assistance and the fact that France had become more actively involved in Nigeria than in Francophone states (1974:3). Still there is a limit beyond which France ceases to be influenced in its foreign and economic policies by sentimentality. It too must strive, like other states, to advance its own economic interests. In this regard, Nigeria with a potentially large internal market and booming oil industry is probably on most counts more inviting to the French than the single-crop economy of stagnant Senegal. Yet, Senghor has tended to perceive flows unrealistically because of his emotional attachment to France. That the French in Senegal are inclined to treat the Senegalese as "grown-up children" may be encouraged by the sentiments of dependency which Senghor has tirelessly cultivated. He has repeatedly pleaded that Franco-phone Africans in general, and more particularly the Senegalese, would like to see that "France remains our major partner, not only in cultural affairs, but in economic matters as well" (1974:3). But economic matters are decided not so much on the basis of sentiments as on real or potential benefits. French involvement in Nigeria, East Africa and, more importantly, its intricate economic and military arrangements with South Africa have been guided solely by this quest to advance its national economic and strategic interests.

There is very little that is disinterested in French technical assistance. While France has steadily discouraged the formation of federations or unions that bring together French- and English-speaking African states, it has supported economic cooperation among countries in the franc zone. For example, it was within the French colonial framework that the Union Douanière Equatoriale (UDE) originated in 1959 before its transformation in 1964 into the Union Douanière et Economique de l'Afrique Centrale (UDEAC), which at the time grouped together Chad, Cameroon, the Central African Republic, Congo, and Gabon. As we have already mentioned, these states are equally members of a common regional central bank which controls their currencies as provided for in their monetary accords with France. With French support, the more affluent UDEAC states such as Cameroon and Gabon contributed to a solidarity fund to help the landlocked and less endowed Chad and the Central African Republic. Although Chad received 65% and the Central African Republic 35% of the contributions to the fund, they remained dissatisfied, feeling that the customs arrangement in UDEAC did not benefit them as much as their partners.

In April 1968, Chad and the Central African Republic left UDEAC to join with Zaire in forming the Union d'Etats Afrique Centrale (UEAC). It was suggested at the time that the United States supported these developments as a means to weaken French domination in Central Africa. The extent of U.S. involvement and continuing presence in Zaire suggests, in fact, that Mobutu could not have embarked on such a venture without American support in one form or another. It should equally be pointed out that given its strategic location, endowment in natural resources, and relatively large population, Zaire's claim to leadership in Central Africa is not entirely without a basis. And Mobutu has assiduously cultivated this role after his seeming success in restoring what appears to be a semblance of stability in that much tormented country.

But if it was in the interest of the United States and Zaire to divide UDEAC by establishing a rival union to it, the opposite could be said for the French. Because of the interpenetration of trade, financial, and cultural arrangements between France and its former colonies (Bretton, 1973; O'Brien, 1972), French pressure can generate results that no other foreign power can match. It was not by accident, therefore, that the Central African Republic returned to UDEAC in December 1968, leaving Chad alone with Zaire in the UEAC. But Chad's membership in the BCEAEC, which was transformed into the Banque des Etats de l'Afrique Centrale (BEAC) after the 1972 monetary accords, and its continuing participation in UDEAC specialized services would suggest that the UEAC is to all intents and purposes a paper organization. The UDEAC states are harnessed to the French system to a degree that makes them collectively dependent on France, and hence deserving of the latter's support.

As an organization, however, UDEAC is not as conspicuous an example of France's continuing control as the Organisation Commune Afrique et Malgache (OCAM). On the surface at least, it could be argued that the UDEAC states occupy a contiguous geographical area which encompasses one of the five regions that the United Nations Economic Commission for Africa has recommended for development planning. From its inception in September 1961 as the Union Africaine et Malgache (UAM), through various stages before becoming OCAM in 1965, however, OCAM has brought together former French colonies, as well as at certain moments Rwanda, Zaire, and Mauritius. With its membership scattered from the west coast of Africa to the Indian Ocean, it was essentially a French-speaking organization which linked these states collectively to France. Concerned mainly with coordinating their ties with the European Economic Community (EEC) and linked by some specialized services, OCAM has never aspired to any form of political integration.

In terms of potential contribution, the defection of Mauritania from OCAM in June 1965 was more than compensated for by the admission of Zaire (then Congo, Kinshasa), at the time when Moises Tshombe was prime minister; and in April 1972, Mauritius also became a member. Not only has France supported OCAM, but it has financed the organization's secretariat and provided needed technical advice and personnel to run its programs (Corbett, 1972:77). In January 1966 an official of the French Ministry of Cooperation sent a message to OCAM leaders and appropriately informed them that "close cooperation between yourselves and with us means making a big contribution to world peace and African unity" (Skurnik, 1972:228). It is perhaps unfortunate that the rhetoric of African unity has become so meaningless that collective subordination to French dictates is viewed as a contribution to unity in the continent.

The structure and composition of OCAM favors French interests to the degree that surpasses its formal ties to the former colonial power. As the most cohesive group within OCAM, the Conseil de l'Entente (see below) provides Houphouët-Boigny with a base to advance the position of the Ivory Coast, a position which is rarely distinguishable from French preferences. Reinforced by the relatively privileged economic position of the Ivory Coast, Houphouët-Boigny has in a sense occupied the leadership position in OCAM. As one observer has commented, "not only did political inequalities reinforce economic inequalities, but political leadership was in the hands of the individual (Houhouët-Boigny) least interested in promoting political integration" within the organization (Jalloh, 1973:160). The French would have of course been reluctant to endorse any advance to political integration, nor are the conditions in such a geographically spread grouping favorable to unification.

As happened with the two colonial federations of French West Africa and French Equatorial Africa, there has not been much economic interdependence among the member states of OCAM. While minor shifts have occurred in the exports of these countries from France to the other EEC countries since the 1960s, regional trade among OCAM members remains very low. (See Table 1.) Despite the evidence of some diversification in trade pattern, OCAM member states will for the foreseeable future maintain their major dependence on France.

The increasing number of defections over the years from OCAM suggests uneasiness in associating with what is clearly a neocolonial organization. After Mauritania left OCAM in June 1965, seven years elapsed before Zaire followed on April 21, 1972; Cameroon on July 1, 1973; Chad on July 3, 1973; the Malagasy Republic on August 4, 1973; and the People's Republic of the Congo on September 22, 1973. While it is significant to note that all these states have been the most vocal in asserting their independence from France, defections from OCAM should not be construed as evidence of readiness finally to cut off all dependence on France. It is one of those curious aspects of Franco-African relations that militantly anti-French rhetoric can be pushed to extremes at the same time that requests for French technical assistance are being made. Throughout 1973, for example, the development of cultural nationalism in Chad,

Table 1. DIRECTION OF OCAM EXPORTS BY PERCENTAGES: 1966 and 1968

From:	To:	1966			1968		
		France	Other EEC	OCAM	France	Other EEC	OCAM
Cameroun		37.6	29.2	2.7	33.7	36.5	8.0
Central African Republic		37.4	12.0	--[a]	38.0	7.4	--[a]
Chad		48.8	6.5	--[a]	63.5	12.1	6.6
Congo		7.5	38.9	n.a.	5.7	47.4	n.a.
Dahomey		52.8	14.6	12.1	36.9	14.6	9.4
Gabon		43.2	17.3	4.3	33.7	15.5	5.9
Ivory Coast		38.8	22.4	3.7	34.5	28.5	5.1
Malagasy Republic		45.8	7.4	3.0	33.5	6.0	4.9
Niger		54.9	12.4	5.8	63.1	13.2	6.5
Rwanda		--[a]	34.4	n.a.	2.5	27.0	n.a.
Senegal		73.8	7.8	4.4	66.3	9.3	8.0
Togo		40.3	37.1	2.3	38.5	43.7	3.0
Upper Volta		18.0	1.5	51.9	14.3	4.7	55.2
Zaire		10.3	50.5	0.6	10.6	53.0	3.3

a. Less than 0.1%.

SOURCES: Secrétariat-Général de l'OCAM, Annuaire OCAM, 1968, and Bulletin Statistique de l'OCAM, No. 15 (Juin 1970).

coupled with official denunciations of French neocolonialism from Ndjaména (formerly Fort-Lamy), made it seem as if relations between the two countries were about to be severed. Yet at the same time, the French were building a military base at Fort Archambault, now known as Sarh, in order to protect President Ngarta Tombalbaye's home area against possible attacks from the Chad national liberation movement based in the northern provinces.

There is no evidence to suggest that Francophone African states are now prepared to sever their ties with France and follow Tanzania in a commitment to self-reliance. Nor are the French, up to a certain degree of course, tired of supporting and exploiting their former colonies. While conceding that OCAM "had been badly shaken by several withdrawals," one observer nevertheless pointed out that the organization remained "more or less under French influence" (Wauthier, 1973:A63). To the extent that these states continue to perceive development from the perspective of short-term benefits, nearly all of them, notwithstanding defections from OCAM and anti-French rhetoric, will opt for the perpetuation of their dependence on France.

INTRAREGIONAL RIVALRY FOR DOMINATION

The struggle between Senegal and the Ivory Coast for the leadership role of French-speaking West Africa surfaced even before the attainment of independence by both countries. As deputies in the French parliament, Senghor and Houphouët-Boigny competed for the role of African spokesman in the National Assembly. As William Foltz has suggested: "That the two men's ideas on a wide variety of subjects were fundamentally different, and that Senegal and the Ivory Coast were rivals for economic leadership within the French West African federation, made their personal rivalry all the more significant and intense" (Foltz, 1965:159). But on the question of maintaining close vertical links with France, both men were in agreement, and their differences were confined to the manner in which such unions were to be arranged.

Yet, unlike Houphouët-Boigny, Senghor was, until the breakup of the Mali Federation, a strong proponent of federalism among African states. His arguments for federalism centered on the fact that it would offer the best hope for eliminating the inequalities which had resulted from colonial conquest. To him, racial and economic equality could only be attained through the formation of federal unions. (See *Marches Coloniaux,* March 27, 1954, p. 814.) This enthusiasm may not have been disinterested, however. Since Dakar and Senegal already benefited from the federation of French West Africa, Senghor's preference for federalism may have been motivated largely by the desire to reinforce the privileged position of his country. That position had given Senegal a prominence which in true economic terms belonged to the Ivory Coast.

This cynical interpretation of Senghor's interest in federalism may be supported by his own subsequent behavior when the Francophone West African federation faced imminent disintegration. If he could not dominate the entire region, at least he would be satisfied with a role which guaranteed him hegemony in part of the region. To this end, he suggested the division of French West Africa into two subregions as follows: the first group of Senegal, Mauritania, Soudan (present-day Mali), and Guinea would maintain Dakar as the capital; while a second, comprising the Ivory Coast, Upper Volta, Niger, and Dahomey, would have their capital in Abidjan. Rather than perpetuate the rivalry between Senegal and the Ivory Coast, Senghor preferred the region to be divided between the two regional powers, allowing each to have its sphere of influence (Senghor, 1954). The intensity of this rivalry virtually guaranteed the failure of broader efforts toward regional cooperation. The failure of the Union Douanière des Etats de l'Afrique Occidentale (UDEAO) was largely attributed to these differences. Officials of the Ivory Coast were eager to develop their transit trade and industries, while Senegal wanted to preserve its own privileged economic position in French-speaking West Africa. (See Mytelka, 1974:305). If complementarity of interests existed between the two countries, it was hardly perceptible, certainly from the standpoint of the leadership.

Senghor's interest in the Mali Federation may have been prompted by two factors: first, his residual enthusiasm for political unification in the region; second, and perhaps more importantly, his belief that such a union—which was initially designed to include Senegal, Soudan, Upper Volta, and Dahomey—would guarantee Senegal a dominant economic and political voice. The moving personalities in the Mali Federation were Senghor and Modibo Keita, who later became president of the independent republic of Mali. Naturally, the French were suspicious of the proposed union, largely because of Keita, whose militancy was viewed with the same apprehension as that of Sékou Touré. The Ivory Coast and France opposed the federation in no mistaken terms.

It should not be understood that the French were opposed to all ideas of federation. After all, it was they who had introduced the experiment in their territories by the creation of French West Africa and French Equatorial Africa. But such unions were acceptable only if they were constituted by French officials or intended to serve French objectives. That Africans could by themselves decide to form political unions at a time when De Gaulle had just assumed the presidency and was setting the Fifth Republic into motion was tantamount to heresy. The militancy of the oath which officials of the Mali Federattion took merely underlined French suspicions. The delegates pledged "to defend everywhere the Mali Federation, to become tireless pilgrims and preachers of political unity, and to *accept the ultimate sacrifice for the realization of African unity*" (emphasis added; Foltz, 1965:102). Although the Mali Federation was to retain its membership in the French community, the professed determination to die for African unity must have frightened Houphouët-Boigny as well as French officials. The latter two thus united to make sure that the federation would never succeed.

Houphouët-Boigny responded by establishing a rival group to weaken the Mali Federation or at least compete with it from a position of strength. As the veteran French journalist Philippe Decraene commented at the time, "Houphouët-Boigny has just decided to set up, under the leadership of the Ivory Coast, a territorial regrouping" which, unlike the Mali Federation stressed economic, and not political, cooperation (*Le Monde,* May 5, 1959). It was known as the Conseil de l'Entente with the objective of harmonizing economic policies among the member states.

Although Dahomey and Upper Volta had been on the verge of joining the Mali Federation, no formal commitment to this effect had been made prior to the launching of the idea of the Conseil de l'Entente. That left considerable scope for French and Ivorian officials to pressure these two states not to join the federation. Dependent on the Ivory Coast for a sea outlet and employment for its migrant workers, the Upper Volta was particularly vulnerable to Ivorian pressures. To their Voltaic counterparts, officials of the Ivory Coast stressed, among other things, the role of Abidjan as a commercial outlet and the employment of migrant workers from the Upper Volta in the Ivory Coast plantations. To the fearful *chefferie* (traditional rulers) of the Upper Volta, it was argued that their traditional roles would be threatened by radicals in Dakar and Bamako. And if such pressures were not sufficient, there was available Ivorian and French money to influence the doubtful. In the words of one commentator: "It is commonly assumed that during this period considerable Ivory Coast funds found their way into Voltaic pockets" (Foltz, 1965:109; see also Thompson, 1969:205). By March 1959, the hope that Upper Volta would joint the Mali Federation had disappeared. For the Upper Volta, it was a question of economic survival. While Dakar and Bamako could only promise a chance at some unspecified, and in any case distant, gains, Abidjan and Paris were ready to guarantee financially that country's existence. This proved to be more attractive and, therefore, acceptable.

The defections of Dahomey and Upper Volta denied the Mali Federation the momentum which might have sustained it over the usually difficult initial stages of political unification. Although the federation officially came into existence in early 1959, it was beset by disagreements which finally culminated in its dissolution in August 1960.

The collapse of the Mali Federation was a disappointment to Senghor on several counts. First, it had vindicated Houphouët-Boigny's argument that such political ventures were premature. Second, whatever belief Senghor had in the wisdom of political unification seems to have been drastically shaken by the events which preceded the final disintegration. All this made Houphouët-Boigny look wiser, more mature, and realistic in his appraisal of the political situation in the continent. The Entente which had been formed to serve as a counteracting force to the Mali Federation in the region suddenly faced no competitor. Despite its loose structure, the Entente has since provided the Ivory Coast with a base to exercise and consolidate its influence in Francophone West Africa. Yet the success of this grouping in its chosen or rather imposed limited objective has been responsible to a considerable extent for the failure of more inclusive integrative efforts in West Africa. That, in a sense, and in view of Houphouët-Boigny's indifference to the idea of political unification in the continent, must be viewed as the raison d'etre of the organization.

PATTERNS OF REGIONAL SUBIMPERIALISM

The dominant role which Houphouët-Boigny plays in Francophone West Africa is institutionalized in his hegemonic position within the Conseil de l'Entente. The Entente was formally created on May 29, 1959, by the Ivory Coast, Dahomey, Upper Volta, and Niger. Togo joined in 1966 as a fifth member. The goal of the organization was appropriately ambiguous. It stated simply that its purpose was to "harmonise relations among member states on the basis of friendship, brotherhood and solidarity" ("Conseil de l'Entente," 1974:16). The Entente is one of the oldest regional groupings in Africa and includes a total population of about 20 million people. It has neither permanent nor formal institutions but conducts its activities through periodic meetings of the presidents and various ministers as well as other officials.

Such ambiguity as evident in the purpose and organization of the Entente need not necessarily be viewed as characterizing a lack of political will. It is sufficiently flexible to permit deployment without difficulty to achieve short- or long-term political objectives, which of course must be favored by the Ivory Coast. The latter has insisted on uniformity of behavior among member states. All the Entente states requested independence from France as a bloc, and in April 1961 all signed agreements with France covering defense, economic matters, education, cultural relations, and so on. Upper Volta did, however, refuse to sign any defense agreements with France (Africa South of the Sahara, 1974:97), no doubt reflecting the fact that it had only joined the organization reluctantly. With the perennial backing of France, the Ivory Coast consequently used economic means to pressure Voltaic leaders to show more conformity in their political attitudes. To this end, the finance minister of the Ivory Coast, who was himself French, refused in early 1961 to pay customs rebates to the Voltaic government as had been agreed upon the previous year (Thompson, 1969:205). As a landlocked state, deprived of natural resources, Upper Volta had no other course but dependence on the economic goodwill of the Ivory Coast and, as its corollary, political subordination.

One of the most significant achievements of the Entente has been its concern for the development of all member states. Its solidarity fund, Fonds de Solidarité, was established with the objective to offer member states "financial assistance based on their resources, and to contribute to the economic stability of all the participating states" ("Conseil de l'Entente," 1974:16). In June 1966, the solidarity fund was transformed into a mutual aid and loan guarantee fund, Fonds d'Entraide et de Garantie des Emprunts du Conseil de L'Entente. Of the total of 650 million francs (CFA) contributed by member states to the fund on the basis of their national revenues, the Ivory Coast alone paid 500 million francs into the fund. Niger, Upper Volta, and Dahomey each contributed 42 million francs, with the remaining 24 million francs coming from Togo. The purpose of the fund is to guarantee loans and foreign investments in order to encourage outside lenders to finance development projects in member states (Africa South of the Sahara, 1974:96-97). With a preponderant proportion of the total coming from the Ivory Coast, the latter's ability to manipulate and dominate the politics of the other member states cannot be doubted. This conclusion need not be surprising, for the Entente exists only because of the Ivory Coast. As Edward Corbett has pointed out, the Entente has "helped Houphouët-Boigny to keep his neighbors in line through the operation of a kitty to which the Ivory Coast is the major contributor" (1972:75).

While the Ivory Coast population is only about one-fifth of the total population of the Entente states, its other statistics are more impressive. Its gross national product of nearly $1.5 billion is more than that of the other four states combined. Bearing in mind that its per capita income of $308 does not reflect the *real* situation of the African population, it is nevertheless interesting to compare it with the $80 for Dahomey, $90 for Niger, $124 for Togo, and $50 for Upper Volta. Moreover, in view of the central location of Abidjan and the attractiveness of the country from the standpoint of foreign investors, this astounding inequality between the Ivory Coast and its partners is likely to be widened or at least maintained for quite some time.

The dependence of Upper Volta on the Ivory Coast is perhaps the most conspicuous of all, a fact which has given Houphouët-Boigny a strong voice in that country's domestic politics. Most of the Francophone African states have traditionally exported primarily to France, with some shifts toward other EEC countries since they associated with that community in 1957. The situation in Upper Volta has been, however, significantly different. In 1966, for example, 50.4% of the exports from Upper Volta went to the Ivory Coast, and by 1968, this percentage had risen to 53.0. These exports consisted mainly of animals and animal products (Jalloh, 1973:162). Nor is this the only example of this dependent relationship. With its relatively large population, the Upper Volta has relied on the Ivory Coast plantations to provide employment for its citizens. To migrant workers from Niger, Upper Volta, and Dahomey, the Ivory Coast is viewed with the same attraction that migrant workers from Malawi, Mozambique, and other southern states view South Africa. It is a place to seek the economic betterment that is out of reach within their own countries.

With due account to obvious economic differences in both situations, it should be noted that the foreign population has played a role in the Ivory Coast economy similar to what it has in the South African economy. Between 1950 and 1965, the foreign population made up 25% of the total population of the Ivory Coast. Equally, it made up 35 to 40% of the active male work force, half of the male work force in urban areas, more than 60% of the work force in urban zones outside of public works, and about half to two-thirds of the work force in the rural plantation areas. Most of these migrant workers come from

Upper Volta (Amin, 1970:284). If the Ivory Coast leadership decided to expel aliens from the country in order to satisfy the demands of some indigenous citizens who feel threatened by this "foreign" presence, as has indeed been done elsewhere in Africa, most notably in the expulsion of aliens by the Ghanaian regime of Kofi Busia in 1970, the results would be acutely disturbing to the Voltaic leadership. For this reason alone, the latter will maintain its dependent relationship with the Ivory Coast.

Whereas the unwieldy and larger OCAM has proved troublesome to control, Houphouët-Boigny has been assured of the solid backing of the Entente states in the pursuit of his political and diplomatic objectives. His long confrontation with Nkrumah, which came to a head during the 1965 summit of the Organization of Arican Unity (OAU) in Accra, was a case in point. Partly because of genuine fears and partly in order to settle old scores, the OCAM states threatened to boycott the Accra summit because Nkrumah allegedly could not guarantee their safety in the Ghanaian capital. It is true that among Nkrumah's freedom fighters in Ghana were opponents of some of these leaders, who along with Nkrumah were determined to remove them from positions of power by any means. But because of the long-standing feud of Houphouët-Boigny and some neighboring leaders against Nkrumah, OCAM members seemed to have gone much further than was necessary in demands for guarantees of their safety in the Ghanaian capital. As Kojo Botsio, one of Nkrumah's senior cabinet ministers commented in regard to the demands of these states, "diplomats cannot go around pointing out people they want deported" from another country (Thompson, 1969:384). In the end, only eight states, including all those of the Entente plus Gabon, Chad, and the Malagasy Republic, boycotted the Accra summit. The solidarity of the Entente behind Houphouët-Boigny, who led the call for the summit boycott, made the defection of some other OCAM members less painful.

Houphouët-Boigny's ascendancy to a position of dominance in French-speaking West Africa is now generally conceded even by Senghor. From a position of strength, he has recently found it harmless to invite his erstwhile rival from Dakar to share the limelight. In a recent speech, Houphouët-Boigny stated that both Senegal and the Ivory Coast had special responsibilities "because of their relatively advanced level of economic development and their determination to share with all in seeking solutions for their urgent problems" (Afrique contemporaine, 1974:16). This is a conciliatory gesture from a leader whose strength makes his power obvious. Senghor is in fact in no position to really share that role with the Ivory Coast, given the stagnant nature of the Senegalese economy.

ABSENCE OF DISTRIBUTIVE JUSTICE

On their own, neither the Ivory Coast nor Houphouët-Boigny would have emerged into any appreciable prominence in the African continent. Much that is frequently attributed to such countries as the Ivory Coast, Senegal, or Zaire ignores both the foreign component in their size and the degree of deprivation internally within these countries. The much-heralded boom, which the Ivory Coast has enjoyed since the 1950s, has been superficially propelled for the benefit of the expatriate population. In this regard, it is interesting to note that by the early 1970s, the French community in the Ivory Coast, or, more accurately, in and around Abidjan, already numbered some 40,000. This represents a twofold increase over the preindependence number of Frenchmen in the country. Theoretically, independence should have created the conditions for the indigenous population to assume a more active role in its development with a corresponding reduction in the extent of dependence on expatriates. In the relatively well-endowed countries, however, the French community has on the contrary grown steadily.

The economic power at the disposal of the French community in the Ivory Coast is well beyond its actual numbers. Although only about 1% of the country's population, the expatriate French community earns something like 40% of the total wages paid in the country. Commerce is literally a French monopoly with other non-French foreigners competing for a closer role. For example, less than 20% of all retailers in Abidjan are Ivorian. This situation is frequently rationalized on the grounds of the contribution of these French residents to the country's development. Between 1950 and 1965, the Ivory Coast enjoyed something like a 9% annual economic growth. But this was essentially an export boom, since during this period exports virtually quadrupled. This type of growth will not automatically "result in an economic 'take-off,' but in an increased external dependency and the blocking of growth" (Amin, 1970:284).

Nor is there much evidence to sustain the notion that an independent capitalist sector has now developed in the Ivory Coast. Given the dependent nature of the economy, capitalism has certainly been extended to the country, which is not to say that it has developed an autonomous capitalist system. As Samir Amin has argued, the emergent class in the Ivory Coast "has no autonomy of its own; it has no being without the European society which dominates it. Here, the workers are African. But the true bourgeoisie is absent, domiciled in Europe, which provides the capital and the men who use it" (Amin, 1971:206-207). Whatever growth such a system has generated has largely benefited the already-established foreign capitalist class. Through the transfer of profits, through the transfer of the savings of the ridiculously high salries paid to Europeans, through dividends, and so on, capital is continually exported to France where the "real bourgeoisie" resides.

The example of the Ivory Coast has for several years now been characterized by Samir Amin as one of "growth without development." In other words, there has been negligible "spillover" from growth to development. According to Amin, such growth is "engendered and kept up from outside, without the construction of socio-economic structures that would enable automatic passage to a still further stage, that of a self-centered and self-maintained new dynamism" (Amin, 1970:288). This situation is concealed by the frequently mentioned comparatively impressive figure for per-capita income of the Ivory Coast. The per-capita income says very little about the *real* economic situation of the country, however.

This fascination with the country has been fostered by tourists, who, however, rarely venture out of Abidjan, a modern and, by any standard, attractive city. In this ideal setting, one observer has wryly commented, the tourist may be treated to well-prepared Parisian cuisine in the Hotel Ivoire and "play chemin-de-fer at the hotel casino, skate at the hotel ice rink, see the latest French movies at the hotel cinema, bowl at the hotel bowling lanes, and swim in the hotel's huge swimming pool" (Muncie, 1973:41). It is a city of startling contrasts, with the most exaggerated inequalities in living conditions and income redistribution. The luxury of Cocody makes a mockery of that other Abidjan suburb, Deux Cents Vingt Logements, nor can the latter be compared with the rural world of some 80% of the population, among whom a yearly income of even half the per capita income is but a dream. It is also in the rural areas where facilities such as schools, hospitals, roads, and other essential services are limited. In short, the preponderant majority, whose income is much below the national average, is also the least beneficiary of essential services.

This situation of exaggerated inequality is by no means confined to the Ivory Coast. Although generally a poor continent, Africa has an incredible concentration of income in the hands of a relative few. In the relatively developed countries of the region, "7 per cent of the African population takes in 40 per cent of the income. . . . In the lesser evolved inland countries, the figures are lower, with the privileged population—2-3 per cent—getting from 15-20 per cent of the income, but the trend toward growing inequality is the same" (Amin, 1974:10-11). It is a development which threatens to undermine the traditional communal spirit of African society. "Within the urban sector, class differences have reached considerable extremes in income distribution and styles of life," argues Peter Gutkind. "Traditional family obligations, although still much discussed, are being eroded rather rapidly as the better-off African workers treat luxuries as necessities at the expense of poorer kin" (1974:13). In a sense, Africans have rapidly embraced the acquisitive spirit of Western society without equally adopting its redistributive aspects. Not only is there a total lack of any notion of income redistribution, but the already well-paid civil servants are seemingly viewed as a group that deserves special services and added facilities.

It is no accident that this inequality is conspicuously evident and most disturbing in the heavily centralized and irrelevant bureaucracies that these states have developed. The positions which colonial officials occupied in the pre-independence period and which distinguished them from the African population are now occupied by blacks who are in turn distinguished from their fellow brethren by an ominous economic barrier. These countries have become, in effect, two societies: the rich and privileged few on one hand, and the overwhelmingly poor majority on the other. An otherwise sympathetic writer has commented that "in Senegal two nations exist as distinctly and separately as ever they did in Disraeli's England. A privileged class, for the most part consisting of higher civil servants . . . set apart from the unskilled and low-skilled workers" (Markovitz, 1969:25). This situation is not limited to Senegal, however. Throughout Francophone Africa, the privileged and their families are guaranteed better health care, receiving questionable *indemnités,* while the already less fortunate are entitled to nothing. The services and facilities which were once reserved for white "functionaries" are today retained for the exclusive use of black "functionaries." Not only have the injustices of preindependence Africa continued, but the exploitation of the poor by fellow blacks has assumed wider and more immediate dimensions.

The hopes that the younger and more educated generation would change, or at least work toward the elimination of the prevailing injustices, appear to have been misplaced. Among this group there is a startling absence of a social conscience; its most vocal members have turned out to be enthusiastic participants in the prevailing system. They demand a bigger share of the pie, not for the most underprivileged, but for themselves. Those who are poor or unfortunate are to all intents and purposes leaderless; their situation, which is already critical, is bound to deteriorate even further. They are the forgotten majority.

Frustrated and desperate for a solution to their plight, the underprivileged have responded with acts of violence. They may be viewing the increasing number of break-ins and robberies in African urban centers as the only means available to them to redress the equilibrium.

Perhaps more important is the extent of frustrations expressed in vandalism —destruction of property and automobiles and so forth. Yet more privileges continue to be accorded to the bureaucracy and their foreign supporters by the political leaders, whose main concern appears to be the retention of political power and the shocking economic benefits it brings to them. The leaders themselves are certain beneficiaries of this situation. For they derive their strength from both the internal and foreign economic sectors, "seeking gains in both, hence favoring development of both, their value judgments being shaped by their personal investment interests and opportunities" (Bretton, 1973:29). Since the overwhelming majority of African leaders cannot claim to be enjoying the genuine support of the electorate, they must seek domestic allies in the bureaucracy and foreign economic interests to sustain them in positions of leadership. Thus the familiar dictum "help me and I will help you," without regard to popular sentiments, is duly respected. Deprived of any meaningful participation in the political process, and thus powerless, the masses count for little or nothing. Taxed heavily to maintain their privileged brethren in inflated bureaucracies, they seem doomed to "take off" into continuing misery.

CONCLUSIONS

This study suggests that subimperialism in Africa is by necessity dependent on foreign powers. In the case of Francophone West Africa, the shift of prominence from Senegal to the Ivory Coast can best be approached and understood within the context of French political and economic interests in the region. The "real" imperialists, just as the "real" bourgeoisie, are resident abroad, while their agents advance their predetermined objectives within the region.

Within the region, the struggle for leadership between Senghor and Houphouët-Boigny has finally been settled in favor of the latter. The collapse of the Mali Federation, and the relative "success" of the Conseil de l'Entente, which has been assured of perennial French backing, have solidly reinforced the position of Houphouët-Boigny as the doyen of politics in the region, with Senghor no doubt delighted to be left with the position of vice-doyen. In this regard, the Entente could be viewed more as an arrangement to sustain Houphouët-Boigny's hegemony than as an attempt to promote the idea of African unification. To the extent that the solidarity or mutual-loan-guarantee fund serves the short-term goals of Houphouët-Boigny's partners in the Entente, their dependence in turn reinforces the dominance of the Ivory Coast. Moreover, the unusual attention and attraction which the international financial community has shown in the Ivory Coast has had a solidifying effect on that country's quest for intraregional supremacy. The result has been the further widening of the gap between the Ivory Coast on the one hand and its neighbors on the other.

Neither the dependence on France nor the hegemonic role in Francophone West Africa has materially affected the economic condition of the majority of Ivorians. The country's boom, which has mainly been confined to its export trade, has largely benefited foreign capitalists and their local agents. Indeed, throughout Africa, the majority has been subjected to economic injustices from their black rulers just as they did from colonial regimes. This situation has been concealed by the illusion of the alleged communal African spirit which makes for a preference to share with one's brethren. The degree of exploitation and conspicuous consumption by the privileged few suggests a necessity for reappraising this hitherto unsubstantiated claims about the persistent communality in African society. That the elites can remain indifferent to such awesome inequality and not view it as a social problem necessitating urgent action indicates that, barring revolutionary upheavals, the prospects of change are indeed limited.

REFERENCES

Africa south of the Sahara (1974). London: Europa Publications.
Afrique contemporaine (1974). No. 71 (January-February).

ALIBERT, J. (1974). "L'évolution de la zone franc en Afrique Noire." Afrique contemporaine (no. 74, July-August).

AMIN, S. (1970). "Capitalism and development in the Ivory Coast." In I.L. Markovitz (ed.), African politics and society. New York: Free Press.

——— (1971). L'Afrique de l'Ouest bloquée. Paris: Minuit.

——— (1974). "The paradox of food imports to agricultural Africa must be eliminated in this decade." Third World, 3(5).

BRETTON, H.L. (1973). Power and politics in Africa. Chicago: Aldine.

"Conseil de l'Entente: Quincième anniversaire du Conseil" (1974). Afrique contemporaine (no. 74, July-August).

CORBETT, E. (1972). The French presence in black Africa. Washington: Black Orpheus.

FOLTZ, W.J. (1965). From French West Africa to the Mali Federation. New Haven, Conn.: Yale University Press.

GUTKIND, P.C.W. (1974). The emergent African urban proletariat (Occasional Paper Series, No. 8, Centre for Developing Area Studies). Montreal: McGill University.

HOUPHOUET-BOIGNY, F. (1957). "Black Africa and the French Union." Foreign Affairs (July).

JALLOH, A.A. (1973). Political integration in French-speaking Africa. Berkeley: Institute of International Studies, University of California.

MARKOVITZ, I.L. (1969). Léopold-Sédar Senghor and the politics of Negritude. New York: Atheneum.

MUNCIE, P.C. (1973). Torches in the night: Educational experiences in Tanzania and the Ivory Coast. London.

MYTELKA, L.K. (1974). "A genealogy of Francophone West and Equatorial African regional organizations." Journal of Modern African Studies, 12(2).

N'DONGO, S. (1972). La "coopération" franco-africaine. Paris: Maspero.

NKRUMAH, K. (1965). Neo-colonialism: The last stage of imperialism. London: Heinemann.

O'BRIEN, R.C. (1972). White society in black Africa: The French of Senegal. Evanston, Ill.: Northwestern University Press.

SENGHOR, L.-S. (1954). "L'avenir de la France dans l'outre-mer." Politique etrangere (October).

——— (1974). "Les rapports africains à la croisée des chemins." Afrique contemporaine (no. 73, May-June).

SKURNIK, W.A.E. (1972). The foreign policy of Senegal. Evanston, Ill.: Northwestern University Press.

THOMPSON, W.S. (1969). Ghana's foreign policy. Princeton, N.J.: Princeton University Press.

TUNTENG, P-K. (1974). "France-Africa, plus ça change. . . ." Africa Report (July-August).

WAUTHIER, C. (1974). "France's year in Africa." In C. Legum (ed.), Africa contemporary record. New York: Africana Publishing.

WORONOFF, J. (1972). West African wager: Houphouët versus Nkrumah. Metuchen, N.J.: Scarecrow Press.

10

SOUTHERN AFRICA:
White Power in Crisis

BEN TUROK
KEES MAXEY

Though we live in turbulent times, it is nevertheless not often that history moves visibly before us. This sense of historical change is felt only when there occurs a lurch in the balance of power on a scale large enough to upset a particular political system for good. The collapse of Portuguese colonialism in Africa is such a case, opening up the way for the emancipation of the black peoples in its former territories and bringing about a massive change in the balance of geo-political forces in the subcontinent of southern Africa. From what was only recently a seemingly all-powerful and compact region of concerted white domination there now emerges a picture of a thoroughly dislocated power structure with even granite South Africa in a crisis of policy.

It was only a year previously that the offensive of South Africa to establish a range of economic, political, and military bridgeheads over the whole area seemed to be gaining ground. Even the campaign for dialogue with black Africa further north was proceeding quietly despite protestations by the Organization of African Unity (OAU). The main thrust of the offensive, however, was within southern Africa itself, taking the form of a carefully dovetailed plan to integrate black and white states in a common economic union buttressed by covert political arrangements.

The prospects of such a union looked dangerously promising, posing a serious problem for the OAU but even more for the liberation movements of southern Africa. In a sense the bold decision to build the Cabora Bassa dam symbolized the confidence of the white regimes that they could jointly exploit the region's vast resources of natural wealth and labor. Symbolic too of their self-confidence was the plan to bring in a million white settlers to manage the mines and industries made possible by the new electric power generated by the dam. But this attempt to turn back the clock of history has failed. Whatever else may now

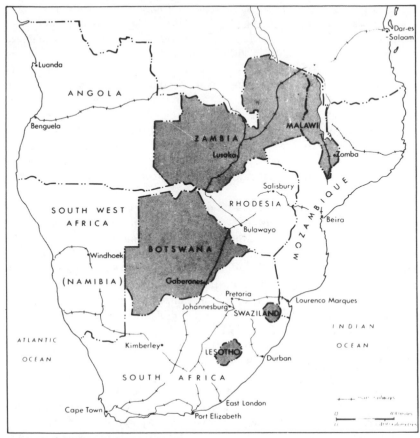

Figure 1: SOUTHERN AFRICA

happen in Mozambique, it is certain that this particular infusion of white support will not take place. Instead, the African liberation movements are consolidating their power bases, and Mozambique and Angola can no longer be included in the block of white domination. Whatever concessions the interim governments of these states have to make to South Africa in order to survive the first years of independence, they can no longer be counted as a reserve area or even a buffer protecting the deep South. Furthermore, there is no certain way to prevent their territories being used by South African militants as a political base in the first instance and for military action later on. Of particular importance in the immediate present is the fact that events in the former Portuguese territories have made Rhodesia and Namibia the loose teeth in the jaws of white power.

The historical record will show that the national liberation movements in southern Africa received their major impetus from the time of the intervention of guerrilla forces. Important as was the political mobilization before that, it seems that in each case it was the physical intervention of guerrillas (even on a modest scale, as in Rhodesia) which created great political strain and raised in sharp form the capacity of the regimes to survive. We do not wish to minimize the significance of nonmilitary struggle. Clearly the negative vote to the Pearce Commission was highly significant, just as the large-scale strike in Namibia in December 1971 marked a turning point in popular awakening. But in the calculations of the white regimes it is primarily the resort to military means which concentrated the political pressures leading to talk of "settlement" and decolonization. We have yet to see whether the same pattern follows in South Africa itself with its highly developed industrial structure and large urban working class, but it seems safe to assume that the politics of white power remain highly sensitive to the strategic-military potentials of the liberation movements.

As we write we are conscious of moving on an escalator with a rapidly changing scenario around us, but we are convinced that whatever current negotiations may produce for Rhodesia, Namibia, and the other states, the subcontinent will remain in a condition of continuous conflict until all the white regimes and especially that of South Africa have fallen. And that particular task remains especially difficult since its ruling class regards itself as indigenous, having no metropole to retreat to, and since imperialist interests still regard this class as the bastion of Western economic, political, and military interests in the region as a whole. (See Brooks, 1974.)

The collapse of Portuguese rule in Mozambique and Angola left South Africa in a quandary. It could persist with its outward thrust seeking to maintain the frontiers of white power on the Zambezi and using Rhodesian borders to build up a low level military-espionage-subversion intervention which could be highly unsettling for the new governments and generally take on what has been called the "Israeli" posture of retaliation for every incursion against the white redoubt. It would be assisted here by the sophisticated base set up in the Caprivi Strip and by the long exposed frontiers of Angola and Mozambique which could be easily breached in the event of any attack on South Africa herself at the now-exposed flanks. On the other hand, she could try for a carefully conducted withdrawal from these troublesome areas with their vast spaces and disadvantageous population ratios favoring black rebellion and rely instead on a diplomatic-political arrangement tending to regional stability, while leaving the South African forces free to defend her own territories. The choice has not been easy, since a glance at a map will show what a huge land mass is lost to white control by such a step, breathtaking in its historical import.

Political pressures from the Western powers have aimed at pushing South Africa toward the latter option, and it has seemed that the OAU has been willing to strike a bargain which would ensure rapid change in Rhodesia and South African disengagement from Namibia. These measures would be accompanied by some kind of stabilization in the area as a whole enabling further exchanges and negotiations over the future of South Africa's blacks to be conducted in ministerial parlors rather than on the battlefield.

There is a great deal of evidence that developments in Rhodesia will be crucial in determining the balance of power in the region as a whole, at least in the short run, and this article therefore gives considerable attention to that country. Rhodesia (or Zimbabwe, as Africans call it) is a landlocked country of some 150,810 square miles and a population of 5,099,000 in the 1969 census. The backbone of the country is a fairly high plateau of about 4,250 feet, sloping down to the Zambezi in the north, to the Sabi and Limpopo rivers in the south, and the Kalahari desert in the west. The borders are as in Table 1.

Of strategic importance is the fact that most of the European-occupied land is in the central plateau while the land around the circumference is either African-occupied or allotted to game reserves. This has meant that as long as African opposition was mainly confined to the urban areas, it could be contained fairly easily, but when the threat was posed from across the borders, from Zambia and Mozambique, the lines of communication proved inadequate for the Rhodesian forces, and the existing institutions of control were insufficient. This was why the South African forces were required even before the Rhodesians had suffered noticeable casualties.

The first attacks by ZANU and ZAPU took place in 1966 when small groups infiltrated into central and western Rhodesia. A further larger incursion was made by a joint force of ZAPU-African National Congress (of South Africa) in the Wankie area near Victoria Falls. It was this attack that obliged Rhodesia to seek South African military support. Another large-scale attack was made by a ZAPU-ANC (SA) in 1968 near Lake Kariba, but this too was crushed by security forces.

In 1970-1971, both organizations reassessed their strategy to ensure greater local support from villagers in future incursions. ZANU began to infiltrate guerrillas into the northeast of Rhodesia through the Tete province of Mozambique with the help of Frelimo. In 1972 they began a series of attacks on farms, white government officers, and African informers and security forces in a wide sweep of country northeast of Salisbury. By March 1975 the security forces had admitted military losses totaling 61 killed and a large number injured. ZAPU made a series of commando raids along the Zambezi, forcing the maintenance of substantial security forces along its whole length and creating a high sense of

Table 1. RHODESIA'S BORDERS

Borders	Contiguous Country	Length (miles)	Special Features
North	Zambia	430	Runs along the Zambezi
West	Point contact with Namibia (Caprivi)	0	
West	Botswana	480	Follows Shashe River in the south
South	South Africa	140	Runs along the Limpopo
East	Mozambique	710	Partly along the Zambezi Valley; then along a mountain range

insecurity and vulnerability among the white population throughout the northern part of Rhodesia.

These military campaigns had a marked effect on morale in the country. Industry was dislocated by the calling up of reserves (in many cases one month in every six), and the black contingents in the army have not proved wholly loyal. After a dance in Salisbury, colored soldiers in battle dress shouted at the police, "Up with terrorists, up with Frelimo, and down with the police" (*Rhodesia Herald*, November 6, 1974). The effect of immigration has been substantial, while emigration has risen, particularly among professionals. Counting white heads has long been an important aspect of Rhodesia's politics, where much depends on the internal solidarity of its 229,000 whites. (See Maxey, 1975.)

HISTORICAL ORIGINS OF WHITE SETTLEMENT

That so small a white settler group should stubbornly entrench itself, defying its former masters and world condemnation, is perhaps remarkable. But it is readily comprehensible if Rhodesia's Unilateral Declaration of Independence (UDI) is seen in the context of white domination in South Africa, and as an extension of it. It may be ironical that South Africa is now pressing for a "settlement," but a white Rhodesia would have been unthinkable without a white base in South Africa itself. It is necessary to go back in time and space to seek the origins of white colonization in the region as a whole, though only the briefest outline can be given here.

White settlement proper began in southern Africa with Jan van Riebeeck's arrival in 1652. Having easily established his refreshment station for the ships of the Dutch East India Company, he was followed by Dutch soldiers and officials who soon expanded their hold inland. They asserted their power and authority over the indigenous Khoikhoi but also imported slaves from East Africa and Asia, thereby introducing a new, more pliable (because more insecure and more anchored) work force into the colony. Le May (1971:7) says: "The heathen savage [referring to the Khoikhoi] had been regarded as a creature of natural inferiority, but savagery was not an irredeemable condition, for the Khoikhoi might learn the white man's language and habits, and adopt his religion. With slavery, inferiority became structured in a social institution in which status became identified with colour."

The slaves had no standing in the civil law of the colony. They could not marry or possess money or goods as property, and they had no access to the law for any purposes. The Khoikhoi were also denied these rights, but it was rather the rigid institutions of slavery which established the rigorous identity of overlordship with white skin. When the Dutch settlers eventually moved further inland and came into conflict with the Xhosa people, they also established a relationship close to slavery upon them, with color playing an important symbolic function. Later, in the nineteenth century, when the Boers (as the

Dutch settlers came to be called in recognition of their local identity) seized large areas of the interior by force, they brought Africans into service as laborers and servants, but denied them the right to reside in these areas when not so employed. They were not permitted to own land, firearms, or horses and required passes signed by their employers. When Boer republics were eventually established in the Transvaal and Free State, Africans were specifically excluded from the franchise.

White domination was by no means a prerogative of Dutch-Boer rule alone. While British rule, established in the Cape in 1806, brought various changes, like the abolition of slavery and the introduction of judicial processes, the essentials of white rule remained. Neither in the eastern Cape where thousands of English settlers sank roots after 1820, nor in Natal, where British annexation (following Boer conquest of the Zulus) led to the introduction of a further contingent of tens of thousands of English settlers, were Africans considered to be other than laborers without rights.

In Natal, a commission of settlers reported in 1854 that, "when not effectively restrained and directed by the strong arm of power, the true and universal character of the natives, as framed by their education, habits and associations, is at once superstitious and warlike. . . . They are crafty and cunning; at once indolent and excitable; averse to labour" (Wilson and Thompson, 1969:383). And labor was what the settlers wanted most. In consequence, the British administration imposed discriminatory taxation which Africans alone had to pay and which yielded more than £5000 a year while further indirect taxes were levied on blankets and other consumer goods (including trousers, which by law they were obliged to possess). Welsh (1971) describes Natal society as a "racial oligarchy dominated in all respects by the colonists, and maintained, in the final analysis, by force." And he asserts that it is wrong to suggest that apartheid is the exclusive product of Afrikaner nationalism: its antecedents were to be found in Natal rather than elsewhere. At any rate, white dominance, in Natal as in the rest of the country, was both repressive and exploitative.

While the Cape and Natal were firmly in British hands and the Transvaal and the Orange Free State came to be set up as Boer republics, there remained peripheral areas which continued to be in dispute. Lesotho came under direct British rule in 1884, to become independent in 1966; Swaziland became British in 1906 until its independence in 1968; and Botswana was taken over in 1896 as a protectorate until independence in 1966. In each case Britain resorted to direct rule to seal the issue after a dispute with the Boer republics. None of these territories gained much significance, however, since they were wholly undeveloped and were mainly labor pools for the South African economy as it developed. Their populations—Lesotho, 1,000,000 (1969), Swaziland, 362,367 (1966), and Botswana, 514,378 (1964)—were small enough not to arouse great interest, and it is only now that minerals are being discovered in Swaziland and Botswana. As their strategic location is coming to be appreciated, these states assume their real significance.

Rhodesia was one of the last parts of Africa to be overtaken by white rule in the process called "the scramble for Africa." Nonetheless, it was of greater significance than Lesotho, Botswana, or Swaziland because it was seen as an extension of South Africa itself.

The modern history of Rhodesia began in 1835 when the Ndebele fled there from the South. They were a cattle-rearing and military people led first by Mzilikazi and later by Lobengula. In the latter half of the century Rhodes, who was in the Cape, determined to make a bid for the rumored Rhodesian gold, at the same time ensuring that neither the Portuguese nor the Boers would move in. One of his business associates, Charles Rudd, arrived in Bulawayo and got Lobengula to sign in October 1888 the notorious Rudd Concession. This granted Rudd mineral rights in the area under Ndebele control and became the basis for the establishment of the British South Africa Company and its endorsement by the British government.

Rhodes wanted to establish a physical presence in Rhodesia, and in 1890 the "Pioneer Column," consisting of 184 English and Afrikaner whites chosen from all over South Africa and accompanied by 300 black auxiliaries, went to Rhodesia. They halted near the Shona village of Harari, which was thereupon named Fort Salisbury after the British prime minister of the time. The participants were paid 7s. 6d. a day and promised a 3,000-acre farm and 15 gold mine claims on arrival. In April 1891, the British government declared it a "British sphere of influence," and Rhodes became chief magistrate. (See Keatley, 1973:113-118.)

The use of chartered companies was a cheap form of imperialist expansion since the expense of control and administration was borne not by government but by the company. At the same time this abrogation of government responsibility set in motion a process leading to ever greater autonomy for Rhodes and the settlers. After continued war the settlers confiscated the Ndebele national cattle herd and this, coupled with increasing resentment in the Shona areas, led to the uprisings (called Chimurenga by Africans) in 1896-1897 which were put down by British troops. It was widely expected that Rhodesia would ultimately become part of South Africa, but in 1922 a referendum of white voters preferred "Responsible Government" as a British colony. With increased participation of settlers in local government and greater authority for the local civil service was coupled a decline in the formal role of the BSAC. Rhodesia came to take on the appearance of an independent state deriving its traditions from South Africa rather than from Britain. The Constitution of 1961 contains the clause: "The law to be administered by the High Court shall be the law in force in the Colony of the Cape of Good Hope on the 10th day of June 1891 as modified by subsequent legislation" (Order in Council, 1961). And the legislative program since 1922 bears a remarkable similarity to South African legislation. Labor laws and the vital Land Apportionment Act of 1930, which divided the country very unequally in relation to population, ensured that the policy of "parallel development" became entrenched in Rhodesia.

SOUTH AFRICA

Institutions of White Power

The characterization of the system of white domination in South Africa remains elusive for the many writing on the problem. Explanations vary from crude notions of conquest as the primary determinant, to race prejudice, to simplistic propositions about capitalist class exploitation, and to a modification of the internal colonialism thesis. Blumer's exposition on the insinuation of industrialization within a rigid racial order has been of considerable assistance, but a satisfactory characterization of the unfolding system *in its modern form* which gives adequate weight to class exploitative relations while explaining the tendency to *increasing* racial inequalities has yet to emerge. We shall not even attempt this task here since we seek primarily to elaborate on those conditions which have shaped the present crisis. Our analysis begins in South Africa itself since that is the baseline for developments in the North.

A new situation arose with the discovery of diamonds in 1870 and the opening of the Witwatersrand gold mine in 1886. It led to a great influx of Europeans first as diggers, then as workers on the mines, when they were opened up in earnest with foreign capital. In just over a decade the African component of the work force reached 100,000 men.

The main priorities in the country were now evident. The large white-owned farms and the burgeoning mining industry required a steady supply of cheap labor. Ready to hand was a voiceless, voteless black population, whose military defeat had gone hand in hand with the erosion of its agricultural and pastoral subsistence economy and upon whom had already been imposed such taxes as would oblige many to seek employment for cash wages in the white-controlled economy. These circumstances were highly conducive to the reinforcement of racial divides between white and black, to the generation of feelings of race prejudice and white superiority.

Further reinforcement was generated by the color bar clause in mining law enacted in 1893 by the Volksraad of the Boer Transvaal Republic, which stipulated that only whites might do the actual blasting (Wilson, 1972:7). Naturally Africans were thereby segregated within the work force, and their wages reflected this at £26 a year in 1897 while the white workers earned 10 times more. Many of these were British worker immigrants with no previous colonial experience, but they soon learned to identify with white superiority particularly when they came to feel threatened by black workers who were prepared to accept very low wages. White wages were extraordinarily high. An economic commission set up in 1914 reported that "Wages on the Witwatersrand are nearly 40% higher than in America and nearly 225% than in any European country" (Houghton, vol. 2, 1972:181).

This wages structure became the model for industry and commerce where white workers gradually established a monopoly control of skilled work. The average annual wage paid in factories in 1915-1916 was (Houghton, 1972):

White	African	Coloured	Asian
£171	£32	£48	£26

To protect these living standards, the white workers of British origin set up trade unions into which they recruited Afrikaner workers, thereby fusing their common interest. Africans were, however, excluded.

The job color bar was confirmed in industry by the Mines and Works Act of 1911 and its amendment of 1926, as a result of union pressure. Africans were excluded from the definition of "employee" in the Industrial Conciliation Act of 1924. Africans were thereby symbolically and legally denied state recognition and excluded from formal collective bargaining. As a result, African unionism never managed to establish itself on a permanent basis. While there have been many strikes over the years, some very extensive, they have not led either to recognition from employers or to lasting material benefits. (The concrete process whereby workers in advanced capitalist societies maintain or even improve living standards needs to be contrasted with the inability of African workers to do the same in South Africa.)

For the many white workers who were not skilled and who were not catered for by the craft unions, the government adopted a "civilized labor policy" which ensured priority for whites in job provision particularly in the expanding state sector. This remains government policy at present so that the public sector provides employment for 40% of economically active whites outside agriculture.

If the white workers in the modern period manipulated these traditions of white privilege to ensure high wages and security, the tradition also ensured that the reverse would apply for Africans. Dominated by a white administration, Africans were unable to resist the pressure of taxes and landlessness which forced them to seek cash wages in the white economy. It was cheap black labor that powered the birth of industrialization in South Africa. Gold, the exotic mineral which had already become the unit of exchange on a world scale, lay deep in the bowels of the earth in very low-grade ore. William Hance (1964) has argued that "the gold industry of the Republic owes its continuance to the availability of large numbers of low-wage labourers. If the gold reefs were situated in the United States they probably would be of interest only to students of geology; they would not be worked." And since gold was the country's first modern industry it set the pattern for the entire industrial labor policy (Wilson, 1972:7). The crux of this policy was migrant labor. Before gold, Africans were indeed recruited seasonally by farmers all over the country. And diamonds also generated a migrant work force with about 10,000 employed at Kimberley by 1874. They were housed in bachelor compounds closed to the public allegedly for security reasons, and the practice continued elsewhere including on the gold mines. Migrant labor was based on the concept that the worker resided essentially in the African reserves (some 13% of the land surface) which had remained under exclusively African occupation after the wars of conquest. The implicit argument of the mineowners was that, since the migrant's family was thus resident elsewhere and earned some income from farming, this income constituted a kind of family allowance, though it was generated neither by the state nor by the employers but by the productive activity of the family itself. This both permitted and justified a policy of paying labor below its cost of reproduction, which made it especially cheap. To achieve this end, the state had to play its part by ensuring that the family remained on the reserves while the wage earner was a migrant. A whole series of laws were designed to achieve this.

There were many other advantages in the migrant labor system, including the easy adjustment of the size of the work force in accordance with the changing tempo of production. African workers were never long enough at any location to develop the kind of continuity required to organize trade unions which might force up wages, and migrancy discouraged the acquisition of skills so that Africans were easily dismissed and replaced from the large pool of unskilled labor.

The Role of the State

Two central aspects of the South African system thus have emerged from our discussion. First, the colonial heritage created a tradition of white authority and privilege which was carried forward into the modern era. Second, industrialization in South Africa was contingent upon the maintenance of a cheap migrant labor system. The greater the intensity of exploitation of black workers, the faster the economy could grow, and the greater the surplus to siphon off for white appropriation.

But such a system could not be left to the whims of laissez-faire. This would have resulted in the urbanization of African workers, leading to pressure on wage levels and demands for political rights. The state therefore stepped in with all its authoritarian traditions derived from the colonial heritage and stamped its will on the lives of Africans.

The result of decades of tuning up the legislation on migrancy is that Africans are subject to prosecution for offenses that are not recognized as such in any other country, nor by any other race in South Africa. There are now 700,000 convictions under the pass laws every year. Most labor is on some kind of contract, and all work-seekers require permits to enter any area outside their residence. Being virtually unable to exercise any selectiveness, they cannot get higher wages by shopping around.

The gold mines are prohibited by law from providing family accommodation for more than 3% of their African work force. The white S.A. Agricultural Union is pressing for a contract system similar to the mines. The railways labor force is largely migrant, and of the 4,600 Africans employed in the Western Cape section in 1971, 4,000 were housed in compounds or transit camps. Wilson (1972:77) estimates that the total number of African migrants in the country is 1,305,000, or 51% of those in registered employment.

The effect of the cheap migrant labor system on white living standards is marked. Over the population as a whole the highest 10% (almost all whites) received 58% of total income in 1971. Comparative GNP per capita stood in

1960 at £1627 for whites and £106 for Africans. Annual consumption per head was £746 for whites and £48 for Africans, while monthly household incomes were £199 for whites and £18 for Africans.

Yet South Africa is a wealthy industrialized country and extraordinarily well endowed in mineral wealth, and not only in gold and diamonds as is commonly thought. She does produce 80% of the capitalist world's gold. But in the Western world she is also the largest producer of platinum, antimony, copper, lead, and zinc. The country's reserves of manganese, chrome, vermalite, and fluorspar are also estimated to be the largest in the Western world, and she produces the second largest amounts of asbestos, vanadium, vermiculite, and sillimanite in the Western world. In uranium, South Africa is a major producer and has the world's largest known deposits. Coal and iron ore deposits are practically inexhaustible, while all the minerals for the production of steel and steel alloys are available. One of the world's largest open-cast copper mines is in the Transvaal, and pithead prices are the lowest in the world. With a million tons of fish caught off the coast of the republic in 1968 and nearly the same amount off South-West Africa, she is the sixth largest fisher in the world.

The total value of minerals produced up to December 1960 exceeded £7,060,000,000, while the annual mineral production in 1969 was £865,000,000. In 1968 South Africa generated 33,000 kilowatt-hours of electricity amounting to 57% of Africa's total and a per-capita consumption equal to that of Western Europe. Its electric power is also among the cheapest in the world.

Cheap power and ready-to-hand raw materials has encouraged the emergence of a powerful industrial base. The motor industry, which was formerly entirely import only, produced 256,000 vehicles in 1969, of which 50% was local content by weight. The clothing industry supplies 90% of local demand, while the textile industry supplies 60% of local demand. In chemicals South Africa had a big start with the manufacture of explosives for mining operations, and its Johannesburg Modderfontein factory, owned by African Explosives, is one of the largest privately owned in the world. SASOL, a state owned corporation making oil from coal (the largest in the world), has developed a large chemical by-products industry.

Industrialization has brought a large number of Africans, colored people (those of "mixed" race), and Asians into the mines and factories, though their race has determined their lower occupational roles and lower wages than their white coworkers. Table 2 gives comparisons in some selected major industries. The inequalities in reward emerge clearly from this table as does the size of the total black work force. But what is also striking is the size of the white work force, which is far from negligible as a factor in production and as an element in the political framework. The size and occupational roles of the white workers has a direct bearing on whether South Africa may be termed a colonial-type system, or whether it is primarily capitalist. We would argue that the white workers ought not to be thought of as settlers, partly on historical grounds but

Table 2. RACIAL COMPOSITION OF LABOR AND WAGES
IN MAJOR SOUTH AFRICAN INDUSTRIES

		Mining and Quarrying	Manufacture	Construction
Whites	No:	61,782	279,700	60,800
Average wage per month		£195.82	£170.81	£178.10
Africans	No:	592,819	644,900	270,000
Average wage per month		£9.48	£29.16	£28.03
Coloreds	No:	6,352	201,300	47,200
Average wage per month		£41.90	£41.16	£61.74
Asians	No:	578	76,500	5,300
Average wage per month		£51.46	£43.58	£79.92

Table adapted from R. First et al., 1973:48.
SOURCE: Republic of South Africa, Department of Statistics, *Statistical New Releases,*
June 16, 1971; June 18, 1971; September 13, 1971.

also because they are thoroughly insinuated into the industrial framework as workers, though of a highly privileged kind.

Table 3 shows how jobs are allocated according to race. It also shows, however, that a large number of whites are still engaged in skilled manual work, and this must affect the characterization of the system as a whole.

The crux of the issue lies in the role of the state as arbiter of occupational roles and status. It is the custodian of white domination at every level. It achieved this early on by a variety of statutory measures and the deliberate stimulation of industry from 1925 onwards, always ensuring that whites got preference in the skilled jobs. Even now, when there is a great scarcity of skilled white labor, Iscor, the government-owned steel corporation, still has a work force consisting of 19,900 whites and 19,000 blacks. The white workers have insisted on the perpetuation of job reservation. For instance, in the engineering industry the Amalgamated Engineering Union maintains a closed shop; and, since Africans are prohibited by law from being members of that union and from acquiring apprenticeship, they are also thereby deprived of the skilled work reserved for its members. Interestingly enough, race prohibition as such does not appear in the industrial agreement, and the union has claimed that it does not practice racial discrimination. This dissimulation is possible because the state provides the legislative backup needed.

But the state does more than ensure the supply of cheap labor and maintain high living standards for whites. It also intervenes at the level of the enterprise —to a degree unusual in a supposedly private enterprise system. State intervention comes not only from infrastructural support in the publicly owned railways, airways, electric power plants, and so forth, but also from the state corporations in steel, chemicals, fertilizers (for farming), and oil from coal. The Industrial Development Corporation (public) is active in numerous other industries, including armaments, which is one of the most important.

Writing in 1965, Pierre van den Berghe (1967:90) said:

Table 3. SOUTH AFRICAN LABOR POPULATION, 1971: DISTRIBUTION BY OCCUPATION CATEGORY AND RACIAL GROUP[a]

Category	Whites		Coloreds		Asians		Africans		Total Population	
	No./% of White Population	% of Whites in Category	No./% of Colored Population	% of Coloreds in Category	No./% of Asian Population	% of Asians in Category	No./% of African Population	% of Africans in Category	No./% of Total Population	% of Population in Category
A	111.7 8.1%	(93.0%)	0.9 0.2%	(0.7%)	2.5 1.5%	(2.1%)	4.9 0.2%	(4.1%)	120.0 2.7%	(100.0%)
B	221.2 16.0%	(67.9%)	22.1 4.9%	(6.8%)	9.1 5.5%	(2.8%)	73.5 2.9%	(22.2%)	325.9 7.2%	(100.0%)
C	533.1 38.5%	(76.5%)	35.9 8.0%	(5.1%)	50.4 30.5%	(7.2%)	78.1 3.1%	(11.2%)	697.5 15.5%	(100.0%)
D	250.4 18.1%	(77.6%)	34.0 7.6%	(10.4%)	6.4 3.9%	(1.9%)	35.9[b] 1.4%	(11.0%)	326.7 7.2%	(100.0%)
E	182.2 13.2%	(12.5%)	194.4 43.4%	(13.3%)	74.1 44.9%	(5.1%)	1,011.2[c] 40.3%	(69.2%)	1,461.9 32.4%	(100.0%)
F	29.9 2.2%	(2.2%)	135.1 30.1%	(10.0%)	11.8 7.1%	(0.9%)	1,174.4 47.2%	(87.0%)	1,351.2 30.0%	(100.0%)
G	31.6 2.3%	(44.9%)	2.9 0.6%	(4.1%)	0.8 0.5%	(1.1%)	35.1 1.4%		70.4 1.6%	(100.0%)
H	25.1 1.8%	(16.2%)	24.1 5.4%	(15.5%)	10.2 6.2%	(6.6%)	95.9 3.8%	(61.8%)	155.3 3.4%	(100.0%)
Total	1,385.2 100.0%	(30.7%)	449.4 100.0%	(10.0%)	165.3 100.0%	(3.7%)	2,509.0 100.0%	(55.6%)	4,508.9 100.0%	(100.0%)

NOTE: Total working population, 4,508,900, made up of whites, 1,385,200 (30.7%); Coloreds, 449,400 (10.0%); Africans, 2,509,000 (55.6%). Population figures in table above are in 000s.

a. Table includes figures for manufacturing, mining and services, but agriculture is excluded.
b. Including "6,400 registered skilled Bantu building workers."
c. Including "2,000 registered learner Bantu building workers."

CATEGORY: A—Professional, with degree or equivalent qualification. B—With some lower professional qualification, including teachers, draughtsmen, nurses, etc. C—Clerical, including bank clerks, plus shop assistants and other nonmanual jobs. Status is that of unskilled nonmanual. D—Skilled manual, jobs usually require formal apprenticeship. This category includes trained (though not apprenticed) African building, dock, and transport workers. E—Semiskilled, including miners, machinists, etc., where there is no formal qualification. Work is learned on the job. It is not a supervisory function in Britain—e.g., bus driver. F—Unskilled, manual. G—Military, police, customs, and excise personnel. Central or local government employees who are not industrial or clerical. H—Domestic workers, including cooks, laundry workers, canteen, hotel workers, but does not include private domestic service.

SOURCE: We are indebted to Mr. P. Lowman of the Labour Research Department, London, for this table. (South African Department of Labour Manpower Survey No. 9, April 1971.)

With an average increase of 6.89 per cent in the value of manufacturing production between 1910 and 1940, South Africa's rate of expansion was over three times faster than that of the United States (2.23 per cent) and Canada (2.06 per cent) and over seven times faster than that of Great Britain (0.87 per cent) during the same period.

Since then, growth has been even more rapid, overtaking almost every other country, with Gross Domestic Product rising to £6,844 million in 1969. The contribution to GDP at factor cost grew at an average annual rate of 10.3% between 1960 and 1968. The physical volume of production grew at 8.9% per annum from 1960 to 1969, while employment grew at 5.3% per annum, indicating big rises in productivity over the same period. (See Africa South of the Sahara, 1971:699).

In a report for the United Nations, Sean Gervasi (1970:1) pointed out that this kind of growth is indicative of a concerted national effort. He suggests that this effort "has been guided by a Government whose apparent intention is to secure a greater degree of economic independence by rapid industrialization. South Africa is a private enterprise economy in name only. The influence of the state in the economy is now paramount."

A survey called "Top Companies," published by the S.A. *Financial Mail* on April 16, 1971, shows the economic power of the state sector in relation to the private sector. As reprinted here in Table 4, companies are ranked by total assets in 1971. (State Corporations are marked with an asterisk.)

Several points are made in the comments accompanying the survey. The state sector is very large. Financial power, however, certainly lies with the mining houses, the banks, and other financial institutions. The only operating industrial companies included in the top 100 were Rembrandt and AE and CI. Although Barclays and Standard are shown to be bigger than De Beers, if comparative size were measured by shareholders' funds, De Beers would emerge nearly 10 times

Table 4. ASSETS OF LEADING SOUTH AFRICAN COMPANIES

	Total Assets in £ Million
Barclays Bank DCO	1,966
*SA Railways & Harbours	1,388
*Escom (Electricity Commission)	983
Standard Bank of SA	683
Anglo-American (gold, etc.)	643
De Beers Consolidated (diamonds, etc.)	590
United Building Society	459
Volkshas (Afrikaans capital)	400
Charter Consolidated (linked with Anglo)	386
S.A. Mutual	376
S.A. Permanent	370
Consolidated Goldfields	339
*Post Office	333
*Iscor	331
Trust Bank (Afrikaans capital)	310
Rand Selections (Afrikaans capital)	291

the size of the two biggest banks. If Anglo and De Beers were combined, as they ought to be since they belong to the same multinational corporation with assets of £2,303,000,000, they would dominate the table, as they in fact do the economy.

To sum up the discussion and draw out the political implications, we find that while the roots of apartheid can be traced back in history, it is the institutions set up by the Act of Union of 1910 that congealed the system in its modern form. After the British imperial army defeated the Boers in 1902, the British government nevertheless concluded that its interests would be best served by the consolidation of white control throughout South Africa with the full participation of the Boers.

The Act of Union created modern institutions of government and white control. With some minor exceptions which have since been abolished, it excluded people of color from the formal political process and reserved voting and representational rights to whites only. As a result the system congealed into one of the most undemocratic, unequal, and authoritarian in the world, with white political power being used to enforce and entrench white privilege in every sphere. Despite differences of perspective between the two major factions of the ruling class, English- and Afrikaans-speaking, there grew a wide-ranging concensus that white supremacy and privilege must be maintained; and this policy filtered down from parliament throughout the organs of government and administration to the lowest levels.

What is more, British foresight in uniting Boer and Briton ensured that there was sufficient white manpower to staff the controlling heights of all public and private institutions. This was no small elite, but a substantial alliance of classes and factions of classes, capable of running the entire power structure including the economic sector. One of the consequences was that the ruling alliance was so large in proportion to the total population and overall development that black advancement had to be choked off by numerous impediments deliberately erected to keep wealth, status, and power in white hands. There was no room for a black middle class. (It may be emerging now that the economy is booming beyond the parameters of white supervision.)

Institutions of "Separate Development"

Black aspirations were not to be suppressed forever, however. Even arrogant white supremacists could see that, and so the model of separate representation and separate development was set up leading to the creation of Bantustans and Urban Bantu Councils for Africans, the Coloured Representative Council for people of mixed races, and the S.A. Indian Council for Asians. Of these, the Bantustans are the most important.

Although "Native Policy" has always upheld the administrative and territorial separation of the reserves, it was Dr. B.J. Verwoerd, prime minister from 1958 to 1966, who gave it new robes. The main object of his initiative was to provide an alternative focus for African political aspirations outside the parliamentary framework, though he also saw the need to offer some alternative to integration in a common society, especially in the light of world criticism. The Promotion of Self-Government Act of 1959 and the Transkei Constitution Act of 1963 were designed to give the impression that viable independent states were envisaged.

However, Dr. Verwoerd's proposals fell on stony ground. The African National Congress rejected it out of hand as fraudulent and mischievous, tending to the regeneration of tribalism and divisiveness among Africans, and it reiterated its demands for full democratic rights. In the reserves themselves the proposals were not taken seriously other than by some chiefs and headmen who were in any case government appointees carrying out official policy. The notion that "independence" might be granted to the reserves, where the hierarchy of tribal tradition had long been emasculated and where dependence on the white economy was total, seemed ludicrous. Years of undermining poverty had also ensured that there was no class of potential collaborators willing to play a neocolonial role. The mantle of "autonomy" and "independence" therefore fell on the shoulders of unpopular chiefs or reluctant recipients like Chief Gatsha Buthelezi.

While the political aspect of "independence" has received much attention, the promised economic development has yet to materialize. Viability is still far off, especially since the eight regional administrations overseeing the Bantustans straddle nearly 300 separate pieces of land, many of them islands in white farming country. The control of expenditure is still largely in the hands of Pretoria-appointed white officials, and it seems that their own salaries and supporting costs take a large slice out of development funds. Of the £57 million allocated for the 1971 development plan two-thirds was set aside for town planning (which includes roads, houses for civil servants, fences, and settlements), while £7.3 million, the next largest amount, was for soil conservation.

Yet the underdevelopment of the Bantustans is immense. In the Transkei, the largest unit, only 34,186 people were in paid employment in 1965, and, of these, 18,000 were in government service. Against this, 257,586 were employed outside the Transkei. In the Bantustans as a whole only 945 jobs were created in secondary industry in the six years before 1968. The contribution made by the Bantustans to the total GNP of South Africa is 2%, and this is by 7,000,000 people, or one-third of the total population of the country. (See United Nations, 1970.) Barbara Rogers (1972:24) says:

> Annual income per capita in the reserves in 1954, excluding remittances of migrant workers, was R25.8 [about £15.2]; if income from the white areas were included, the figure would be R48 [about £28.2] p.a. . . . It therefore appears that there was probably a net decline in actual income over those six years; taking into account the fall in money values, the decline in real income per capita was considerable. . . . The reserves are also becoming increasingly dependent on sources of income in the white economy; whereas in 1960-1 the ratio of domestic income from migrant workers was 47:53, by 1966-7 this had become 42:58, a significant swing in the direction of increased dependence on the white economy.

The Bantustans are not only far from viable; they do not even have a basis for self-sustaining growth. And if development were forced from above, say by an infusion of foreign capital, it would seriously undermine the supply of labor to the white economy, which is already under some pressure in this respect. In 1972 South Africa was employing nearly half a million "foreign" Africans: Lesotho, 131,749; Malawi, 131,291; Mozambique, 121,708; Botswana, 31,960; Swaziland, 10,108; Rhodesia, 6,200 (House of Assembly Debates, Hansard, June 14, 1973).

The Bantustans are also faced with the disadvantage of being universally sited far from the sources of raw materials (other than timber), transport, power, piped water, and the kind of infrastructure that boosted development in the white areas. Their fate seems to be one of continuing stagnation and poverty.

But the most important objection to the Bantustan scheme is political. Africans ask why they should give up their claim to the rest of South Africa and particularly that 2.8% in which 80% of the industry is located and which employs 80% of the industrial labor force, or why they should forget about the steel industry, which has an output of ingot steel reaching nearly five million tons in 1969 and which produces among the cheapest steel in the world. Steel has aided development in the new goldfields in the Orange Free State and provided the raw material for the expanding engineering industry, which in turn has facilitated the mechanization of white agriculture, the development of secondary industry, and the expansion of transport (Cole, 1966:430). With industry expanding fast and now substantially the biggest contributor to the GNP, its location in what are called the white urban complexes, which also have the three main harbors, has led to self-generating growth on a considerable scale.

In agriculture too there can be no comparison in the fertility and productivity of Bantustan lands with white farms. The amount of cultivated land in each case is 2.01 hectares in the Bantustans against 9.56 million hectares in the white areas, while there are 11.18 million hectares of natural pastures in the Bantustans against 78.97 million hectares in the white areas.

Nor can we ignore the matter of national sentiment. Africans are unlikely to give up forever those areas in which their forefathers lived centuries ago and which present-day generations have helped to build into their modern wealthy form.

The policy of Separate Development does not include the provision of separate independent territories for the two million colored people nor for the 620,000 Asians. History did not leave them reservations and they have become wholly integrated into the white-controlled economy even though residential segregation has forced them into separate urban townships and Group Areas.

For these "nationalities," separate political institutions have been devised. The Coloured Persons Representative Council was set up in 1969 consisting of 40 elected and 20 nominated members. At the first election the strongly antiapartheid Labour party won a clear majority of the elected seats. But support from the block of government-nominated members for the collaborationist Federal party gave the latter an overall majority to form the council's executive committee.

The council has a budget and works together with the Administration of Coloured Affairs (largely manned by senior white civil servants). The proceedings of the council have been stormy with boycotts and walkouts by the Labour party, which constantly attacks government policies. Mr. Sonny Leon, leader of the Labour party, has said:

> Every year we make recommendations to the government, and every year they're turned down. Some minor concessions have been granted. And they've increased our budget, which they control. But one of the cruellest ironies is that more and more white administrative staff are employed to run the C.R.C., and their salary bill is far higher than the salary bill of all C.R.C. members, including the executive, put together. [Randall, 1973:33]

Mr. Leon maintains that the central issue remains that the colored people seek full universal franchise and representation in parliament, and this the government is equally determined to refuse. The government's objective in forming the council was to encourage a sense of a separate identity among coloreds. But this has failed. Instead, the council is seen as yet another "dummy" institution, and coloreds are increasingly identifying politically with the Africans, "whose arms are open to us," says Mr. Leon.

When first constituted, the South African Indian Council had no elected element at all and consisted of 25 government-nominated members. It was an advisory body only and, since it tended to expound government policies, was treated with public obloquy. As a measure to counter criticism, a new system of electoral colleges was set up in 1974—there were no voters' rolls—to elect 15 of the 30 council members. The rest continue to be government appointees. However, even the chairman of the 1974 council, Mr. H.E. Joosub, a government apologist on most issues, was moved to say that the Indian community believed the new body had changed little and that they would remain voiceless in the administration of their own affairs. (See *Johannesburg Star*, September 7, 1974.)

Both these councils, colored and Indian, are now in crisis. In the Indian Council there was an angry response to a speech by Mr. Vorster, who warned them against a policy of confrontation. An executive member, Mr. A. Rajbansi said: "Anything short of a say in the country's legislative processes is unacceptable. We don't believe in 'parallel' development. If the basis is dishonourable, then we may have to abandon this course and follow the path of confrontation. This is because the Government is not listening to us" (*Johannesburg Star*, November 30, 1974).

RHODESIA

White Minority Rule

We have noted the considerable continuity in historical experience and institutional framework shared by Rhodesia and South Africa. But there is a most important difference: the white ruling class in Rhodesia is much smaller, constituting only 4.5% of the total population, as compared to 19% in South Africa.

This is why geography is so important in understanding the situation there, and we shall give this dimension rather more than usual space. While the basic distribution of land was decided in the early days of the Pioneer Column, it was entrenched in law in the Land Apportionment Act of 1931. This act set up several categories of land, the most important of which were land for purchase by Africans, land for purchase by Africans or whites, tribal reserves, and white-only land. Because of the low proportion of whites to Africans, land was the main instrument of social control in addition to being the main source of wealth. In 1963, when the ruling United Federal Party proposed that the Land Apportionment Act be repealed, it lost the election to the Rhodesian Front (Ian Smith's party), which fought on a platform of racial separation. The Rhodesian Front then replaced the act with an even more rigid Land Tenure Act in 1969. (See Palmer, 1969:43; 1974.)

Since the land question is central to our analysis, some hard data may be useful. Land is presently divided into three main categories: white land and African land, 70,230 square miles each, and national (that is, state) land, 10,340 square miles, which is largely game reserve. According to the 1969 Census, the population was distributed as shown in Table 5. All the towns and cities are in the white land area, with a population distribution as shown in Table 6.

According to figures given in these tables, the white population is therefore predominantly urban though heavily outnumbered even in the cities. Density of African population is relatively high in the Tribal Trust land though also significantly in the white land area, while the number of whites in the African areas is negligible. The implications for security and perpetuation of white rule are obvious.

Perhaps even more decisive is the fact that immigration of whites to Rhodesia never attained significant levels. Between 1946 and 1951 white population grew from 83,500 to 138,000, with immigration reaching a peak in 1960. Since then, immigration has slowed down until the inflow just balances the outflow.

Surprisingly enough, this small white population, which several decades

Table 5. RHODESIAN LAND DIVISION BY RACE
(Density in persons per square mile in parentheses)

	Africans	Whites	Coloreds and Asians
White land	1,730,140	224,794	23,453
	(28.5)	(3.7)	(0.5)
African land			
Tribal trust	2,921,840	2,100	157
	(46.6)	(0.3)	(−)
Purchase land	135,610	91	32
	(23.6)	(0.3)	(−)

Table 6. RHODESIAN URBAN POPULATIONS BY RACE

Town	Africans	Whites
Salisbury	280,000	96,800
Bulawayo	187,000	49,700
Others (ten towns)	189,000	33,300
Total	656,000	179,800

earlier had rejected union with South Africa, began to press the British government for even more local powers in the early 1950s. They also had in view an amalgamation with Northern Rhodesia and Nyasaland, from which direct British rule would be eliminated. However, Britain preferred the federal structure and pushed this through against bitter opposition from the African populations in Northern Rhodesia and Nyasaland.

Nevertheless, the Federation of the Rhodesias and Nyasaland brought rapid development to Southern Rhodesia. In 1957-1958, the annual gross output of federal manufacturing industry was £127 million, of which £105 million was in Southern Rhodesia. The Kariba Dam was also a creation of the federation, and its first generating plant was located in Southern Rhodesia as was the first parliament, the new university, and all the administrative headquarters. Africans in the other two states reacted vigorously to the growing authority of Southern Rhodesia, and the Monckton Commission was forced to propose in 1960 that secession was not incompatible with federation. As a result, Malawi (ex-Nyasaland) and Zambia (ex-Northern Rhodesia) seceded immediately prior to becoming independent. In 1965, the unilateral Declaration of Independence (UDI) was Southern Rhodesia's response to these developments.

This period of constitutional juggling did not go unremarked by the African people of Southern Rhodesia. The Southern Rhodesian African National Congress was led by Joshua Nkomo. It was influenced by the style and traditions of the South African body of the same name and was particularly articulate on the land question. It also opposed strongly the legislation which was entrenching race discrimination ever more rigorously. It was banned in 1959, to be followed by the National Democratic party in 1960. This was banned too, to be followed by the Zimbabwe African Peoples Union (ZAPU), which was also banned in 1962, though it regrouped in exile in Zambia. In 1963 the breakaway Zimbabwe African National Union (ZANU) was formed under the leadership of the Rev. Ndabaningi Sithole. Both organizations were under constant police harassment, and their leaders were either jailed or detained in remote camps. British attempts to "settle" with the Smith regime in Rhodesia received an overwhelming defeat in 1971, when the British-appointed Pearce Commission went through what was expected to be a largely formal exercise in seeking African opinion on a new formula that had the effect of legitimating UDI. The most important aspect of this rejection was that it revealed a fundamental and deep distrust by Africans of white promises and protestations of good faith. Africans also objected to the proposals on the grounds that they had had no part in their formulation (Mlambo, 1972). It was doubtless these considerations that loomed large when decolonization in Portuguese Africa led to talks in Lusaka in November 1974 between representatives of Ian Smith and various African movements.

Political Economy of White Minority Rule

Unlike South Africa, Rhodesia is a poor country. Per-capita income in 1972 was about £150, although white incomes are about ten times that of Africans. This means that the white elite is even more parasitic than in South Africa, and this is borne out by the statistics (for March 1974) given in Table 7.

The Southern Rhodesia economy has been based upon cheap labor from its inception. One of the first problems which the white settlers faced was how to induce Africans to work for them. Some African laborers were brought with the Pioneer Column from South Africa. Others were forced to work, and this was one cause of the 1896-1897 uprisings. A hut tax was placed on all African families. In 1903, the administration tried to quadruple this tax in order to "conduce to more continuous labour by the native," but this move was stopped by the British government. Taxation and rents on land occupied by Africans but "owned" by the British South Africa Company, coupled with "hints" for native commissioners to chiefs and headmen were useful means of improving the supply of labor before the First World War. As Africans came into the money economy, the problem became one of control of labor. Until the Industrial Conciliation Act of 1960, all Africans were excluded from the definition of "employee," as in South Africa and were subject to the provisions of the Masters and Servants Act of 1901. Even now, the Industrial Conciliation Act

Table 7. RACIAL COMPOSITION OF LABOR AND WAGES IN
MAJOR RHODESIAN INDUSTRIES

	Numbers of Employed		Average Annual Wage	
Sector	Africans	Europeans	Africans	Europeans
Agriculture	345,700	4,700	£ 101.	£ 2,257.
Mining	56,900	3,630	284.	3,811.
Manufacturing	124,900	22,720	404.	3,222.
Electricity/Water	5,100	1,800	383.	3,613.
Construction	63,500	8,580	361.	3,101.
Finance/Insurance	3,500	8,620	584.	2,738.
Distribution/Hotels	63,600	22,920	361.	2,409.
Transport	21,100	11,220	584.	3,196.
Public Administration	29,000	12,500	425.	2,775.
Education	27,200	7,130	586.	2,593.
Health	8,600	3,870	501.	2,093.
Domestic service	129,300	––	231.	––
Other	30,100	10,880	334.	2,269.
Total	909,000	118,600	£ 256.	£ 2,786.

SOURCE: Monthly Digest of Statistics. October 1974. Tables 14, 15, 16a, 17a.

covers only about 40% of the labor force. Furthermore, although Africans are able to form registered trade unions, they can only do so if the union in question is nonracial. However, the control of the unions is vested in the more highly paid and qualified workers, who are mostly white. Those unions which Africans control are for very poorly paid sectors. As a result, the number of African engineering apprentices, for example, is very low indeed. (See Arrighi, 1970:197-234; Ball, 1967:88-108.) It is doubtless this model of labor relations that is now preferred by the South African Trade Union Council.

The distribution of incomes according to race shows the same characteristics as in South Africa. According to recent work at the University of Rhodesia the projected Poverty Datum Line (PDL) for an average African family of six is £54.9 a month. Even if both parents are working the average income will fall below this figure in practice. Rural Africans are the worst off, and in 1968 the average rural income per head for Africans in cash and kind was about £11 per annum (Sutcliffe, 1971), which roughly corresponds to £35 for an economically active person.

The South African migrant labor system finds its mirror image even in the details of Rhodesian implementation. African urban townships have always been located some distance away from the cities (usually a bicycle ride away), but in recent years the Bantustan approach has been adopted. In the case of Salisbury, for example, it is proposed to locate a large African township in the Seki Tribal Trust Land about 15 miles from the city so that workers could commute while the responsibility for maintenance would be that of the "tribal authorities" (reported by the Select Committee on Decentralization of the Rhodesian Parliament).

Bantustan policies also have their echo here in the policy of "Communal Development" in the rural areas which are the responsibility of the local African councils under the local chief. However, here too the heritage of the past in the shape of the undermining of the traditional chiefs in the first instance and the later return of certain circumscribed powers have so discredited the system that they carry little weight. If Bantustan policies carry little conviction in South Africa, they have even less in Rhodesia, where there can be no possibility of dismemberment of the country. It is not even put forward as a serious proposition by the regime.

Faced with a rising armed and political struggle at home and lacking a policy of decolonization acceptable to critics abroad, Rhodesia's white minority faces a questionable future. We would even ask whether there is any prospect for the whites as a distinguishable group in that country, and the contrast with South Africa looms large here.

White Rhodesians do not have the same deep roots as their South African counterparts despite a common recent history. Evidence on emigration shows that every crisis has generated a distinct exodus which the regime cannot afford. In 1963, 18,000 whites emigrated; and in the period 1961-1964 a total of 55,700 left, while there was an influx of 30,000 during the same period.

Furthermore, only 21% of those over 21 years of age at the time of the 1969 census were born in Rhodesia and had roots there. Over 50% of those who had arrived in 1966 had left by March 1969, and there has been a greater proportion of immigrants from Portugal, Italy, and Greece in recent years—that is, from the poorest countries of Europe—who bring no capital with them which might tie them down. We suspect that if it were not for the stringent exchange controls limiting the cash which can be taken out by emigrants, the exodus would be far greater. As it is, it seems that many who leave permanently do so under the pretext of taking an extended holiday, thereby drawing the larger allowances allowed for such purposes.

This sense of futility in a last ditch stand for a white Rhodesia seems to be gaining ground in South Africa itself. Coupled with the fears of a sort of knock-on effect of successes by the liberation movements which draw ever closer to South African borders, there is the feeling that South African troops would be too vulnerable in Rhodesia in the long run. Rhodesia takes on the appearance of an exposed outpost rather than a front line for South Africa, and Vorster has been pragmatic enough to sense the change in the balance of power in the region as a whole. This is not to say that Rhodesia will be jettisoned, only to suggest that the greatest flexibility will be deployed to defuse the crisis that has built up there in the heat of recent years and to keep the African states tied up in negotiations. In the words of South Africa's state president, "It is in the interests of the whole of Africa—especially Southern Africa—that the current tense situation which has arisen from terrorist activity from Zambia should return to normal" (Sprack, 1974:80).

THE LONG ARM OF MOZAMBIQUE

Settlement of some kind in Rhodesia would make it easier for South Africa to keep up its pressure to ensure a noninterventionist policy by a Frelimo government. There must be an expectation in South Africa—and in Britain—that the cessation of guerrilla activities by ZANU and ZAPU would lead to stabilization permitting the ending of sanctions and the involvement of the Frelimo government in economic relations with both Rhodesia and South Africa. This is certainly the aim of the Vorster regime, which has already taken steps to strengthen the dependence of Mozambique's economy on South African resources. If this scheme fails, Mozambique could become a base for wide-ranging activity by liberation movements penetrating all southern Africa.

The economy of Mozambique has long been integrated structurally with that of South Africa. (See Clarence-Smith, 1974.) One reason has been the need for the Rand to have an outlet to Lourenço Marques, which led to the opening of a railway in 1894. This was followed up by a convention signed by the Portuguese government which has remained the basis for economic relations between the two countries. In return for a guarantee that 50% of the Rand's exports would pass through Lourenço Marques, the Witwatersrand Native Labour Association

(WNLA), an employers' organization, was allowed to recruit Mozambican workers for the mines. Recruitment had already been intense for decades, with 80,000 or three-quarters of the mining labor force coming from Mozambique before the Boer War, but the convention fixed a maximum of 100,000. Labor from this area has been extremely reliable, since the region is desperately poor with sandy, infertile soil, and there has been no alternative to migrant earnings for a long time.

By 1960 it was estimated by the South African government's Foreman Committee that a total of 220,000 legal and clandestine Mozambican workers were in South Africa, constituting 22.4% of gold mine workers and 43.3% of the coal miners. These workers' salaries were an important ingredient in Mozambique's foreign earnings, amounting to £4.8 million in 1968. More important, however, are the earnings from the transportation of goods, which amounted to £28.7 million in 1968, of which a large proportion came from South Africa. Tourism from South Africa and Rhodesia is also important, bringing in £1.4 million in 1968. All these constitute passive, largely nonproductive activities which have not generated economic growth up to now. As a result, the trade balance with South Africa has been in increasing deficit (it would have been worse but for the export of petroleum products to South Africa), while the South African market is important for Mozambique timber, sisal, and fruit.

By the end of the 1960s, South Africa had become the principal investor in Mozambique, with Anglo-American participating in the production of explosives and cashew nuts, in fisheries, and in petroleum prospecting. But the most important project of all, one which will be the major indicator of how relations between the two countries are moving, is the Cabora Bassa dam project with all the planned ancillary development work. Anglo-American dominates the consortium building the dam, and the South African Electricity Supply Commission has undertaken to buy the bulk of the electric power, which is expected to amount to 1,700 megawatts by 1980. It will also make the Zambezi River navigable from the Rhodesian border to the sea, a major inducement to development in itself. It is likely that the dam will be Mozambique's best bargaining weapon in the future, though it could also be the prize for which the remaining racist regimes in southern Africa would be willing to foment the greatest mischief. An independent Mozambique will have no choice however but to seek to establish a dominant position in any remaining economic relationship with South Africa or it will flounder into humiliating economic dependency and political suicide. On the other hand, a firm attitude by a Frelimo government would encourage Africans in Rhodesia as well as in Swaziland and the other small states who lie in the palm of South Africa's economic power (Brooks, 1974).

THE ROLE OF THE WESTERN POWERS

The concern of the Western powers with southern Africa derives from three main considerations: protection of investments and profits, maintenance of essential sources of raw materials, and defense. Each of these factors has in the past led to the bolstering of white minority regimes throughout southern Africa, and it is a new experience to see pressures being exerted on Smith and Vorster to make significant gestures to African aspirations even to the point of negotiating with liberation movements committed to armed struggle. It requires a considerable adjustment to the political horoscope to interpret this shift of posture and it will be some time before the image clears.

The only certainty is that the Western powers seek above all the stabilization of the situation in southern Africa, which has been threatened by the action of the liberation movements. If this means the recognition of African governments where white rule was previously thought indispensable, this adjustment will be made, though measures will also be taken to assure the remaining white regimes that their security has not been forgotten. As elsewhere, Western policy is pragmatic and self-interested, though its lines of thought are not always clear to the observer. In the case of southern Africa there is, however, a clear need to protect investments which have accumulated over time. The extent of foreign investment in South Africa in particular has been well documented, and only the major points need to be brought out here. (See First et al., 1973.)

Britain remains South Africa's main source of foreign investment, and by 1970 sterling area investment totalled £1,983 million or 58% of all foreign investment. The dollar area accounted for 15%, while Western Europe owned 21%. Foreign investment has continued to increase steadily, and in 1971 the annual net inflow rose to £447 million compared to an annual average of £93 million in 1965-1967. Much of this capital is direct investment by large corporations which participate in existing firms or create new ones. This kind of investment is notable for its stability, and the profits are generally plowed back into finance expansion. To some extent this explains why South African capital formation seems to be becoming increasingly self-sustaining with foreign inflows dropping from 53% in 1946-1949 to about 11% in 1974.

The rate of return on direct British investments remained at 10% or above in the period 1960-1968, producing for Britain more profit than any other overseas area. Only Australia ranks higher as an outlet for direct British investment. Rates of return on American capital invested directly in South Africa were 18.6% compared with the average world rate of 11%.

Investment and trade go together. Britain is still South Africa's main trading partner, and in the last decade the annual turnover almost trebled from £252 million in 1961 to £650 million in 1971, accounting for 29% of South Africa's export. The pattern of trade follows a long-standing imbalance in products, with exports made up largely of raw materials (minerals) and food and wine while imports are machinery and capital goods.

The exports provide the clue to the other major interest of the Western powers, the mineral wealth of southern Africa. (See Lowenstein and Gervasi, 1972.) Developments in the United States reveal the trend particularly graphically. Although the United States was considered largely self-sufficient in most commodities at the turn of the century, rapid industrialization generated an insatiable demand for raw materials. The ratio of net imports to consumption, for all minerals except gold, shows a change from an excess of 1.5% in 1900-1909 to a deficit of 14.0% in 1961. This shift to dependence on foreign supplies by the developed West marks one of the most significant economic changes of our time. It also explains the pressures on U.S. foreign policy to ensure the steady supply of raw materials. This applies even more to countries like Britain, West Germany, and Japan, where total output has risen very rapidly in the past decades and where raw materials are few.

In relation to the situation in southern Africa and Zambia the needs of the Western powers are for conditions which will guarantee these raw materials. If we include Zaire and Malagasy in this subcontinent the production of minerals as a percentage of non-Communist world production (1969) is as follows: gold, 68.8%; gem diamonds, 63.6%; industrial diamonds, 64.3%; cobalt (contained), 56.7%; chromite, 31.5%; vanadium, 29.4%; platinum group metals, 28.4%; vermiculite, 30.7%; antimony, 27.9%; copper, 22.0%; and uranium, 17.0%.

In the case of South Africa alone, the United States uses a substantial proportion of South Africa's uranium, antimony, chromite, diamonds, and asbestos, and these could not be easily replaced. Britain imports from South Africa large quantities of antimony, platinum, asbestos, clay, and chromium and seems to be increasingly dependent on these supplies. The same is true for Germany and to a lesser extent Japan.

Last, we come to the military-strategic aspect. While the West is clearly anxious to ensure that the governments in southern Africa remain friendly, ready to support the West in any global conflict, there is also great concern that these governments should be stable. At this time of stress and tension, it seems that at least the latter requirement is being met; hence, increased political attention is being given to the region, and the world strategic importance of southern Africa continues to loom large in Western thinking. Military liaison and cooperation is increasing despite the criticism made of South Africa at the United Nations and elsewhere. In 1974 the first Franco-South African joint naval exercises were carried out, and in the same year the two biggest-ever peacetime exercises between the British and South African navies also took place. Furthermore, the United States formally abandoned its support for the arms embargo against South Africa, and NATO extended its sphere of interest to the South Atlantic covering the Cape sea route.

In 1974 *Esquire* magazine revealed the Nixon Administration's strategic perspectives, and the vital section of the magazine article, dealing with "Option 2" and headed "General Posture," is worth recording here even though the document relates to 1970, that is, before the changes in Mozambique and Angola (Szulc, 1974):

> We would maintain public opposition to racial oppression but relax political isolation and economic restrictions on the white states. We would begin by modest indications of this relaxation, broadening the scope of our relations and contacts gradually and

to some degree in response to tangible—albeit small and gradual—moderation of white policies. Without openly taking a position undermining the United Kingdom and the U.N. on Rhodesia, we would be more flexible in our attitude toward the Smith regime. We would take present Portuguese policies as suggesting further changes in the Portuguese territories. At the same time we would take diplomatic steps to convince black states of the area that their current liberation and majority-rule aspirations in the south are not attainable by violence and that their only hope for a peaceful and prosperous future lies in closer relations with white-dominated states. We would emphasize our belief that closer relations will help to bring change in the white states.

While it may be assumed that the underlying policy of support for white rule remains unchanged, it is evident that the wholly unanticipated loss of the former Portuguese territories has severely jolted U.S. strategy. On the one hand, South Africa's urging for a defense alliance with NATO becomes more compelling. On the other, account must be taken of the knock-on effect of the successes of the liberation movements.

The complexity of these events and the fact that so many strands from the whole subcontinent are now being drawn together in unexpected ways make it hazardous in the extreme to try to predict which tendency will gain the ascendancy. Superficially it seems that suddenly opposing sides are pressing for the same outcome: a settlement in Rhodesia and Namibia. One can read into this a grand conspiracy or, as we prefer, the conjuncture of a number of differing interests and perspectives all of which stand to gain by the diminution to Smith's power and the legitimation of the functioning of the Zimbabwe liberation movement.

Shifting the focus further south, we can see how the new balance of power in southern Africa is generating new pressures, internal and external, on white domination in South Africa, once so arrogant and aggressive in posture in relation to the rest of Africa. (See Turok, 1973.) There are increasing contradictions in the system of apartheid as it has developed over time; there are political pressures from the black states, which cannot easily coexist with a regime of white rule; and there are pressures from the Western states for the reasons mentioned. Above it all, there is the clamor of the liberation movements for freedom for their peoples and for a social revolution to end poverty and exploitation. As we write, important moves are being made to set in motion high level negotiations to "settle" some of these problems; but the main point we have been trying to make is that no matter what happens in these negotiations, it is the effects on the root structures that will determine whether history has really moved.

APPENDIX

SOUTH AFRICA'S ECONOMIC RELATIONS WITH ITS NEIGHBORS

Botswana

Population:	514,000 (1964)
Labor:	Total in employment: 54,103
	Total in employment in S.A. 25,955 (i.e., 48.0%)
Trade:	In S.A. Customs Union and most trade directed there. With the opening of the road to Zambia this may change substantially.
Investment:	Largely from S.A. (Anglo-American Corp.)

Lesotho

Population:	1,000,000 (1966)
Labor:	Total in employment: 82,700
	Total in employment in S.A. 80,700 (i.e., 97.6%)
Trade:	In S.A. Customs Union and all trade directed there.
Investment:	Minimal.

Swaziland

Population:	370,000 (1966)
Labor:	Total in employment: 80,000
	Total in employment in S.A. 20,000 (i.e., 25%)
Trade:	In S.A. Customs Union.
	Imports £ 20 million.
	Exports £ 25 million.
Investment:	Not recorded.

South-West Africa

Population:	610,000 (1966)
Labor:	Most are employed in the country.
Trade:	In S.A. Customs Union. 80% (approx.) of the imports are from S.A.
Investment:	61% of investment in mines is foreign.
	53% of investment in fisheries is foreign.
	The rest is either South African or local.

Rhodesia

Population:	5,310,000 (1970)
Labor:	Was a large importer of foreign African labor.

During 1950-1969	Male and Female	Male Only
From Malawi	111,280	48,700
From Mozambique	69,870	27,950
From Zambia	23,460	5,400

Trade: Pre-UDI

	Imports	Exports
Total	£ 216.47 million	£ 236.64 million
S.A.	£ 52.73 million	£ 17.06 million (7.2%)

REFERENCES

Africa south of the Sahara (1971). London: Europa Publications.

ARRIGHI, G. (1970). "Labour supplies in historical perspective: A study of proletarianization of the African peasantry in Rhodesia." Journal of Development Studies, (April 6):197-234.

BALL, T. (ed., 1967). Rhodesian perspective. London: Michael Joseph.

BROOKS, A. (1974). "The new southern Africa: Opportunities and dangers." Paper presented to the Conference on Portuguese Africa, London, December 7.

CLARENCE-SMITH, W.G. (1974). "South Africa and Mozambique, 1960-1970." Paper delivered at the Institute of Commonwealth Studies, London, February 17.

COLE, M. (1966). South Africa. London: Methuen.

FIRST, R.; STEELE, J.; and GURNEY, C. (1973). The South African connection: Western investment in apartheid. London: Penguin.

GERVASI, S. (1970). Industrialization, foreign capital and forced labour in South Africa, 1970 (UN document E70.11.K.8).

HANCE, W.H. (1964). Geography of modern Africa. New York: Columbia University Press.

HOUGHTON, D.H., and DAGUT, J. (eds., 1972). Source material on the South African economy (2 vols.). London: Oxford University Press.

KEATLEY, P. (1973). The politics of partnership. London: Penguin.

LE MAY, G.H.L. (1971). Black and white in South Africa. London: B.P.C.

LOWENSTEIN, G., and GERVASI, S. (1972). Southern Africa in the world economy. Oxford: Institute of Commonwealth Studies, Oxford University.

MAXEY, K. (1975). The fight for Zimbabwe. London: Rex Collings.

MLAMBO, E. (1972). No future without us: The story of the African National Council of Zimbabwe. London.

PALMER, R.H. (1969). "War and land in Rhodesia." Trans-African Journal of History, 1.

––– (1974). "Land and racial domination in Rhodesia, 1937-1974. Paper delivered at the University of Zambia History Seminar, October 16.

RANDALL, P. (1973). A taste of power. Johannesburg: Spro-cas Johannesburg.

ROGERS, B. (1972). The Bantu homelands. London: International Defence and Aid Fund.

SPRACK, J. (1974). Rhodesia: South Africa's sixth province. London: International Defence and Aid Fund.

SUTCLIFFE, R.B. (1971). Report (No. 33). Oxford University Institute of Economic Statistics.

SZULC, T. (1974). Why are we in Johannesburg? Esquire (October).

TUROK, B. (1973). "South Africa: The search for a strategy." In R. Milibrand and J. Saville (eds.), The socialist register. London: Merlin.

United Nations, Unit on Apartheid (1970). Bantustans in South Africa. (UN Publication 26/70).

VAN DEN BERGHE, P. (1967). South Africa: A study in conflict. Berkeley: University of California Press.

WELSH, D. (1971). The roots of segregation. London: Oxford University Press.

WILSON, F. (1972). Labour in the South African gold mines. Cambridge: Cambridge University Press.

WILSON, M., and THOMPSON, L. (eds., 1969). The Oxford history of South Africa (2 vols.). London: Oxford University Press.

11

SOCIOECONOMIC EFFECTS OF TWO PATTERNS
OF FOREIGN CAPITAL INVESTMENTS, WITH
SPECIAL REFERENCE TO EAST AFRICA

TAMAS SZENTES

Institute for World Economics
Hungarian Academy of Sciences

The role and effects of foreign capital investment in developing countries form one of the most complex and delicate problems in development policy. Simplified answers to this question may easily lead to a false orthodoxy and have disastrous consequences in actual policy.

Simplifications concerning this question may be found in two versions:

(1) There is the version of orthodox "pure" economics, which sees the problem as the need for external financial resources and the transfer of technology. This view attributes almost exclusively positive effects to the import of foreign capital and personnel. It is deeply rooted in the orthodox apologetic concept of "underdevelopment," which asserts that the present state of developing countries is simply an earlier and lower, but natural, stage of growth, compared to that of the developed countries; it does not search for origins of the problem in the historical development of the international capitalist division of labor. (See Szentes, 1973.)

The political recommendation following from this concept is quite simple: Even if there be some relatively negative side effects temporarily, such as the demonstration effect, real development (breaking into the "vicious circle") depends on the inflow of foreign capital and personnel,

AUTHOR'S NOTE: An earlier version of this paper was presented at a conference on "The Use of Foreign Funds in Economic Development in the East African Countries—Kenya, Uganda, Tanzania, Zambia," organized by the African Institute for Economic Development and Planning (UN) and held at Dar es Salaam in May-June 1972. The conference paper has been shortened and edited and is reproduced with the permission of the author and the director of the institute.

which creates a "hospitable climate of investment" for foreign investors. This in fact means giving the latter a free hand, retaining at most an indirect influence on their activity via monetary and fiscal policy.

(2) Simplification concerning the role of foreign capital follows also, however, from a one-sided critique of colonialism. This version takes into account the fact of the exploited and disadvantageous position of the countries in question in the international capitalist division of labor, but it neglects the structural background of the latter as well as the shifts of power factors within it, and thus cavalierly suggests prompt and complete disengagement from the international capitalist system without considering the historical context, the conditions, and the costs of such a disengagement.

The present paper, by investigating briefly the changing background, the motives, the structural aspects, and the socioeconomic results of foreign private investments, with some specific examples from East Africa, aims at focusing attention on the need for a careful analytical approach in appraising particular investment proposals. It seeks to contribute modestly to the formulation of a realistic progressive policy. Such a policy must bear in mind not only the direct but also the indirect effects, both positive and negative, and should not restrict the issue of foreign private investments to the consideration of the acute shortage of development resources on the one hand or the objective of national economic independence on the other. Development and independence (and let us add the trend to socialism) move in the same direction in the long run, even if in the short run there seem to be contradictions in their immediate needs in a concrete situation.

THE BACKGROUND AND EFFECTS OF THE "COLONIAL TYPE" OF INVESTMENT PATTERN

The "colonial type" of direct investments[1] —as is well known—was the vehicle of a particular international division of labor which was embodied in the colonial system and was the expression of the historical development of capitalism at a given period of time. In the last decades of the nineteenth and the first decades of the twentieth century, agriculture and mineral production in the leading countries of world capitalism of the time did not keep pace with the rapid growth of industrial production. In addition, there was an increasing shortage of markets, the most characteristic problem of the capitalist system. Both problems led to a push toward a "solution" in the international arena by acquiring both sources of supply and markets for manufactured goods in the nonindustrialized countries.

On the other hand, the more the internal laws of capital accumulation asserted themselves in the most developed capitalist countries of the time, the more the strange twins of unemployment and the underutilization of part of the accumulated capital as its concomitants, along with the tendency of the falling

rate of profit, became apparent. Thus besides the acquisition of external resources of raw materials and foodstuffs and of foreign markets, an outward-
oriented capital flow (and, by means of emigration to the colonies, a labor flow
as well), plus a search for investment opportunities promising a higher rate of
profit, became imperative.

Capital export, playing the decisive role in this international division of labor,
has a double function (Goncol, 1966): (1) "to bridge the gap between the
increasing need for industrial raw materials and the need for expanding markets
for the products of modern large-scale industry" and (2) to be "a safety valve of
internal over-accumulation . . . a factor counter-acting the tendency of the
depreciation of capital" and of the fall in the rate of profit. The former aims at
ensuring the preconditions for undisturbed reproduction, that is, the marketing
condition and the raw material supply; the latter aims at defending capital and
ensuring profit making. There is, however, an antagonistic contradiction between
the two functions: the operation of the one is detrimental to the other.

Capital export is not only a means of financing the export surplus; it is also a
mode of realizing profit. While the former function tends to expand the market
and, at the same time, restore temporarily the equilibrium of international trade,
the latter function tends to restrict the market and upset the equilibrium.

As a result of the fact that "in the epoch of imperialism commodity exports
are subordinated to capital exports, or more exactly, that commodity exports
subserve the purposes of capital exports, the uppermost of which is the acquisition of super-profits" (Goncol, 1966:12), radical changes have taken place in the
whole structure of the world economy. While in the preimperialist stage of the
capitalist international economy the debtor-creditor relationship was basically
the consequence and function of the international exchange of goods, in the
imperialist stage on the contrary tne international exchange of goods has become
more and more the function of the debtor-creditor relationship. With this change
of roles, however, the content and the conditions of the mechanism of this
relationship have also changed. Now the Ricardian assumption of the unlimited
capacity of the world market and of the harmonious equalization between the
flows of money and commodity, restoring international equilibrium, has come
to be nonsensical, just as has the assumption of a mechanism in which the
international specialization of production would be governed by so-called comparative advantages.

Since capital export by the metropolitan countries is necessarily accompanied
by the repatriation of profits, a coordinated rate of accumulation and growth in
the two sectors of the capitalist system of international division of labor—that is,
in the industrial metropolitan centers and the primary-producing periphery—
cannot be assured ceteris paribus except by a steadily increasing flow of capital
exports counteracting the outflow of profits. A steadily increasing flow of
capital exports leads, however, to the cumulative process of overborrowing and
overlending.

The increase in the interest charges and the annual repayment liabilities as the consequence of the inflow of loan capital is but one of the manifestations of cumulative indebtedness. As soon as further borrowing serves the immediate purpose of repaying former loans, the inflow of loan capital ceases to be a potential counterforce to the systematic outflow of profits. Instead, it further aggravates the financial imbalance.

If the regular outflow of profits is to be compensated for by a constant increase in the inflow of fresh investment capital to bolster up the balance of payments, the consequent problem is not only that "this would have to be an increase ad infinitum—otherwise when it stopped, a balance of payments crisis would occur" (Yaffey, 1970:187)—but also that there could be an *unlimited growth of foreign property* within the national economy.

Unless the "assimilation," in one way or another, of this foreign capital is assured or unless its nationalization *without* compensation takes place, the increasing inflow of foreign investment capital leads not only to the growth of the explicit burden of remitted profits (rents, dividends, and so on) but simultaneously also to the implicit burden of the growth of industrial or commercial assets in foreign ownership. This sort of implicit indebtedness is even more serious in the sense that it grows *sponte sua.*

The internationalization of the process of capital circulation and production by means of capital export contains certain built-in factors which objectively determine not only the world economic structure born under the sign of this internationalization but also its further transformation.

Above and beyond the disequilibrium and cumulative indebtedness resulting from the inflow and accumulation of foreign capital, there are additional negative effects from the colonial type of movements. During the colonial period, private capital from the metropolitan country, flowing into the secured territories and supported directly by the economic policy of colonial administration, gave rise to the well-known enclave sectors producing primary products for export and creating, in the "ocean" of precapitalistic relations, a new, more developed mode of production: capitalistic commodity production. There can hardly be any doubt that the introduction of a more developed mode of production, the transition to market economies, and the linkage to the international economy are definitely phenomena of development. Therefore in the analysis of colonial investments a distinction must be made between these and other elements of real development and the particular forms and conditions in which they have been realized. Consequently it is "only" the particular forms and conditions with their results which shall be criticized.

The above distinction helps in understanding the apparent contradiction: why, in general, the more intensive the penetration of foreign capital has been, the higher the level of commodity production, accumulation, GNP per capita, etc. has become on the one hand, and the more marked the disastrous socioeconomic consequences have been on the other. This contradiction can be observed quite well in East Africa (even if many additional factors, like differences in climatic and soil conditions, are to be taken into consideration), where the much greater extent of the penetration of foreign capital (and settlers) made Kenya's economy more developed than that of Uganda or Tanganyika, but at the price of more painful sacrifices and conflicts and a negative heritage of colonialism.

We are faced with a specific dialectics of development and underdevelopment, not only in the sense of Frank's enlightening concept (1967)—that is, as the dialectical relationship between the development of the metropolitan centers and the underdevelopment of the colonial periphery—but also in the sense that within the latter the steps of real development were taken in forms, under conditions, and with consequences that have erected new obstacles to further development.

1. First of all, the colonial conditions of foreign investments meant not only that the transformation of the old, traditional mode of production was much more painful than otherwise, but also that it failed to be complete and did not result in a new and complete socioeconomic formation. See, for example, the process of land alienation connected with the establishment of reserves and the practice of forced labor in Kenya for the interest of foreign investors, which consequently did not result in true "primitive accumulation" like that in England in the past (Woddis, 1960; Rweyemanu, 1971; Iliffe, 1969).

2. The colonial conditions of foreign investments included, secondly, a monopolistic position and intensive support by colonial administration for the investors from the colonizing country, preventing thereby potential rivals—from outside or inside—from competing. The lack of competition not only worked against technical development but subordinated even more directly the investment policy in the colonial country to the actual interests of the colonizer, who determined and, if necessary, radically changed the production structure quite independently of local interests.

The direction and tempo of Tanganyika's economic development, for example, reflected her constitutional status and the changes in it. In the German period a vigorous inflow of (German) private capital took place (Yaffey, 1970:52), attracted to the country as a potential "No. 1 colony" of Germany. This made ivory and rubber the main export products and launched the sisal industry as an independent source for cordage supply. In the period between the two World Wars there was only a reduced inflow of private capital and grants-in-aid from Britain, for whom Tanganyika meant only one of the many colonies, and moreover one with an unfamiliar and less safe status as a mandate under the League of Nations.

3. A further and more serious consequence of the foreign investments in the colonial period is the well-known concentration of the economic key positions, the so-called "commanding heights," in foreign hands. As a colonial heritage of the new independent states, this situation has considerably reduced the sphere of national decision making within the national economies, made the implementation of development programs and economic policies subject to the reaction and behavior of foreign capital and expatriates, and served as a source of internal or external conflicts.

There are many examples of this control of the "commanding heights" in the economy of East Africa by foreign companies and settlers: the Brooke Bond tea plantations, the Ralli Brothers, and Lord Delamere's estates, the subsidiaries of Lonhro, the affiliates of Unilever, the business group of Smith-Mackenzie, the British-owned commercial banks, and so on ("Who Controls Industry in Kenya," 1968; Seidman, 1969). A suggestive figure indicating the positions of foreign capital in Tanzania is given by Yaffey (1970:97): By 1964 paid-up equity capital was £23,225,000, 52% of which was held by residents outside East Africa. (How much was owned by expatriate residents in Kenya or Uganda is not known.)

What obviously follows from the fact that key positions are in foreign hands is the extreme vulnerability of the whole economy and the high degree of uncertainty in development planning, due to unforeseeable reactions of foreign investors. Reference can be made here, for example, to the sudden flight of foreign private capital in 1964 in Tanganyika, draining off about one-third of the potential investment sources.

4. The outflow of a considerable part of investment incomes, the drain of most of the investable surplus, is a consequence that has already been referred to. That its negative impact on the balance-of-payments position of the country concerned can hardly be counteracted by an adequately increasing inflow of fresh capital has already been pointed out.

The growth of foreign assets in the countries in question seems to be attributable much more to the reinvestment of retained profits—that is, to the absorption of the expropriated surplus produced locally—than to the influx of new capital. And this is so in spite of the normally low proportions of retention (Yaffey, 1970:207).

Foreign investors preferred those spheres of investment (like banking, insurance, and importing) promising a high rate of profit with little initial investment. But however high the rate of return and however small the initial capital was, in the event of nationalization they normally make a claim on compensation even for the loss of future profits. In Tanzania, for example, the Standard and the Barclay Banks demanded more than five million pounds as a compensation for future profits (Davidson, 1975:37).

The question of compensation for future losses, however, might rather be raised by the national governments of developing countries. A rather obvious case seems to present itself when the conditions of future mining have deteriorated because of the gross exploitation of natural resources by colonial capital. It seems to me that the expropriation and exploitation of natural resources by foreign capital therefore, though normally fused with other forms of exploitation,[2] can be distinguished as a specific form and as disguised waste of the national assets, the detrimental effects of which are felt only when the growth of the relevant national industry comes to be faced with the problem of a narrowing raw material basis and the problem of increasing "national costs" of raw materials due to the too early and export-oriented exploitation of local resources.

The impact of foreign investments on the accumulation sources and actual capital formation cannot, of course, be assessed simply by comparing the inflow of capital and the outflow of profit, or the repatriation versus the retention of investment incomes. On the negative side, additional, mostly disguised forms of income drain should be added (such as special price systems, bookkeeping manipulations, overinvoicing imports brought from affiliated companies, under-invoicing exports sold to the latter, remittances to overseas head offices for managerial and consultancy services, general head-office expenses, directors' fees, agency fees, royalties, and similar payments), while items on the positive side (like the income-generating effect and the transfer of technology, mana-gerial skill, and technical know-how) are rather questionable, not only with respect to their actual dimensions but with respect to their very existence. To assess the indirect effects of colonial investments on the sources of accumulation is possible, however, only in the context of the socioeconomic structure which has resulted from these investments.

5. The most disastrous consequence of the colonial type of investment is the peculiar socioeconomic structure itself which it has brought about. This struc-ture is characterized by the lack of internal integration, which manifests itself in (a) the dualism of capitalist and precapitalist socioeconomic sectors,[3] (b) the wide and long-lasting coexistence of export economies and subsistence economies side by side, and (c) the distortion of the sectoral pattern of economy and the weakness of intersectoral links.

The dualism and distortion of the economy (and society) are obviously the results of the historical fact that, instead of the internal self-evolution of economy (and society) it was the colonial penetration of *foreign* capital which gave rise in certain spheres to the capitalist mode of production and linked the economies in question to the world market. Consequently, these changes which would have been positive per se, as well as their conditions and results, were not determined by the internal laws of development, but instead by an external factor, the interests of foreign capitalists. To understand why colonial invest-ments led to various distortions and the preservation of traditional elements, it is of course not necessary to attribute, in general, an a priori sinister intention to foreign investors who, as Nurkse (1958) correctly emphasizes, were mainly guided in their investment policy by simple business considerations. The prefer-ence in investment policy for the sectors producing, at a low capital intensity, primary products for export followed quite obviously from the actual conditions of an increasing demand for primary products outside the country versus the limits of the local market, the outward orientation of infrastructure, auxiliary services and institutional pattern, and the availability of cheap, unskilled labor versus the expensiveness and risk of applying costly machines to be transported from overseas and requiring qualified workers. Even if these conditions were made possible by prior brute force (such as land alienation and forced labor), they could be taken for granted by the individual investors, and they were reproduced by the very investment policy adjusted to them. A spontaneous, cumultive process started to lead to and reproduce structural distortions and the preservation of "traditional" economies.

Owing to the enclave-character of the "modern" sector, foreign capital came into conflict with the precapitalist socioeconomic remnants only insofar as they happened to fall directly within the sphere of its own activity. In this case it destroyed them or put them into its own service, often with the help of colonial administration. It was not interested, however, in the complete transformation of the precapitalistic relations, because its own growth was governed by laws independent of the latter.

This is why and how dualism and socioeconomic distortions have necessarily resulted from the colonial investments,[4] producing thereby further negative effects via the mechanism of the dual system.

6. It is not only the character of the sectors developed by colonial investments which has limited the sphere of expansion of the local market but also the very mechanisms of the dual system itself. The main points of these limitations are the following:

(a) In general, an export-oriented primary production, by its very nature, could create only to a limited extent linkages and spread effects within the country's economy. Most of the linkage effects have been transferred into the metropolitan country, where the processing and consumption of the products took place, and where most of the equipment, instruments, and machines came from (Singer, 1964).

(b) Even the indirect linkage-effects via the spending of personal incomes of those engaged in the sector concerned remained very limited due not only to the repatriation of personal savings of expatriates and to the low real-wages level of local labor "frozen" mostly in unskilled categories but also to the heavy bias for import consumption of those in higher income brackets.

(c) The low level of real wages resulted partly from the monopolistic position of foreign companies and settlers in employing manpower and partly from the pressure exerted by the traditional subsistence sector functioning as an ample source of cheap labor. (The latter is one of the reasons for the preservation of the traditional sector.) The rise in real wages was particularly restricted in the case of plantation systems, operated on the basis of a large supply of cheap unskilled labor. For example, in Tanganyika the basic rate of pay of wage workers in the sisal plantations remained stationary for the eight years 1951 to 1958 (Woddis, 1960). That is, even nominal wages proved to be quite rigid for a long period.

(d) The migrant labor system (Szentes, 1964) resulting from dualism, adjusted to the need of colonial investors, has also had an impact on market conditions by its influence on wages and consumption. It relies on the subsistence economies as basic or additional sources of living and security, and it transfers certain consumption habits biased for imported commodities. It also has an impact on the rural surplus-producing capacity and on the "learning process" in general.

(e) Owing to colonial investment and economic policy, the conditions of operation of the preserved traditional sector have deteriorated in a way that there is increasing need for the transformation of the subsistence economies into market economies, even though there has been a reduced ability to make such a transformation.

Land alienation, widely practiced in many countries (particularly in East Africa in Kenya), was one of the most direct factors in deterioration. By reducing the available land, it led in many places to the disruption of shifting cultivation patterns, excessive exploitation of the fertile lands and pastures, soil erosion, and a diminishing return of crop production and animal husbandry as well as the appearance of population pressure. (See East African Royal Commission, 1955; Aaranovitch and Aaranovitch, 1947; Brown, 1959.) The migrant labor system has also decreased, by the concomitant absenteeism of young labor, the sector's capacity to produce marketable surplus. The higher competitiveness of foreign-owned economies, the preference of foreign trading companies (as well as most of the consumers) for imported commodities, the bias of the whole pattern of market institutions, infrastructure and banking and credit system for the export-import business made it by no means easier for the subsistence economies to bring the surplus actually produced systematically to the local market.

(f) A decline of the traditional handicraft industries (United Nations, 1958)—such as domestic weaving and household utensils production—followed from similar circumstances, particularly from the suppressing competition of imported products and, if any, those produced locally by foreign enterprises. This has further reduced the sphere of traditional economic activities without giving rise to new ones on the spot and has reduced the internal division of labor in general, as well as the facility of mobilizing locally the unemployed labor in rural areas in off-seasons.

(g) The unfavorable pattern of consumers' demand, biased heavily for imported goods and characterized by a great number of missing links, is an obvious consequence of the abnormally open character of the economy and society, resulting from the colonial type of investment and the mass presence of foreign capital and personnel. The demonstration effect is a phenomenon widely referred to in literature. How the latter gave new impetus, new subjects, or new media even to those consumers' propensities rooted in the traditional sector (such as ostentation, conspicuous consumption, ritual consumption) should be equally stressed.

7. As to domestic capital formation, the limiting effect of the colonial type of investments as well as the mechanism of the dual system manifests itself in various ways:

(a) The repatriation of profits and personal savings (referred to above) is only the most obvious one.

(b) Another one is the misallocation of resources between the productive and unproductive sectors—that is, a strong gravitation of foreign (and also local) capital toward the "parasitic forms of investments" attached and adjusted to the enclaves, as in service enterprises, banking, and insurance (Yaffey, 1970:40-41).

The dissipation of local labor and "entrepreneurship" in "parasitic" occupations (such as domestic service, odd jobs, huckstering, begging, and prostitution) around the expatriate centers is also a characteristic form and manifestation of the misallocation of national resources potentially available for productive accumulation.

(c) The specialization in primary production, brought about by colonial investment, leaves by its very nature limited scope for technical development and for the rise of internal and external economies. The effects of this specialization in terms of the limited generation and spread of technical development and of internal and external economies restrict the rise of national productivity and reduce "vertically" the potential resources of accumulation (Singer, 1964), while the limited need by the primary producing enclaves for supplementary productive activities reduces "horizontally" as well potential resources of accumulation, in the sense that systematic surplus (profit) production is restricted to only a few branches. The allocation of the processing of the primary products in question—and the attached commercial, transport, and communication apparatus—to the metropolitan country means the transfer of those additional sources of accumulation based materially upon the product itself. This transfer gives the metropolitan country additional sources of income and accumulation which originally do not belong to her potentials. The consequent expansion of economic activities over and beyond their "natural limits" in the latter leads to the expansion not only of profitable investment opportunities but also of the sources of state revenues, such as taxation (Bogmar, 1965).

Due to the impact on the quality of labor and the so-called "learning process," colonial investment failed to give sufficient impetus to the rise of labor productivity. The applied technique required unskilled workers while the migrant labor system prevented them even from accumulating certain job experiences over a considerable time.

(d) The strong demonstration effect of the expatriates' behavior discouraged the wealthier indigenous strata from personal savings, or induced them (particularly those belonging to the non-European immigrant minorities) to keep the saved amounts in foreign banks, instead of using them for productive investments in the country.

(e) The lopsided development of infrastructure and services as adjusted to the needs of the direct investments in the enclave sectors made the realization of surplus and its conversion into productive investment extremely difficult in other sectors. That, for example, the transport and marketing facilities, the energy supply, as well as the banking and insurance pattern in East Africa have been mostly designed to service the export-import business of foreign investors is a well-known fact. It is enough to look at the map of the main roads and railways in East Africa, running from the export-crop-producing areas to the ports, and to look at the distribution pattern of energy, credit, and insurance businesses. In Kenya more than 80% of electric power was sold in the Nairobi-Mombasa enclave areas at the time of independence. Even in 1969 two-thirds of credits were directly involved in export-import trade. In Uganda and Tanzania, too, productive activities outside the enclaves could hardly obtain credit facilities. In 1965, 50% of the loans to the private sector was directed to wholesale and retail trade in Tanzania (Seidman, 1968).

8. Demographic development, manpower and employment patterns have been also strongly influenced by the direct investments of the colonial type and the socioeconomic dualism stemming from the latter.

(a) "Population pressure" is a relative phenomenon, manifested in certain tensions in land tenure, food supply, employment, and educational facilities. It is due both to the increased rate of population growth and to the failure of the "modern" sector to induce adequate transformations in other sectors and expand sufficiently its own facilities.

The higher rate of population growth has resulted from the striking change in the death rate, which has been pushed down—though not sufficiently yet—by improvements in health services in and via the "modern" sector, and from the maintenance of the birth rate, which is still influenced by moral laws and ancient customs deeply rooted in the "traditional" sector. Such a divergence could have hardly been long lasting without the peculiar character of the "modern" sector as fashioned by the colonial investment pattern.

The failures of the "modern" sector in making necessary transformations and expansions are complex. Enclave investment not only has taken away land and labor from other productive sectors oriented toward subsistence or the local market, reducing thereby the means of production and local means of subsistence, and reducing also the labor-absorbing capacity both "horizontally" (access to land) and "vertically" (cottage industries, handicrafts) but has also involved built-in factors reducing the growth of labor-absorbing capacity within the enclaves as well. Such built-in factors are the limitation to vertical development both upward and downward, and those critical obstacles follow from the income drain and the increasing difficulties in marketing. In addition, the diversion of production from producing for local consumption aggravated the food supply problem, while applied technology, particularly that in plantations, set limits to the rise in the productivity of land (Woddis, 1960:37; Batten, 1947).

Consequently, a cumulative tendency of labor oversupply in the unskilled categories resulted both from the effect of the colonial investments on the economy and society outside the enclaves (by increasing population growth, worsening conditions for self-subsistence, and so on) and from the very nature of these investments, which keep down the rate of growth and limit the labor-absorptive capacity within the enclaves, while being accompanied by increasing outward suction effect.

(b) The patterns of employment, wages, and labor class adjusted themselves to the emerging migrant labor system, reflecting clearly the fact that, given the lack of internal integration, the two sectors were out of gear.

(c) The qualitative aspect of employment—that is, the striking shortage of skilled labor—is no less related to the type of foreign direct investment than the quantitative one. The peculiar character of the "modern" sector resulting from the latter has limited the "learning process" not only within but also outside the enclaves. It failed to give the development of public education the positive inducements which otherwise and normally the growth of a modern sector could have given. Instead, it contributed to the transplantation of an irrelevant, biased system of education; and by putting into operation the migrant labor system, it made on-the-job training uneconomical and extremely difficult, if not impossible.

9. Because it is well known, it is almost needless to add how much the direct investments of the colonial type have distorted also the foreign trade pattern of the countries concerned. The distortion of the foreign trade pattern, reflecting that of the structure of the economy as a whole, manifests itself in:

(a) The disproportionate weight and crucial role of foreign trade in economic process (i.e., a heavy foreign trade dependence).

(b) The heavily concentrated commodity-composition of exports, accompanied by rather widely structured imports.

(c) The heavy and irrational concentration of the geographical distribution of foreign trade.

As to the weight and role of foreign trade, the former is disproportionate to the actual level of gross domestic product (GDP). The contribution of exports to gross national product (GNP) and the ratio of imports to GDP may illustrate but hardly express fully the degree of trade dependence. For example in East Africa the ratio of exports to GDP averaged 18% for Kenya, 36% for Uganda, and 41% for Tanzania between 1954 and 1964 (United Nations, 1970).

The trade dependence is aggravated by the high level of export dependence on a few primary products making up the bulk of exports. For example, in East Africa between 1961 and 1963 the share of agricultural primary products in the export of Kenya averaged 79%, that of Uganda 88%, and that of Tanzania 83% (FAO, 1965). Even in 1965 more than 75% of the exports of East African countries depended on two commodity groups (United Nations, 1969).

The high level of concentration of export and import markets in one or a few developed countries which are great distances from the countries concerned clearly showed the bilateral dependence and subordinated position of the latter, resulting from the colonial investments. In 1960 the United Kingdom shared 25% in the exports and 36% in the imports of Kenya, and 16% and 34% in those of Uganda respectively. In 1961, 36% of Tanganyika's export went to the United Kingdom, and more than 37% on her imports were of U.K. origin (Economic Development of Kenya, 1963; Economic Development of Uganda, 1962; United Nations, 1964).

The negative consequences of the distortions in foreign trade pattern appear not only in the fact and degree of dependence, vulnerability, uncertainty, and tension via trade relations, including the danger of political pressures as well as the transfer of business cycle fluctuations, but also in the overemphasis on external economic relations and the costs involved.[5]

10. A further consequence of direct investment by foreign capital in the colonial period is the emergence of parallel structures of economy in neighboring countries, as fragmented, supplementary appendages for the metropolitan economy and competitive units for each other. This was so even in the case of the East African countries, in spite of their being in a relatively fortunate position by virtue of belonging—as a whole region—to the same metropolitan country and of sharing common services and a sort of subcenter.

Parallel structures of a competitive rather than complementary character represent one of the most serious obstacles to regional integration and a rational participation in the international division of labor.

11. The foreign direct investment of the colonial type have made, of course, an impact on the structure of society as well.

Social transformation following the rise of capitalistic relations in the enclave sectors not only was more painful as a result of having been governed by foreign interests but also resulted in a misbirth: the old did not completely disappear, and the new was built not on the ruins but among the remnants of the old. In addition, the penetration and strengthening of the new did not occur evenly everywhere, and even where the old was ousted by the new, it still retained its influence. Thus modern relations became associated with traditional conditions. Just as the breaking up of the old forms of economy failed to be followed by a completely new and full economic formation—in fact, the old and new forms remained side by side—so, in the same way, substantial remnants of the old structure of society have survived.

The capitalist element, which, through the penetration of foreign monopoly capital, became predominant in the heterogeneous structure, affected and restricted horizontally the economic "breeding ground" of the precapitalistic elements (the traditional tribal subsistence economy, village communities, or feudal economies) in accordance with its own interests. It also exercised, of course, a certain vertical effect—"at the bottom" mainly through the migrant workers, that is, male labor leaving the traditional economy for temporary wage employment, and "at the top" through feudal landowners and chiefs who, in order to get rich, started trading with goods, land, labor, and money or took part in the colonial administration. This effect, however, proved too weak to induce a genuine social transformation. The economic sphere of such a transformation became, from the outset, a very difficult terrain, owing to the nature of the "modern" sector, and partly because the effect itself, which "at the top" involved the appearance of a strange way of life, and "at the bottom" meant employment and exploitation by foreigners. This was, though, to some extent offset by the bonds and the cohesive forces of the old society, which often became stronger and tighter when on the defensive.

Consequently, neither a genuine national bourgeoisie nor a real urban proletariat could develop. Instead, in accordance with the limited contact of the enclaves with various traditional elements and communities, a fragmented, heterogeneous structure of society emerged, with a number of subsocieties.

The migrant-labor system and the employment situation in the "modern" sector retarded the development of a real urban proletariat by keeping most of the wage workers still tied to the sphere of traditional farming. Segregation, the depressing existence and rivalry of foreign capitalists, and the various obstacles to a complete transformation of the economy restricted the rise of local bourgeois elements mainly to the sphere of parasitic activities and intermediary roles. Insofar as even the latter were filled up mostly by expatriates, namely non-European foreigners (such as the Asian expatriates in East Africa), it created not only further limits for social mobility but also increased confusion and interference between the movement of social and "racial" elements.

The rather general preference for nonproductive fields and for administrative and other activities in career building follows quite obviously from the enclave character of economic growth and explains the rapid rise, after independence, of a bureaucratic elite.

12. There are also, of course, political aspects of the social structure distorted by enclave-investment. The relatively wide scope for political shifts and sudden changes (such as coups) due to the weakness of the internal class-basis of political regimes and the relatively wide-open gate for external influences may seem to be related too indirectly to the affects of foreign investments. Regional differences, with concomitant tribal conflicts, are, however, much more directly attributable to the investment policy of foreign capital.

THE BACKGROUND AND EFFECTS OF AN EMERGING NEW PATTERN OF FOREIGN PRIVATE INVESTMENTS

In recent years there has been a shift in the investment pattern of foreign capital. It is extremely difficult to ascertain whether the final consequences will be positive or negative. It is even more difficult to present wide and unambiguous documentation on the impact of this new pattern of foreign investments. Nevertheless, the logic of theoretical analyses, the conclusions reached by analogy with similar empirical experiences in other regions, certain statistical figures, and a number of case studies seem to offer sufficient evidence to allow us to point to a negative impact and to foreseeable dangers, which may however be averted if an effective counterstrategy comes into operation.

Although it would be too early to speak of the rise of a new system of international division of labor, particularly in the case of Africa, where the elements of the "classic" pattern of extractive imperialism are still predominant, the increasing difficulties in the operation of the latter and its advancing dilution by new elements lead us to ask: what sort of international division of labor would exist if the observable trends continued, and how could the developing countries benefit from it?

Though the extraction of mineral raw materials, particularly those of strategic importance, remains one of the most important activities of foreign companies and large international consortia in the developing countries rich in natural resources,[6] the marked bias of their investment policy against plantation investments[7] and, instead, for investments in certain manufacturing industries[8] already points to an emerging new pattern. Similarly, a shift in their choice of techniques can also be observed in terms of their industrial investments: Relatively high capital-intensity characterizes the new industrial enterprises, which are mostly last-stage assembly and/or processing plants.

The industrial ventures of foreign companies, as well as the transfer of industrial technology as materialized in the former, indicate that the monopoly of metropolitan countries over industry, versus the primary-producing periphery, is being relaxed a bit, or rather replaced by another one.

In addition, considerable changes have taken place with respect to the origin and character of foreign capital in Africa: The monopolistic position of the former colonizer's capital has been increasingly replaced by the less exclusive dominance of multinational corporations[9] or international monopolies, leaving more space in their service, but less independence, for local enterpreneurs and others, and reflecting the growth of a "collective" neocolonialism; behind all this is the aspiration of U.S. monopolies to "take over" (Nkrumah, 1965), as well as the need for new methods in the era of national independence and East-West competition.

The diversification in the origin of foreign capital after independence and the increasing role of U.S. capital have been accompanied by the shift in character of foreign capital in favor of the affiliates of large-scale and vertically integrated industrial corporations.

In many countries the decline of private investments by former colonizers and the outflow or nationalizations of the capital of smaller-scale colonial enterprises, trading houses, transport firms, and, particularly, individual settlers mark the same process.

The apparent tolerance of the new foreign investors and multinational corporations is accompanied by measures taken by African governments aimed at expanding the public sector and increasing the national participation or the role and control of the state in the economy. Moreover, in many cases, the multinationals are willing to step into partnership with the state and even accept minority ownership. This new policy is, of course, to a great extent forced by the new conditions,[10] but it partly reflects also a certain reorientation of business interests. The same applies to the attitude of multinational corporations concerning regional integration.

In addition to the postwar change in the leadership of world capitalism, the rise and growth of a socialist world system, the collapse of colonial empires, the general expansion of state monopoly capitalism, and the rise and rapid growth of international monopolies, there is no doubt that the scientific and technical revolution has been one of the decisive factors behind the emerging new patterns of investments. Its various effects on the colonial type of international division of labor and the position of primary-producing countries are sufficiently familiar so as to make it unnecessary to repeat them. Its effects on the dimensions and pattern of production, the increasing internationalization of the production process and the fronts of competition, however, need to be stressed here.

The development of productive forces leading to the internationalization of the reproduction process is an objective tendency independent of, although influenced by and also affecting, the actual socioeconomic formations. Under capitalism this internationalization has been started and pushed forward by the fundamental problem of the system—i.e., the market problem—and governed by its main motive force—i.e., profit.

In general, the extent to which international economic relations become the built-in factors of the reproduction process of individual national economies—or rather, vice versa, the extent to which the latter take part in the internationalized reproduction process—depends on the number and sizes of the missing links in the "national" system of reproduction process; these missing links are, horizontally, the lack of entire producing branches to meet local demands and, vertically, the lack of complexity and the discontinuity of the various existing branches. Specialization creates new units but also new missing links.

Due to the general growth of productive forces, to the expanding dimensions of production and producing units, and to the dimensional requirements of up-to-date technology (in terms of both supply and demand), as well as to the rapid expansion of demand via the demonstration effect, the increasing number of missing links is more and more characteristic of all national economies. The weaker or stronger position in the capitalist system of international cooperation and the distribution of benefits from it depend, however, to a great extent on the location of the missing links. This explains why the most powerful monopolies strive for, and competition among the most advanced capitalist countries aims among other things at, catching and monopolizing the most important, decisive links in the expanding and more internationalized reproduction process at the expense, if necessary, of leaving or even creating missing links in less important spheres.

The scientific and technical revolution has changed the pattern of leading industries, given rise to new ones, and created new centers of technological research and development. It has been demonstrated by it where the decisive links are.

The warning signs of an emerging new international division of labor of capitalism appear not only in the shifting pattern and policy of foreign investments in the developing countries but in other spheres as well. This new international division of labor eventually may completely replace the present and already outdated division of labor, one between industrial and primary producing countries. It will instead be a division of labor between the centers of scientific and technological progress and the periphery of all those countries relying on the regular imports of the technical achievements and scientific results of the former. Although it may add new features to the economy of developing countries by a certain type and level of industrialization, it may result in an even wider gap between center and periphery than the present one.

Since the "dimensional" aspects of scientific-technical development have become more and more decisive, the "law of uneven development"—as outlined by Lenin—appears in a somewhat new context. The feasibility of "catching-up" refers not only to the question of a jump in the application of technology but also to the question of the dimensions of economic units. Unless the integration of smaller units takes place, the gap to be jumped over is getting wider simply because of dimensional aspects of the new technology. This trend obviously favors the big countries against the smaller ones. The technological gap has widened not only between industrial and primary-producing countries but also between the U.S. and other developed countries (Adams, 1969). This process has been accompanied by the increasing concentration and centralization of capital and research capacities in the hands of the biggest U.S. companies[11] and their expanding penetration via direct investments, joint ventures, partnerships, and so on into the Western European economies and the former spheres of interest of the latter.

The rapidly increased role in economic development, in technological research and product development, and in the centers of technical progress in general has induced the most powerful companies to expand or even specialize their activities in this field, requiring thereby expanding markets for the materialized knowledge and technology.

The installation of last-stage assembly or processing plants with relatively capital-intensive techniques in the developing countries, the increasing proportion in trade of those export products with a more or less monopolized technical advantage for the producer, the expanding export trade of licenses, patents, technical know-how, managerial and consultancy services, and so on all reflect the same process.

In the case of the vertically integrated corporations that are expanding their capital goods production at home, market interests quite clearly suggest that they promote the growth of consumer-goods-producing industries with capital intensive techniques abroad. So also do these interests seek to continue to block the development in the periphery of the capital-goods-producing sector, particularly those industries capable of serving as the centers of technical progress for the local national economy.

Let us look at the effects or consequences likely to follow from the emerging new pattern of foreign investments, leaving aside for the moment the efforts of national governments to struggle against the tendencies based on the new pattern.

1. The emerging pattern of foreign direct investments, contrary to the expectations concerning their more international—i.e., less bilateral—character, will not widen but in fact limit the sphere of national decision making.

The question of foreign control—i.e., the shift outside the country of the locus of some types of decision making—is related, of course, to the power of the foreign firm and its government supporting it, relative to the government of the host country. Although, as a result of decolonization, foreign governments have lost the means of direct and "legal" administrative interventions, the power base behind the new ventures may have actually increased. This is obvious in an economic sense, since multinational corporations, particularly the vertically integrated ones, are not only stronger than national companies and competitive private firms in terms of capital, technical know-how, marketing influence, and bargaining position but also more capable of maneuvers on an international scale. And insofar as the new ventures belong to U.S.-based corporations (which is not yet characteristic of tropical Africa), an increased power base even in terms of government support (including military threats) seems to be obvious.

Multinational corporations tend to centralize control over and impose a hierarchical system upon national economies. They are able to close up shop in one country and move to another, to create parallel capacities in neighboring countries, to slow down production expansion in one country in favor of another, and so on. Since they extend over several units of national economies, they easily escape political regulation by governments in terms of any one unit. Due to their high capacity for internal financing they can free themselves to a great extent even from outside financial control (Arrighi, 1967:4).

Their multinational character and the increased independence of national control do not mean, however, that ownership and control are internationally dispersed throughout the corporate system. As Magdoff (1969) points out, capital as a fundamental part of a particular set of production relations which can be maintained in existence only through a sufficiently powerful apparatus of coercion (i.e., the state) must have nationality just like the states of today do. Consequently, the corporate hierarchy involves the centralization of high-level decision making in the very home base—namely, the metropolitan city from where status, authority, income, and consumption patterns radiate out to the periphery. In other words, it is the developing countries—and some of the relatively weaker developed countries, too[12]—which are to be confined to the subordinate position, a sort of "branch plant status" in the international hierarchy of corporations.

Multinational corporations not only control the decision making over the part of the local national economy which belongs, by direct investments, to their sphere of ownership but also influence governmental decisions in other sectors as well. Their actual capacity to influence local governments in shaping economic policy and law is ensured by the wide international network of their activity; the complexity of intertwined business interests (Nkrumah, 1965; Seidman, 1969; Shivji, 1970); the support, open or disguised, given to them by the home government and its military power; the explicit or implicit interrelationship, in many cases, between direct investments on the one hand, and financial and technical assistance, on the other[13]; and the vulnerable, excessively "open character" of the economy and society in the host developing countries. These factors explain why state control and participation, partial nationalizations, and majority ownership do not necessarily alter the actual location of decision making and bring the sector concerned under the real control of national government.

Nationalizations do not necessarily interfere with the interests of multi-national corporations. If the managerial control of enterprises wholly or partially owned by the state remains in the hands of multinational corporations or their agencies, they may still enjoy the various advantages and security of operating inside the public or parastatal sector, directing the business activity and investments of the latter in conformity with their own interests, establishing new business connections with their home bases and affiliates, acquiring profitable investment opportunities in fields left for private investors, and keeping competition away from the latter.[14] Partnership with the state, built-in positions in the public sector, and management control in parastatal bodies may give greater security than any declared guarantee against nationalization. It is understandable why multinational corporations pay so much attention to influencing the information and management structure of parastatals,[15] to supplying parastatals and economic ministries with technical assistance people, and to keeping control over the training of managerial staff.

2. The new investment pattern seldom leads to a reduction of the outflow of investment incomes or to a considerable improvement in domestic capital formation. Though, in principle, in most cases, the higher level of the surplus-producing capacity of the new industrial ventures might give a basis for rapidly expanding reinvestments and also government revenues (by taxation, profit sharing, and so on) to be invested in other sectors, while state control over foreign exchange transactions via parastatal bodies might narrow down the repatriation of profits, in practice these possibilities are seldom realized.

The multinational corporations, even given state control and partnership in parastatals, still have various, mostly disguised or indirect, opportunities for shipping out investment income.

On the one hand, those disguised forms of income drain already used in the past and mentioned above (such as bookkeeping manipulations, over- or underinvoicing, and royalties) are even more widely employed by international vertically integrated companies, especially if in partnership with the state. On the other hand, the double bias of industrial investments (i.e., for applying capital-intensive techniques and against establishing local centers of capital goods production), together with other restraints on the "learning process," opens new fields for and creates new forms of income drain which are, or seem to be, connected with the problem of technology and skill. The "cost of servicing of human capital" (Helleiner, 1967) and payments for management and technical skill, patents, licenses, trade marks, consultants, and so on may actually absorb a considerable part of the surplus and, in spite of their "cost" appearance, include de facto profits.

Close cooperation with and influence on local government may ensure additional advantages and disguised profit opportunities via such things as tax holidays, accelerated depreciation allowances, overvalued exchange rates, low interest rates, easy access to public funds, concessions on import duties, and government protection against "outside" competition in the local market and against the labor movements as well (including bans on strikes, frozen wages, and so forth).

The misallocation of resources and manpower is not less characteristic of the new pattern than it was of the colonial one. Even worse, the high propensity to unproductive expenditures and employment has been widely transferred into the public and parastatal sectors, which may be seen in the rapid disproportionate growth of headquarters expenditures in these sectors, involving the cost and salary structure, the employment pattern, and so on.

3. Instead of bringing about an internal integration of the socioeconomic structure, foreign investments of the new pattern seem to reinforce internal dualism and partial and "outward" integration (i.e., the integration of parts only of national economies within the international capitalist economy).

Both the location of the new plants and their character in terms of production linkages tend rather to a further disintegration in both a regional and a sectoral sense. In Kenya, for example, about 60% of the employment and manufacturing establishments were located in Nairobi and Mombasa. In Tanzania 89% of industrial plants were established in five towns: Dar es Salaam, Tanga, Moshi, Mwanza, and Morogoro (Seidman, n.d.:5). The income gap between urban center and rural areas tends to increase as a result of the new investments too.

The orientation of the new investments toward the import-substitutive light industries (particularly those producing luxury or near-luxury items for the high-income elite) or the first-stage processing of primary products for export make even more serious the lack of central links in the chain of the vertical structure of production. Where there is a lack of domestic industries that manufacture capital goods, machines, tools, and equipment, the adoption of capital-intensive techniques leads to an intensification of import orientation. And since the imported capital-intensive techniques with their relatively high technical level (relative to the general level of education in the country) mean the exclusion of local labor from the training process or at least the restriction of this training process to a narrow worker elite, the old mechanisms which ensure the predominance of those sectors and techniques that produce hardly any linkage effects are, strangely enough, left unchanged in the rest of the economy.

This method of industrialization, instead of creating the central links in the process of industrial (and agricultural) development—that is, capital-goods-producing industries determining the technical and productivity level and expanding both the productive capacity and the future labor-absorbing capacity of the national economy as well as the local market—implants in the national economy only the superstructural elements of industry (almost just as "alien" bodies as the "enclave" sectors); and thus it hinders the process of socioeconomic integration and has, as one of the results, the tendency to limit the market relations and linkage effects among sectors.

4. The tendency toward limited local-market relations manifests itself in the impact of this investment pattern on

(a) The import sensitivity of the national economy.

(b) The volume and composition of the labor force employed.

(c) The "traditional" rural sector.

(d) The other branches and economic units of the urban sector.

The increase in import sensitivity—which follows from the fact that the operation of the capital-intensive technique depends on the importing of machines, equipment, means of transport, and sometimes even of raw materials and fuels—aggravates the export dependence of the national economy and results in the cumulative strengthening of the enclave character of the export sectors.

As a result of the shift toward capital-intensive techniques, the absorptive capacity of the modern sector decreases in relative terms, while in the composition of employees a change takes place in favor of the highly paid employees and skilled elite workers. This leads to a decrease in exactly that sort of purchasing power—i.e., the purchasing power of those in the lower income brackets (due to the relative shrinking of their employment and the freezing or fall of real wages)—which would induce a demand for local products and thereby the development of industries producing for the domestic market and which would also induce a transformation of "traditional" economies. On the other hand, the purchasing power biased for imported goods—i.e., the purchasing power of expatriates operating or training for the advanced techniques and of the local elite—increases.

The growing rural-urban gap and the employment bias in favor of a narrow worker elite involve a cumulative chain reaction with the biased investment choices. The former, by limiting the expansion of demand for other than consumer goods of relative luxury, reinforces investment preferences, while the latter contributes to the growth of a gap. A similar relationship seems to exist between the preference for capital-intensive techniques and the reluctance to invest in capital-goods production. The application of imported specialized machinery diverts demand from simple capital goods that could be produced locally. The lack of local capital-goods production favors the imports of specialized machinery. The import bias follows, of course, also from the business links between local and overseas companies.

The process of the transformation and integration of the "traditional" sector is strongly impeded by the relative contraction of the employment opportunities of the unskilled labor trying to move out of that sector and by the structural shift of purchasing power and demand (at the expense of the potential market of the products of the "traditional" sector). Contacts and relations may even be reduced between the "traditional" and "modern" sectors which were formerly realized by the migrant labor system and the marketing of occasional surplus products and simple handicraft products of the "traditional" sector for the urban low-income strata.

This type of "industrialization" involving capital-intensive light industries also makes its influence felt in other parts of the urban sector. Thus the domain of the local small and handicraft industries continues to contract, and the small or medium capital belonging to a few "national" entrepreneurs (or rather to the local "racial" minorities) who are engaged in the processing or marketing of local products is either ousted from its activity or compelled to turn elsewhere.[16] As a rule, the labor force of the new light industrial plants is not recruited from among the self-employed artisans or handicraft workers engaged in the same trade (even if they do exist, as in the case of textile, clothing, and shoe industries); thus, not only is the stage of guilds and factories missing (very understandably of course) in the development process but the phase of labor-intensive handicraft cooperatives and small-scale plants of light industry is also missing. As a consequence, products are ousted from the market and their producers dropped from among those having their own purchasing power. This process is a negative one not only because it is painful (other societies also have had to undergo similar painful processes) but because, instead of promoting the expansion of the internal social division of labor, it works rather in the direction of its contraction.

The self-employed artisans and handicraft workers as well as the migrant laborers who have lost their jobs are usually reemployed not by the emerging productive branches which ousted them from their former activities but rather by the "traditional" sector or in nonproductive sectors (first of all, in domestic service).

Due partly to the shift of demand toward imported goods and partly to its decreasing competitiveness against large-scale enterprises (which use capital-intensive techniques and can pay higher wages and take greater risks), small and medium capital engaged in producing local products is compelled either to retreat into other branches (mainly to the service industries or the retail trade of imported goods) or to come under the control of foreign capital. The result is again not the expansion of production linkages and market relations between the sectors and branches (a concomitant of the apparently similar process of concentration) but instead their contraction.

5. The emerging new pattern of investments fails to lead to the changes required for socioeconomic development and social justice with respect to human labor and employment. Insofar as it tends to reproduce the disintegrated dual structure and fails to integrate the rural "traditional" sector into a new, dynamic modern sector, it does not help in harmonizing the economic and the social-moral-cultural factors behind population growth and thereby influence fertility and mortality rates.

The limited sphere of industrial growth—involving the bias against capital goods production, the character of the new industries, and the techniques applied in them—reduces both the expansion of employment facilities inside the industrial sector and their ability to promote the expansion of employment facilities outside, in other sectors.

Figures for the period between the mid-fifties and the mid-sixties show that the rate of growth of employment considerably lagged behind the rate of growth of population and that of real product. The relatively static and periodically declining wage employment accompanied by rising wages reflects a shift in the employment pattern. The increase in wages seems to benefit mostly or exclusively a narrow worker elite, while its impact on profits is negligible. As a result of capital-intensive techniques and the still low general level of wages, the wage bill constitutes only about 20% of the total cost of manufacturing industries in Africa (Seidman, n.d.:269). The transfer of capital and technology is not accompanied by an international transfer (i.e., equalization) of wage and labor standards.

On the one hand, the influence on local government by international companies can result in restrictive labor legislation keeping union activity and wages down as an inducement to foreign investors, while, on the other hand, wage increases which are attributable to capital-intensive techniques tend to be limited to a narrow stratum only.

The shift in the pattern of labor demand toward the qualified categories, as a result of the new ventures and also of the policy of replacing foreign personnel by nationals in a number of posts in economic management and administration,[17] has not resulted in a sound demand pattern which might stimulate the building up of a system of public education and vocational training adjusted to the needs of a dynamic economic development. The "missing links" have remained characteristic features not only in the industrial structure but also in the pattern of the labor force. In the former they prevent the economic linkage effects from coming into operation and strengthen outward orientation, while in the latter they disrupt the "social linkage effect" and hinder both the natural supply of skilled labor and a general and simultaneous upgrading of the entire labor force.

In addition to semiskilled workers experienced only in simple technical operations, the new industries demand only a small number of qualified and specialized workers and not a core of mobile and versatile skilled workers with wide, complex professional knowledge and practice. But it is exactly the latter who would be able to fill its own ranks by training the less-qualified and less-experienced workers and promote the supply of the higher categories of the labor force (technicians, foremen, workshop managers) partly by its own further education.

The advancing replacement of expatriates and the increasing involvement and upgrading of nationals, together, unfortunately in many places, with the further expansion of bureaucracy, has brought about abrupt and disproportionately increasing demands for administrators. This, in turn, has stimulated, together with the income expectations attached to such posts, the overproduction of unspecialized bureaucrats.

Changes of this nature give new scope for social differentiation and induce among the workers the separation of a narrow elite from the uneducated masses and increase, on the other hand, the danger of bureaucracy alienated from society. They do not stimulate the development of public education and the formation of a widely based pattern of vocational training comprising interlocking vertical grades.[18]

The new pattern of investments seems to set limits to the "learning process" not only horizontally (as explained above) but also vertically. Since most of the industrial plants as affiliates or branch plants are linked to the overseas centers where technological decisions are made, or they are managed by expatriate technical and managerial staff implementing ready-made technology, there is hardly any room for technological experimentations, innovations, and research.

The transfer of technology and skill which otherwise could be an important factor promoting economic development is carried out within the analyzed pattern of foreign investments in a way that increases dependence on outside forces.

6. The negative effects of the new pattern of investments on foreign trade and economic relations have been already referred to in many respects. Despite the import-substitutive character of most of the new industrial ventures, the tendency of the growth of imports, being faster than that of exports, follows from the very pattern of investments, not only because of the high import component of the new investments and the heavy reliance on imported technology and skill, but also due to the unfavorable influence on consumption patterns and the failure to expand internal linkages.

Growing balance-of-payments problems, increasing reliance on primary exports as foreign-exchange sources for imports, and expanding and deepening dependence on the trade with and assistance from the metropolitan centers are the most striking consequences, if no counteracting efforts are made.

Insofar as the new pattern reinforces the overseas orientation of economic relations—namely, toward the industrial centers where skill and capital are to come from—it works also against the regional integration and economic cooperation of neighboring countries. This is so even if the formation of larger units easing and economizing the penetration of multinational corporations, as well as the establishment of region-wide markets for last-stage processing and assembly plants and access to the markets of additional countries, may well fit the interests of foreign capital. As long as "structural decisions" remain influenced by the latter, duplicative industrial investments (if following from the actual business considerations of international companies) can hardly be avoided within the region to be integrated.

7. Finally, as to the social impact of the new pattern of foreign investments, it seems to follow from what has been already said that the process of social integration cannot unfold. Instead, the new investments tend to reinforce social—as well as economic—dualism, and have already led to an increasing inequality of income distribution between urban and rural populations, between the various groups of wage and salary earners, and among the regions.

Though the new industries gave rise to a new stratum of working class, a relatively qualified and privileged elite group, the absence of a proletariat in the classical sense of the term has remained characteristic. The marginally or partially proletarianized lower stratum still representing the overwhelming majority has been filled up by new outflows from rural areas, while the "central links" between the former and the new upper stratum are missing. Consequently the worker elite (unlike labor-aristocracies in developed capitalist countries) has its position not on top of a pyramid-like stratification but rather in a "vacuum."

The transformation of the rural sector is still impeded by the lack of production linkages with the modern sector and the weakness of stimuli from the latter. Both ways of development for the rural population—i.e., via wage employment and market production—have been made more difficult: the former by the absolute or relative decrease of employment facilities and the latter by the reinforced diversion of demand from rural produce.

The suppression of competition of the new industrial plants established by foreign capital, protected and privileged by government or in partnership with it, and the rising labor costs as well as the shifting patterns of consumption have increased the disadvantages of smaller-scale industrial enterprises and handicraft industries and set new obstacles for a national industrial bourgeoisie to arise in the characteristic way. Instead, economic and state administration, as well as retail and service industries attached and subordinated to the activity of foreign capital, have become or remained the zones of the emergence of bourgeois strata in the sector.

IS THERE ANY COUNTERSTRATEGY POSSIBLE FOR NATIONAL GOVERNMENTS?

The analysis of the negative effects of foreign direct investments both of the colonial pattern and the emerging new one should assist the outlining of a possible counterstrategy in realistic terms, instead of leading to vague academic judgments only. Fortunately some elements of such a strategy seem already to be taking shape in the practice of a few progressive national governments, while the relevant experiences of socialist countries may also contribute to it.

A realistic economic policy, even a general and long-run strategy, can only be elaborated in concrete terms related to the country concerned. Let me focus nonetheless on a few key general conclusions that may be drawn from the above analysis.

1. Foreign direct investments both of the colonial and the new patterns have functioned as the vehicles of international cooperation and division of labor. Although the actual conditions under which the latter has been realized, and consequently its direction and content, are of a great and apparently growing disadvantage for developing countries, it is definitely *not* autarky, and probably not complete disengagement from capitalist metropoles, that is the realistic and exclusive alternative. Not only is the actual feasibility of artarky or complete

disengagement rather dubious, in view of structural relations, but their rationality and necessity are also highly questionable, with regard to the present stage of science and technology as well as international situation. Those who suggest a complete disengagement as a general alternative seem to underestimate the growing dimensions of production, science, and technology and the concentration of their centers in the advanced sector of capitalist world economy.

Since international communication, and the international flow of technical knowledge and scientific achievements, are a condition sine qua non of rapid development in our age, it is not an alternative to international cooperation but, instead, an alternative to its present "vehicles" which is to be sought.[19]

2. Developing countries need the transfer not only of adequate technology and skill but also of financial resources (an inflow, rather than an outflow). Since most of the negative effects of the analyzed form of capital import follow, as we have seen, from the growth of foreign ownership and influence within the country, (i.e., from direct investments), the import of loan capital seems to represent a much better solution for the problem.

3. Nevertheless, foreign direct investments are not merely an inherited reality to be reckoned with; they may also be a necessity in a given time and situation. The further question, therefore, is how to use foreign investment capital outside the colonial and neocolonial patterns discussed above and how to limit its negative effects. It seems to me that for the latter there are two decisive factors:

(a) The "assimilation" of foreign capital, i.e., its final absorption into national and social ownership, which can be achieved by various methods.

(b) An effective control from both above and below, and planned influence over its activity, which require an adequate information and management system, a capable research and advisory apparatus attached to the top leadership, and a reasonably well-established and operating planning machinery. All these seem to suggest a high priority in the development program for education and training.

4. Taking into consideration the cumulative dangers and consequences of a high degree of coincidence of bilateral links, and the concentration process in the capitalist world economy, it is not a matter of indifference which national origin direct investments have, and to what extent the various economic links (capital import, trade, technical assistance, and so on) are concentrated.

5. Since an unfavorable bias in investment policy may follow—as it does—not only from a deliberate adjustment to foreign interests but also from the spontaneous market forces rooted in the given structure, no counterstrategy can be successful without involving the structural transformation of the economy.

6. Bearing in mind the dimensional problems of industrialization and technical development, integration and regional cooperation between developing countries appear not only as a possible means for decreasing dependence on advanced capitalist countries but as an objective requisite for "catching up" as well.

NOTES

1. By "colonial" type of investments is meant investment both in the sectors producing primary products for export and in the infrastructure erected to meet the needs of the latter. Throughout this paper "direct investments" refers to investments that result in the rise and growth of capitalistic assets under foreign ownership.

2. Such as repatriation of investment incomes, royalties, and disguised drains via special pricing systems. The repatriated dividends from the Zambian copperbelt have amounted to about £400 million since 1928, although hardly more than £30 million of foreign risk capital has flown into the country for investments in the copperbelt. In addition, the British South Africa Company, by having obtained mineral rights, received royalty payments of about £80 million between the 1920s and 1964 (Boldon, 1969). As to the special pricing systems a marked example was the posted-price calculations of the international oil monopolies (Harab, 1968:91-107).

3. Contrary to Boeke's sociological dualism as well as the idea of technological dualism of Eckhaus, Higgins, and others, it is the Sachsian interpretation—i.e., dualism in a socioeconomic sense—which seems to be relevant and acceptable. In the dual system the "precapitalistic" sector has been subordinated to and functioning for the capitalist one, which means that it is no more an intact, real original precapitalism. (See Boeke, 1953; Eckhaus, 1965; Higgins, 1965; Sachs, 1964.)

4. There is no meaningful interpretation of "underdevelopment" without relating it to these structural effects of colonial investments. And without it there is no meaningful interpretation of colonialism either.

5. The abnormal proportion of overseas deliveries and business relations results in considerable and regular losses by shipping freights, insurance costs, and so on and even through banking operations. For the latter, see Yaffey, 1967.

6. Ann Seidman (1970) points to the rapid expansion of foreign private investments in Africa's mineral deposits in the postindependence period and the increasing multinational character of the new ventures often supported by international financial institutions.

7. Contrary often to the interests of local colonial settlers, and European plantation owners, the multinational corporations have tended to encourage export-oriented cash-crop production by African farmers.

8. Industrial output expanded rapidly in Africa, at a rate of about 7.4% per annum (as compared to 4.5% in advanced countries) in the period of 1948-1968. Manufacturing output expanded even faster, at a rate of about 8.5% per annum (United Nations, 1968).

9. There is already a quite wide and comprehensive literature on the increasing role of multinational corporations and their impact on developing as well as developed countries. Among others, see Magdoff, 1969; Nymer and Rowthorn, 1970; Nymer, 1971; Shaw, 1971; Kidron, 1965; Friedmann and Kalmanoff, 1961; Essack, 1970; Arrighi, 1967; Adam, 1971.

10. This is a point often missed in some radical critiques on neocolonialism and multinational corporations. See, for example, Shivji, 1970; Rodney, 1971; Saul, 1971; Szentes, 1971.

11. In the ten most advanced OCED countries the 100 biggest companies share 70-90% of the total amount spent on research and development in the processing industries (J. Nyilas, 1969:163).

12. That this danger exists also for developed countries such as Canada is stressed, for example, in the Watkins Report ("Foreign Ownership and the Structure of Canadian Industry," 1968). It points to the fact that the most serious cost resulting from foreign (U.S.) ownership is the loss of control over an important segment of Canadian economic life. Though foreign direct investments contributed to the present standard of living, their inherent tendency is to shift decision-making power in the private sector outside Canada. Kari Levitt (1968) arrives at a similar conclusion by stating that the new mercantilism of American corporate empires undermines national sovereignty.

13. Over and beyond the opportunity for the companies to influence the aid (and trade) policy of their home governments and make them use financial and technical assistance as a means to ensure a "good atmosphere" for direct investments in the recipient countries, there is another popular way of influencing local policy and investment "atmosphere." It is via the government advisers, various experts, and other technical assistance staff whose links, contacts, and common interests with foreign companies, in most cases, are not restricted to

those of their nationality. As a rule, the greater the coincidence between the origin of technical assistance and that of foreign investments, the greater the danger that the interests of foreign companies are represented even inside the local government.

14. The anticompetitive character of the multinational corporation is particularly enhanced if key positions inside the management and administration of public and parastatal sectors are held by their agents.

15. Paul Semonin (1971) points out that the corporations are extending their management structures into the government sphere itself.

16. Seidman (1968), by referring to F. Raikes' report, mentions the example of the disastrous impact of modern shoe and sandal factories on small handicraftsmen producing shoes of leather or worn-out rubber tires.

17. This policy has been partly forced by national aspiration and government measures, but partly followed voluntarily by foreign companies intending to refurbish their image, obtain political protection, and acquire reliable allies for the future.

18. There is, of course, considerable progress in this field, following, however, not from, but rather achieved in spite of, the mechanism of actions and interaction described. This progress results from government measures contrary to, offsetting, or counteracting the above tendencies. Such measures are those taken for the expansion of general education, the transformation of the structure of public education, the development of technical and vocational training, the formation of sounder wage and income proportions, the curb on bureaucracy, and the prevention of the strengthening and enrichment of the elite. The results and, of course, the attending conflicts, too, can be observed, as in Tanzania, where progressive state intervention is particularly well developed.

19. Such "vehicles" have already been operating not only among socialist countries but between socialist and capitalist countries as well, for mutual benefits. These "vehicles" include a number of forms of economic and technical cooperation (such as production and license sharing, marketing and service cooperation, and common technological research) but without foreign ownership and also special organizations and institutions but without foreign control over national production.

REFERENCES

AARANOVITCH, S., and AARANOVITCH, K. (1959). Crisis in Kenya. London.

ADAM, G. (1966). "Uj technika, uj struktura." ("New techniques, new structure"). Kozgazdasagi (Budapest).

——— (1971). "The world corporation problematics: Apologetics and critique." Trends in World Economy (no. 5, Budapest).

ARRIGHI, G. (1967). "International corporations, labour aristocracies and economic development in tropical Africa." In D. Horowitz (ed.), The corporations and the cold war. Unpublished papers, University College, Dar es Salaam.

BATTEN, T.R. (1947). Problems of African Development. London.

BOEKE, J.H. (1953). Economics and economic policy of dual societies. New York.

BOGNAR, J. (1965). "The future place and role of the developing countries in the world economy." In Studies on developing countries. Budapest: Centre for Afro-Asian Research of the Hungarian Academy of Sciences.

BOLDEN, S. (1969). "Zambia's lost millions." The Nationalist (September 1, Dar es Salaam).

BROWN, K. (1959). Land in Southern Rhodesia. London.

DAVIDSON, B. (1975). "How the Arusha Declaration has worked so far." Uchumi, 1(1).

East African Royal Commission (1955). Report, 1953-1955 (Cmd. 9475). London.

ECKHAUS, R.S. (1965). "The factor-proportions problem in underdeveloped areas." American Economic Review (September).

Economic Development of Kenya (1963). Report of the IBRD mission. Baltimore: Johns Hopkins Press.

Economic Development of Uganda (1962). Report of the IBRD mission. Baltimore: Johns Hopkins Press.

ESSACK, A.K. (1970). "200 super corporations which dominate the capitalist world." Africa and the World, 54(6).
Food and Agriculture Organization (1965). The state of food agriculture. Rome.
"Foreign ownership and the structure of Canadian industry" (1968). Paper prepared for the Privy Council Office. Ottawa: Queen's Printer.
FRANK, A.G. (1967). "Sociology of development and underdevelopment of sociology." Catalyst (3).
FRIEDMANN, W.G., and KALMANOFF, G. (1961). Joint international business ventures. New York: Columbia University Press.
GONCOL, G. (1966). "On the transformation of the capitalist world economy" (Studies in International Economics). Budapest: Hungarian Academy of Sciences, Institute of Economics.
HARAB, F.A. (1968). "The international oil price mechanism." Acta Oeconomica Academiae Scientaiarum Hungaricae, 3(1):91-107.
HELLEINER, J. (1967). "New forms of foreign private investment in Africa" (ERB 67.12). University College, Dar es Salaam.
HIGGINS, B. (1965). "The dualistic theory of underdeveloped areas." Economic Development and Cultural Change (January).
HILFERDING, R. (1947). Finanzkapital. Berlin.
ILIFFE, J. (1969). Tanzania under German rule. London: Cambridge University Press.
KIDRON, M. (1965). Foreign investments in India. London: Oxford University Press.
LEVITT, K. (1968). "Dependence and disintegration in Canada." New World Quarterly, 4(2).
MAGDOFF, H. (1969). "Notes on the multinational corporation." Monthly Review (October).
MORGAN, D.J. (1963). "British private investments in East Africa: Report of a survey and a conference." London: Overseas Development Institute.
NKRUMAH, K. (1965). Neo-colonialism: The last stage of imperialism. London: Nelson.
NURKSE, R. (1958). "Some international aspects of the problem of economic development." In S. Agarwala and R. Singh (eds.), The economics of underdevelopment. London: Oxford University Press.
NYILAS, J. (1969). "Korunk Vilaggazdasaga I." Kozgazdasagi (Budapest).
NYMER, S. (1971). "The multinational corporation and the law of uneven development." In J.N. Bhagwati (ed.), Economics and world order. New York: Macmillan.
NYMER, S., and ROWTHORN, R. (1970). "Multinational corporations and international oligopoly: The non-American challenge." In G.P. Kindleberger (ed.), The international corporation: A symposium. Cambridge: Massachusetts Institute of Technology Press.
RODNEY, W. (1971). "Some implications of the question of disengagement from imperialism." Maji Maji (no. 1).
RWEYEMANU, J.F. (1970). "Tanzania: Economy and society in the pre-independence period." Unpublished manuscript, University of Dar es Salaam.
––– (1971). "The political economy of foreign private investment in the underdeveloped countries." African Review, 1(1):108-118.
SACHS, I. (1964). Patterns of public sector in underdeveloped economies. New York: Asia Publishing House.
––– (1965). Foreign trade and economic development of underdeveloped countries. New York: Asia Publishing House.
SAUL, J. (1971). "Who is the immediate enemy." Maji Maji (no. 1).
SEIDMAN, A.W. (1968). "Industrial strategy and rural development." Unpublished manuscript, University College, Dar es Salaam.
––– (1969). "Comparative development strategies in East Africa." Unpublished manuscript, University College, Dar es Salaam.
––– (1970). "Old motives, new methods: Foreign enterprises in Africa today." In C.H. Allen and R.W. Johnson (eds.), African perspectives. London: Cambridge University Press.
SEMONIN, P. (1971). "Nationalizations and management in Zambia." Maji Maji (no. 1).
SHAW, R. (1971). "Foreign investment and global labor." Columbia Journal of World Business (no. 4).

SHIVJI, I.G. (1970). "Tanzania: The silent class struggle." Cheche (University of Dar es Salaam).
SINGER, H.W. (1964). International development: growth and change. New York: McGraw-Hill.
SZENTES, T. (1964). "Migrant-labour system in black Africa." Indian Journal of Labour Economics, 7.
——— (1971a). The political economy of underdevelopment. Budapest: Akademiai Kiado.
——— (1971b). "Status quo and socialism." Maji Maji (no. 2).
United Nations (1958). Special study on economic conditions in non-self-governing territories.
——— (1964). Economic bulletin for Africa, 4(January).
——— (1968). Economic bulletin for Africa, 7(1 and 2).
——— (1969). Economic bulletin for Africa, 9(1).
——— (1970). Economic bulletin for Africa, 10(1).
VAN DE LAAR, E. (1969). "Growth and income distribution in Tanzania since independence." Unpublished manuscript, University College, Dar es Salaam.
"Who controls industry in Kenya" (1968). Report of a working party. Nairobi: East African Publishing House.
WILLIAMS, R. (ed., 1968). May Day manifesto 1968. London: Penguin.
WODDIS, J. (1960). Africa: The roots of revolt. London: Lawrence and Wishart.
YAFFEY, M.J.R. (1967). "Foreign exchange loss through banking operations: The case of Tanzania" (Unpublished E.R.B. paper, no. 67.3). University College, Dar es Salaam.
——— (1970). Balance of payments problems of a developing country: Tanzania. Munich: Weltforum Verlag.

12

A BIBLIOGRAPHICAL GUIDE TO THE STUDY
OF THE POLITICAL ECONOMY OF AFRICA

CHRIS ALLEN
University of Edinburgh

"**Political economy**" is open to rather narrow definitions, ranging from the tendency to regard it as a preserve of Marxist writers alone (for example, Szentes, 1971) to a sterile attempt to quantify modernization theory along the lines suggested by Coleman (1967). Since the political economy approach to the study of African economies, societies, and states is still a relatively recent, minority trend, and since it must draw on the large body of work that is derived from other approaches, it seems more fruitful at present to define it in deliberately broad terms. The body of work, then, to which this is a guide is marked by the following methodological and analytical features: a concern with the temporal dimension, with how change may occur and be induced; a concern with the ways in which systems and phenomena are reproduced, or reproduce themselves, rather than an assumption that this does not require explanation; a concern with the economic bases of ostensibly noneconomic phenomena; a concern with holistic theories as much as, or more than, with middle range analysis; and a sensitivity to disciplines other than one's own. In terms of subject matter, the approach is marked by a stress on the themes of underdevelopment, imperialism, and class formation and action; more generally, with questions not merely of the distribution of power and wealth, but with the origins and morality of this distribution, and with the means to change it. It is therefore usually associated with a radical political commitment, particularly a socialist commitment (see Waterman in Gutkind and Waterman, 1975, an important general reader in African political economy).

Much of the most important material on the political economy of Africa has been, and will continue to be, produced by Marxists. This bibliography, like the volume in general, is more wide-ranging since it seeks to be a critical guide to the most significant publications in this field. Inevitably I have had to select a relatively small list from a much larger set of books and articles, not only because space is limited, but because the treatment of different topics in African political economy has been so uneven as to force one at times to include only some of the more valuable items on one topic while listing weaker material on a neglected field. I have confined my listing to material in what are still the main academic languages in African studies—English and French—and I have preferred short items in English that are relatively easy to obtain where this does not involve a significant lessening of quality, especially when they are themselves useful guides to the literature. There is inevitably some idiosyncrasy in my choice, and a limit to my acquaintance with the literature. I hope neither will greatly reduce the usefulness of this guide, which, while intended to stand on its own, is best used in combination with another, more narrowly focused on radical material and national case studies (such as the paper by Allen in Gutkind and Waterman, 1975).

This introduction is organized by topic, moving from underdevelopment and its origins to its contemporary economic manifestations, and the means suggested or adopted to escape from it. There follow sections dealing with material which is concerned mainly with the contemporary social, political, and ideological consequences of underdevelopment in Africa.

Underdevelopment, Imperialism, and Colonialism

African underdevelopment owes its origins principally to the expansion of European economic activity from the sixteenth century onwards (Rich and Wilson, 1967; Wallerstein, 1973, 1974; Hymer and Resnick, 1971; Patnaik, 1972; Kay, 1975). The process of incorporation and subordination of African economies is analyzed briefly in Amin (1972) and at length in Rodney (1972), which deals also with the social, intellectual, and political consequences of this process, discussed less comprehensively by Goody (1971), Buttner (1970), and Coquery-Vidrovitch and Moniot (1974), a useful Marxist general history from 1800. Among regional studies only Sheriff (1971) and Wayne (forthcoming) deal with East Africa. By contrast, West Africa has two excellent non-Marxist studies by A. Hopkins (1973) and Sundstrom (1975), plus a useful general history in Ajayi and Crowder (1973-1974), to add to Rodney (1970) and to Suret-Canale's classic Marxist account (1961), the first volume of a very valuable if rather thickly documented study of West African economic and political history. To these should be added three studies of individual states which discuss the relationships between economic and political change: Wilks (1975), Person (1968), and Barry (1972).

This latter topic has formed part of a lengthy debate on African modes of production, and the relative analytical importance of hunting, agriculture, and trade (Meillassoux, 1960, 1964, 1972, 1973; Terray, 1972; Rey, 1971; CERM, 1969; Coquery-Vidrovitch in Gutkind and Waterman, 1975; Pollet and Winter, 1971). For trade and markets generally, Meillassoux (1971) is a wide-ranging collection with an important introduction, while trade and state formation is dealt with, usually in case study form, by Terray (1974), Ehrensaft (1972), A. Hopkins (1968), Hymer (1970), and Dupré and Rey (1973). For slavery, see Meillassoux (1975), Bazin (1974), Klein (1971), Rodney (1966), and Mason (1973). This last topic is also—as with many of those above—part of African social history. As Klein (1972) points out, however, it is rare to find a work concerned primarily with this field. Social stratification is discussed in Amin (1973a), Diop (1971, 1972), Tuden and Plotnicov (1970), and Ehrensaft (1972), the last for Nigeria only; while African merchants figure in Reynolds (1974), Amin in Meillassoux (1971), and Rivière (1971).

The importance of the slave trade for both British development and African (and Caribbean) underdevelopment is debated in Rodney (1968, 1972), Engerman (1972), and Sheridan (1972); for the smaller East African trade, see Sheriff (1971) and Wolff (1974). The transition to "legitimate commerce" marks the beginning of modern imperialism. Discussion of this from Marx onwards is far too extensive to list: useful surveys are Barratt-Brown (1970, 1972, 1974), Kemp (1967), and Owen and Sutcliffe (1972), while Fieldhouse (1973) is a valiant if unsuccessful critique. The phenomenon of imperialism itself is rarely treated within a specifically African context, the great bulk of the historical material being made up of narrowly descriptive case studies of particular areas, metropolitan powers, companies, or individuals. Volume 5 of Gann and Duignan (1969-1974) is a bibliographical guide to such material, while Volume 1 contains good case studies by Flint, Hargreaves, and Newbury. There is another useful bibliography by Gardinier in Gifford and Louis (1971), a dull orthodox collection on French imperialism and colonialism. Of much greater sophistication and importance are Suret-Canale (1971, 1973), Coquery-Vidrovitch (1970, in Gann and Duignan, 1969-1974, Volume 2), and Amin (1973b) on the economic bases of French colonialism. For British colonialism, East Africa is better covered (by Brett, 1973; Rweyemamu, 1973; Wolff, 1974; Van Zwanenberg, 1974; Leys, 1975; Lubetsky in UEA, 1972) than is the West (A. Hopkins, 1968, 1973; Kay, 1972; Williams, forthcoming).

Central and southern Africa are beginning to be fully analyzed, after a long period of at best liberal historiography. For the most part such analyses occur in articles and conference papers rather than as extended studies, as with Trapido (1971), Harold Wolpe (1972), Legassick (1974), Wilson (1972), and the uneven collections in ICS (1970-1974) for South Africa. Rhodesia is covered by Emmanuel (1972a), Arrighi and Saul (1973), Phimister (1974), Kosmin (1974), and Van Onselen (1974a); Angola is covered by Boavida (1972). Material on colonial social history again overlaps with that on economic history and social differentiation (see "Underdevelopment and Social Change" below), but there are a general survey in Davidson (1969a) and a brief bibliography in Klein (1972).

Contemporary Underdevelopment

Theories of underdevelopment habitually suffer from a variety of dualism, asserting that capitalism in Africa, Asia, or Latin America is qualitatively different from that in industrialized countries (Wallerstein, 1974). Amin comes closest to avoiding this (though Floret, 1974, would disagree) in his two crucial volumes on contemporary capitalism (1973a, 1974a). More overtly dualist, but nonetheless essential reading, are Szentes (1971), a painstaking general account of the genesis of contemporary mechanisms of underdevelopment, and the work of Dos Santos (1970, in Bernstein, 1973) and Frank (1970, 1974). (See Laclau, 1971, for a sophisticated critique.) All of these owe a considerable debt to earlier Marxist writers (see, for example, the comments in Leys, 1975, and Foster-Carter in De Kadt and Williams, 1974) and particularly to Baran (1957). They are all attacked, on the key issue of the possibility of industrialization, by Warren (1973), though the subsequent debate shows his attack is ill-founded.

Among the mass of studies of African economies, relatively few consider economic institutions and processes as part of the reproduction of underdevelopment. Amin has written several important case studies from this perspective (1965, 1967a, 1970a, 1970b, 1973b, and Amin and Coquery-Vidrovitch, 1969), as has Seidman, who combines general material (1969, 1974b, and Green and Seidman, 1968) with studies of trade and foreign firms (1971, in Allen and Johnson, 1970) and case studies of East Africa (1972) and Zambia (1973, 1974a). Other important country studies include Rweyemamu (1974), Yaffey (1970), and Green in Allen and Johnson (1970) for Tanzania; Cliffe in Harris (forthcoming) for Kenya and Tanzania; Leys (1975) and ILO (1972) for Kenya; and Bondestam (1974b) for Ethiopia. West Africa is covered by Amin (above) and by Suret-Canale (1973, 1974), who has also written on Guinea (1970). There is an interesting debate on the Ghanaian and Ivorian economics by Berg and Green in Foster and Zolberg (1971), and both Hugon (1968) and Kom (1972) write on Cameroun from different radical standpoints; finally, Williams (forthcoming) has several narrow but useful essays on Nigeria, with an excellent general introduction. The material on Rhodesia noted earlier is also relevant here, as is Sutcliffe (1971), and the series of important recent specialized studies by Clarke (1974a, 1974b, 1974c), P. Harris (1974a, 1974b), Riddell (1974), and R.J. Davies (1974). While these do not yet make up a coherent political economy of Rhodesia that can replace Arrighi's brief and slightly dated account (Arrighi and Saul, 1973), they are an important development in an area in which academic work has usually avoided challenge to empiricist orthodoxy and government policy. The corresponding trend in South African studies, which owes much to earlier Marxist, focuses more on the creation and maintenance of apartheid and the South African state. There are, however, important studies by Legassick (1974), and in R. Harris (forthcoming), Wolpe (1972), Johnstone (1970), First, Steele, and Gurney (1972), Trapido (1971), Asheron (1969), and Rob Davies (1973).

Almost all that is written on particular mechanisms of underdevelopment (trade, investment, aid, and so on) is wholly uncritical, as Szentes (1971) shows. Among critical studies, the majority is concerned with partial reforms suggested by often superficial (though detailed) critiques. Seers and Joy (1971) is a paradigm case, and Byres (1972) is an example of how useful such material can be. That which remains covers the field unevenly. Terms of trade are discussed by Emmanuel (1972b) and Yaffey (1970), and the problems of monoculture by Essang (1967), Haslemere Group (1972), Lawrence (in RDRC, 1974), and Amin (1973b); for the particular problem of trade with the EEC, see Barratt Brown (1972). Foreign investment and foreign firms are covered by Evans (1971), Van der Laar (1971), Arrighi and Saul (1973), Dunning (1971), Schatz (1969), Goncharov in Gutkind and Waterman (1975), Yaffey (1970), ILO (1972), Sklar (forthcoming), Suret-Canale (1974), and Cronje, Ling, and Cronje (1975); see also the contents of the *Review of African Political Economy*, 1975, 1(2). Foreign public investment (aid) is dealt with by Byres (1972), Payer (1974), Corbett (1973), and Suret-Canale (1974); for the Tanzanian experience see Niblock (1971), and for suppliers' credits Cohen and Tribe (1972). Technology transfer is discussed in Helleiner (1968), Vaitsos (1974), Cooper (1973), Muller-Plantenburg (1971), and ILO (1972). Oni (1966), Gershenberg (1972), and Loxley in Uchumi (1972) are studies of banking, while Amin (1967b, 1969), Diop (1972), Leys in CAS (1972), and Akeredolu-Ale in Williams (forthcoming) focus on African businessmen.

Several of the country studies cited above have important sections on the rural economy (for example, Seidman, 1972; Leys, 1975; Amin, 1967a). Further analyses can be found in rural material cited below on planning, politics, and social differentiation, particularly those on East Africa. Village and locality studies are plentiful, but only rarely are they of sufficient general importance to be cited in the space available here: Hill (1972), Bondestam (1974a), Rey (1971), and Copans (1975) are good examples. Studies of larger scope include Hill (1963, 1970), Berry (1975), Pelissier (1966), and RDRC (1975); for the political economy of famine see Cliffe (1974) and Comité Info Sahel (1974).

Finally, an area of gross neglect in African political economy has been women's economic activity and its effects on social and sex-role differentiation and on women's political power. Boserup (1970) and Mintz (1971) are good general accounts, while Little (1974) is a survey of earlier work, showing clearly its limitations and biases. The recent work tends to be in the form of narrow case studies and to be still unpublished: characteristic of those available are Hill (1969), Maher (1974), Wipper (1972), Obbo in UEA (1972), Remy in Williams (forthcoming), and Mbilinyi in UEA (1970).

Ending Underdevelopment

This section covers three fields: reformist strategies, (apparently) socialist strategies, and revolutionary decolonization. As most of the material to be mentioned could be placed elsewhere, this is a somewhat arbitrary section; the issue is, however, a major one in the political economy of Africa. Reformist strategies tackle the effects of underdevelopment piecemeal and fail largely through lack of control of the economy, through neglect of countervailing tendencies in other sectors than that under reform, and because of the class or sectional interests of ruling groups. These points are brought out in Seidman (forthcoming) and in studies on planning by Van Arkadie and Leys (Seers and Faber, 1972), Green in Foster and Zolberg (1971), and Uchumi (1972). Equally important are studies of nationalization and parastatals by Sklar (1975), Shivji in Gutkind and Waterman (1975), Van Arkadie (1971), Packard in Uchumi (1972), and Loxley and Saul (1975), and material on agricultural development policy in RDRC (1974), Essang (1970), De Decker (1968), Raikes and Meynen in UEA (1972), Holmquist (1972), Meister (1972), Bondestam (1974a), Stahl (1974), IDS (1973), and Leonard (1972). Socialist strategies, discussed generally in Thomas (1974), have been claimed for Guinea, Mali, Algeria, and Tanzania, though in no case is there consensus on the validity of the claim. The best documented of the sectoral strategies is rural development, for which see Duprat (1973), Lucas (1973), and Ageron (1972) for Algeria; De Decker (1968) and Suret-Canale (1970) for Guinea; Ernst (1975) for Mali; and RDRC (1974), Cliffe and Saul (1972), Raikes (1975), and Shivji (1975) for Tanzania. Investment and industrial policies are discussed by Rweyemamu (1973), Akkache (1971), and Clegg (1971), and the problems of planning in Zolberg (1968) and Uchumi (1972). Overall assessments of Tanzania have been made by Arrighi and Saul (1973) and Cliffe in Harris (forthcoming); of Algeria by Maschino and M'Rabet (1972); and of Mali by Jones (1972).

Revolutionary decolonization, claimed by Fanon as the only means of ending underdevelopment (1965; discussed in Lucas, 1971), is still largely unstudied. Algeria has already been mentioned, while the former Portuguese colonies have been treated almost entirely in political or military terms, though there is useful material in Rudebeck (1974) and Davidson (1969b, 1972). These discuss also political and military problems, best dealt with by the late Amilcar Cabral (1969, 1972, 1973a, 1973b); see also Arrighi and Saul (1973), Saul (1974), and Davidson (1974).

Underdevelopment and Social Change

The incorporation of different African societies into the international capitalist economy at different times and by differing means results in marked local variations in the patterns and direction of social differentiation and other forms of social change. Furthermore, the stress within colonial economic policy on the continued use of primitive accumulation, in combination with the partial and uneven nature of the transformation of precapitalist economic and social structures, had added to local variations in social change a markedly ambiguous overall character. This has not yet had any theoretical treatment, even in the fundamental analyses of Amin (1973a, 1974a), beyond that in the material cited under African modes of production. Despite this local specificity and general ambiguity, attempts have been made to identify processes of peasantization and rural social differentiation, of proletarianization, and of the formation of an African bourgeoisie, resulting in much valuable work. (For uneven but useful collections of such work, see Abdel-Malek, 1971, and UEA, 1972.)

The merits or faults of early general work on class are discussed in Kitching (1972) and Cohen (1972), and its results summarized in Barbé (1964). Peasantization is covered generally by Post (1972) and in important case studies by Rey (1971), Bundy (1972), Phimister (1974), Leys (1975), Lubetsky in UEA (1972), Berry (1975), Aronson (1971), and Copans (1975). Other material on rural class structures is provided by Awiti (1973), D. O'Brien (1975), Essang (1970), Stavenhagen (1969), Feldman in Oxaal, Barnett, and Booth (1975), Shivji (1975), Ernst (1975), and Derman (1972). Rural class consciousness is rarely discussed, more perhaps because of failures of perception by political scientists and anthropologists than because of its absence. It is best studied (in the literature) through the material above and in that on rural revolt, such as Fox, De Craemer, and Ribeaucourt (1965) and Verhagen (1967, 1969) on Zaire; Williams and Beer in Williams (forthcoming) and Beer (forthcoming) on Nigeria; and Fanon (1965), Saul (1974), and Davidson (1974) on liberation movements. The much wider category of rural dissent and riot has generated far too many studies to allow for a representative sample here; as a single example, there is a particularly interesting set on colonial Ghana (Johnson, 1972; Simensen, 1974; Kilson in Foster and Zolberg, 1971; Rhodie, 1968; Shaloff, 1974).

Proletarianization is the process of becoming dependent on the sale of one's labor power in rural as well as urban contexts. The former, characteristic of settler economies, is described in Arrighi and Saul (1973) and Clarke (1974a). The latter has a prolific literature under such disguises as urbanization, labor migration, and labor commitment, much of it useful at best for its data. The process of migration and its relationship with the uneven impact of under-development are described in Amin (1972, 1974b), Gibbal (1974), Osoba (1969), Heisler (1970), and Wayne (forthcoming), among many others; but there is still no general account of the formation of an urban proletariat, or even of the growth of the work force of a particular town. Instead we have a few studies in prewar labor history (Cohen and Hughes, 1971; Van Onselen, 1973, 1974a, 1974b; Phimister, 1971; Clayton and Savage, 1975) and rather more of the 1940-1960 period (Sandbrook and Cohen, 1975; Joseph, forthcoming; Cohen, 1974; Allen in Allen and Johnson, 1970). Contemporary studies included valuable unpublished theses by Peace, Lubeck, and Jeffries; their work can be found in Sandbrook and Cohen (1975) and Jeffries (1975) and in Peace in De Kadt and Williams (1974). There are other important case studies by Grillo (1974), Sandbrook (1974), Mapolu (1972), Mihyo (1974), Burawoy (1972a, 1972b), and Waterman in Williams (forthcoming), covering the sociology and politics of workers and their organizations. For the economic aspects, the most useful work is by Weeks (1971a, 1971b, 1972, 1973); see also Allen in CAS (1972).

Recently there has been belated attention paid to the non-wage-earning urban poor, incorrectly referred to as either the lumpen proletariat or the informal sector (ILO, 1972). For discussion of the uses of these concepts see Cohen and Michael (1972) and R.J. Davies (1974); for the nature and activity of the groups concerned, see Le Brun and Gerry (1975), Williams in De Kadt and Williams (1974), Gibbal (1974), Hart (1973), R. O'Brien (1973), Furedi (1973), and Gutkind (1967, 1973, 1975).

The least understood major social category in contemporary Africa is probably Fanon's "national bourgeoisie"; confusion is reflected in the numerous terms used for the group by academics. Fanon's scarifying comments (1965) remain among the most illuminating, disordered though they be; also generally valuable are Amin (1973a) and First (1970), plus the case studies by Shivji (1975), Diop (1971, 1972), Meillassoux (1970), Amin (1967a), Leys (1975), Rivière (1971b, 1971c), and Williams in Allen and Johnson (1970). Evidence that this category is a class, or one in formation, is indirectly provided by much of the material above on economic policy and planning (see also Prewitt in UEA, 1972; Nduka in Gutkind and Waterman, 1975) and by the material on their political activity and ideologies (see below). Other material can be gleaned from "elite" studies, despite their narrowness and notion of class as merely social rank. Miller (1974) is a typically uncritical survey, while Oppong (1973) and Clignet (1970) are case studies in techniques of elite closure through marriage and education; for historical data see Wallerstein and Kilson in Volume 2 of Gann and Duignan (1969-1974).

Politics of Underdevelopment

This section is concerned with the patterns of distribution of power that result from underdevelopment, and with the mechanisms through which this pattern is created, reproduced, or attacked. At the level of the nation-state and below, these mechanisms are mainly formal institutions, notably the state, together with the means of influencing beliefs, and (mainly at the local level) less formal institutions based on caste, kinship, patronage, and sectional interest. I have discussed above the actions and institutions of the rural and urban poor; this section therefore centers on the issue of the origins and reproduction of the existing power distribution. It will also deal with international politics, though briefly, since most international relations work on Africa can be safely neglected.

General analysis of domestic politics is still largely in the hands of theorists of the modernization, nation-building, or political development schools, whose work combines shallowness with commitment to the values and interests of current (nonsocialist) ruling groups. Heeger (1974) provides a suitably banal survey, and Kesselman (1974) and Tipps (1973) offer interesting critiques. The best of these schools, however, provide considerable insight into the behavior of ruling groups and their institutions (Zolberg, 1966; Huntington, 1968) and offer case studies which transcend the limitations of their theories (as with Kilson, 1966; Zolberg, 1964; Sklar, 1963; Apter, 1963; Willame, 1972; and much of Coleman and Rosberg, 1964, and Lofchie, 1971). Political economists have by contrast neglected general analysis, where the best account is still—after sixteen years—Fanon, 1965 (which is well discussed in Staniland, 1969a, and Lucas,

1971). Also useful, but too brief, are First (1970), Arrighi and Saul (1973), and Copans (1972).

We are better served with analyses and case studies of more restricted scope, especially Leys's brilliant study of Kenyan politics (1975), which also contains brief treatments of several important analytical problems, notably that of the postcolonial state (see also Alavi, 1972; Shivji, 1975). This latter is profoundly influenced by the nature of the transfer of power, well illustrated in Wasserman (1973a, 1973b), and by the use of parties as means of controlling radical mass discontent and its reflection among the intelligentsia (Furedi, 1973; Kraus, 1971; Post and Jenkins, 1973) and as vehicles of elite self-interest (Rathbone, 1973; Marshall, forthcoming; Scott, 1972; Kilson, 1966; Leys, 1975). In turn, this accounts for the reason why parties and African political systems prize patronage (a readily abused concept discussed in Sandbrook, 1972, 1974; Kaufman, 1974; Alavi, 1973; D. O'Brien, 1975) and ethnic political mobilization or "tribalism" (Wallerstein, 1972; Melson and Wolpe, 1972; Leys, 1975). Also relevant in this context are the use of unions by their officers for self-advancement (Sandbrook, 1974; Sandbrook and Cohen, 1975) and the use of rural institutions such as cooperatives, extension services, and the like, to enhance the wealth and power of richer farmers (see agricultural policy in the section on "Ending Underdevelopment" above). This last theme, and the question of the local bases of political power are discussed in the recent series of studies of local politics, many of considerable quality and perception (Schumacher, 1975; Lamb, 1974; Vincent, 1971; N. Hopkins, 1972; Dunn and Robertson, 1973; Staniland, 1975; D. O'Brien, 1971, 1975).

Politics since independence has been marked by the use of state power to create a bourgeoisie, a topic which is dealt with indirectly in much of the material above, but which lacks a general study. Also characteristic have been the growth of authoritarian political behavior (including violence) and military intervention. The former is illustrated in most country studies of the last decade (for example, Post and Vickers, 1973; Chomé, 1973), while the latter is discussed in general and with good case studies in First (1970) and in Yannopolous and Martin (1972). Further case studies by Terray (1964), Lewis (1972), Decalo (1973a), and Martin (1972) show the importance of combining both military and nonmilitary factors in explaining coups. There is no satisfactory general account of military regimes, nor, indeed, of most of the main military governments in, for example, Nigeria or Ghana; for Zaire see Willame (1972) and Chomé (1973), and for a brief general survey, see Decalo (1973b). Politics in southern Africa have been changing rapidly since the coup in Portugal, though the basic cause of change remains the great increase in African guerrilla and other activity (see the section on "Ending Underdevelopment" above and Minter, 1974; Good, 1974; Turok, 1974; Johns, 1973). Broader accounts of politics in the various territories can be found in the work of Cabral and Davidson already cited, in Bowman (1974) for Rhodesia, and in Boavida (1972) and Marcum (1969) for Angola; there is at present no satisfactory account of South African politics. Outside the South, radical political movements are rare, even among workers and peasants (see the section on "Underdevelopment and Social Change" above); of the various radical parties, only the UPC of Cameroun has been adequately studied (Joseph, 1973), though there is material on the Sudanese Communist party in First (1970). For an interesting general discussion of revolutionary movements in underdeveloped countries, see Wertheim (1974).

The political position and activity of women has been as greatly neglected as their economic role, academics thereby showing again their tendency to absorb and reflect elite attitudes (see on this Clarke, 1974c; and Cohen and Hutton in Oxaal, Barnett, and Booth, forthcoming). There is no major work on this topic, though Wipper (1972) and Rosalda and Lamphere (1974) are good collections, and there are valuable individual studies by Wipper (1971), Boal and Van Allen in Jacquette (1974), Ardener (1973), Dobert (1970), Rivière (1968), and Mbilinyi (1972, 1973).

The study of ideology is difficult and tends in African contexts to be replaced by studies of attitudes, notably of elite groups. The material in the section on "Underdevelopment and Social Change" concerning workers and peasants contains much that is relevant to a study of their ideologies, though the discussion is very tentative (see, for example, Allen, Peace, and Jeffries in Sandbrook and Cohen, 1975). On religion see Hodgkin in Gutkind and Waterman (1975), Rodinson (1974), Colonna (1974), and Fox, De Craemer, and Ribeaucourt (1965). There is no general work on the ideologies of African bourgeoisies, though Benot's study of "state" ideologies (1969) comes closest; and Prewitt and Mohiddin in UEA (1972), Mohan (1966), Schwarz (1974), and Nduka and Osoba in Gutkind and Waterman (1975) are all helpful. Further insight can be gained from discussion of African intellectuals and writers: see Reeves (1974), Case (1973), and Obiechina (1974).

Finally, there is international politics, which in this context I shall take to cover foreign influence and intervention, African foreign policy and foreign relations, and the particular problem of southern Africa. The basis of external influence on African states is, of course, the latter's underdevelopment and dependency, already discussed above (though worth mentioning again are Green and Seidman, 1968, and—on neocolonialism more generally—Jenkins, 1970, and Nkrumah, 1965). There is also a considerable literature in this field stemming from peace research, largely unknown to Africanists: Galtung (1971), Hveem (1973), Käkönen (1974), and Senghaas (1974) are both examples of and guides to such material. Case studies of foreign intervention tend to be justificatory; for critical studies of the Congo events, see Weissman (1970) and C. O'Brien (1962), and for less intentionally revealing accounts of American activity see Attwood (1967) and Darlington (1968). France is covered by Corbett (1973) and Chaffard (1969), with interesting case studies from Spero (1973) and R. O'Brien in Abdel-Malek (1971). "Aid" and influence are discussed by Payer (1974) and Niblock (1971) on Tanzania; Chinese assistance and foreign policy are not discussed at length with any sympathy, but Ogunsanwo (1974) is a useful source of data. There are also very few studies of African foreign policy that are not both theoretically crude and largely descriptive: Mohan (1969) covers Ghana; Ameillon (1964) Guinea; and Bailey (1975) and Hoskyns in Cliffe and Saul (1972) Tanzania. For the special case of southern Africa, Cervenka (1973) is a thin and uneven but representative collection, and Shaw (1974) is an adequate survey of recent writing; other useful discussion can be found in Minter (1972, 1974), Bowman (1968), Good (1974), Gervasi (1973), and First, Steele, and Gurney (1972).

REFERENCES

ABDEL-MALEK, A. (ed., 1971). Sociologie de l'impérialisme. Paris: Anthropos.
AGERON, C.R. (1972). "Agriculture socialiste et auto-gestion rurale en Algérie." Compterendu trimestrielle des séances de l'Academie des Sciences Outre-mer, 31(3):499-524.
AJAYI, J.F.A., and CROWDER, M. (eds., 1973-1974). History of West Africa (2 vols.). London: Longmans.
AKKACHE, A. (1971). Capitaux étrangers et libération economique: l'expérience algérienne. Paris: Maspero.
ALAVI, H. (1972). "The state in post-colonial societies." New Left Review, 74:59-81.
––– (1973). "Peasant classes and primordial loyalties." Journal of Peasant Studies, 1(1):23-62.
ALLEN, C., and JOHNSON, R.W. (eds., 1970). African perspectives. Cambridge: Cambridge University Press.
AMEILLON, B. (1964). La Guinée, bilan d'une indépendence. Paris: Maspero.
AMIN, S. (1965). Trois expériences africaines de développement. Paris: Presses Universitaires.
––– (1967a). Le développement du capitalisme en Côte d'Ivoire. Paris: Minuit.
––– (1967b). "Le développement du capitalisme en Afrique Noire." L'Homme et la Société, 6:107-119.
––– (1969). Le monde des affaires sénégalaise. Paris: Minuit.
––– (1970a). "Development and structural change: The African experience." Journal of International Affairs, 24(2):203-223.
––– (1970b). The Maghreb in the modern world. Harmondsworth: Penguin.
––– (1972). "Underdevelopment and dependence." Journal of Modern African Studies, 10(4):503-524.
––– (1973a). Le développement inégal. Paris: Anthropos. Review by P. Hugon in Revue Tiers-Monde, 1974, 58:421-434.
––– (1973b). Neocolonialism in West Africa. Harmondsworth: Penguin.
––– (1974a). Accumulation on a world scale (2 vols.). New York: Monthly Review. Review by C. Palloix in L'Homme et la Société, 1970, 18:197-208.
––– (ed., 1974b). Modern migration in western Africa. London: Oxford University Press.
AMIN, S., and COQUERY-VIDROVITCH, C. (1969). Histoire economique du Congo 1880-1968. Paris: Anthropos.
APTER, D.E. (1963). Ghana in transition. New York: Atheneum.
ARDENER, S.G. (1973). "Sexual insults and female militancy." Man, 8(3):422-440.
ARONSON, D.R. (1971). "Ijebu-Yoruba urban-rural relationships and class formation." Canadian Journal of African Studies, 5(3):263-280.
ARRIGHI, G., and SAUL, J.S. (1973). Essays on the political economy of Africa. New York: Monthly Review.

ASHERON, A. (1969). "Race and politics in South Africa." New Left Review, 53:55-68.
ATTWOOD, W. (1967). The reds and the blacks. London: Hutchinson.
AWITI, A. (1973). "Economic differentiation in Ismani." African Review, 3(2):209-239.
BAILEY, M. (1975). "Tanzania and China." African Affairs, 74(294):39-50.
BARAN, P. (1957). The political economy of growth. New York: Monthly Review.
——— (1958). "On the political economy of backwardness." In A. Argawala and S. Singh (eds.), The economics of underdevelopment. New York: Oxford University Press.
BARBE, R. (1964). Les classes sociales en Afrique noire. Paris: Editions Sociales.
BARKER, J.S. (1973). "Political factionalism in Senegal." Canadian Journal of African Studies, 7(2):287-303.
BARRATT BROWN, M. (1970). After imperialism (2nd ed.). London: Merlin.
——— (1972). Essays on imperialism. Nottingham: Spokesman Books.
——— (1974). The economics of imperialism. Harmondsworth: Penguin.
BARRY, B. (1972). Le royaume du Waalo. Paris: Maspero.
BAZIN, J. (1974). "War and servitude in Segon." Economy and Society, 3(2):107-144.
BEER, C. (forthcoming). The politics of peasant groups in Western Nigeria.
BENOT, Y. (1969). Idéologies des indépendances africaines. Paris: Maspero. See also Revue Tiers-Monde, 1974, 15(57):135-170.
BERNSTEIN, H. (ed., 1973). Underdevelopment and development. Harmondsworth: Penguin.
BERRY, S.F. (1975). Customs and socioeconomic change in Western Nigeria. Oxford: Oxford University Press.
BOAVIDA, A. (1972). Angola: Five centuries of Portuguese exploitation. Richmond, Canada: Liberation Support Movement.
BOKSERUP, E. (1970). Woman's role in economic development. London: Allen and Unwin.
BONDESTAM, L. (1974a). "People and capitalism in the north-eastern lowlands of Ethiopia." Journal of Modern African Studies, 12(3):423-439.
——— (1974b). "Underdevelopment and economic growth in Ethiopia." Kroniek van Afrika, 1:20-35.
BOWMAN, L.W. (1968). "The subordinate state system of southern Africa." International Studies Quarterly, 12(3):231-261.
——— (1974). Politics in Rhodesia. Cambridge, Mass.: Harvard University Press.
BRETT, E.A. (1973). Colonialism and underdevelopment in East Africa. London: Heinemann.
BUNDY, C. (1972). "The emergence and decline of a South African peasantry." African Affairs, 71(285):369-388. See also ICS, 1973.
BURAWOY, M. (1972a). The colour of class in the copper mines. Manchester: Manchester University Press.
——— (1972b). "Another look at the mineworker." African Social Research, 14:239-287.
BUTTNER, T. (1970). "The economic and social character of precolonial states in tropical Africa." Journal of the Historical Society of Nigeria, 5(2):275-290.
BYRES, T. (ed., 1972). Foreign resources and economic development. London: Cass.
CABRAL, A. (1969). Revolution in Guiné. London: Stage One.
——— (1972). "Identity and dignity in the national liberation struggle." Africa Today, 19(4):39-47.
——— (1973a). Return to the source: Selected speeches. New York: African Information Service.
——— (1973b). "Fruits of a struggle: Notes for a history." Marxism Today, 17(1):13-21 (and Tricontinental, 31).
CASE, F.I. (1973). "La bourgeoisie africaine dans la litterature de l'Afrique occidentale." Canadian Journal of African Studies, 7(2):257-266.

Centre of African Studies (1972). Developmental trends in Kenya. Edinburgh University: Centre of African Studies.

CERM (1969). Sur le mode de production asiatique. Paris: Editions Sociales.

CERVENKA, Z. (ed., 1973). Land-locked countries of Africa. Uppsala: Scandinavian Institute of African Studies.

CHAFFARD, G. (1969). "L'homme des affaires secrètes." Nouvel Observateur, 258-260.

CHOME, J. (1973). L'ascension du Mobutu. Paris: Maspero.

CLARKE, D.G. (1974a). Contract workers and underdevelopment in Rhodesia. Gwelo, Rhodesia: Mambo Press.

––– (1974b). Domestic workers in Rhodesia. Gwelo, Rhodesia: Mambo Press.

––– (1974c). "Settler ideology and African underdevelopment in post-war Rhodesia." Rhodesian Journal of Economics, 8(1):17-38.

CLAYTON, A., and SAVAGE, D.C. (1975). Government and labour in Kenya 1895-1963. London: Cass.

CLEGG, I. (1971). Workers' self management in Algeria. London: Allen Lane.

CLIFFE, L. (1974). "Feudalism, capitalism and famine in Ethiopia." Review of African Political Economy, 1(1):34-40.

CLIFFE, L., and SAUL, J.S. (eds., 1972). Socialism in Tanzania (2 vols.). Nairobi: East African Publishing House.

CLIGNET, R. (1970). "Education and elite formation." Pp. 304-330 in J. Paden and E. Soja (eds.), The African experience. Evanston, Ill.: Northwestern University Press.

COHEN, D.L., and TRIBE, M.A. (1972). "Suppliers' credits: Ghana and Uganda." Journal of Modern African Studies, 10(4):525-541.

COHEN, R. (1972). "Class in Africa: Analytical problems and perspectives." Socialist Register, 230-256.

––– (1974). Labour and politics in Nigeria, 1945-71. London: Heinemann.

COHEN, R., and HUGHES, A. (1971). Towards the emergence of a Nigerian working class, 1897-1939 (Faculty of Commerce and Social Science Occasional Papers D7). Birmingham: Birmingham University.

COHEN, R., and MICHAEL, D. (1973). "The revolutionary potential of the African lumpen-proletariat: A sceptical view." IDS Bulletin, 5(2/3):31-42.

COLEMAN, J.S. (1967). "The resurrection of political economy." Mawazo, 1(1):31-40.

COLEMAN, J.S., and ROSEBERG, C.G. (eds., 1964). Political parties and national integration in tropical Africa. Berkeley: University of California Press.

COLONNA, F. (1974). "Cultural resistance and religious legitimacy in colonial Algeria." Economy and Society, 3(3):233-252.

Comité Info Sahel (1974). Qui se nourrit de la famine en Afrique? Paris: Maspero.

COOPER, C. (1973). Science, technology and development. London: Cass.

COPANS, J. (1972). "Economies et luttes politiques de l'Afrique noire contemporaine." L'Homme, 12(3):119-131.

––– (1975). Organisation du travail agricole et stratification sociale dans les villages Wolof Mouride. Paris: Maspero.

CORBETT, E.M. (1973). The French presence in black Africa. Washington: Black Orpheus Press.

COQUERY-VIDROVITCH, C., and MONIOT, H. (1974). L'Afrique noire de 1800 à nos jours. Paris: Presses Universitaires.

CRONJE, S.; LING, M.; and CRONJE, G. (1975). Lonrho: Portrait of a multinational. London: Julian Friedmann.

DARLINGTON, G. (1968). African betrayal. New York: David McKay.

DAVIDSON, B. (1969a). The Africans. London: Longmans.

––– (1969b). The liberation of Guiné. Harmondsworth: Penguin.

––– (1972). In the eye of the storm. London: Longmans.

――― (1974). "African peasants and revolution." Journal of Peasant Studies, 1(3):269-290.
DAVIES, R.J. (1974). "The informal sector in Rhodesia: How important?" Rhodesia Science News, 8(7):216-220.
DAVIES, Rob (1973). "The white working class of South Africa." New Left Review, 82:40-59.
DECALO, S. (1973a). "Regionalism, politics and the military in Dahomey." Journal of Developing Areas, 7(3):449-478.
―――(1973b). "Military coups and military regimes in Africa." Journal of Modern African Studies, 11(1):105-126.
De DECKER, H. (1968). Nation et développement communtaire en Guinée et au Sénégal. Paris: Mouton.
De KADT, E., and WILLIAMS, G.P. (eds., 1974). Sociology and development. London: Tavistock.
DERMAN, W. (1972). Serfs, peasants and socialists. Berkeley: California University Press.
DIOP, M. (1971, 1972). Histoire des classes sociales dans l'Afrique de l'ouest (Vol. 1, Le Mali; Vol. 2, Le Sénégal). Paris: Maspero.
DOBERT, M. (1970). "Civic and political participation of women in French-speaking West Africa." Unpublished Ph.D. dissertation. George Washington University.
Dos SANTOS, T. (1970). "The structure of dependence." American Economic Review, 60(2):231-236.
DUNN, J., and ROBERTSON, A.F. (1973). Dependence and opportunity: Political change in Ahafo. Cambridge: Cambridge University Press.
DUNNING, J.H. (ed., 1971). The multinational enterprise. London: Allen and Unwin.
DUPRAT, G. (1973). Revolution et autogestion rurale en Algerie. Paris: Armand Colin.
DUPRE, G., and REY, P.P. (1973). "Reflections on the pertinence of a theory of the history of exchange." Economy and Society, 2(2):131-163.
EHRENSAFT, P. (1972). "The political economy of informal empire in pre-colonial Nigeria, 1807-1884." Canadian Journal of African Studies, 6(3):451-490.
EMMANUEL, A. (1972a). "White settler colonialism and the myth of investment imperialism." New Left Review, 73:35-57.
――― (1972b). Unequal exchange. London: New Left Books. Review by C. Palloix in Bulletin of the Conference of Socialist Economists, 1972. 2(1):67-94.
ENGERMAN, S.L. (1972). "The slave trade and British capital formation in the eighteenth century." Business History Review, 46(4):430-443.
ERNST, K. (1975). Tradition and progress in the African village. London: Hurst.
ESSANG, S.M. (1967). "The lessons of the cocoa crisis." Nigerian Journal of Economic and Social Studies, 9:235-242.
――― (1970). "The distribution of earnings in the cocoa economy of Western Nigeria." Unpublished Ph.D. dissertation, Michigan State University.
EVANS, P.B. (1971). "National autonomy and political development: Critical perspectives on multinational corporations in poor countries." International Organisation, 25(3):675-692.
FANON, F. (1965). Wretched of the earth. London: MacGibbon and Kee.
FIELDHOUSE, D.K. (1973). Economics and empire 1830-1914. London: Weidenfield and Nicholson.
FIRST, R. (1970). Barrel of a gun. London: Allen Lane.
FIRST, R.; STEELE, J.; and GURNEY, C. (1972). The South African connection. London: Temple Smith.
FLORET, J. (1974). "Samir Amin ou le cheval de Troie des bourgeoisies nationales." Sous le drapeau de socialisme, 62:40-42.
FOSTER, P., and ZOLBERG, R. (eds., 1971). Ghana and the Ivory Coast. Chicago: University of Chicago Press.

FOX, R.C.; De CRAEMER, W.; and RIBEAUCOURT, J.M. (1965). "The second independence: A case study of the Kwilu rebellion in the Congo." Comparative Studies in Society and History, 8(1):78-109.

FRANK, A.G. (1967). Capitalism and underdevelopment in Latin America. New York: Monthly Review.

——— (1969). Latin America: Underdevelopment or revolution. New York: Monthly Review.

——— (1974). On capitalist underdevelopment. Delhi: Oxford University Press.

FUREDI, F. (1973). "The African crowd in Nairobi: Popular movements and elite politics." Journal of African History, 14(2):275-290.

FURTADO, C. (1965). "Development and stagnation in Latin America: A structuralist approach." Studies in Comparative International Development, Monograph Series, 1(11).

GALTUNG, J. (1971). "A structural theory of imperialism." Journal of Peace Research, 8(2):81-118.

GANN, L.H., and DUIGNAN, P. (1969-1974). Colonialism in Africa, 1870-1960 (vols. 1-3, 5). Cambridge: Cambridge University Press.

GERSHENBERG, I. (1972). "Banking in Uganda since independence." Economic Development and Cultural Change, 20(3):504-523.

GERVASI, S. (1973). "South Africa looks north." Free Southern Africa, 1:17-29.

GIBBAL, J.N. (1974). Citadins et villageois dans la ville africaine. Paris: Maspero.

GIFFORD, P., and LOUIS, W.M. (eds., 1971). France and Britain in Africa. New Haven, Conn.: Yale University Press.

GOOD, K. (1974). "Settler colonialism in Rhodesia." African Affairs, 73(290):10-36.

GOODY, J. (1971). Technology, tradition and the state in Africa. London: Oxford University Press. Review by E. Terray in Annales, 1973, 28(5):1331-1338.

GREEN, R.H., and SEIDMAN, A. (1968). Unity or poverty? Harmondsworth: Penguin.

GRILLO, R.D. (1974). African railwaymen. Cambridge: Cambridge University Press.

GUTKIND, P.C.W. (1967). "The energy of despair." Civilisations, 17:186-211, 380-402.

——— (1973). "From the energy of despair to the anger of despair." Canadian Journal of African Studies, 7(2):179-198.

——— (forthcoming). "The view from below: Political consciousness of the urban poor in Ibadan."

GUTKIND, P.C.W., and WATERMAN, P. (eds., 1975). African social studies: A radical reader. London: Heinemann.

HARRIS, P.S. (1974a). Black industrial workers in Rhodesia. Gwelo, Rhodesia: Mambo Press.

——— (1974b). "Ten popular myths concerning the employment of labour in Rhodesia." Rhodesian Journal of Economics, 8(1):39-48.

HARRIS, R. (ed., forthcoming). The political economy of Africa.

HART, K. (1973). "Informal income opportunities and urban employment in Africa." Journal of Modern African Studies, 11(1):61-89.

Haslemere Group (1972). Coffee: The rules of neocolonialism. London: Haslemere Group.

HEEGER, G.A. (1974). The politics of underdevelopment. New York: St. Martins; London: Macmillan.

HEISLER, H. (1970). "A class of target proletarians." Journal of Asian and African Studies, 5:161-175.

HELLEINER, G.K. (1968). "New forms of foreign investment." Journal of Modern African Studies, 6(1):17-27.

HILL, P. (1963). The migrant cocoa farmers of southern Ghana. Cambridge: Cambridge University Press.

——— (1969). "Hidden trade in Hausaland." Man, 4(3):392-409.

——— (1970). Studies in rural capitalism in West Africa. Cambridge: Cambridge University Press.

——— (1972). Rural Hausa. Cambridge: Cambridge University Press.
HOLMQUIST, F.W. (1972). "Towards a political theory of rural self-help development in Africa." Rural Africana, 18:60-79.
HOPKINS, A.G. (1968). "Economic imperialism in West Africa: Lagos 1880-92." Economic History Review; 21:580-606. See discussion with J.F.A. Ajayi and A. Austen, Economic History Review, 1972, 25(2):303-312.
——— (1973). An economic history of West Africa. London: Longmans.
HOPKINS, N.S. (1972). Popular government in an African town. Chicago: University of Chicago Press.
HUGON, P. (1968). Analyse de sous-développement en Afrique: Cameroun. Paris: Presses Universitaires.
HUNTINGTON, S.P. (1968). Political order in changing societies. New Haven, Conn.: Yale University Press.
HVEEM, H. (1973). "The global dominance system." Journal of Peace Research, 10(4):319-340.
HYMER, S.H. (1970). "Economic forms in pre-colonial Ghana." Journal of Economic History, 30(1):33-50.
HYMER, S.H., and RESNICK, S. (1971). "International trade and uneven development." Pp. 473-494 in J. Bhagwati et al. (eds.), Trade, balance of payments and growth. Amsterdam: North Holland Publishing.
Institute of Commonwealth Studies (1970-1974). The societies of southern Africa in the nineteenth and twentieth centuries (5 vols.). London: Institute of Commonwealth Studies.
Institute of Development Studies (1973). An overall examination of the special rural development programme. Nairobi: Institute of Development Studies.
International Labor Organization (1972). Employment, incomes and equality in Kenya. Geneva: International Labor Organization. Reviewed by C. Leys in African Affairs, 1973, 72(289):419-429.
JACQUETTE, J.S. (ed., 1974). Women in politics. New York: Wiley.
JEFFRIES, R. (1975). "Ghanian workers: 'Labour aristocracy' reconsidered." Review of African Political Economy, 1(2).
JENKINS, R. (1970). Exploitation. London: MacGibbon and Kee.
JOHNS, S. (1973). "Obstacles to guerilla warfare: A South African case study." Journal of Modern African Studies, 11(2):267-303.
JOHNSON, T.L. (1972). "Protest, tradition and change: The southern Gold Coast riots, 1890-1920." Economy and Society, 1(2):164-193. Discussion with R. Stone, Economy and Society, 1974, 3(1):84-105.
JOHNSTONE, F.R. (1970). "White prosperity and white supremacy in South Africa today." African Affairs, 69(275):124-140.
JONES, W.I. (1972). "The mise and demise of socialist institutions in rural Mali." Geneve-Afrique, 11(2):19-44.
JOSEPH, R. (1973). "Radical nationalism in Cameroun: The case of the UPC." Unpublished D.Phil. dissertation, Oxford University.
——— (forthcoming). "Settlers, strikes and sans-travail: The Douala riots of 1945."
KAKONEN, J. (1972). The political economy of colonialism in Ghana. Cambridge: Cambridge University Press.
——— (n.d.). The mechanisms of neocolonialism. Mantta: Finnish Peace Research Association.
KAUFMAN, R.R. (1974). "The patron-client concept and macropolitics." Comparative Studies in Society and History, 16(3):284-308.
KAY, G. (1975). Development and underdevelopment. London: Macmillan.
KEMP, T. (1967). Theories of imperialism. London: Dobson.
KESSELMAN, M. (1973). "Order or movement? The literature of political development as ideology." World Politics, 26(1):139-154.

KILSON, M.L. (1966). Political change in a West African state. Cambridge, Mass.: Harvard University Press.
KITCHING, G. (1972). "The concept of class and the study of Africa." African Review, 2(3):327-350.
KLEIN, M. (1971). "Slavery, the slave trade and legitimate commerce in late nineteenth century Africa." Etudes d'histoire africaine, 2:5-28.
––– (1972). "African social history." African Studies Review, 15(1):97-112.
KOM, D. (1972). Le Cameroun: Essai d'analyse economique et politique. Paris: Editions Sociales.
KOSMIN, B.A. (1974). "The Inkoya tobacco industry of the Shanowe people: A case study of the displacement of a precolonial economy." African Social Research, 17:554-577.
KRAUS, J.P. (1971). "Cleavages, crises, parties and state power in Ghana." Unpublished Ph.D. dissertation, Johns Hopkins University. See also Foster and Zolberg, 1971.
LACLAU, E. (1971). "Feudalism and capitalism in Latin America." New Left Review, 67:19-38.
LAMB, G. (1974). Peasant politics. London: Julian Friedmann.
LeBRUN, O., and GERRY, C. (1975). "Petty-commodity producers and capitalism." Review of African Political Economy, 1(3).
LEGASSICK, M. (1974). "South Africa: Capital accumulation and violence." Economy and Society, 3(3):253-291.
LEONARD, D.K. (1972). "The social structure of the agricultural extension service in the Western Province of Kenya." African Review, 2(2):223-243.
LEWIS, I. (1972). "The politics of the Somali coup." Journal of Modern African Studies, 10(3):383-408.
LEYS, C. (1975). Underdevelopment in Kenya. London: Heinemann.
LITTLE, K. (1974). African women in towns. Cambridge: Cambridge University Press.
LOFCHIE, M. (ed., 1971). The state of the nations. Berkeley: University of California Press.
LOXLEY, J., and SAUL, J. (1975). "The political economy of the parastatals." Review of African Political Economy, 1(2). Early version in East African Law Review, 5(1/2):9-37.
LUCAS, P. (1971). Sociologie de Frantz Fanon. Algér: Société Nationale d'Edition et Diffusion.
––– (1973). "Réforme agraire en Algérie." L'Homme et la Société, 27:131-142.
MAHER, V. (1974). Women and property in Morocco. Cambridge: Cambridge University Press.
MAPOLU, H. (1972). "The organisation and participation of workers in Tanzania." African Review, 2(3):381-417.
MARCUM, J. (1969). The Angolan revolution (Vol. 1). Cambridge: Massachusetts Institute of Technology Press.
MARSHALL, J.M. (forthcoming). The political economy of dependence, Ghana, 1945-66. Available in draft as an M.Sc. thesis, 1972, from the Institute of Social Studies, The Hague.
MARTIN, M.L. (1972). "The Uganda military coup of 1971." Ufahamu, 2(3):81-121.
MASCHINO, T.M., and M'RABET, F. (1972). L'Algérie des illusions: La révolution confisquée. Paris: Maspero.
MASON, M. (1973). "Captive and client labour and the economy of the Bida emirate." Journal of African History, 14(3):453-472.
MBILINYI, M.J. (1972). "The 'new woman' and traditional norms in Tanzania." Journal of Modern African Studies, 10(1):57-72.
––– (1973). "Education, stratification and sexism in Tanzania." African Review, 3(2):327-340.
MEILLASSOUX, C. (1960). "La phénomène économique dans les sociétés traditionelles d'autosubsistence." Cahiers d'études africaines, 4:38-67.

––– (1964). Anthropologie économique des Gouro de Côte d'Ivoire. Paris: Mouton. Review by J. Suret-Canale in La Pensée, 1967, 135:94-106.
––– (1970). "A class analysis of the bureaucratic process in Mali." Journal of Development Studies, 6(2):91-110.
––– (ed., 1971). ·The development of indigenous trade and markets in West Africa. London: Oxford University Press.
––– (1972). "From reproduction to production." Economy and Society, 1(1):93-105.
––– (1973). "On the mode of production of the hunting band." Pp. 187-203 in P. Alexandre (ed.), French perspectives in African studies. London: Oxford University Press.
––– (ed., 1975). L'esclavage dans l'Afrique precoloniale. Paris: Maspero.
MEISTER, A. (1972). "Characteristics of community development and rural animation in Africa." International Review of Community Development, 27-8:75-132.
MELSON, R., and WOLPE, H. (1972). Nigeria: modernisation and the politics of communalism. East Lansing: Michigan State University Press.
MIHYO, P.B. (1974). "The workers' revolution in Tanzania." Maji Maji (Dar es Salaam), 17:1-61.
MILLER, R.A. (1974). "Elite formation in Africa." Journal of Modern African Studies, 12(4):521-542.
MINTER, W. (1972). Portuguese Africa and the West. Harmondsworth: Penguin.
––– (1974). "Imperial network and external dependency: Implications for the Angolan liberation struggle." Africa Today, 21(1):25-39.
MINTZ, S.W. (1971). "Men, women and trade." Comparative Studies in Society and History, 13(3):247-269.
MOHAN, J. (1966). "Varieties of African socialism." Socialist Register, 220-266.
––– (1969). "Ghana, the Congo and the United Nations." Journal of Modern African Studies, 7(3):369-406.
MULLER-PLANTENBERG, U. (1971). "Technologie et dépendance." Critiques de l'économie politique, 3:68-82.
NIBLOCK, T.C. (1971). "Aid and foreign policy in Tanzania." Unpublished Ph.D. dissertation, Sussex University.
NKRUMAH, K. (1965). Neo-colonialism: The last stage of imperialism. London: Nelson.
OBIECHINA, E. (1974). Culture, tradition and society in the West African novel. Cambridge: Cambridge University Press.
O'BRIEN, C.C. (1962). To Katanga and back. London: Hutchinson.
O'BRIEN, D.C. (1971). The Mourides of Senegal. Oxford: Oxford University Press.
––– (1975). Saints and politicians. Cambridge: Cambridge University Press.
O'BRIEN, R.C. (1973). "Unemployment, the family and class formation in Africa." Manpower and Unemployment Research in Africa, 6(2):47-59.
OGUNSANWO, A. (1974). China's policy in Africa, 1958-71. London: Cambridge University Press.
ONI, O. (1966). "Features of Nigeria's financial institutions: A Marxist approach." Nigerian Journal of Economic and Social Studies, 8(3):383-402.
OPPONG, C. (1973). Marriage among a matrilineal elite. Cambridge: Cambridge University Press.
OSOBA, S.O. (1969). "The phenomenon of labour migration in the era of British colonial rule." Journal of the Historical Society of Nigeria, 4(4):515-538.
OWEN, R., and SUTCLIFFE, R. (eds., 1972). Studies in the theory of imperialism. London: Methuen.
OXAAL, I.; BARNETT, A.; and BOOTH, D. (eds., 1975). Beyond the sociology of development. London: Cass.
PATNAIK, P.U. (1972). "External markets and capitalist development." Economic Journal, 82(328):1316-1323.

PAYER, C. (1974). The debt trap. Harmondsworth: Penguin.
PELISSIER, P. (1966). Les paysans du Sénégal. Sainte-Yrieix: Imprimerie Fabrègue.
PERSON, Y. (1968). Samori: Une révolution dyula. Dakar: IFAN.
PHIMISTER, I.R. (1971). "The Shamva mine strike of 1927." Rhodesian History, 2:65-88. See also his 1975 Ph.D. dissertation on African miners in Rhodesia, Salisbury University.
——— (1974). "Peasant production and underdevelopment in Southern Rhodesia 1890-1914." African Affairs, 73(291):217-228.
POLLET, E., and WINTER, G. (1971). La société Soninke. Brussels: Institut de Sociologie.
POST, K.W.J. (1972). " 'Peasantisation' and rural political movements in western Africa." European Journal of Sociology, 13(2):223-254. (See also pp. 337-341.)
POST, K.W.J., and JENKINS, G.D. (1973). The price of liberty. Cambridge: Cambridge University Press.
POST, K.W.J., and VICKERS, M. (1973). Structure and conflict in Nigeria, 1960-65. London: Heinemann.
RAIKES, P. (1975). "Ujamaa vijijini and rural socialist development." Review of African Political Economy, 1(3).
RATHBONE, R. (1973). "Businessmen in politics: Party struggle in Ghana, 1949-57." Journal of Development Studies, 9(3):391-402.
REEVES, G. (1974). "The East African intellectual community." Unpublished Ph.D. dissertation, Edinburgh University.
REY, P.P. (1971). Colonialisme, neocolonialisme et transition au capitalisme. Paris: Maspero.
REYNOLDS, E. (1974). Trade and economic change on the Gold Coast, 1807-74. London: Longmans.
RHODIE, S. (1968). "The Gold Coast cocoa holdup, 1930-31." Transactions of the Historical Society of Ghana, 9:105-118.
RICH, E.E., and WILSON, C.H. (eds., 1967). The Cambridge economic history of Europe (Vol. 4). Cambridge: Cambridge University Press.
RIDDELL, R. (1974). "Poverty and the wage structure in Rhodesia." Rhodesia Science News, 8(7):201-205.
RIVIERE, C. (1968). "Promotion de la femme guinéene." Cahiers d'études africaines, 31:406-427.
——— (1971a). "Les bénéficaires du commerce dans la Guinée precoloniale et coloniale." Bulletin de l'IFAN, 33(2):257-284.
——— (1971b). "Les mécanismes de constitution d'une bourgeoisie commercante en Guinée." Cahiers d'études africaines, 43:378-399.
——— (1971c). "Comportements ostentatoires et style de vie des élites guinéenes." Cultures et Developpement, 3(3):415-443.
RODINSON, M. (1974). Islam and capitalism. London: Allen Lane.
RODNEY, W. (1966). "African slavery and other forms of social oppression on the upper Guinea coast in the context of the Atlantic slave trade." Journal of African History, 7(3):431-443.
——— (1968). West Africa and the Atlantic slave trade. Nairobi: East African Publishing House.
——— (1970). A history of the upper Guinea Coast 1545-1800. Oxford: Oxford University Press. Review by Y. Person in African Historical Studies, 1971, 4(3):669-690.
——— (1972). How Europe underdeveloped Africa. London: Bogle-L'Ouverture. Reviews by E.A. Alpers and B. Magubane in Ufahamu, 3(3):97-144.
ROSALADA, M.Z., and LAMPHERE, L. (eds., 1974). Women, culture and society. Stanford: Stanford University Press.
RUDEBECK, L. (1974). Guine-Bissau: A study of political mobilisation. Uppsala: Scandinavian Institute of African Studies.

Rural Development Research Committee (1974). Rural co-operation in Tanzania. Dar es Salaam: Tanzania Publishing House.

RWEYEMAMU, J.F. (1973). Underdevelopment and industrialisation in Tanzania. Nairobi: Oxford University Press.

SANDBROOK, R. (1972). "Patrons, clients and factions: New dimensions of conflict analysis in Africa." Canadian Journal of Political Science, 5(1):104-119.

――― (1974). Proletarians and African capitalism: The case of Kenya 1960-72. Cambridge: Cambridge University Press.

SANDBROOK, R., and COHEN, R. (eds., 1975). Towards an African working class. London: Longmans.

SAUL, J.S. (1974). "African peasants and revolution." Review of African Political Economy, 1(1):41-68.

SCHATZ, S.P. (1969). "Crude private neo-imperialism: A new pattern in Africa." Journal of Modern African Studies, 7(4):677-688.

SCHUMACHER, E.J. (1975). Politics, bureaucracy and rural development. Berkeley: University of California Press.

SCHWARZ, A. (1974). "Mythe et realite des bureaucraties africaines." Canadian Journal of African Studies, 8(2):255-284.

SCOTT, J.C. (1972). Comparative political corruption. London: Prentice-Hall.

SEERS, D., and FABER, M. (1972). The crisis in planning (2 vols.). London: Chatto and Windus for Sussex University Press.

SEERS, D., and JOY, L. (1971). Development in a divided world. Harmondsworth: Penguin.

SEIDMAN, A. (1969). An economics textbook for Africa. London: Methuen.

――― (1971). "Prospects for Africa's exports." Journal of Modern African Studies, 9(3):409-428.

――― (1972). Comparative development strategies in East Africa. Nairobi: East African Publishing House.

――― (1973). Alternative development strategies in Zambia. Madison: University of Wisconsin Land Tenure Center.

――― (1974a). "Import-substitution industry in Zambia." Journal of Modern African Studies, 12(4):601-631.

――― (1974b). "Key variables to incorporate in a model for development." African Studies Review, 17(1):105-121.

――― (forthcoming). "Changing theories of political economy in Africa."

SENGHAAS, D. (1974). "Peace research and the Third World." Bulletin of Peace Proposals, 2:158-172.

SHALMOFF, S. (1974). "The income tax, indirect rule and the Depression: The Gold Coast riots of 1931." Cahiers d'études africaines, 54:359-375.

SHAW, T.M. (1974). "Southern Africa: Co-operation or conflict." Journal of Modern African Studies, 12(4):633-655.

SHERIDAN, R.B. (1972). "Africa and the Caribbean in the Atlantic slave trade." American Historical Review, 77(1):15-35.

SHERIFF, A.M.H. (1971). "The rise of a commercial empire: An aspect of the economic history of Zanzibar 1770-1873." Ph.D. dissertation. London: London University.

SHIVJI, I. (1975). Class struggles in Tanzania. London: Heinemann.

SIMENSEN, J. (1974). "Rural mass action in the context of anti-colonial protest: The Asafo movement of Akim Abuaka." Canadian Journal of African Studies, 8(1):25-41.

SKLAR, R.L. (1963). Nigerian political parties. Princeton, N.J.: Princeton University Press.

――― (1975). Corporate power in an African state. Berkeley: University of California Press.

SPERO, J.E. (1973). "Dominance-dependence relationships: The case of France and Gabon." Unpublished Ph.D. dissertation, Columbia University.

STAHL, M. (1974). Ethiopia: Political contradiction in agricultural development. Uppsala: Political Science Association.

STANILAND, M. (1969a). "Single-party regimes of political change: The PDCI and Ivory Coast politics." Pp. 135-185 in C. Leys (ed.), Politics and change in developing countries. Cambridge: Cambridge University Press.

——— (1969b). "Frantz Fanon and the African political class." African Affairs, 68(270):4-25.

——— (1975). The lions of Dagbon: Political change in northern Ghana. Cambridge: Cambridge University Press.

STAVENHAGEN, R. (1969). Les classes sociales dans les sociétés agraires. Paris: Anthropos.

SUNDSTROM, L. (1975). The exchange economy of precolonial tropical Africa. London: Hurst.

SURET-CANALE, J. (1961). L'Afrique noire, occidentale et centrale (2nd ed.). Paris: Editions Sociales.

——— (1970). La république de Guinée. Paris: Editions Sociales.

——— (1971). French colonialism in tropical Africa. London: Hurst.

——— (1973). Afrique noire: De la colonisation aux independances 1945-60 (Vol. 1). Paris: Editions Sociales.

——— (1974). "Difficultés du néocolonialisme française en Afrique tropicale." Canadian Journal of African Studies, 8(2):211-233.

SUTCLIFFE, R.B. (1971). "Stagnation and inequality in Rhodesia 1946-68." Bulletin of the Oxford University Institute of Economics and Statistics, 33(1):35-56.

SZENTES, T. (1971). The political economy of underdevelopment. Budapest: Akademia Kiado.

TERRAY, E. (1964). "Les révolutions congolaises et dahoméenes." Revue française des sciences politiques, 14:917-942.

——— (1972). Marxism and "primitive" societies. New York: Monthly Review.

——— (1974). "Long-distance exchange and the formation of the state: The case of the Abron kingdom of Gyaman." Economy and Society, 3(3):315-345.

THOMAS, C. (1974). Dependence and transformation. New York: Monthly Review.

TIPPS, D.C. (1973). "Modernisation theory and the study of national development." Comparative Studies in Society and History, 15(2):199-226.

"Towards socialist planning" (1972). Uchumi (Dar es Salaam), 1:23.

TRAPIDO, S. (1971). "South Africa in a comparative study of industrialisation." Journal of Development Studies, 7(3):309-320.

TUDEN, A., and PLOTNICOV, L. (eds., 1970). Social stratification in Africa. New York: Free Press.

TUROK, B. (1974). Strategic problems in South Africa's liberation struggle. Richmond, Canada: Liberation Support Movement.

Universities of East Africa (1970-1973). Universities of East Africa Annual Social Science Conference: Proceedings. (Published by the host institution in each year.)

VAITSOS, C.V. (1974). Intercountry income distribution and transnational enterprises. London: Oxford University Press.

Van ARKADIE, B. (1971). "The role of the state sector in the context of economic dependence." Institute of Development Studies Bulletin, 3(4):22-37.

Van der LAAR, A. (1971). "Aspects of foreign private investment in African development." Kroniek van Afrika, 3:159-176.

Van ONSELEN, C. (1973). "Worker consciousness in black miners: Southern Rhodesia, 1900-20." Journal of African History, 14(2):237-256.

——— (1974a). "African mine labour in Southern Rhodesia, 1900-33." Unpublished D.Phil. dissertation, Oxford University.

——— (1974b). "The 1912 Wankie colliery strike." Journal of African History, 15(2):275-289.

Van ZWANENBERG, R. (1974). "The development of peasant commodity production in Kenya 1920-40." Economic History Review, 27(3):442-454.

VERHAEGEN, B. (1967, 1969). Rébellions au Congo (2 vols.). Brussels: Crisp.

VINCENT, J. (1971). African elite: The big men of a small town. New York: Columbia University Press.

WALLERSTEIN, I. (1972). "Social conflict in post-independence black Africa: The concepts of race and status reconsidered." In E.Q. Campbell (ed.), Racial tensions and national identity. Nashville, Tenn.: Vanderbilt University Press.

––– (1973). "Africa in a capitalist world," Issue, 3(3):1-11.

––– (1974). "Dependence in an interdependent world." African Studies Review, 17(1):1-26. See also Comparative Studies in Society and History, 1974, 16(4):387-415.

WARREN, W.M. (1973). "Myths of underdevelopment: Imperialism and capitalist industrialisation." New Left Review, 81:3-45. Discussion by A. Emmanuel and others, New Left Review, 1974, 85:61-104.

WASSERMAN, G. (1973a). "Continuity and counter-insurgency: The role of land reform in decolonising Kenya 1962-70." Canadian Journal of African Studies, 7(1):133-148.

––– (1973b). "The independence bargain: Kenya Europeans and the land issue, 1960-62." Journal of Commonwealth Political Studies, 11(2):99-120.

WAYNE, J. (forthcoming). "Colonialism and social structural change in Kigoma region, Tanzania."

WEEKS, J.F. (1971a). "The problems of wage policy in developing countries with special reference to Africa." Economic Bulletin of Ghana (n.s.), 1(1):31-44.

––– (1971b). "Wage policy and the colonial legacy." Journal of Modern African Studies, 9:361-387.

––– (1972). "Employment, growth and foreign domination in underdeveloped countries." Review of Radical Political Economics, 4(1):59-70.

––– (1973). "An exploration into the nature of the problem of urban imbalance in Africa." Manpower and Unemployment Research in Africa, 6(2):9-36.

WEISSMAN, S. (1970). American foreign policy in the Congo. Ithaca, N.Y.: Cornell University Press.

WERTHEIM, W.F. (1974). Evolution and revolution. Harmondsworth: Penguin.

WILKS, I. (1974). Asante in the nineteenth century. Cambridge: Cambridge University Press.

WILLAME, C. (1972). Patrimonialism and political change in the Congo. Stanford, Calif.: Stanford University Press. Review by B. Nimer in International Journal of African Historical Studies, 1973, 6(2):315-334.

WILLIAMS, G.P. (ed., forthcoming). Nigeria: Economy and society.

WILSON, F. (1972). Labour in the South African gold mines. Cambridge: Cambridge University Press.

WIPPER, A. (1971). "The politics of sex: Some strategies employed by the Kenyan power elite." African Studies Review, 14(3):463-482. See also Journal of Modern African Studies, 1971, 9(3):429-442.

––– (ed., 1972). "The roles of African women: Past, present and future." Canadian Journal of African Studies, 6(2).

WOLFF, R.D. (1974). The economics of colonialism: Britain and Kenya, 1870-1930. New Haven, Conn.: Yale University Press.

WOLPE, H. (1972). "Capitalism and cheap labour power in South Africa." Economy and Society, 14:425-456.

YAFFEY, M.J.H. (1970). Balance of payments problems of a developing country: Tanzania. Munich: Weltforum Verlag.

YANNAPOLOUS, T., and MARTIN, D. (1972). "Régimes militaires et classes sociales en Afrique," Revue française des science politique, 22(4):847-882.

ZOLBERG, A.R. (1964). One party government in the Ivory Coast. Princeton, N.J.: Princeton University Press.
––– (1966). Creating political order. Chicago: Rand McNally.
––– (1968). "The political use of economic planning in Mali." Pp. 98-123 in H.G. Johnson (ed.), Economic nationalism in new states. London: Allen and Unwin.

ABOUT THE CONTRIBUTORS

CLAUDE AKE is a Nigerian who is currently Associate Professor of Political Science at Carleton University, Ottawa, and the University of Dar es Salaam. He has previously taught at the University of Nairobi and Columbia University (where he also obtained his Ph.D.). He is Research Director of the African Association of Political Science. He is author of *A Theory of Political Integration* and *Political Science as Imperialism* (forthcoming), and various articles on political theory and political economy.

CHRIS ALLEN obtained his M.A. at Oxford in 1968. He was Research Fellow at Nuffield College in 1968-1970 and Lecturer in Political Science at Ahmadu Bello University (Northern Nigeria) in 1970-1971. He has been Lecturer in the same field at the University of Edinburgh since 1972. He was joint editor of *African Perspectives* (Cambridge, 1970) and *Developmental Trends in Kenya* (Edinburgh, 1972). He has also contributed to *African Affairs, Review of African Political Economy,* and various collective works. One of his main interests continues to be trade unionism in Africa.

LIONEL CLIFFE is Reader in Politics at the University of Zambia and was formerly Director of Development Studies, University of Dar es Salaam. He was editor of (and contributor to) *One Party Democracy* (with John Saul); he also edited the two-volume *Socialism in Tanzania* and *Rural Cooperatives in Tanzania.* He is one of the founding editors of the newly established *Review of African Political Economy.*

ROBIN COHEN grew up in South Africa. His first degree was from the University of Witwatersrand. He subsequently studied at the London School of

Economics (M.Sc.) and the University of Birmingham (Ph.D.). From 1967 to 1969 he conducted research in Nigeria while a Lecturer at the University of Ibadan. He is currently Senior Lecturer in Sociology at the University of Birmingham. He has published *Labour and Politics in Nigeria* (1974) and coedited *The Development of an African Working Class: Studies in Class Formation and Action* (forthcoming). His latest research concerns problems of development on the island of St. Helena in the South Atlantic.

CATHERINE COQUERY-VIDROVITCH is Maitre de Conférences and Directeur, U.E.R., Géographie, Histoire et Sciences de la Société, Université de Paris VII. She is the author of *La découverte de l'Afrique noire atlantique des origines au XVIIIe siècle* (Julliard, 1965 and 1971); *Brazza et la prise de possession du Congo: La mission de l'Ouest Africain, 1883-1885* (Mouton, 1969); and *Le Congo français au temps des grandes compagnies concessionnaires, 1898-1930* (Mouton, 1972); and is coauthor (with S. Amin) of *Histoire économique du Congo, 1880-1968* (IFAN-Dakar, Anthropos 1970) and (with H. Miniot) of *L'Afrique noire de 1800 à nos jours* (PUF, Nouvelle Clio, 1974). She has also published numerous articles on the social and economic history of precolonial and contemporary Africa and on problems of the Third World.

PHILIP EHRENSAFT is currently a professor of sociology at the Université du Québec à Montreal. He previously taught at McGill University (1971-1976) and the University of California, Santa Cruz (1970-1971) and received his Ph.D. from Columbia University. He is author of a number of journal articles tracing the economics of Africa and Latin America.

PETER C.W. GUTKIND is Professor of Anthropology, McGill University, Montreal. He obtained his M.A. at the University of Chicago and his Ph.D. at the University of Amsterdam. He is author of *The Royal Capital of Buganda* (Mouton, 1963) and *Urban Sociology* (Van Gorcum, 1974) and is coauthor (with A.W. Southall) of *Townsman in the Making* (East African Institute of Social Research, 1957), and (with D.G. Jongmans) of *Anthropologists in the Field* (Van Gorcum, 1967). His major interest is African urban studies.

BERNARD MAGUBANE is a native South African. He obtained his B.A. at the University of Natal in 1958 in the fields of sociology and native administration and his M.A. in 1964 and his Ph.D. in 1967, both at UCLA. He was a Lecturer at the University of Zambia, 1967-1969 and Visiting Lecturer at UCLA in 1970. He has also worked for the American Friends Service Committee in California and was a Research Assistant in the School of Public Health, UCLA. He has contributed a chapter on "Politics of Football: The Durban and District African Football Association" in Leo Kuper's *An African Bourgeoisie* (Yale, 1965). Papers dealing with social change in Africa have appeared in *African Social*

Research, Race, East African Journal, The American Anthropologist, and *The African Political Review.* He is now teaching at the University of Connecticut at Storrs.

KEES MAXEY lives in England. He studied chemistry at St. Andrews University, Scotland, where he gained a B.Sc. (Hons.). At present he is an analytical chemist with a photographic manufacturing company. He is a member of the British Labour Party and an elected member of the Essex County Council. He is author of *From Rhodesia to Zimbabwe* (Fabian Research Series, 1972) and *The Fight for Zimbabwe: The Armed Conflict in Southern Rhodesia since UDI* (Rex Collings, 1975).

TAMAS SZENTES was born at Dunakeszi, Hungary. He obtained his M.A. in 1955 and his Ph.D. in 1959. From 1955 to 1962 he was an editor for Economics Publishers, Budapest, and since 1962 he has been teaching economics at the University, Budapest. He is currently Professor of Development Studies in the Department of International Economy. Between 1967 and 1971 he was Professor of Economics and Head of the Department, University of Dar es Salaam. He is author or coauthor of sixteen books, including, the English monograph, *The Political Economy of Underdevelopment* (Akademiai, 1971 and 1973), which has been translated into Polish, Russian, German, and Italian. In addition, he has published at least a hundred papers in the scholarly presses. His main interest is development strategies.

P-KIVEN TUNTENG comes from the Cameroon. He obtained his B.A. at Ryerson in 1967, his M.A. at the University of Ottawa in 1970, and his doctorate in political science at the University of Geneva in 1972. From 1972 to 1974 he was Assistant Professor of Political Science, Institute of International Relations, University of Yaounda, Cameroon. He currently teaches at Vanier College, Montreal, and at the University of Ottawa. He has published in *Transition, Race, Civilizations, The British Journal of Sociology,* and *Caribbean Studies.* His main interest is French-speaking Africa and French politics and development strategies.

BEN TUROK is a South African and a graduate engineer. But politics called, and he became first a Provincial Councillor representing Africans and then National Secretary of the Congress of Democrats. He was sent to prison, where he took a degree in philosophy, and then took a masters in political science in Tanzania, where he went into exile for several years. He has published largely on South Africa in various books and journals.

IMMANUEL WALLERSTEIN is Distinguished Professor of Sociology at the State University of New York, Binghamton. He formerly taught at McGill University, Montreal, and at Columbia University. Among many honors, he is a former president of the African Studies Association of the U.S.A. and in 1975 was awarded the Sorokin Prize by the American Sociological Association. He has published extensively and is the author of the recently published (and much acclaimed) *The Modern World System: Capitalist Agriculture and the Origins of the European World-Economy in the Sixteenth Century* (Academic Press, 1974). His other many publications are equally well known. His present interest is the study of history and society.

GAVIN WILLIAMS was born in Pretoria. He has studied at Stellenbosh and Oxford. He taught at Durham University but has recently moved to St. Peter's College, Oxford. He has edited (with E. de Kadt) *Sociology and Development* (Tavistock, 1974). He has also edited a set of essays on *Nigeria: Economy and Society* (forthcoming) and contributed papers to books and journals. His research has been in Nigeria, and his interest is the theory and practice of socialism, class analysis, and political economy.